GOVERNORS STATE UNIVERSITY LIBRARY

W9-AKL-840

3 1611 00352 3369

Issues in Clinical Child Psychology

Series Editor: Michael C. Roberts, University of Kansas, Lawrence, Kansas

For further volumes, go to
http://www.springer.com/series/6082

William P. Erchul · Brian K. Martens

School Consultation

Conceptual and Empirical Bases of Practice

Third Edition

GOVERNORS STATE UNIVERSITY
UNIVERSITY PARK, IL

 Springer

William P. Erchul
Department of Psychology
North Carolina State University
Raleigh, NC 27695-7650
william_erchul@ncsu.edu

Brian K. Martens
Department of Psychology
Syracuse University
Syracuse, NY 13244-2340
bkmarten@syr.edu

LC
1027.55
.E73
2010

ISBN 978-1-4419-5746-7   e-ISBN 978-1-4419-5747-4
DOI 10.1007/978-1-4419-5747-4
Springer New York Dordrecht Heidelberg London

Library of Congress Control Number: 2010922793

© Springer Science+Business Media, LLC 2010
All rights reserved. This work may not be translated or copied in whole or in part without the written permission of the publisher (Springer Science+Business Media, LLC, 233 Spring Street, New York, NY 10013, USA), except for brief excerpts in connection with reviews or scholarly analysis. Use in connection with any form of information storage and retrieval, electronic adaptation, computer software, or by similar or dissimilar methodology now known or hereafter developed is forbidden.
The use in this publication of trade names, trademarks, service marks, and similar terms, even if they are not identified as such, is not to be taken as an expression of opinion as to whether or not they are subject to proprietary rights.

Printed on acid-free paper

Springer is part of Springer Science+Business Media (www.springer.com)

*To some influential teachers who inspired
us to dig deeper and reach higher:*

Willard R. Thurlow
Victor R. Wendt
WPE

Joseph C. Witt
C. Dean Miller
BKM

Preface

As considered here, consultation is an indirect model of delivering psychological and/or educational services. Within this model, a specialist (consultant) and staff member (consultee) work together to optimize the functioning of a client in the staff member's setting and to increase the staff member's capacity to deal with similar situations in the future. In schools, for example, a psychologist may consult with a teacher about a student in the teacher's classroom. The practice of school consultation has burgeoned since its formal introduction into public education during the 1960s. Today, graduate training programs in various specialties of psychology and education require coursework in consultation, and many professionals in these areas spend some portion of their day engaged in consultation.

Consultation can be a powerful tool for delivering specialized services in schools, but only when the consultant possesses a requisite level of skill and sophistication. In preparing this volume, we envisioned its major purpose as reducing the level of naiveté typically experienced by the beginning school consultant. Toward that end, we offer a systematic approach to school consultation that targets much of the information needed for one to consult in a competent manner. The reader should note that our use of the somewhat ambiguous term *school consultant* is intentional and recognizes that consultants working in schools today represent a variety of professional disciplines. The primary intended audiences for this book, however, are school psychologists and clinical child psychologists, although psychologists having other specialties are likely to find its content useful. A clear secondary audience is educational specialists, including counselors, special educators, and school social workers. What the reader must have to benefit from our approach is a solid background in psychology, a content area of expertise from which to draw, and well-developed human relations skills.

We believe the overall method of school consultation detailed in this book is different from others that have been published previously. In stating that it is different, we are not claiming that it is wholly original. Our goal instead has been to incorporate the most useful conceptual and/or empirically supported principles of known consultation approaches into a single model that is particularly relevant to school-based practice. More specifically, the model of school consultation we promote attempts to integrate aspects of the historically separate models of mental health consultation and behavioral consultation, along with principles of interpersonal influence, social support, and organizational psychology. In our model, the effective practice of school consultation is linked to the accomplishment of three interrelated tasks – the problem-solving, social influence, and support and development tasks.

Structurally, this volume is comprised of three major sections. The first of these consists of four chapters that describe foundational information, including historical and conceptual information (Chap. 1) as well as the contemporary context for school-based service delivery, including tiered systems of intervention and response to intervention (Chap. 2); using interpersonal influence in consultation (Chap. 3); and understanding the school as a setting for consultation (Chap. 4). The second section, comprised of Chaps. 5–8, documents important processes and outcomes of school consultation. Chapters 5 and 6 present our integrated model of consultation, focusing on elements of mental health consultation, behavioral consultation, professional support, problem solving, social influence, and the organizational context. Moving away somewhat from these core elements, Chap. 7 provides information on assessment issues and strategies of particular relevance to consultation, and Chap. 8 describes the importance of and provides practical models for selecting effective school-based interventions. Chapters 9 through 11 form the third section. Key participants in school consultation, teachers and students, are described in Chaps. 9 and 10, respectively. Chapter 11 contains a transcribed consultation case study that illustrates many aspects of school consultation in general and the integrated model in particular. Chapter 12 is an epilog that reviews important points and looks ahead to the future effective practice of school consultation. New to this third edition are Chaps. 2 and 7.

We have been very heartened by the positive reactions of students and colleagues to earlier editions of *School Consultation: Conceptual and Empirical Bases of Practice*. For example, Hintze (1998) wrote: "In reviewing the text, I found myself reflecting on what was being proposed from a variety of perspectives: 'how much easier this is going to make my teaching,' 'this is just the type of book students have been asking for,' 'that's exactly what I experienced as a practitioner,' or 'I wish I had a book like this when I was being trained.'" Meyers and Coleman (2004) noted: "Erchul and Martens offer an astute and scholarly discussion of school-based consultation…after reading this thought-provoking book, one is left with an enhanced theoretical understanding of consultation and is thus better prepared to practice with confidence and a clear sense of purpose." We hope that readers of the third edition will find it just as useful.

We have heard that one of the strengths of the earlier editions lay in its concise presentation of many topics germane to school consultation. That emphasis is retained here, but we also acknowledge there is much more to consultative practice than a single source can adequately cover. Therefore, instructors selecting this book for their graduate-level courses may wish to supplement it with others. We suggest the following sources for deeper coverage of indicated topics: Caplan and Caplan (1993/1999; mental health consultation); Kratochwill and Bergan (1990; behavioral consultation); Sheridan and Kratochwill (2007; conjoint behavioral consultation); Jimerson, Burns and VanDerHeyden (2007; response to intervention); Grigorenko (2008; Individuals with Disabilities Education Improvement Act of 2004); and Erchul and Sheridan (2008a; school consultation research).

Books are seldom the result only of their authors' efforts, and with this in mind, we wish to express our gratitude to several individuals. Stephanie Asbeck, Priscilla Grissom, and Lynne Myers are thanked for their careful proofreading, editing, and indexing efforts. We also appreciate Blair Johnson's help in preparing Fig. 6.1. We thank Judy Jones, Garth Haller, and other staff members at Springer for their considerable assistance in putting our ideas into print.

Throughout our careers we have been intellectually sparked by the scholarly contributions of Gerald Caplan (1917–2008) and Bertram H. Raven. Gerald Caplan, late Professor of Psychiatry at Harvard Medical School and originator of the modern practice of mental health consultation, has been a primary influence on our understanding of the interpersonal, organizational, and preventive aspects of consultation. Bert Raven, Professor of Psychology Emeritus at the University of California, Los Angeles, and renowned social psychologist, has greatly enhanced our view of the role that social influence plays in consultation. We are grateful to these gentlemen for both their kindness and insights into human behavior that led us to develop our integrated model of school consultation.

We also wish to acknowledge the many talented doctoral students – now our colleagues – with whom we have collaborated over the years. The diligent efforts and insights of Seth Aldrich, Scott Ardoin, John Begeny, Megan Bennett, Tracy Bradley, Sandy Chafouleas, Teri Chewning, Sheila Clonan, Edward Daly, Florence DiGennaro Reed, Kim Getty, Priscilla Grissom, Andrea Hiralall, Richard Hollings, Mary Cathryn Murray, Lynne Myers, Ami O'Neill, Derek Reed, Susan Smith Scott, Caryn Ward, Michelle Whichard, and Kristen Wilson have contributed immeasurably to the development of our model.

Finally, Bill Erchul would like to thank his wife, Ann Schulte, for the continued support of his many activities as well as for her clear-headed thinking on consultation, schools, and school psychology. Brian Martens would like to thank his wife, Rosemarie, for her continued help and support as well as her invaluable (and often humorous) insights as a master problem solver and enthusiastic life partner.

Raleigh, NC   William P. Erchul
Syracuse, NY   Brian K. Martens

The authors and publisher are grateful to Wiley/Blackwell/John Wiley & Sons, Inc. for permission to reproduce Table 3 (p. 238) and Figure 4 (p. 240) from B. H. Raven, "The Bases of Social Power: Origins and Recent Developments," which appeared in Vol. 49 of the *Journal of Social Issues*. Copyright © 1993 by Wiley/Blackwell/John Wiley & Sons, Inc.

About the Authors

William P. Erchul is a Professor of Psychology at North Carolina State University and served as the Director of Training of NCSU's School Psychology Program (1987–2004). He received his BA in Psychology and Communication Arts from the University of Wisconsin-Madison, and his Ph.D. in Educational Psychology with a specialization in School Psychology from the University of Texas at Austin. He has worked for the Human Interaction Research Institute in Los Angeles and has been a consultant to various school systems, public agencies, and private businesses. Dr. Erchul is a Fellow of the American Psychological Association and the American Academy of School Psychology, a recipient of APA's Lightner Witmer Award (given in recognition of early career research contributions to the field of School Psychology), a recipient of the North Carolina School Psychology Association's Excellence in Staff Development Award, a member of the Society for the Study of School Psychology, and has been recognized at the college level as an outstanding faculty researcher at NCSU. He has been President of the American Academy of School Psychology; President of the North Carolina Inter-University Council on School Psychology; Vice-President of Publications, Communications, and Convention Affairs of APA's Division of School Psychology; and Executive Producer of *The Conversation Series* for the Division of School Psychology. Dr. Erchul is a licensed health service provider psychologist and has been board certified in school psychology by the American Board of Professional Psychology. His primary research program centers on interpersonal processes and outcomes associated with psychological consultation. Dr. Erchul has produced over 100 journal articles, chapters, books, and other scholarly works. He has been associate editor of the APA journal, *School Psychology Quarterly*; senior editor of the *Handbook of Research in School Consultation*; and guest editor of special issues of the *School Psychology Review* and the *Journal of Educational and Psychological Consultation*. He also serves or has served on the editorial review boards of six scholarly journals.

Brian K. Martens is a Professor of Psychology at Syracuse University. He served as Director of Training for the School Psychology program from 1998 to 2007 and as Associate Chair and Chair of the Psychology Department from 2007 to 2009. Prof. Martens received the 1990 Lightner Witmer Award from Division 16 of the American Psychological Association for outstanding early research contributions and is a Fellow of the Association and a member of the Society for the Study of School Psychology. He received the Editorial Appreciation Award from *School Psychology Review* in 2002, was appointed to the board of directors of the Society for the Experimental Analysis of Behavior from 1995 to 2003, and was named one of 90 distinguished alumni at the 90th Anniversary Celebration of Teachers College at the University of Nebraska in 1997. He was named Faculty Advisor of the Year in the College of Arts and Sciences in 2007, received the Excellence in Graduate Education Faculty Recognition Award in 2006, and was named Outstanding Teacher of the Year at University College in 1995. Prof. Martens serves on the Professional Advisory board of the May Institute and was a 2007 Catalyst Scholar for the School Psychology Research Collaboration Conference. He has published over 100 articles, books, and chapters concerned with translating findings from basic operant research into effective school-based interventions, functional assessment and treatment of children's classroom behavior problems, and the instructional hierarchy as a sequenced approach to training basic academic skills. Prof. Martens is a past Associate Editor for the *Journal of Applied Behavior Analysis* (1993–1996) and *School Psychology Quarterly* (1991–1994) and currently serves as Editor of the *Journal of Behavioral Education*.

Contents

Part I Background

1 Introduction to Consultation 3

The Effectiveness of Human Services Consultation 5

Historical Influences on the Human Services Consultant Role 6

    Theoretical Issues.. 6

    Professional Issues 7

    Pragmatic Issues... 8

Historical Influences on the School Consultant Role 9

    Developments from the 1940s Through the 1970s 9

    Developments During the 1980s and 1990s 10

    Contemporary Developments 11

Reconceptualizing Consultation for Today's Schools 12

    Historical Summary 12

    Our Definition of School Consultation 12

    Assumptions of Our Approach to School Consultation....................... 13

    Topics Not Addressed in Our Approach to School Consultation 14

The Rest of the Book 15

2 Problem Solving and Response to Intervention 17

Establishing a Context for RTI and the Modern Practice of School
Consultation 18

    Prevention as a Philosophical Influence 18

    NCLB and IDEIA 2004 as Legislative Influences.............................. 19

    Empirical Influences 20

Problem Solving.. 21

    What is Problem Solving? 21

    Problem-Solving Teams.. 22

RTI 24

    What is RTI? 24

    RTI Systems of Implementation 24

    Tier-Based Service Delivery Within RTI.. 25

    Assessment and Intervention Methods Within RTI 28

Conclusion 29

3 Promoting Change in Schools 31
    Changing Beliefs, Attitudes, and Behaviors Within Consultation 31
        The Need for Consultee Change 31
    Helping the Consultee to Change 33
        Collaboration: What Is It? 33
        Should Consultants Influence Consultees and the Process
        of Consultation? 34
        Relevance of These Five Studies for School Consultants 38
        A Clarification of Our Position 39
        Are There Ethical Questions and Issues of Professional Dissonance
        Regarding the Use of Influence in Consultation? 39
        If It Is Not a *Collaborative* Relationship, Then What Is It? 40
        The Egalitarian Virus 41
    General Strategies for Effecting Changes in Human Systems 41
        Empirical–Rational Approach 42
        Normative–Reeducative Approach 42
        Power–Coercive Approach 42
        Relevance of Chin and Benne's Strategies for School Consultants 43
    The Bases of Social Power and Their Application
    to School Consultation 43
        An Introduction to Social Power Bases and Social Influence 43
        Coercive Power and Reward Power: Impersonal Forms 45
        Coercive and Reward Power: Personal Forms 47
        Legitimate Power: Position, Reciprocity, Equity,
        and Responsibility-Dependence 48
        Expert Power and Referent Power: Positive Forms 49
        The Expert–Referent Power Dilemma 50
        Expert and Referent Power: Negative Forms 50
        Informational Power: Direct and Indirect Forms 51
        Empirical Studies of Raven's (1992, 1993)
        Social Power Bases Applied to School Consultation 52
        Relevance of Social Power Base Research Studies
        for School Consultants 54
    Other Means of Influence 54
        Invoking or Reducing the Power of Third Parties 54
        Preparatory Devices: Setting the Stage for Social Influence 55
        The Mode of Influence 57
    A Power/Interaction Model of Interpersonal Influence
    and Its Application to School Consultation 57
        The Motivation to Influence 57
        Assessment of Available Power Bases 59
        Assessment of the Available Bases in Relation to Target, Power,
        Preferences, and Inhibitions 59

Preparing for the Influence Attempt 59
Choice of Power Bases and Mode in Influence Attempts 60
Assessing the Effects of Influence 60
Conclusion 60
Notes 61

4 The School as a Setting for Consultation 63
Organizational Traditions in the Public School System 64
Classical Organizational Theory 64
The Human Relations Movement 66
Organizational Behavior Theory 70
The Service Structure of Public Schools 71
Available Services 71
The Refer-Test-Place Sequence 74
The Role of Consultation 76
School Consultation from an Administrative Perspective 76
Factors Influencing the Use of Consultation Services 76
The Three Paradoxes of School Consultation 78

Part II Consultation Processes and Outcomes

5 Bases of an Integrated Model of School Consultation 83
Community Mental Health and Mental Health Consultation Bases 83
Population-Oriented Preventive Model 84
Crisis Model 85
Support Systems Model 86
Caplan's Model of Mental Health Consultation 86
How the Mental Health Consultant Offers Support to Consultees 90
Behavioral Psychology and Behavioral Consultation Bases 91
Problem-Solving Model 91
Application of Behavior Modification in Natural Settings 92
Bergan's Model of Behavioral Consultation 92
Interpersonal Influence and Social Power Bases 96
Summary of the Bases of an Integrated Model
of School Consultation 97
Achieving Entry in School Consultation: Entering
the Service Delivery Network 97
Assessing the School as an Organization:
Some General Considerations 98
Negotiating the Contract 100
Achieving School-Level (Physical) Entry 101
Achieving Classroom-Level (Psychological) Entry 102

6 Model Description and Application 105
　A Critical Appraisal of Consultation Models 105
　　Mental Health Consultation 105
　　Behavioral Consultation 107
　　The Consultative Relationship 110
　An Integrated Model of School Consultation 110
　　Precursors to School Consultation 113
　　The Problem-Solving Task 115
　　The Social Influence Task 117
　　The Support and Development Task 120
　　Outcomes of School Consultation 124

7 Assessment in School Consultation 127
　Functional Behavior Assessment 129
　　Indirect Assessment Phase 131
　　Direct Assessment Phase 132
　Systematic Formative Evaluation 134
　Brief Experimental Analysis 136

8 Selecting Effective School-Based Interventions 141
　Effectiveness of Intervention Alternatives 142
　　Results from Meta-Analytic Reviews 142
　　The Role of ABA in School-Based Intervention 143
　Conceptual Models of Children's Learning and Behavior Problems ... 144
　　Academic Intervention Models 144
　　Behavioral Intervention Models 147
　　Limitations of ABA Approaches to School-Based Intervention ... 151
　Implementation Issues 151
　　Conceptual Relevance 152
　　Treatment Strength 153
　　Treatment Acceptability 153
　　Treatment Integrity 154

Part III Key Participants in Consultation

9 Teachers as Consultees 159
　Perspectives on Teachers and Teaching 159
　　The Complexity of Classroom Teaching 159
　　The Rewards of Teaching 161
　　Major Challenges Facing Teachers Today 162
　　Teacher Recruitment, Attrition, and Retention 164
　　Implications for the School Consultant 164
　Perspectives on Teachers and School Consultation 165
　　Three Views on Why Teachers Seek Consultation 165
　　Teacher Expectations for Consultation 167

What Teachers Do Before Seeking Consultation 169
Factors that Distinguish Teachers Who Participate
in Consultation from Those Who Do Not 170
Increasing the Effectiveness of Consultation with Teachers 171
Adapting Consultation to the Teacher's Schedule:
The 15-Min Consultation 171
Consulting as Part of a Prereferral
Intervention/Problem-Solving Team 172
Increasing Knowledge/Skill Transfer and Maintenance 174
Providing Consultative Support to Teachers 176

10 Students as Clients 177
Legislation Governing Service Delivery in the Schools 178
Educational Approaches to Classification 180
Rationale for Classifying Special Needs Students 181
Overview of Childhood Disabilities 182
Students Classified as Learning Disabled 185
Students Classified as Emotionally Disturbed 187
A Contextual Model of Student Achievement 189
Variables Limiting Individualized Instruction 189
Variables Related to Student Achievement 190

11 Consultation Case Study 193
Problem Identification Interview: February 18 194
An Analysis of the First Interview 202
Problem Analysis Interview: March 4 204
An Analysis of the Second Interview 212
Problem Evaluation Interview: April 9 214
Child Measures 214
Teacher/Consultation Case Measures 215
Conclusion 215

12 Epilog: The Effective Practice of School Consultation 217

References 221

Author Index 245

Subject Index 253

Chapter 1
Introduction to Consultation

Consultation ... denote[s] the process of interaction between two professional persons – the consultant, who is a specialist, and the consultee, who invokes his help in regard to a current work problem with which the latter is having some difficulty, and which he has decided is within the former's area of specialized competence. The work problem involves the management or treatment of one or more clients of the consultee, or the planning or implementation of a program to cater to such clients. (Caplan, 1963, p. 470)

The chapter begins with psychiatrist Gerald Caplan's definition of consultation, not because it is the best definition for our purposes, rather because it provides a starting point, both historically and conceptually, from which to view the role of the school consultant. Historically speaking, perhaps the earliest systematic approach to human services consultation began in 1949 in Israel where Caplan and his small clinical staff were assigned the challenging task of attending to the mental health needs of 16,000 adolescent immigrants. Complicating this assignment were the facts that these adolescents were housed at more than 100 residential institutions, transportation within the country was often problematic, and there were about 1,000 initial requests for assistance. In confronting these obstacles to the traditional model of referral/diagnosis/psychotherapy of individual clients, Caplan reasoned that available professional resources would need to be used more effectively (Caplan, 1970).

In response to these circumstances, a different model of delivering mental health services emerged. Rather than meeting individual clients at the clinic in Jerusalem, Caplan and his staff traveled to many institutions and met there with the referred teenagers and their caregivers (later termed *consultees*). Supportive, collegial discussions with the caregivers about the adolescents often resulted in the caregivers returning to work with a new, enhanced perspective that led to their more effective management of client problems. By concentrating his staff's professional energies on consultative activities that improved the functioning of caregivers, Caplan believed that the mental health of many more clients could be positively affected than it was possible through traditional one-on-one therapy. He also found that much more pertinent information was obtained when meeting with caregivers on-site as opposed to a clinic (Caplan & Caplan, 1993/1999).

Conceptually, Caplan's 1963 definition and later elaborations (Caplan, 1964, 1970; Caplan & Caplan, 1993/1999) specify the unique and essential features of the

W.P. Erchul and B.K. Martens, *School Consultation,* Issues in Clinical Child Psychology, DOI 10.1007/978-1-4419-5747-4_1, © Springer Science+Business Media, LLC 2010 mental health consultation relationship. These features distinguish consultation from the relationships and contracts inherent to other professional activities such as supervision, teaching, and psychotherapy. First, the consultative relationship is essentially triadic, with the involvement of a consultant and one or more consultees and clients. Consultees typically lack the training and experience that consultants possess, and they may be professionals or paraprofessionals representing various fields, including education, nursing, law, or medicine. Second, the optimal working relationship is coordinate and nonhierarchical; ideally, there is no power differential between consultant and consultee. Third, consultee work-related challenges rather than personal problems form the basis for consultative discussion. Fourth, the consultant has no administrative responsibility for or formal authority over the consultee. Thus, the ultimate professional responsibility for the client's welfare remains with the consultee, not with the consultant. Fifth, the consultee retains the freedom to accept or reject whatever guidance the consultant may offer. In other words, consultation is considered to be a voluntary relationship. Sixth, messages exchanged between consultant and consultee are to be held in confidence, unless the consultant believes someone will be harmed if silence is maintained. Finally, consultation has a dual purpose – to help the consultee with a current professional problem and to equip the consultee with added insights and skills that will permit him or her to deal effectively with similar future problems, preferably without the consultant's continuing assistance.

Gerald Caplan's historical and conceptual contributions to mental health consultation are unprecedented (Erchul, 2009). Notwithstanding, it is also true that the field of consultation has progressed considerably from these early beginnings, benefiting along the way from the views of many other theorists, practitioners, and researchers. Today, consultation maintains a high profile within school, clinical, community, counseling, and organizational psychology, as well as within related mental health fields (e.g., social work, psychiatric nursing) and many areas of education (e.g., special education, school counseling). For example, a school psychologist may consult with teachers about effective management strategies in order to prevent classroom disruptions. A clinical psychologist may be contracted initially to conduct psychological testing in a school, but later may be asked to consult with special education teachers who instruct adolescents with impulse control problems. A community psychologist may consult with elected officials about the ways to reduce violent crime in the downtown area at night. A counseling psychologist employed at a university counseling center may consult with residence hall advisers to help them identify and assist those students who do not effectively handle the pressures of university life. A special educator may consult with a classroom teacher about how to instruct a student who has a moderate learning disability.

There are many external indicators of the growth and popularity of consultation in the human services. Searching the PsychINFO database (January 2000–January 2009) using the word *consultation*, we found 7,893 references in a keyword search, including 432 dissertations. Well over 100 books on human services consultation have been published since 1967, including about 20 since 2000. There are currently two professional journals that focus primarily on aspects of consultation: *Consulting*

Psychology Journal: Practice and Research and *Journal of Educational and Psychological Consultation.* There are several other journals that routinely publish articles on human services consultation, including *American Journal of Community Psychology, Journal of Primary Prevention, Journal of School Psychology, School Psychology Quarterly,* and *School Psychology Review* (Zins, Kratochwill, & Elliott, 1993). With respect to practice issues, school psychologists typically spend about 20% of their time engaged in consultation and report that consultation is one of the most (if not the most) preferred of their service delivery activities (Fagan & Wise, 2007; Gutkin & Curtis, 2009).

This short introduction establishes a context for the rest of this chapter and fore-shadows the content of chapters that follow. Other topics examined in Chap. 1 are the effectiveness of consultation, historical antecedents of the general human services consultant role and the specific school psychological consultant role, our definition of school consultation, and finally, our assumptions as authors.

The Effectiveness of Human Services Consultation

As helping professionals, we live in an era that promotes "evidence-based practice" (Norcross, Beutler, & Levant, 2006) and the use of "evidence-based interventions" (Kratochwill et al., 2009). Thus, before investing the required time and energy in learning how to consult, the reader might ask, "Does consultation work?" In other words, is there empirical evidence indicating that positive effects accrue to clients and consultees when a specialist works directly with one or more consultees who in turn work directly with one or more clients? Before providing an answer, it is important to note first that conducting consultation research is difficult, and regrettably, many studies are flawed, both conceptually and methodologically (Erchul & Sheridan, 2008b; Gresham & Noell, 1993; Lewis & Newcomer, 2002; Reddy, Barboza-Whitehead, Files, & Rubel, 2000). As just one example, because consultation represents an attempt to benefit a third party (client) through change in a second party (consultee), one often cannot determine whether client change resulted from consultant effort or some other factor instead.

Accepting this less-than-ideal state of consultation outcome studies, however, there is ample evidence indicating that consultation is an effective treatment. Some of this evidence is based on *meta-analysis,* a statistical method for summarizing the effects of a treatment across large numbers of original research studies that investigated the treatment (Smith & Glass, 1977). For each study included in a meta-analysis, the change in performance due to a particular treatment is calculated as the mean of the treatment group minus the mean of the control group divided by the standard deviation of the control group. These *effect size (ES) statistics* are then averaged across studies examining a common treatment procedure to indicate the mean effectiveness of that procedure in standard score units. For example, an *ES* of 1.0 would indicate that the treatment group, on average, outperformed the control group by one standard deviation unit on whatever outcome measure was used (e.g., teacher rating of student, achievement test score). Translating this $ES = 1.0$ example to percentile ranks, the mean score of the treatment group could have fallen at the 84th percentile and that of the control group the 50th percentile. A negative ES would indicate that the treatment group scored lower than the control group, whereas a zero ES would indicate that there was no group difference.

Medway and Updyke (1985) examined the results of 54 controlled studies of psychological consultation published from 1958 to 1982 that were conducted in schools, clinics, and other organizations. These studies collectively reported 83 consultee outcome measures and 100 client outcome measures. Medway and Updyke's key findings included: (1) the average ES was 0.55 for consultees and 0.39 for clients; (2) consultees demonstrated functioning/satisfaction >71% of untreated controls; and (3) clients had outcome measure scores that were more favorable than 66% of their controls.

The effectiveness of consultation is arguably greater when one focuses on results obtained from school consultation research only. For example, Sibley (1986, reported in Gresham & Noell, 1993) found average ESs of 0.60 for consultees and 0.91 for clients across 63 studies of school consultation. Adapting meta-analytic procedures for single-case designs, Busse, Kratochwill, and Elliott (1995) reported an average client ES of 0.95 for 23 cases of teacher consultation. Though not a meta-analysis, Sheridan, Welch, and Orme (1996) completed a comprehensive review of 46 school consultation outcome studies published from 1985 to 1995 and noted that 67% of all reported outcomes were positive, 28% were neutral, and only 5% were negative. Thus, outcome research on consultation published over a five-decade period has consistently documented the effectiveness of the approach.

Historical Influences on the Human Services Consultant Role

In order to understand the modern-day context for consultation within psychology and related fields, it is necessary to review some of the historical factors beginning in the 1950s that led to its acceptance and adoption as a significant role for many specialists. Here, we present some relevant and intertwined theoretical, professional, and pragmatic considerations.

Theoretical Issues

Thomas Szasz's (1960) conceptualization of psychopathology is often credited with challenging the assumptions of traditional psychological treatment, which was strongly aligned with the medical model (Hersch, 1968). In what Szasz termed the "myth of mental illness," mental illness does not reflect an organic disease entity as much as problems with living that are psychosocial in nature. It is therefore important to assess behavior as normal or abnormal within a social, situational, and moral context rather than only within an individual's psyche. Importantly, this view suggests that normal and abnormal behavior share the same processes of development, maintenance, and change. On a broader level, Szasz's revolutionary outlook demystified psychopathology and the role of the psychiatrist as well as emphasized the role of social institutions in the development of abnormal behavior.

A second, related issue concerns the rise of sociological and ecological models of abnormal behavior. The medical model, as applied to psychological treatment, began to lose support in the 1950s when sociological research substantiated clear linkages between the occurrence of mental illness and variables such as socioeconomic status, education, nutrition, and dysfunctional social networks. For example, Hollingshead and Redlich (1958) documented that aggressive, rebellious, and psychotic behavior was much more prevalent in the lower socioeconomic classes than in the middle and upper classes. These developments drew attention to variables outside the traditional individual-centered realm of mental health professionals, and provided credibility to nontraditional intervention programs by allied health professionals.

A third theoretical issue that facilitated the development of the human service consultant role was the rise of behavioral psychology. By the mid-1960s, psychoanalysis had begun to decline and behavior therapy was on the upswing. The behavioral perspective, in contrast to psychodynamic thought, views abnormal behavior as a function of environmental events and emphasizes learning and learning-based therapies. These therapeutic processes are specific, and mental health paraprofessionals (e.g., teachers, parents) can be trained to use many of them. Furthermore, behavioral treatments demonstrate relatively large, positive treatment effects. Very importantly, the emergence of behavioral psychology brought therapy out of the clinic setting, making possible the closer monitoring of treatment implementation and outcome. It also broadened the scope of potential clients and potential change agents (Gutkin & Curtis, 1982; Hersch, 1968; Tharp & Wetzel, 1969).

Professional Issues

There are at least three professional issues relevant to the emergence of the human services consultant role. The first is the problem with the clinical diagnosis of psychopathology, stemming from the early demonstrations that client assignment to specific DSM I and II diagnostic categories was generally unreliable (e.g., Zubin, 1967), and that symptomatology often failed to discriminate among diagnostic categories (e.g., Zigler & Phillips, 1961). Also, because the client's socioeconomic status rather than his or her diagnosis was shown to be the best predictor of the type of treatment received (Hollingshead & Redlich, 1958), many began to question the utility of diagnosis by highly trained mental health professionals prior to treatment (Hobbs, 1964).

Second, there was a failure on the part of mental health professionals to specify therapeutic goals and processes. As more therapies became available in the 1960s, it became less clear whether the overriding goal of psychological treatment was to reduce inner stress, cure mental illness, reorganize the patient's personality, remove symptoms, or promote mental health. With respect to therapeutic processes, active treatment components often were not identified or, in the case of behavior therapy and existentialism, polar opposite concepts were advanced as critical for treating mental illness (Hersch, 1968). Confusion for the field and the public ensued, with one result being the greater acceptance of nontraditional forms of therapy, such as encounter groups (Lieberman, Yalom, & Miles, 1973).

Third, the lack of demonstrated therapeutic outcomes for psychotherapy (Eysenck, 1952) led some to question its value and, in some cases, pursue other treatment options. One impact of Eysenck's findings, then, was to legitimize other forms of helping relationships, including basic human relations training (Carkhuff, 1969) and mutual help groups (Caplan & Killilea, 1976). Eysenck's classic study also focused psychology's efforts on demonstrating the benefits of psychotherapy, which others later documented (e.g., Smith & Glass, 1977).

Pragmatic Issues

One might specify three pragmatic reasons why the consultant role emerged in psychology and allied fields. First, there was the realization that there were insufficient numbers of trained mental health professionals to implement the medical model on a large scale (Albee, 1959). Even if there had been adequate personnel, there was the concern that psychotherapy as a means of addressing widespread mental health problems was ineffective and inefficient. As Hobbs (1963) stated, "A profession that is built on a 50-minute hour of a one-to-one relationship between therapist and client...is living on borrowed time" (p. 3). Complicating this situation was the discovery that the majority of individuals who needed help often failed to contact service providers (Hersch, 1968).

Second, during the 1960s there was a growing awareness of the differential delivery of mental health services among the rich and poor. Sociological research indicated that more serious mental health problems and risk factors were significantly overrepresented in the lower classes, but irrespective of diagnosis, the poor client received a quick treatment such as electric shock and the rich client received extended (and often costly) psychotherapy (Hollingshead & Redlich, 1958). During this time it seemed as though psychotherapy was appropriate only for a circumscribed client population – one that was young, attractive, verbal, intelligent, and successful (YAVIS).

Third, there were demonstrations of the successful use of paraprofessionals in various studies, suggesting that less formally trained individuals could contribute meaningfully to the prevention and treatment of mental disorders. In particular, researchers showed that parents, teachers, and teacher assistants could be trained to modify children's behavior in specific settings (e.g., Cowen et al., 1975; Hobbs, 1966).

   The culmination of all the above factors, which illustrate dissatisfaction with the traditional means of delivering mental health services, was a revolution termed the *community mental health movement.* This movement was officially sanctioned in 1963 when President John Kennedy signed into law the Community Mental Health Centers Act (P.L. 88-164) and continued until federal funds were reduced or reallocated in the early 1980s. Most importantly for our purposes, P.L. 88-164 specified consultation as one of five essential services that community mental health centers had to provide in order to receive federal monies. This provision gave consultation formal recognition and legitimized the placement of consultants in mental health agencies and schools. The community mental health movement also is acknowledged for its emphasis on: (1) population-oriented prevention (i.e., primary, secondary, and tertiary); (2) social support systems, which can lessen the risk of mental illness through the sharing of tasks and mobilization of resources; and (3) crisis intervention, which establishes a brief timeframe for action (Erchul & Schulte, 1993; Gallessich, 1982; Schulberg & Killilea, 1982).

Historical Influences on the School Consultant Role

Other notable trends occurred within public education and school psychology from the 1940s to the present. Many of these reflect changes in federal law and the resulting changes in school-based service delivery. In general, these trends have served to increase the need for psychologists and other professionals who consult with school personnel about educational and psychological issues.

Developments from the 1940s Through the 1970s

Seventy years ago, children with disabilities generally were excluded from education, as there was no mandate to serve this population. During the 1940s and 1950s, school psychology was viewed as the attempt to apply concepts and methods from clinical psychology to school adjustment problems. Beginning in the 1960s, state and federal funding became available to support special education programs, and school psychologists assumed the role of diagnostician. The passage of several states' laws that protected the educational rights of children with disabilities led to the authorization in 1975 of P.L. 94-142, the Education for All Handicapped Children Act (renamed the Individuals with Disabilities Education Act [IDEA], P.L. 102-119, in 1990). This law increased the number of children to be served and required multidisciplinary team evaluation procedures as well as a continuum of services to be provided in schools. Although many of these services were of a pull-out variety (where students with disabilities were sent to special classrooms), through its "least restrictive environment" provision, the law did provide the impetus for mainstreaming efforts. *Mainstreaming* refers to the integration of children with disabilities into regular education classes. P.L. 94142/IDEA broadened the potential role of school psychologists to include consultation, but at the same time established the school psychologist's primary role as "gatekeeper" for special education (Fagan & Wise, 2007).

As an aside, it must be stated that there have been numerous problems associated with the school psychologist's traditional role as gatekeeper. Practical and logistical issues have included increased caseloads and backlogs of outstanding assessments; lengthy delays for receipt of services; the likelihood of students in need of services deemed ineligible for them; and the high cost of evaluation-placement relative to other available services, such as the Title I reading program. It also has been acknowledged that the commonly used standardized tests have poor psychometric properties, and the results obtained from them are often of little use in making programming decisions and monitoring student progress. Within the ranks of school psychologists, there has been dissatisfaction over the reality that most are trained broadly but used narrowly. With the effectiveness of special education placements being questioned for some time, it is understandable that organizations such as the National Association of School Psychologists have pressed for an expanded role for school psychologists. Much more positively, there is a growing body of research demonstrating the manipulable influences on academic achievement and the educational applications of behavior analysis and intervention. This type of research certainly holds promise for the even greater involvement of school psychologists as consultants (Fagan & Wise, 2007; Martens, Witt, Daly, & Vollmer, 1999; Reschly, 1988; Tindall, 1979).

Developments During the 1980s and 1990s

Many changes were observed in public education in the 1980s. Perhaps as a result of state and federal cuts in the education budget, there emerged a greater focus on teacher accountability and a major rethinking of national educational goals, with a decided emphasis on outcomes. Within special education, there was rapid growth evidenced in mildly handicapped populations, particularly in the specific learning disability category. Responses to this trend included increased mainstreaming efforts as well as the initiation of prereferral intervention and prereferral intervention teams. The major purpose of prereferral intervention (also known as intervention assistance) was to promote mainstreaming by offering greater professional support to the classroom teacher. Also noticeable during the 1980s was the *Regular Education Initiative* (REI), a movement whose adherents believed that most mildly disabled students can and should receive instruction in the regular classroom. It should be clear that the concepts of mainstreaming, prereferral intervention, and REI emphasize the provision of consultative support to regular education teachers (Lloyd, Singh, & Repp, 1991; Reschly, Tilly, & Grimes, 1999; Zins, Curtis, Graden, & Ponti, 1988).

During the 1990s, seeds were sown for additional educational reforms. The 1997 amendments to IDEA (P.L. 105-17; IDEA 1997) helped to legitimize a consulting role for school psychologists, in that the amendments defined "psychological services" as including the development and implementation of positive behavioral supports and behavior intervention plans for students. The 1997 amendments also specified that triennial reevaluations of students in special education could be based on existing information and previous evaluations, if deemed appropriate by school personnel and parents. This provision theoretically served to decrease the time spent in formal psychoeducational assessment and thereby potentially increase the time spent in intervention and consultation activities (Fagan & Wise, 2007; Hoff & Zirkel, 1999).

Contemporary Developments

Since 2001, two very important acts of federal legislation concerning public education have been enacted. The first, the No Child Left Behind Act (NCLB; P. L. 107–110), specifies that the educational skills and progress of *all* children – regardless of disability status – be measured annually, with performance-based rewards and punishments issued to teachers and schools. It is clear that NCLB has institutionalized data-based decision-making and has raised the stakes for accountability in US public schools. The second, the Individuals with Disabilities Education Improvement Act (IDEIA 2004; P.L. 108-446), has opened the door to reconceptualizing the category of specific learning disability. IDEIA 2004 Part B regulations allow a response-to-intervention (RTI) approach to take the place of the traditional IQ/achievement discrepancy for eligibility determination. Briefly, *RTI* is a series of steps/tiers: (1) the classroom teacher implements scientific, research-based instruction/intervention with the student; (2) the student's academic progress is measured; (3) if the student does not show improvement, the intervention is intensified; (4) the student's progress is measured again; and (5) if the student still has not improved (i.e., responded), then he/she is eligible for special education services or a formal psychoeducational assessment that may result in special education placement (Burns & Gibbons, 2008; Fuchs, Mock, Morgan, & Young, 2003; Kratochwill, Clements, & Kalymon, 2007). Although we shall elaborate on this issue in Chap. 2, at this juncture it can be readily seen how the success of RTI depends on the skill of the specialist who consults with a classroom teacher.

Schools today face many challenges. There is increased concern over school violence and discipline problems, unprecedented diversity reflected within student populations, heightened accountability for both student and teacher performance, personnel shortages, and a substantial reduction in available funding. These and other emerging issues strongly suggest that there will be a need for school-based consultants for years to come (Erchul & Sheridan, 2008a; Esquivel, Lopez, & Nahari, 2007; Larson, 2008).

Reconceptualizing Consultation for Today's Schools

Historical Summary

Some of the more critical developments distilled from the preceding historical review are summarized in the following 12 points:

1. Over time, there has been a greater emphasis placed on social and situational determinants of behavior.
2. There is often no clear connection between assessment and treatment, suggesting that formal diagnosis and classification are unnecessary for effective treatment.
3. Many traditional, commonly used standardized assessment instruments have been shown to lack adequate psychometric properties, and thus are of little value in deciding on programming options and in monitoring client progress.
4. There has been a growing reliance on therapeutic methods other than psychotherapy.
5. Human services have been delivered increasingly in naturalistic settings rather than in clinic settings.
6. Direct care providers, rather than highly trained specialists, increasingly have been viewed as primary change agents.
7. The aims of population-oriented prevention can be served well through the provision of social support.
8. Crisis intervention has shown that effective psychological services can be delivered within a short time frame.
9. Experience with IDEA's multidisciplinary assessment teams and prereferral intervention teams suggests a clear benefit to sharing expertise and information among professionals representing different specialties.
10. The specification of treatment goals, procedures, and outcomes has become increasingly important as accountability for services looms larger in education and psychology.
11. The higher accountability for teacher performance, as reflected in NCLB, demands that consultants support teachers in their professional role.
12. The evolution of IDEA, from 1975 to the present, has served to institutionalize consultation as an essential service to be provided by school-based professionals.

Our Definition of School Consultation

These 12 points constitute a strong rationale for the delivery of psychological and educational services in schools via a consultation approach. As a step toward operationalizing this approach, we offer the following definition:

> School consultation is a process for providing psychological and educational services in which a specialist (consultant) works cooperatively with a staff member (consultee) to improve the learning and adjustment of a student (client) or group of students. During face-to-face

interactions, the consultant helps the consultee through systematic problem solving, social influence, and professional support. In turn, the consultee helps the client(s) through selecting and implementing effective school-based interventions. In all cases, school consultation serves a remedial function and has the potential to serve a preventive function.

Assumptions of Our Approach to School Consultation

The approach to consulting in schools presented in this book draws on our experiences as practicing consultants and researchers of processes and outcomes associated with psychological consultation. In presenting this approach, we wish to alert readers to our biases:

1. We promote a scientist–practitioner viewpoint by providing guidance for consultative practice whenever possible that is based on research findings rather than conjecture (Erchul & Sheridan, 2008a). As the title of this book implies, we believe our approach is based on solid conceptual ground and, where possible, relevant empirical findings.
2. We view successful school consultation as involving a combination of social influence and professional support within a problem-solving context. We refer to the resulting approach as an "integrated model of school consultation." What is specifically integrated in the model are two theoretically distinct approaches to consultation (i.e., Caplan's mental health consultation (1970; Caplan & Caplan, 1993/1999) and Bergan's behavioral consultation (1977; Bergan & Kratochwill, 1990)), as well as two general approaches to consultative practice (i.e., social influence and professional support) regarded by some as mutually exclusive concepts.
3. In contrast to a view taken in earlier editions of this volume, we believe that the integrated model of school consultation is highly appropriate for, and, in fact, intended for, internal consultants. An *internal* consultant is defined as one who spends most of his or her time working at a site that is the setting for consultation, although how consultees view the consultant frequently is a key factor as well (Brown, Pryzwansky, & Schulte, 2006). School psychologists, for instance, often are difficult to characterize strictly as internal or external consultants because they are more appropriately placed on an internal–external continuum (Alpert & Silverstein, 1985). For example, one school psychologist may be assigned full time to a single school (internal), but another may consult only 2 days each month with a particular school but has done so for 18 years, so is considered a regular staff member (external and internal). Particularly given this edition's emphasis on social influence (Chap. 3), problem-solving models and RTI (Chap. 2), and direct client assessment measures (Chap. 7) as well as a new case study (Chap. 11), the relevance of the integrated model to the internal consultant should be clear.
4. We believe the elements of Caplan's mental health consultation approach are useful for understanding relationship and system-level issues within consultation.

Many others (e.g., Brown et al., 2006; Davis & Sandoval, 1992; Heller & Monahan, 1977; Marks, 1995; Meyers, Parsons, & Martin, 1979) have offered similar endorsements.

5. Because of their documented effectiveness, we believe psychological interventions employing behavior analytic principles are well suited for use by professionals in school settings. This view, developed more fully in Chap. 8, is shared by others writing about school consultation, including Bergan and Kratochwill (1990), Sugai and Tindal (1993), and Watson and Sterling-Turner (2008).

6. We recognize the significance of multicultural and cross-cultural factors in school consultation (e.g., Ingraham, 2000; Ingraham, 2008; Ramirez, Lepage, Kratochwill, & Duffy, 1998) and, although we have not explicitly incorporated these factors into the integrated model, we encourage all consultants to assess the role of diversity issues in practice. In particular, Ingraham's (2000) five components for culturally competent school consultation offer a useful supplement to the ideas discussed in this volume. Our endorsement of diversity issues notwithstanding, we also encourage consultants to adopt a scientist–practitioner perspective to critically examine evidence for the construct validity of "cultural competence," as Frisby (2009) has so thoughtfully done.

Topics Not Addressed in Our Approach to School Consultation

The integrated model put forth in this book will prove useful to school consultants when applied to many situations, but does not claim to be equally useful to all. Important applications not addressed in this book include the following:

1. The approach is not an organization development model, although it assumes a basic understanding of the school as an organization in which consultation is provided. For example, in Chap. 4, we describe the school and note its importance as a setting for consultation, but we do not offer guidance on how the consultant can then engage in typical organization development activities such as survey feedback and team building. The key issues pertaining to organization development in schools have been discussed recently by Curtis, Castillo, and Cohen (2008), Illback and Pennington (2008), and Meyers, Proctor, Graybill, and Meyers (2009).

2. Although we apply an ecological framework to understanding the classroom and school as systems, we do not apply this framework to understand the family as a system, despite its clear importance to the overall effort of school consultation. Others who promote this valuable perspective include Christenson and Sheridan (2001), Esler, Godber, and Christenson (2008), and Sheridan and Kratochwill (2008).

3. It is not our intention to provide comprehensive coverage of any single consultation model, as other authors have (see, for example, Brown et al., 2006; Crothers, Hughes, & Morine, 2008; Dougherty, 2009). As noted previously, we emphasize

and draw on major elements of two well-established models – Caplan's mental
health consultation and Bergan's behavioral consultation.

4. There are many skills and much content knowledge that underlie the successful
practice of school consultation and a single volume unfortunately cannot be detailed
enough to address them all. Toward that end, we believe a serious student of school
consultation would benefit from reading supplementary materials that deal in depth
with topics such as interviewing and supportive communication, functional assessment, curriculum-based measurement, evidence-based academic and behavioral
interventions, response to intervention, and special education law.

The Rest of the Book

A major purpose of this book is to reduce the level of naiveté typically experienced
by the beginning school consultant. Toward that end, we attempt to provide a systematic approach to consultation that emphasizes the information necessary for one
to practice competently as a school consultant.

The book is divided into three sections. The first section is comprised of four
chapters that describe important background information, including the modern
context for school consultation, especially given provisions of NCLB and IDEIA
2004 (Chap. 2); how one can produce change employing social influence (Chap. 3);
and what it takes to understand the school as a setting for consultation (Chap. 4).
The second section, consisting of Chaps. 5–8, explains significant processes and
outcomes of school consultation. Chapters 5 and 6 focus on the integrated model of
consultation, emphasizing the elements of professional support, problem solving,
social influence, and the organizational context. Chapter 7 provides an overview of
direct client assessment techniques used in the contemporary practice of school
consultation. Recognizing that a mutually respectful relationship between professionals is a necessary but not sufficient condition for effective school consultation,
Chap. 8 provides guidance on how to select interventions and how to evaluate their
effectiveness relative to treatment outcome, integrity, and social validity.

The third section includes Chaps. 9–11. The key participants in school consultation, teachers and students, are the focus of Chaps. 9 and 10, respectively. Chapter
11 offers an actual two-interview school consultation case study and includes an
analysis of consultant behavior during each interview. An epilog chapter, summarizing important points and looking toward the future practice of school consultation, concludes the volume.

As noted earlier, the context for the practice of school consultation has shifted
dramatically over time and largely in response to acts of federal legislation. IDEA
1997 and IDEIA 2004, for example, are credited for having mandated elements of
practice such as positive behavioral interventions, strategies, and supports; functional behavioral assessment; and scientific, research-based interventions within a
multi-tiered RTI framework (Martens & DiGennaro, 2008). These topics – and the
new context for school consultation – are our focus as we proceed to Chap. 2.

Chapter 2
Problem Solving and Response to Intervention

The practice of school consultation today is quite different from that of the 1990s. Why is that the case? How has school consultation changed? It is the goal of this chapter to explore these complex questions.

Our explorations lead us to consider problem solving, response to intervention (RTI), and school consultation. However, our coverage of each in this chapter is intentionally unequal. Problem solving, for example, is introduced here and covered in more depth in Chaps. 5, 6, and 9. Likewise, school consultation is the focus of this entire book and its treatment in this chapter is minimal, as it instead provides a backdrop for the other two topics. That leaves RTI.

If you have not visited schools recently, or do not visit them regularly, you may be unaware of the ubiquitous presence of RTI. A brief definition of RTI is "the systematic use of assessment data to most efficiently allocate resources in order to improve learning for all students" (Burns & Gibbons, 2008, p. 1). In RTI, "students are exposed to multi-tiered interventions in general education settings to determine which students need what services delivered, with how much intensity, and for how long" (Gresham, 2009, p. 206). In a short time, RTI has greatly affected the way services are delivered to students, and certainly the practice of school consultation has been changed as a result.

It is important to realize that the RTI literature is already voluminous and continues to expand rapidly. Thus, we cannot comprehensively present RTI as much as introduce it along with related topics and offer a context for how together they mesh with the contemporary practice of school consultation. We proceed by describing (1) contextual influences on RTI and the contemporary practice of school consultation; (2) aspects of problem solving; (3) fundamental characteristics of RTI; and (4) relationships between and among problem solving, RTI, and school consultation.

W.P. Erchul and B.K. Martens, *School Consultation,* Issues in Clinical Child Psychology,
DOI 10.1007/978-1-4419-5747-4_2, © Springer Science+Business Media, LLC 2010

Establishing a Context for RTI and the Modern Practice of School Consultation

To explore the intertwined nature of RTI and school consultation, we build on background information presented in Chap. 1 using the framework of philosophical, legislative, and empirical influences advanced by Erchul and Sheridan (2008b).

Prevention as a Philosophical Influence

From its earliest beginnings, consultation in the human services has been concerned with preventing mental illness and educational failure (Zins & Erchul, 2002). *Primary prevention*, for instance, refers to lowering the rate of new cases of a disorder in a population over a period of time by counteracting harmful effects before they have an opportunity to produce the disorder (Caplan, 1964). School consultation has been shown to operate at the primary prevention level by demonstrating reductions in the number of referrals for special education services in a particular school following consultation with regular education teachers (e.g., Ponti, Zins, & Graden, 1988). Although the terms primary, secondary, and tertiary prevention basically have been replaced with the terms universal, selective, and indicated prevention, respectively (see Chap. 5), the recurring message is that consultants often work with consultees on existing problems to prevent future problems from occurring. Prevention, then, has always been a significant undercurrent in the consultation literature (Erchul & Sheridan, 2008b).

Certain elements of RTI also reflect the importance of prevention. First, the special education category of *specific learning disability* (SLD) historically has relied on documenting the presence of an IQ-achievement discrepancy. This conceptualization is acknowledged as psychometrically flawed and embodies a reactive "wait-to-fail" approach by withholding interventions until a child's achievement drops significantly below his or her IQ (Gresham, 2009). The Individuals with Disabilities Education Improvement Act of 2004 (IDEIA 2004) offers an alternate way to conceptualize SLD using RTI. Specifically, within RTI, a child suspected of SLD is presented with evidence-based interventions implemented with integrity. If the child responds favorably, then the learning difficulty is thought to have been treated successfully before a full-blown learning disability could develop. If the child responds poorly to these interventions, however, he or she is deemed eligible for further evaluation and assistance (including special education). The proactive, front-loading of intervention resources found in RTI thus is very consistent with a prevention/early intervention philosophy that utilizes an at-risk rather than deficit orientation (Gresham).

Another aspect of RTI that reflects a preventive orientation is the multitier system of intervention, specifically in its foundational tier (i.e., tier 1). Although we describe the system of tiers in greater detail later on, at this point it is sufficient to grasp that *universal screening* occurs in tier 1. With the universal screening of academics, for instance, all students receive brief measures of academic and/or behavioral competency that are evaluated at the level of the classroom or school building to answer these questions: (1) How many students are responding to the instruction provided?; (2) Is the instruction effective?; (3) How many students are at risk for failure?; and (4) Who are the students needing further assessment and possibly greater supports? (Ikeda, Neessen, & Witt, 2008). The described screening procedure represents a clear example of a primary/universal prevention activity within RTI.

NCLB and IDEIA 2004 as Legislative Influences

Several specific federal laws enacted since the early 2000s have led to notable educational reforms such as RTI that in turn have affected school consultation. The two laws considered here are the 2001 reauthorization of the Elementary and Secondary Education Act (better known as No Child Left Behind or NCLB) and IDEIA 2004. When compared to their immediate predecessors, these laws shifted the focus of schools' documentation from *how* their programs deliver educational services to the *results* they produce (Reschly & Bergstrom, 2009).

NCLB (2001)

The major contribution of NCLB is that it has made the US educational system accountable for learning by setting academic performance goals for all students and establishing rewards and sanctions for educational professionals to meet these goals. A driving assumption behind NCLB is that all students can learn, and all schools must be proficient in teaching basic reading and mathematics skills by the 2013–2014 academic year. Science-based practice in the classroom is the means by which this change is to occur. Some positive indicators of the impact of NCLB thus far include: (1) school personnel taking outcomes of student learning very seriously, (2) schools frequently conducting large-scale assessments and collecting a considerable amount of student data, and (3) school personnel using these data in decision making at both individual and system levels (Tilly, 2008). The high-stakes aspects of NCLB bode well for greater use of school consultation services and fostered the introduction of RTI later on in IDEIA 2004.

Along these lines, Burns and Gibbons (2008) made the salient point that "although RTI was born in special education law, it was conceived in the No Child Left Behind Act" (p. 4). Some NCLB provisions that are regarded as having facilitated the development of RTI are: (1) frequent collection and review of data; (2) accountability for results, such as through tracking a school's adequate yearly progress; (3) use of science-based instructional and intervention strategies; (4) reading instruction targeted toward five empirically based component areas; (5) emphasis on prevention and early identification/treatment of academic problems; and (6) public reports of student achievement by individual school, breaking these data down by categories such as student race/ethnicity, English language proficiency, and disability category (Reschly & Bergstrom, 2009).

IDEIA (2004)

A special education law, IDEIA 2004 is the current reauthorization of the Education for All Handicapped Children Act of 1975 (P.L. 94-142). The regulations for IDEIA 2004 Part B, released in August 2006 for implementation during the 2006–2007 academic year, present several implications for school consultation. The first of these, of course, is that RTI was introduced as an acceptable substitute for the time-honored IQ/achievement discrepancy eligibility determination for SLD. Although IDEIA 2004 links RTI exclusively to SLD identification, Reschly (2008) argued incisively that because the law specifies that RTI can be used *prior to* or as a part of the referral process, one cannot know ahead of time if a child has an SLD, and therefore RTI rightfully applies to all high-incidence disability categories. High-incidence disabilities include SLD, speech/language impairment, mental retardation, and other health impairment; these categories account for about 70% of all disabilities in the population within the age group of 3–21 (National Center for Educational Statistics, 2009). This line of thought has been instrumental in advancing an expanded role for school psychologists that involves them in more consultation, problem solving, and RTI activities.

Second, IDEIA 2004, like its predecessor, IDEA 1997, promotes *positive behavior support* (PBS). Positive behavior support is "an application of a behaviorally based systems approach to enhance the capacity of schools, families, and communities to design effective environments that improve the link between research-validated practices and the environments in which teaching and learning occur" (Office of Special Education Programs, n. d.). The objective of PBS is to establish and sustain primary/universal (i.e., school-wide), secondary/targeted (i.e., small group), and tertiary/indicated (i.e., individual) support systems that improve lifestyle results for all children and thereby produce meaningful educational and behavioral change (Simonsen & Sugai, 2009). Evaluations of school-wide PBS programs have shown that 84% of students annually receive one or fewer office referrals for major rule violations when primary/universal support is in effect (Horner, 2007, cited by Simonsen & Sugai). We highlight PBS because it illustrates both (1) how a multitiered system of intervention found in RTI can apply to behavioral as well as academic problems and (2) that consultation constitutes a viable means by which this type of service can be delivered (e.g., Knoff, 2008).

Empirical Influences

From provisions of the federal laws just reviewed, it is evident that we live in a time that heralds scientifically based professional practice. Other terms used to denote this orientation include "evidence-based intervention," "empirically supported treatment," "empirically validated therapy," and "evidence-based practice" (Erchul

& Sheridan, 2008b). Most importantly, this viewpoint dictates that a professional's actions should be informed by the best available research, and it is a view that is integral to the fields of mental health (Norcross, Beutler, & Levant, 2006), professional psychology (APA Presidential Task Force on Evidence-based Practice, 2006), and school psychology (Kratochwill et al., 2009). As scientist–practitioners, we hope that everyone undertaking RTI and school consultation will embrace this orientation.

Apart from this general commitment to science guiding practice, however, what are some specific empirical influences on RTI and school consultation? Reschly and Bergstrom (2009) presented eight such influences:

1. Applied behavior analysis;
2. Behavior assessment, curriculum-based measurement (CBM), and formative evaluation;
3. Principles of learning and instruction;
4. Meta-analysis findings;
5. Direct instruction;
6. Reading instruction;
7. Learning strategies; and
8. Consultation methods for problem solving.

Each listed area is a domain onto itself and to which many graduate degree programs dedicate an entire course! We shall not elaborate further on these empirical influences here, but do address each content area elsewhere in this book. It is evident that these research foundations influenced policy developments in the late 1990s to early 2000s, which then influenced federal law in the early- to mid-2000s Reschly & Bergstrom, (2009).

The activity of problem solving is fundamental to both school consultation (Brown, Pryzwansky, & Schulte, 2006) and RTI (Burns, Deno, & Jimerson, 2007). Next, we introduce problem solving by presenting a definition and key aspects as well as elements of problem solving carried out in a team-based format.

Problem Solving

What is Problem Solving?

In general, *problem solving* is a systematic process, wherein an issue of concern is identified, clarified, and analyzed to the point an appropriate strategy is selected or devised and then implemented to address the problem. Following implementation of the strategy, its impact on the problem is evaluated.

In psychology and education, problem solving may be usefully depicted through a series of questions, such as:

1. Is there a problem and what is it?
2. Why is the problem happening?

3. What can be done about the problem?
4. Did the intervention work? (Tilly, 2008, p. 18)

These questions correspond to four stages: problem identification, problem analysis, plan implementation, and problem evaluation (Bergan, 1977; Bergan & Kratochwill, 1990). It should come as no surprise that these problem-solving stages constitute essential features of RTI and school-based problem-solving (i.e., behavioral) consultation (Erchul & Schulte, 2009; Kratochwill, Clements, & Kalymon, 2007). Problem solving and the four stages are addressed in detail within the context of the integrated model of school consultation in Chaps. 5 and 6.

Problem-Solving Teams

Formal team-based problem solving in schools has been evident at least since the mid-1970s' enactment of P.L. 94-142, which required multidisciplinary teams to decide on student eligibility for and placement in special education (Gravois, Groff, & Rosenfield, 2009). Beginning in the 1980s, this group decision-making format evolved to also include prereferral intervention teams (PITs), which were intended to support teachers, decrease inappropriate referrals to special education, and help difficult-to-teach students in the regular classroom (e.g., Graden, Casey, & Christenson, 1985). Although group composition can vary, a PIT often includes the referring teacher, regular education teachers, special education teachers, school psychologist, other specialists, and a school administrator. Following a PIT's problem-solving discussion, it is assumed the classroom teacher will deliver an intervention to the student. Interestingly, a survey of state departments of education indicated that 86% of states now either require or recommend PITs, but most do not offer any guidance about how to implement them (Truscott, Cohen, Sams, Sanborn, & Franks, 2005). We present other information about PITs in Chap. 9.

Burns, Wiley, and Viglietta (2008) further distinguished PITs from problem-solving teams (PSTs). They noted that PSTs are more closely aligned with behavioral consultation (Bergan & Kratochwill, 1990) and its systematic problem analysis component in particular, and are more concerned with identifying interventions that produce positive results for children. In contrast, Burns et al. view the role of PITs as much more focused on special education referral issues.

Despite these apparent and important fundamental differences, PITs and PSTs have much in common, and it is clear that the extant research literature on PITs has implications for the practice of RTI, most specifically that a paradigm shift is required as teams move from a special education eligibility framework to one of identifying interventions that work. A sampling of this literature reveals that: (1) PITs can vary considerably in terms of member composition, overall goals, and interventions developed (Truscott et al., 2005); (2) PITs have demonstrated success in producing outcomes such as improving student academic achievement and lowering referral rates for special education (Burns & Symington, 2002); (3) PIT members perceive their own teams as functioning well and PITs in general as constituting an effective service delivery model (Bahr, Whitten, Dieker, Kocarek, & Manson, 1999); (4) teachers feel their opinions are often devalued by other team members; (5) teachers believe PIT-developed interventions are frequently unclear, redundant, or not tailored to the individual student; and (6) teachers experience frustration that PITs do not always take responsibility for intervention implementation and/or outcomes (Slonski-Fowler & Truscott, 2004). This mixture of accomplishments and challenges leads to many opportunities as PITs "become" PSTs in the RTI era.

Speaking of PSTs, two recent studies documented the importance of feedback provision as a way to increase procedural integrity and enhance RTI outcomes in a team-based format. First, using a multiple baseline design across three schools, Burns, Peters, and Noell (2008) sought to increase the implementation integrity of a problem-solving process by giving performance feedback. Feedback was provided to PSTs in the form of graphs of the percentage of behaviors specified on a 20-item procedural checklist that had been observed in the previous meeting. Improved procedural integrity resulted immediately from the introduction of performance feedback, with the PSTs showing an average increase in implementation of 78% of the checklist behaviors. However, feedback on procedural integrity did not greatly increase team behaviors related to student progress monitoring, intervention effectiveness evaluation, or treatment integrity assessment.

In a related PST study, Duhon, Mesmer, Gregerson, and Witt (2009) used a multiple baseline design across eight cases to assess the effect of performance feedback on establishing teacher treatment integrity and reestablishing it after it had dropped to an unacceptable level. Feedback on intervention implementation was delivered publicly to individual teachers during weekly PST meetings. Results showed that performance feedback was successful in improving or maintaining high levels of treatment integrity in all cases. Perhaps most significantly, these levels of teacher treatment integrity were associated with enhanced student academic performance on targeted skills as measured by researcher ratings. Duhon et al. concluded that the group setting for feedback provision established a context (and the social support/pressure) for teachers to carry out interventions with a high degree of integrity.

There is much more to learn about team-based problem solving in the present era of high-stakes accountability prompted by NCLB and IDEIA 2004. Given the emerging empirical foundation regarding PSTs, in current practice it would appear important to (1) train team members so that they can contribute meaningfully to the problem-solving process, (2) clarify for members the specific purpose/function of the PST, (3) follow scripts or manuals to consistently guide the process and offer feedback regarding procedural integrity, (4) select and faithfully implement intervention plans that are conceptually relevant and evidence based, (5) monitor treatment plan integrity and provide feedback when needed to improve implementation, and (6) directly assess student outcomes to measure RTI (Burns et al., 2008; Gravois et al., 2009; Martens & DiGennaro, 2008).

RTI

It has taken a considerable portion of this chapter to build a foundation for understanding RTI and the modern practice of school consultation. In this section, we discuss RTI itself, focusing on central components, basic approaches, tiers of service delivery, and typical assessment and intervention methods.

What is RTI?

RTI is "the practice of (1) providing high-quality instruction and intervention that match students' needs and (2) using students' learning rate over time and level of performance to make important educational decisions" (Buffum, Mattos, & Weber, 2009, p. 14). These decisions may include offering more intense interventions in the regular education classroom and determining whether a student should enter special education.

According to Reschly and Bergstrom (2009), the critical components of RTI are:

1. Provision of interventions to students via multiple tiers that reflect varying levels of intervention intensity and measurement precision;
2. Specification of goals and objectives for treatment that stem from a mixture of federal, state, and local standards;
3. Universal screening of all students to evaluate both current educational practices and the risk status of individual students;
4. Identification of student academic, behavioral, and/or emotional regulation needs as indicated by a discrepancy between expected and actual performance;
5. Selection and faithful implementation of evidence-based interventions that target student academic, behavioral, and/or emotional regulation needs;
6. Utilization of frequent progress monitoring with appropriate measures in order to assess the movement toward goals and changing either goals or interventions depending on the progress noted;
7. Recognition of some variability across specific RTI models relative to their comprehensiveness in contributing to educational decision making; and
8. Expectation that RTI data will be used to evaluate individuals, classrooms, and schools to make important educational decisions.

RTI Systems of Implementation

Once universal screening has determined a student needs additional support, there are two primary ways to deliver interventions in RTI: the problem-solving system and standard protocol system (Buffum et al., 2009). Understandably, more relevant to the purpose of this book is the *problem-solving system*, in which the problem-solving method is followed – as in behavioral consultation – to analyze and operationally define a student problem, select/design and implement a treatment plan with integrity, and assess the effectiveness of the plan (Gresham, 2009). As carried out within a team context, the problem-solving approach tends to require greater training of school personnel, but the resulting interventions tend to reflect their greater input and potential commitment as well Buffum et al., (2009).

A second major way to implement RTI is through a *standard protocol system*, in which a recognized set of evidence-based instructional approaches is applied to address student academic problems (Jimerson, Burns, & VanDerHeyden, 2007). For example, there are a number of standard protocol approaches shown to be effective in remediating severe reading problems in young readers, and a major advantage of this approach over the problem-solving approach may be its better quality control over instruction (Gresham, 2009). The standard protocol approach also may involve more straightforward staff training and decision making (Buffum et al., 2009).

Tier-Based Service Delivery Within RTI

RTI assumes that minor student problems can be solved using fewer resources and more serious student problems can be solved using greater resources (Tilly, 2008). To play out this assumption, services delivered to students in RTI are organized by a graduated series of steps or tiers. Although three- and four-tier RTI models have been reported in the literature, there is emerging support for a standardized three-tier model (Burns et al., 2007). Given this conceptualization, tier 1 describes the least intense level of intervention (e.g., regular education curriculum) and tier 3 describes the most intense level (e.g., long-term individual intervention). Besides the intensity of student needs and resulting intervention, the major differences between tiers are the proportions of students participating and the precision of measurement of student progress at each tier (Reschly & Bergstrom, 2009).

There is no shortage of visual representations of the tiers of RTI, variously depicted as a three-dimensional triangle (e.g., Burns & Gibbons, 2008), two-dimensional inverted triangle (e.g., Malecki & Demaray, 2007), cone (e.g., Graden, Stollar, & Poth, 2007), or pyramid (e.g., Buffum et al., 2009). Due to this variability, we shall not reproduce a particular version here in a figure. Rather, we proceed by describing the general characteristics of a three-tier RTI model and then summarizing them in Table 2.1.

Tier 1

Because all children in general education classrooms are clients in tier 1 (i.e., primary/universal prevention emphasis), the focus here is on the quality of research-based instructional practices in the core curriculum. *Benchmark assessment* and/or

Table 2.1 Characteristics of a Generic Three-tier RTI Model

Tier	Population	Description	Assessment
1	All students (academic and behavioral needs for 80–90% of students are handled at tier 1)	Primary/universal/core program: provide excellent core instruction through evidence-based curricula and instructional practices, address minor problems using a best practices approach and sharing strategies that work for other teachers	Benchmark assessment done at least 3 times per year; and data are used to plan services at core and consider progress monitoring of selected students
2	5–15% of students	Secondary/targeted/supplemental level: address moderate problems using small-group evidence-based interventions	Progress monitoring done at least monthly
3	1–5% of students	Tertiary/indicated/intensive level: address severe problems using intensive, individualized evidence-based interventions	Progress monitoring done at least weekly, plus informal classroom-based assessments

Note. Adapted from Buffum et al. (2009), Burns and Gibbons (2008), and Tilly (2008)

universal screening of students on basic skills should occur at least three times a year, and results of these evaluations are helpful to (1) evaluate the effectiveness of core instruction, (2) identify those students experiencing difficulties in order to address their needs immediately, and (3) establish school-based norms to facilitate the setting of academic performance goals. Individual growth over time is documented through *progress monitoring*, which allows one to see the extent to which instruction has supported a student in meeting goals in the core curriculum and at what rate. In tier 1, a teacher may give extra support and time to an "at-risk" student who is failing to meet established performance goals. It is estimated that 10–20% of students will not respond to tier 1 science-based instructional practices, so they will be moved to services provided at the more intensive tiers. Percentages or proportions are used to help schools refine their instructional practices. Core instruction is effective when it meets 80% or more of the students' needs. Until core instruction attains this level, schools must not begin to try to address small group and individual needs because the reality is that they lack the resources to do so (Buffum et al., 2009; Burns & Gibbons, 2008; Tilly, 2008).

Tier 2

Tier 2 serves 5–15% of students and has a secondary/targeted prevention emphasis. This tier incorporates the core curriculum instruction of tier 1 along with supplemental instruction, which often includes small group research-based interventions. When feasible, these groups should be formed around similar student skill deficits, and progress monitoring should occur at least monthly. A student's response to tier 2 interventions is typically evaluated using a *dual discrepancy approach*, which means both the (1) level of progress and (2) rate of growth over time relative to predetermined criteria are considered. For example, if a first grade student is below criterion on a measure of oral reading fluency (e.g., reading fewer than 30 words/min) and displays a growth rate slope that is more than one standard deviation below the average rate for other first graders, then the conclusion is that progress is inadequate. If after a reasonable period of adjusting the intervention the selected intervention(s) is not working, the student may be moved to tier 3 or to an entirely different core curriculum. Of course, if the student has responded (i.e., the interventions have produced clear gains), he or she may be returned to the core program of tier 1 (Buffum et al., 2009; Burns & Gibbons, 2008; Tilly, 2008).

Tier 3

The remaining students (approx. 5%) are served in tier 3, which has a tertiary/indicated prevention emphasis. This tier consists of the core curriculum supplemented by intensive instruction/intervention, which is often delivered one-on-one and with no more than three students to one educator. The main differences between tiers 2 and 3 do not relate to the interventions themselves but rather to their intensity, duration, and frequency, with tier 3 interventions typically being more intense, more frequent, and of longer duration. Progress monitoring also takes place more often – it is recommended that specific skills be assessed weekly if not more frequently. A dual discrepancy approach again is usually used to determine student responses to intervention. Those who are successful in tier 3 may be reintegrated into tier 1 or 2, but those who fail to meet criteria following intensive, repeated intervention may remain in tier 3 or be referred for special education evaluation (Buffum et al., 2009; Burns & Gibbons, 2008; Tilly, 2008).

Additional Considerations

There are several other points relevant to a discussion of tiers within RTI. First, because of RTI's origins as an alternative to diagnosing SLD, it is logical but wrong to think of RTI as pertaining only to academics. RTI addresses socio-emotional and behavioral functioning as well and many RTI models clearly make this point (e.g., Graden et al., 2007). Second, how long a student stays at tier 2 or tier 3 is, of course, related to his or her responsiveness to the selected intervention, the amount of time the team estimates the student will need to reach the goal, and whether the student has other circumstances that the team wants to consider. However, some guidelines for the length and modality of treatment at tier 2 is 30-min sessions 3 days/week in groups of 3–6 students for 6–8 weeks, and at tier 3 is 30-min sessions 5 days/week in smaller groups or individually for 6–8 weeks (Buffum et al., 2009). Obviously, these multiweek "doses" of intervention may be repeated as necessary, always keeping in mind that the goal is for the intervention to help the student to catch up to peers.

Assessment and Intervention Methods Within RTI

The assessment and intervention methods commonly seen in RTI and school consultation are extensive and varied and are the central focus of Chaps. 7 and 8, respectively. In concluding this introduction to RTI, we offer some general thoughts about its assessment and intervention techniques.

Relative to assessment, RTI makes extensive use of CBM in universal screening and progress monitoring. CBM offers a precise, direct way to assess student functioning and progress in basic academic skill areas. CBM probes of 1–3 min each can be administered repeatedly to measure skills such as oral reading fluency, spelling, math computation, and writing. A popular CBM measure within RTI is the Dynamic Indicators of Early Literacy Skills (DIBELS; Good & Kaminski, 2002), which assesses seven areas and can generate graphical displays of data to gauge both individual and school-wide performance. When compared to traditional norm-referenced assessment, advantages of CBM include being more closely related to the curriculum, more sensitive to smaller changes in performance, and shorter in duration (Merrell, Ervin, & Gimpel, 2006). Another advantage of CBM is its greater utility to teachers and parents who generally grasp the missing skills that CBM assesses, and then connect more readily with appropriate interventions for those skills.

Another common evaluation technique in RTI is *functional behavioral assessment* (FBA). FBA is a systematic way to collect information about antecedents (i.e., what happens before a student's behavior), behaviors (i.e., what the student is doing), and consequences (i.e., what happens after the behavior) in order to specify causal reasons for the behavior and then intervene to foster acceptable alternative behavior (Witt, Daly, & Noell, 2000). FBA has its origins in the fields of developmental disabilities and applied behavior analysis, and thanks to provisions of IDEIA 2004 (e.g., PBS), it is commonplace in school-based practice today (Steege & Watson, 2008). Within RTI, FBA appears to be useful in developing interventions in tier 2 (Rathvon, 2008) and tier 3 (Buffum et al., 2009). Although there may be a tendency to think that FBA applies only to the assessment of behavioral problems, its relevance to academic problems is also abundantly clear (e.g., Daly, Witt, Martens, & Dool, 1997). Other techniques related to FBA (e.g., brief experimental analysis of behavior, systematic formative evaluation) are presented in Chap. 7.

Relative to interventions within RTI, there is a plethora of evidence-based interventions available to address academic and behavioral problems of school-aged children (Morris & Mather, 2008). Although we expand on the possibilities in Chap. 8, meta-analytic results have shown effect sizes of 0.70 and higher for a variety of these interventions based on applied behavior analysis; direct, systematic, and explicit instruction; problem solving, and behavior assessment. Effect sizes above 0.50 have been documented for various interventions that target math skills, writing skills, and learning strategies (Reschly & Bergstrom, 2009). This area of knowledge changes rapidly, but fortunately the *What Works Clearinghouse* (http://ies. ed.gov/ncee/wwc) and *Intervention Central* (http://www.interventioncentral.org)

websites make available useful current information. Finally, we would like to reinforce the message that the effectiveness of any evidence-based intervention hinges on its fidelity of implementation (i.e., treatment integrity) (Martens & McIntyre, 2009). This statement is particularly true when the intervention is delivered through an intermediary (e.g., teacher) rather than a specialist, as is nearly always the case in school consultation and RTI.

Conclusion

To close this chapter, we summarize our views on the relationships between and among the interrelated constructs of problem solving, RTI, and school consultation. First, *problem solving* underlies both RTI and consultation and, in fact, problem solving is a core task within our integrated model of school consultation. Although RTI and problem solving are used as synonyms in certain contexts (Reschly & Bergstrom, 2009), not all RTI involves a problem-solving process in that a standard protocol approach may be used instead (Gresham, 2007). Also, RTI may be portrayed as a system of tiered interventions that makes use of problem solving at each level, whereas problem solving also can be a stand-alone process that advances through the stages/questions described earlier (Reschly & Bergstrom). Furthermore, early approaches to problem solving (e.g., behavioral consultation) were not devised with today's RTI multitiered system of interventions in mind, although clearly they have been useful in conducting prereferral interventions since the 1980s (Kratochwill et al., 2007).

Second, it is apparent that RTI incorporates problem solving and its effective implementation calls for the same skills as those required in school consultation. Finally, we regard *school consultation* as the overarching construct of the three in that problem solving is one aspect of consultation and, although all RTI activities invoke consultation to some degree, not all school consultation focuses on RTI issues. This position is echoed by Gutkin and Curtis (2009) who stated: "It is apparent that a [problem solving]/RTI model is not only consistent with, but in fact dependent on, the delivery of effective consultation services by school psychologists and other educational specialists for successful implementation" (p. 594).

Although a school consultant needs to be well versed in the many issues surrounding RTI, we do not believe that school consultation will ever become synonymous with RTI. In promoting this view, we intend to introduce some healthy skepticism about the long-term viability of RTI, as have others (e.g., Reynolds & Shaywitz, 2009). On a grander scale, Gene Cash, a past President of the National Association of School Psychologists, has proclaimed, "RTI is a wonderful service delivery model, but it is not the future of school psychology" (2009, p. 2). Problem solving, on the other hand, is more likely to endure as a core characteristic of consultation and an essential means to deliver specialized services to students, and that it is why it is central to the integrated model of school consultation.

Importantly, this chapter has promoted the view that school consultation now takes place in an era of high-stakes, team-based service delivery that demands evidence-based practice. These circumstances are very different from those that originally gave rise to consultation (e.g., Caplan, 1963), and understandably may lead one to question some fundamental assumptions of consultation described in Chap. 1. For example, because within RTI an evidence-based intervention must be used and be implemented faithfully, a teacher is no longer free to reject an intervention from a PST because it is unfamiliar, time consuming, or philosophically unappealing (Martens & DiGennaro, 2008). Likewise, confidentiality of communications within consultation may not be possible because so many school personnel comprise a PST and information and opinions are freely shared (Caplan, Caplan, & Erchul, 1995).

From content presented thus far in this book, it may be surmised that the school consultant's role may be characterized as that of a change agent (Conoley, 1981b). To realize this role fully, the consultant must understand how to accomplish change through the exercise of interpersonal influence, and this is the focus of Chap. 3.

Chapter 3
Promoting Change in Schools

The central purpose of this chapter is to demonstrate that a primary role of a consultant is to serve as a change agent in the school. By "change," we are referring to the purposeful alteration of beliefs, attitudes, or behaviors of children, adolescents, and adults who are part of the school setting. Given our definition of school consultation presented in Chap. 1, the consultant acts in a direct, face-to-face manner to change the beliefs, attitudes, or behaviors of the adults who are consultees. In turn, consultees work with students, intervening directly in classroom-based problems. To serve as an effective change agent, the consultant needs to understand interpersonal influence and how it relates to the consultant/consultee relationship.

We begin by offering a rationale for why it is important to focus on consultee change in consultation. Next, the unique nature of the psychologist–teacher consultative relationship is examined and issues surrounding social influence in consultation are explored. We then present three frameworks for understanding and promoting change: (1) Chin and Benne's (1969) general strategies for effecting change in human systems; (2) French and Raven's (1959; Raven, 1965) bases of social power model; and (3) Raven's (1992, 1993) power–interaction model of interpersonal influence. Elements of these frameworks are applied throughout the chapter to the practice of school consultation.

Changing Beliefs, Attitudes, and Behaviors Within Consultation

The Need for Consultee Change

The phrase, "psychological services in schools," historically has meant delivering direct clinical services to children and adolescents, including psychological assessment, counseling, and psychotherapy (Fagan & Wise, 2007). However, a more recent theme in the school psychology literature is that the provision of comprehensive school psychological services depends on the psychologist's ability to offer indirect services to adult caregivers (Conoley & Gutkin, 1986). The term *indirect services* refers to psychological services, in which a party other than the psychologist

W.P. Erchul and B.K. Martens, *School Consultation*, Issues in Clinical Child Psychology, DOI 10.1007/978-1-4419-5747-4_3, © Springer Science+Business Media, LLC 2010 is the primary intervention agent providing treatment directly to clients. Examples include consultation, prereferral intervention, in-service training, program evaluation, and research. Conoley and Gutkin noted that the increasing viability of indirect services is due to several well-documented factors, including:

1. There are not enough fully trained professionals to offer direct therapeutic treatment to those clients who need it.
2. Lesser-trained individuals, who are often readily available and less expensive to hire, can offer quality direct services to clients if given appropriate training, support, and supervision.
3. Indirect psychological services, when implemented well, can create ripple effects that may include nonprofessional or paraprofessional staff learning new skills and passing them along to others, as well as the generalization and successful application of these new skills to novel problems they will encounter in the future.

So how can the effective provision of indirect psychological services be facilitated? The *Paradox of School Psychology* holds that "to serve children effectively, school psychologists must, first and foremost, concentrate their attention and professional expertise on adults" (Gutkin & Conoley, 1990, p. 212). Consequently, the successful delivery of indirect services "depend[s] to a large extent on psychologists' abilities to influence the behavior of third-party adults" (Conoley & Gutkin, 1986, p. 403). Along these lines, we contend that *influence is necessary in school consultation in order to increase the probability that teachers will function effectively as intervention agents as well as engage in activities that potentially lead to the prevention of student academic failure and mental illness.*

With respect to teachers serving as effective intervention agents in their classrooms, consider some common explanations for why they may *fail* as intervention agents:

1. They may lack essential skills, such as how to observe students systematically or how to implement evidence-based interventions. Even if teachers possess adequate skills, they may not display them for a variety of reasons.
2. They may hold unrealistic beliefs about children with special needs, such as believing that a child with a diagnosis of attention-deficit/hyperactivity disorder (ADHD) will never learn to read, or a student with a learning disability will not show significant academic gains until the child's home environment improves. Caplan (1970) referred to these stereotypical, self-fulfilling prophecies as "themes."
3. They may harbor unusual attitudes toward support specialists, such as what these specialists can achieve with students with disabilities in special education classrooms is "magical" and simply cannot be replicated in their own classrooms (Martens, 1993b).

Thus, to address skill and performance deficits and to alter misguided beliefs and attitudes such as those listed, one can see how critical it is for school consultants not only to understand interpersonal influence but also to possess the skills needed to implement influence strategies (Hughes, 1992; O'Keefe & Medway, 1997). Also, the context of IDEIA 2004 and RTI (see Chap. 2) indicates that the "consult and hope" era of school consultation is over; consultants now have a clear professional responsibility to ensure that teachers implement evidence-based interventions with integrity (Martens & DiGennaro, 2008).

With respect to teachers playing a role in preventing student educational failure and promoting mental health, much of the same logic applies. For example, adoption of a classroom-based Tier 1/universal prevention approach (i.e., activities aimed at preventing the emergence of educational and psychological problems in all class members) may require an alteration of a teacher's perception of the value of prevention and the corresponding activities needed to achieve it. Similarly, a teacher would not be expected to effectively implement a Tier 2/selective prevention approach (i.e., early detection and treatment of problems in at-risk students) unless properly trained to carefully observe student behavior. We shall return to the topic of prevention in Chap. 5; at this juncture, however, the message should be clear that effective school-based intervention and prevention activities rarely occur solely on the basis of teachers having the proper information. Rather, the exercise of influence is needed in order to achieve change.[1]

Helping the Consultee to Change

But what about "helping"? Shouldn't not we always "collaborate" when we consult? Should the consultant influence consultees and the process of consultation? Aren't school consultants expected to assist, and even "empower," teachers instead of influence them? Aren't there ethical issues involved when we as consultants influence others? This next section explores these questions.

Collaboration: What Is It?

In our view, *collaboration* is a term that many freely use, but very few have operationally defined in a meaningful way (Erchul, 1999). One clear exception to this generalization is Schulte and Osborne (2003), who comprehensively reviewed the literature to glean the various meanings of collaboration. They proposed six different, though overlapping, views of collaboration that exist within consultation:

1. Equal-but-different roles for consultant and consultee;
2. Consultant as a peer facilitator;
3. A unique service-delivery model that differs from consultation;
4. Consultant-structured consultee participation;
5. Participants' shared assent to variable roles; and
6. Participants having equal value/equal power.

Because of space limitations, we cannot offer detailed descriptions of or comparisons among these six views. We wish to reinforce Schulte and Osborne's point, however, that these meanings of collaboration have been implicit or otherwise obscured in the literature. As a result, when one speaks of being "a collaborative consultant," a shared understanding cannot be assured and this lack of precision in language has implications for both practice and research (Schulte & Osborne). Gutkin (Gutkin, 1999a, 1999b; Gutkin & Curtis, 2009) in fact has criticized our reticence to use the term *collaboration* when he himself does not offer a clear operational definition of this term. In sum, we believe the definitional boundaries for what constitutes *consultation* are more distinct than those for *collaboration*, and, although we shall continue to make references to collaboration, we prefer to discuss aspects of consultation instead.

Notwithstanding the multiple views and often fuzzy definitions, it is clear that some notion of collaboration is relevant to achieve consultee behavior change. For example, when referring to 1940s' organizational research on the involvement of factory managers and supervisors in decision making in order to reduce their resistance to change, Schulte and Osborne (2003) stated, "collaboration was seen as a way for a consultant to exert influence and induce change without eliciting…resistance from the consultee because there was no attempt to directly or overtly change consultee beliefs or actions" (p. 121). Therefore, inviting the consultee to actively participate – one view of collaboration – has been recognized for decades as a way to successfully achieve social influence within consultation.

Should Consultants Influence Consultees and the Process of Consultation?

The simple answer to this question is "yes." School-based consultation research studies published over the past 35 years indicate that positive outcomes of school consultation result when the consultant uses "strategic interpersonal communication" (Daly & Wiemann, 1994) and "dyadic social influence" (Barry & Watson, 1996) to persuade consultees and actively direct the overall process of consultation. Although different studies have used different measures of influence, some positive effects or correlates of a consultant exerting influence include: accurate problem identification, leading to plan implementation and problem resolution; consultee perceptions of overall satisfaction with consultation and the consultant as effective; consultant perceptions of the consultee as more willing to collect baseline data and to implement a treatment plan; observed treatment implementation (i.e., integrity) by teachers; and improvements in student behavioral and academic performance. In the sections that follow, we describe a sampling of this research, specifically five studies presented in chronological order.

Early Process–Outcome Studies

Bergan and Tombari (1976) applied the Consultation Analysis Record (CAR; Bergan & Tombari, 1975) to examine messages spoken by school-based behavioral consultants and then relate indices based on them to consultation outcomes. However, in order to understand the context for their study, it is necessary to briefly describe both behavioral consultation and the CAR. Behavioral consultation (Bergan, 1977; Bergan & Kratochwill, 1990) is essentially a four-stage, systematic problem-solving process involving a consultant and consultee. The stages of behavioral consultation include three separate interviews, each of which contains specific objectives that a consultant is expected to address. The four stages are problem identification, problem analysis, plan implementation, and problem evaluation, with formal interview types corresponding to all but plan implementation (see Chap. 5 for additional information).

The CAR (Bergan & Tombari, 1975) is the only verbal interaction coding system designed exclusively for use in consultation research and practice, and it classifies independent clauses that are spoken into four categories: message source, message content, message process, and message control (Chap. 5 again offers additional information). It bears noting that message control refers to how one person influences another person through greater use of elicitors (i.e., clauses that request action or information) than emitters (i.e., clauses that provide information). The *index of interview control* (i.e., message control) is defined as one's proportion of elicitor-coded clauses to overall clauses. Within behavioral consultation, it is assumed that the effective consultant will guide the problem-solving process through the skillful use of elicitors (Bergan & Kratochwill, 1990).

In their seminal study, Bergan and Tombari (1976) used the CAR to code the verbal behaviors of 11 behavioral consultants working with classroom teachers on whose watch 806 students were referred for psychological evaluation because of various academic and behavioral difficulties. Of these total cases, 43% achieved problem identification within behavioral consultation; 31%, plan implementation; and 30%, problem solution. Perhaps the most often cited findings from this study are: (1) the single best predictor of whether an intervention plan was implemented was the occurrence of problem identification ($r = 0.76$), and (2) the single best predictor of problem solution was the occurrence of plan implementation ($r = 0.98$). Clearly, what the behavioral consultant accomplishes in the problem identification interview (PII) has implications for the eventual success of consultation.

For our purposes, it is equally interesting to note that of four consultant effectiveness indices devised by Bergan and Tombari (1976), the index of interview control presented the highest correlations with the occurrence of problem identification ($r = 0.40$) and problem solution ($r = 0.29$) as well as the second-highest correlation with plan implementation ($r = 0.27$). In other words, a consultant's ability to influence the course and direction of interviews through elicitors was linked significantly to the accomplishment of important consultation outcomes. It is especially noteworthy that consultant message control was associated with problem identification because "[c]onsultants successful in identifying problems were almost invariably able to solve those problems" (p. 3).

In a second study, Erchul (1987) expanded on Bergan and Tombari's (1976) findings regarding interview control and influence by utilizing a relational communication framework. Relational communication examines how the process of face-to-face communication unfolds (e.g., through interruptions, topic changes/other's acceptance of topic changes, requests/other's compliance with requests) rather than through a content analysis of the actual spoken messages (Rogers & Escudero, 2004). Unlike the CAR, relational communication coding systems look at how the recipient of a message responds, thus providing information on the interaction between two people (Martens, Erchul, & Witt, 1992).

Within the Rogers and Farace (1975) relational communication coding system, the variable *domineeringness* is defined as the number of Person A's one-up messages (i.e., bids to define the dyadic relationship) divided by the total number of A's messages; it is considered an index of *attempted influence*. *Dominance* for A is defined as the proportion of one-down messages (i.e., acceptance of the other's relational definition) by Person B to all one-up messages offered by A; it is considered to be an index of *successful influence* (Erchul, Grissom, & Getty, 2008). Although it is well beyond the scope here to explain the details of relational communication coding systems, suffice it to say that the assignment of one-up and one-down codes to individual messages is based on others' systematic study of interpersonal communication processes.

Erchul (1987) used a modified version of the Rogers and Farace (1975) coding system to study eight school consultants who worked with one consultee each across the three behavioral consultation interviews (Bergan & Kratochwill, 1990). Three interesting findings emerged. First, consultants had higher domineeringness and dominance scores than consultees across all three interviews, a finding that challenged earlier held beliefs that the consultative relationship is supposed to be collaborative and nonhierarchical. Second, consultant dominance scores correlated 0.65 with consultee perceptions of consultant effectiveness, suggesting that more influential consultants were viewed more favorably by consultees. Third, consultee domineeringness scores correlated −0.81 with consultant perceptions of the extent to which consultees followed through with the collection of baseline data on clients. This result indicates that consultees' attempts to influence consultants were associated with lower consultant evaluations of consultee participation in baseline data collection.

In a third investigation, Fuchs, Fuchs, Bahr, Fernstrom, and Stecker (1990) showed that forms of behavioral consultation in which the consultant is directive or "prescriptive" can facilitate effective classroom interventions for students having problems such as inattention, low motivation, or poorly developed academic skills. These researchers compared the effects of three levels of behavioral consultation, involving students and teachers representing grades 5, 6, and 7. All three levels of consultation included a standardized intervention package, so that teachers could use a consistent strategy to address specific student behaviors. The lowest level of consultation services consisted of the first two stages of behavioral consultation (problem identification and problem analysis) but did not offer assistance in implementing or assessing the effects of the intervention. The intermediate level of consultation services offered all elements of the lowest level and added consultant visits to the classroom in order to facilitate the implementation of the treatment. The highest level of consultation services included all aspects of the intermediate level and added a component, in which the consultant conducted a formative evaluation to modify the treatment if needed.

Fuchs, Fuchs, Bahr, et al.'s (1990) results indicated that the intermediate and highest levels of consultation (i.e., the more prescriptive versions) resulted in greater improvemenlts in students' problem behaviors. Specifically, with greater consultant involvement and control over the process, (1) student behavior improved significantly relative to an untreated control group, and (2) postintervention independent observation of student behavior revealed significant decreases in the discrepancy between target student and normal peer behavior. They concluded that a prescriptive approach to consultation is highly recommended for use in schools where "stress is high, expertise in consultation is low, and consultation time is nonexistent" (p. 511). Our experience suggests that this description applies to many schools in which consultation occurs.

Contemporary Process–Outcome Studies

The more complex answer to the question, "Should consultants influence consultees and the process of consultation?" is, "Yes, but it depends in part on the stage of consultation." Below we describe two school-based behavioral consultation studies from Lehigh University's Project PASS (Promoting Academic Success for Students; DuPaul et al., 2006; Jitendra et al., 2007) that elaborate on this answer and offer a more modern perspective on the interpersonal dynamics of school consultation.

Erchul et al. (2007) studied the connections between verbal interaction patterns in the initial behavioral consultation interview (i.e., PII) and the outcomes of consultation involving students with ADHD. Similar to Erchul (1987), they adopted a relational communication research perspective and focused on the variables of domineeringness and dominance. Based on findings such as those of Bergan and Tombari (1976) and Erchul (1987), it was predicted: (1) consultant PII dominance would be positively related to consultation outcomes and (2) teacher PII dominance would be negatively related to consultation outcomes.

Erchul et al. (2007) coded 42 PIIs using the Rogers and Farace (1975) relational communication coding system. All cases were taken from the Project PASS Intensive Data-based Academic Intervention (IDAI) consultation model, in which research-based academic interventions were designed within a data-driven framework that supplied ongoing feedback to teachers [similar in some ways to Fuchs, Fuchs, Bahr, et al.'s (1990) most prescriptive version of consultation]. Participants were 42 elementary school students with ADHD, 42 teachers, and 5 consultants. PII domineeringness and dominance were computed for teachers and consultants and then correlated with four outcome variables. The application of more stringent statistical criteria reduced this dataset to 31 cases prior to analyses.

With regard to relational communication variables, Erchul et al. (2007) found that within consultant/teacher dyads, one person's successful influence (i.e., dominance) was negatively associated with the other's successful influence ($r = -0.36$). This finding means that as one person's influence increases, the other's decreases, a relational pattern that supports the existence of a cooperative, leader/follower relationship in school consultation. Also, teacher PII dominance correlated significantly with: (1) teacher ratings of intervention effectiveness on the Behavior

Intervention Rating Scale (BIRS; Elliott & Von Brock Treuting, 1991) ($r = 0.48$), and (2) teacher ratings of student progress-to-target behavior using goal attainment scaling (Kiresuk, Smith, & Cardillo, 1994) ($r = 0.33$). There was also a negative association between teacher PII dominance and teachers carrying out interventions with integrity ($r = -0.32$).

In contrast to some other studies using similar methodologies, Erchul et al. (2007) documented teachers' influence over consultants during the PII was linked to important outcomes. The more teachers directed conversation during the PII and consultants followed that direction, the more favorable were teacher perceptions of intervention effectiveness and student progress. These findings were discussed in light of the explicit focus of these interventions being on students' academic rather than behavioral problems, a focus that may not have always been the teachers' highest priority, given that all students were diagnosed with ADHD. The authors also noted more generally how the context for school consultation in the 1980s differs from the context today.

In a follow-up study, Erchul et al. (2009) investigated the associations between verbal interaction patterns in the second behavioral consultation interview (i.e., problem analysis interview or PAI) and the outcomes of consultation involving students with ADHD. Although there was some attrition, the same participants were involved in this study as in Erchul et al. (2007). The sample included 4 consultants, 20 teachers, and 20 elementary school students with ADHD. It is important to note that in the PAI stage of Project PASS IDAI consultation, the consultant proposes several research-based interventions and then asks the teacher to choose the intervention(s) believed to be the most appropriate to his or her classroom situation. This strategy appears to add a new element of interview control/influence to behavioral consultation.

Erchul et al. (2009) coded audiotaped PAIs using the Rogers and Farace (1975) coding system, and domineeringness and dominance were calculated. Significant results were: (1) teacher domineeringness correlated -0.66 with consultant observations of teacher treatment integrity; (2) teacher dominance correlated -0.63 with teacher-rated BIRS intervention acceptability; (3) teacher dominance correlated -0.61 with teacher-rated BIRS intervention effectiveness; and (4) consultant dominance correlated 0.59 with consultant observations of teacher treatment integrity. Unlike Erchul et al. (2007), who found teacher influence within the PII (i.e., initial interview) to be positively associated with outcomes, teacher PAI influence was negatively associated with outcomes. In addition, a consistent finding across both studies was that teacher PII dominance and PAI dominance were negatively associated with treatment integrity – a key element of RTI that is discussed in greater detail in Chap. 8.

Relevance of These Five Studies for School Consultants

Collectively, Bergan and Tombari (1976), Erchul (1987), and Fuchs, Fuchs, Bahr, et al. (1990) make it clear that the effective school consultant needs to be a skilled and persuasive communicator in order to facilitate successful problem identification, intervention selection/implementation, and problem resolution within consultation. Given a more contemporary context, the results of Erchul et al. (2007) and Erchul et al. (2009) refine this assessment by indicating favorable outcomes of school consultation are associated with teachers' influence over consultants during the problem identification stage (assuming successful problem identification also has occurred), and with consultants' influence over teachers during the problem analysis/ intervention selection stage. This conclusion is tempered, however, by the finding that teachers' influence over consultants is negatively correlated with treatment plan integrity during both stages. A significant implication for the school consultant, then, is that although it is important to understand and follow a teacher's frame of reference to identify a student's problem, it is equally important to exert one's influence to maximize the odds of a teacher's successful implementation of evidence-based interventions.

A Clarification of Our Position

To avoid misunderstanding, we wish to clarify several points. First, it is mainly the process of consultation rather than its content that is important for the consultant to influence. Second, we certainly are not suggesting that consultants should ignore or fail to listen attentively to what consultees say; instead, consultants are to establish an interview framework in which consultees are free to respond to and elaborate on issues of mutual concern. Third, although there is value in the consultant structuring the interview format, we are not implying that the consultant frequently "tells the consultee what to do," as some have interpreted the cited line of research to suggest (see, for example, Henning-Stout, 1993). Crises certainly will present themselves in schools, prompting a consultant to act in a highly directive manner. However, that is neither the predominant type of consultation studied in this research nor the general approach to consultation we advocate. In reality, very few school consultant messages are orders or instructions; instead, most are assertions and questions that offer support, extend previous discussion, or initiate new topics (Erchul, 1987).

Are There Ethical Questions and Issues of Professional Dissonance Regarding the Use of Influence in Consultation?

We realize our view of the role of social influence within school consultation may not be universally shared (e.g., Gutkin, 1999a). Although some may claim that the school consultant–consultee relationship must be an "equal" one (e.g., Friend & Cook, 2000), others have argued forcefully that practical and organizational constraints inherent in schools typically preclude this ideal (Caplan & Caplan, 1993/1999; Harris & Cancelli, 1991). Also, those who promote the value of equality within consultation may erroneously consider "equal" to mean "the same as," when the reality is that consultant and consultee have different levels of need, information, and skills, and thus different roles to perform within consultation (Zins & Erchul, 2002).

Perhaps the main reason human service consultants feel uneasy when adopting a social influence perspective is that it is unrelated, and perhaps antithetical, to their professional training (Martin, 1978). To this, we would add that the use of social influence often raises difficult ethical questions for the consultant (Erchul, 1992b; Hughes, 1986; Hughes & Falk, 1981). Consider these examples: Is the consultee being "deceived" or "manipulated" when the consultant exerts influence for the good of the client? Is the consultee's autonomy as a professional inappropriately restricted when the consultant uses influence strategies? Can the consultant's exercise of influence negatively affect important outcomes for the consultee or client? These are difficult questions for a consultant to answer, just as they are for a psychotherapist (Haley, 1987), supervisor (Holloway, 1995), or teacher (Friedrich & Douglass, 1998) who uses a social influence framework to guide his or her professional actions.

The crux of the matter is that any strategy that is effective in changing behavior can be used unethically. When a consultant uses influence strategies to alter another's behavior, it should be clear that these strategies must be used in a responsible and ethical manner (Kipnis, 1994). As practicing consultants, we have found it helpful to measure the responsibility of our professional actions within an *empowerment philosophy* (Roach & Elliott, 2009; Witt & Martens, 1988). A philosophy of empowerment, as applied to consultation, relates to the belief that consultees already possess many basic strengths and eventually will solve their own problems if the consultant helps them develop those strengths by alerting consultees to existing resources and how they may be used (Dunst & Trivette, 1987). In other words, the consultant uses his or her power and influence to make consultees more powerful and influential. Within school consultation, the point has been made that frequently the consultant is attempting to solve a teacher's problem in influencing students (Erchul & Raven, 1997). In our view, making consultees more powerful and influential is a very responsible and ethical goal within the practice of consultation.

If It Is Not a Collaborative Relationship, Then What Is It?

Although we acknowledge the importance of interpersonal flexibility and responsiveness when working with various types of consultees and situations (cf. Hughes, Erchul, Yoon, Jackson, & Henington, 1997), we believe that for much school consultation, research supports the development of a working relationship that is best characterized as *cooperative* (Zins & Erchul, 2002). Support for a cooperative relationship within school consultation comes from relational communication process research, which has shown a common interactional pattern to be a complementary, leader/follower consultant/consultee relationship (e.g., Erchul & Chewning, 1990). Moreover, this pattern may be described as classically antagonistic, in that as one participant is more influential, the other is less influential (Erchul et al., 2007).

In promoting a cooperative relationship, we first note the need for the school consultant to develop facilitative, respectful partnerships with consultees, who must feel safe enough to discuss problems arising in their professional roles. Second, once a common understanding of trust and mutual respect has been established, it is critical for the consultant to lead the course of consultation using his or her knowledge of social influence, the problem-solving process, and continued professional support.

A sampling of the process–outcome school consultation research presented earlier suggests that favorable consultation outcomes occur when (1) consultees actively participate in consultation via the interview structure put in place by the consultant (particularly in the problem identification stage, as documented by Bergan & Tombari, 1976), and (2) consultees follow the lead of the consultant (particularly in the problem analysis/intervention selection stage, as documented by Erchul et al., 2009). Relating the described cooperative relationship to the collaborative relationship within school consultation, we consider particularly relevant views of collaboration to be *consultant-structured consultee participation* and *shared assent to variable roles* (Schulte & Osborne, 2003).

The Egalitarian Virus

Another helpful vantage point from which to view the cooperative consultative relationship is the egalitarian virus (Barone, 1995). In explaining his failure to challenge a teacher's claim that "peanut butter cures attention-deficit hyperactivity disorder" (p. 35), school psychologist Stephen Barone proposed that a disease he termed the *egalitarian virus* paralyzes otherwise competent professionals, causing them to wither in the face of strong but perhaps uninformed opinions. According to Barone, unrealistic ideas regarding the display of expertise permeate the schools today. These ideas include the belief that the specialized expertise of each staff member is directly interchangeable with that of any other, and that any person's opinion should be afforded equal rather than due consideration. The implication for school consultants who wish to maintain a cooperative relationship is to act as content experts when necessary and not downplay their specialized knowledge but, at the same time, attempt to understand and respect the consultees' unique strengths and weaknesses. A consultant who recognizes the significance of the egalitarian virus is unlikely to view collaboration within consultation in terms of participants having *equal value/equal power* (Schulte & Osborne, 2003).

General Strategies for Effecting Changes in Human Systems

Having established a rationale for why achieving change is important within consultation, and why the exercise of interpersonal influence is necessary to achieve this change, we step back to examine issues of change more generally. One often-referenced perspective on change in human systems is that of Chin and Benne

(1969). They examined philosophical views present throughout history that have undergirded numerous theories of influence and then proposed a three-part typology that captures the essence of those theories. Chin and Benne termed their resulting approaches *empirical–rational, normative–reeducative*, and *power–coercive*. The critical difference among the approaches is the motivation the influencing *agent* attributes to the *target* of the influence attempt.

Empirical–Rational Approach

The underlying philosophy of *empirical–rational* approaches is that people are essentially rational and will change their behavior when the change is justifiable to them on an intellectual level. In other words, if a person thinks that it is logical and important to change, he or she will do so if given the proper information. It is only ignorance and superstition that act to prevent behavior change from occurring (Chin & Benne, 1969). A consultant who uses empirical–rational approaches typically disseminates information and techniques to consultees, thus reinforcing Sir Francis Bacon's view that "knowledge is power."

Normative–Reeducative Approach

Normative–reeducative approaches assume that people are active organisms who depend on new knowledge as well as a variety of noncognitive, sociocultural determinants to arrive at a decision of whether to change. When using these approaches, therefore, the influencing agent tries to change the target's attitudes, values, and feelings at a personal level, and norms and significant relationships at the social level (Chin & Benne, 1969). For example, a consultant might rely on a facilitative consultative relationship to persuade a teacher to change a current ineffective instructional practice, or attempt to make the teacher more aware of values and norms present in the school that could affect his or her decision to adopt a new course of action. Importantly, a consultant who subscribes to these approaches believes that, in most cases, the consultee has much of the required information; the focus is on helping the consultee utilize these resources more effectively. In summary, the normative–reeducative view incorporates the empirical–rational view and adds to it a distinctively social element, thereby recognizing the importance of "knowledge *and people* as power."

Power–Coercive Approach

Although empirical–rational and normative–reeducative approaches deal with the role of power in influencing others, both types reject the notion of power as coercive and nonreciprocal. In contrast, *power–coercive* approaches generally assume that the target will change when presented with sanctions that are political or economic in nature, or when made to feel guilty or shameful for not changing. The influencing agent may take these steps when it is apparent that the target believes that it is not in his or her best interests to change. Although power–coercive approaches have been associated with tyrannical leaders of the past, it is also important to note that they have formed the basis of nonviolent strategies for change such as those advocated by Henry David Thoreau, Mahatma Gandhi, and Martin Luther King, Jr. (Chin & Benne, 1969). Unless clearly serving as an advocate for a disenfranchised group (see, for example, Conoley, 1981a), a school consultant who uses power–coercive strategies will be more subtle. For instance, when a consultant informs a consultee that his or her presence in the school has been fully authorized by the principal, the consultee may interpret this message to mean that whatever guidance the consultant offers must be followed or else trouble will result.

Relevance of Chin and Benne's Strategies for School Consultants

The school consultant's job would be extremely easy if a consultee needed only the proper information in order to act on and resolve a work-related problem. Although simple, straightforward problems may be solved using only an empirical–rational approach, in our experience the problems brought to a school consultant are rarely this simple or straightforward. Having the "proper information" is helpful only to a point; often it must be augmented with other elements such as the provision of professional support, guidance, skill building, and feedback, as well as the application of influence in order to accomplish change. For this reason, we regard the exclusive use of, and overreliance on, empirical–rational change strategies in consultation as shortsighted and naive.

Instead, the skillful integration of all three approaches to effect change appears to underlie the successful practice of school consultation. How the consultant integrates these types of strategies, however, is not well established. Although an empirical basis for their application to consultation has been slow to develop, French and Raven's (1959; Raven, 1965) bases of social power model and Raven's (1992, 1993) power–interaction model of interpersonal influence do offer useful conceptual perspectives through which to view issues of influence in school consultation.

The Bases of Social Power and Their Application to School Consultation[2]

An Introduction to Social Power Bases and Social Influence

According to Mintzberg (1983), the best known framework for examining social power is the typology of social power bases developed originally by French and Raven (1959) and later expanded by Raven (1965). *Social influence* is defined as a change in the beliefs, attitudes, or behaviors of a target of influence, which results from the action or presence of an influencing agent. *Social power* is the potential for social influence to occur. It bears noting that social influence is a ubiquitous aspect of human interaction, existing within all known cultures (Wosinska, Cialdini, Barrett, & Reykowski, 2001).

Before presenting the French and Raven social power typology in detail, we wish to interject that, in school consultation, it is social *influence* rather than social power that really matters. In other words, social power offers a useful means to study social influence, but an understanding of power alone does not help the consultant much. As will be seen later in this chapter, it is critical for the school consultant to enact *influence strategies* based on an understanding of power bases.

French and Raven's (1959) model contains six bases of power that the influencing agent (Person A) can utilize in changing the beliefs, attitudes, or behaviors of a target (Person B).

1. *Coercive power* is based on Person B's perception that Person A can punish B if B does not comply.
2. *Reward power* is based on B's perception that A can reward B if B complies.
3. *Legitimate power* is based on B's obligation to accept A's influence attempt because B believes A has a legitimate right to influence, perhaps because of A's professional role or position.
4. *Expert power* is based on B's perception that A possesses knowledge or expertise in a specific area of interest to B.
5. *Referent power* is A's potential to influence B based on B's identification with A and/or desire for such identification.
6. *Informational power* (Raven, 1965) is A's potential to influence B because of the judged relevance of the information contained in A's message. Informational power is attributed to A by A providing B with a logical explanation or new information favoring change.

Expert power and informational power are similar and can be rather easily confused. In both types, B thinks, "I will do as A suggests because that is the best way to address this problem." The critical distinction, however, is that with expert power, B thinks, "I don't really understand exactly why, but A really knows this area so A must be right"; with informational power, B thinks, "I listened carefully to A and see for myself that this is clearly the best way to address this problem."

French and Raven (1959; Raven, 1965) further suggested that, as compared to the other bases of social power, the changed behavior stemming from informational power can be maintained without continued social dependence upon the influencing agent. B essentially has internalized the new behavior and will continue in that manner even if B were to forget that the impetus for the change came originally from A. For the five other bases of power, the changed behavior is socially dependent upon the influencing agent (e.g., "I am doing this differently because A *has told me* to do it this way"). The form of social dependence will differ according to the power base used: "I feel obligated to do as A requests" (legitimate), "A knows what is best for me" (expert), "A has experience similar to mine, so we should see eye-to-eye on this issue" (referent), "A will punish me if I don't do it this way" (coercive), and "A will do something nice to me if I do as A asks" (reward). For reward and coercive power, there is an additional distinction. In order for these bases of power to operate, B must believe that A is able to observe whether B has complied or not. Thus, for these two bases of power, A's surveillance of B is essential.

An initial attempt to apply French and Raven's social power model to the practice of school consultation was made by Martin (1978). He proposed that only expert and referent power constitute bases for a consultant's influence over a teacher-consultee. Because social psychological research has indicated that expert power tends to be highly restricted in range (i.e., only a small number of areas of expertise are usually attributed to any one person), Martin advised consultants to develop advanced knowledge of a limited number of topics, and to try to confine their consultation to these areas of "true" expertise. Because other research demonstrated that referent power has a wide range (i.e., one who has accrued referent power can potentially influence the beliefs, attitudes, and behaviors of another across many aspects of daily life), Martin suggested that consultants should develop this form of power by spending time with consultees in a variety of settings and activities in order to enhance their professional work relationship.

The main reason Martin (1978) dismissed coercive, reward, and legitimate power as irrelevant to the psychologist–teacher consultative relationship is that these types of power are associated with supervisory, hierarchical relationships. Because the psychologist hired by the school system typically occupies a staff position rather than a line authority position, these three types of power are simply irrelevant. It should be noted that Martin's analysis did not consider informational power, which French and Raven (1959) mentioned as a type of influence, but not a power base. Erchul and Raven (1997) proposed an alternate view: given the further development of French and Raven's original social power model, various forms of coercive, reward, and legitimate power, as well as informational power, can play important roles in school consultation. We continue by presenting the expansion of the original model as well as Erchul and Raven's applications of the updated power model to school consultation. These ideas are previewed in Table 3.1.

Coercive Power and Reward Power: Impersonal Forms

The original forms of coercive and reward power, now called "impersonal" forms (Raven, 1992, 1993), refer to B's perception that A is capable of delivering tangible punishments and rewards, respectively. In contrast to Martin (1978), Erchul and Raven (1997) suggested that it is shortsighted to dismiss the relevance of the impersonal forms of coercive and reward power within school-based consultation. After all, an early description of behavioral consultation in schools (Tharp & Wetzel, 1969) included some concrete suggestions for how the consultant can modify the consultee's behavior through the application of positive reinforcement and punishment.

Table 3.1 Further Differentiation of the Bases of Social Power (Raven, 1992, 1993) and School Consultation Examples

Further Differentiated Power Base	Definition and Consultation Example
Impersonal reward	B's perception that A is capable of delivering tangible rewards. *Example*: Consultant, very pleased with how much effort teacher has put forth in consultation, brings in a box of extra classroom supplies for her to use. Of course, the supplies are rewarding, but reward *power* stems from teacher's expectation that there will be additional supplies provided if there is further compliance.
Impersonal coercion	B's perception that A is capable of delivering tangible punishments. *Example*: Subtly, or not so subtly, the consultant communicates the expectation that a failure to follow recommendations could lead to a negative report or poor performance review.
Positive expert	B's perception that A possesses knowledge or expertise in a specific area of interest to B. *Example*: Teacher views consultant as knowledgeable because of her doctoral degree in school psychology.
Positive referent	A's potential to influence B based on B's identification with A and/or desire for such identification. *Example*: Teacher is likely to follow consultant's direction in consultation because she wishes to enter the field of school psychology herself in order to consult with teachers.
Direct information	A's potential to influence B because of the judged relevance of the information contained in A's message. *Example*: Teacher views consultant's treatment plan as likely to succeed – not because of the consultant's expertise or other factors – but because the teacher made up her mind long ago that boys with ADHD always benefit from a classroom point system.
Formal legitimacy	B's perception that A has a right to influence based on A's professional role or organizational position. *Example*: Teacher sees consultant's role as implying the authority to make recommendations that the teacher should feel obligated to follow.
Legitimacy of dependence	B's perception that there is an obligation to help people like A who cannot help themselves and who are dependent upon others. *Example*: Consultant asks for teacher's help in assisting a student through consultation because the student's test scores do not qualify him for a special education placement.
Legitimacy of reciprocity	B's perception that he/she is obligated to respond in-kind for what A has done already to benefit B. *Example*: Consultant has spent several lengthy sessions with the teacher working out a reasonable intervention plan, so now teacher feels an obligation to implement the plan as well as possible.
Legitimacy of equity	B's perception that he/she is obligated to respond to A's request due to an imbalance of expended effort and possible inconvenience incurred previously by A. *Example*: Consultant has spent much time working with teacher developing an intervention plan, but teacher has failed to start implementation, causing consultant to return to classroom unnecessarily to begin what would have been an initial evaluation of the plan. Teacher, perhaps feeling guilty, begins plan implementation immediately.

(continued)

Table 3.1 (continued)

Further Differentiated Power Base	Definition and Consultation Example
Personal reward	A's liking and personal approval of B is important to B, and B believes that approval is more likely if B follows A's recommendations. *Example*: Consultant compliments teacher for collecting baseline data for 5 days, as was recommended. Teacher feels good about such compliments and hopes and expects further approval for future compliance.
Personal coercion	B is very concerned about A not liking or disapproving of B, and expects that noncompliance will result in such disapproval. *Example*: Consultant expresses disapproval when teacher has not implemented the intervention as agreed upon previously. Teacher finds such disapproval painful, and expects even more severe disapproval if she does not follow subsequent recommendations.

Note. Absent from this list are negative expert, negative referent, and indirect informational power, three other forms of power discussed by Raven (1992, 1993)

Also, at some level, the consultee may be concerned about the consequences of failing to follow the suggestions offered by the consultant or failing to implement interventions developed jointly during consultation. For instance, despite the commonly assumed confidential nature of consultation, word may spread quickly through informal social networks within a school about a consultee's failures to profit from consultation. Staff members may attribute a particular consultee's long-standing failure to improve classroom management via consultation to his or her unwillingness to work effectively with the consultant. This in turn may negatively influence the consultee's future relationships with these coworkers. Fortunately, successes arising from consultation may be communicated – and possibly rewarded – through these same networks (Erchul & Raven, 1997).

Coercive and Reward Power: Personal Forms

Two newer types of coercive and reward power are labeled "personal" forms by Raven (1992, 1993), and refer to B's perception that A's personal disapproval and approval, respectively, can potentially influence B. Approval from someone whom we like can be as rewarding as a tangible reward, just as rejection or disapproval from someone we like can serve as a powerful basis for coercive power (Raven & Kruglanski, 1970). For example, within behavioral consultation (Bergan & Kratochwill, 1990), a consultant may choose to compliment a consultee for keeping accurate baseline data on a client, but later may confront that same consultee for repeatedly failing to implement an intervention with integrity (Gresham, 1989). These actions may result in consultee attributions of the personal forms of reward power and coercive power, respectively. It may also be that, given the generally acknowledged supportive nature of the consultative relationship, the use of the personal form of reward power may be more frequent than the use of the personal form of coercive power (Erchul & Raven, 1997).

Legitimate Power: Position, Reciprocity, Equity, and Responsibility-Dependence

The term *formal legitimate power* refers to an agent's potential to influence a target based on the target's belief that the agent has a right to influence based on professional role or organizational position (French & Raven, 1959). For example, a firefighter is attributed legitimate power by those trapped in a burning building, allowing him or her to take whatever actions deemed necessary to achieve a successful rescue. The external consultant, in particular, may draw on formal legitimate power on occasion (Erchul & Raven, 1997). The consultant who relies on legitimate power ("position power") is attempting to project an image that suggests, "I am a consultant, and I am trying to do my job – to help you do your job better. As a consultee, you should feel obligated to consider what I have to offer." However, we would not expect a school consultant ever to be explicit in the use of legitimate position power. In all probability, this blatant use of legitimate position power would be resented by the consultee, and could result in very disastrous consequences. But even if legitimate position power is not made explicit, some consultees may feel that they should follow the consultant's advice. When the consultant is a member of a healing profession, consultee attributions of legitimate power may be more likely (Gallessich, 1982).

In Raven's (1992, 1993) more recent development of the bases of power model, he has gone beyond legitimate position power to promote three other types of legitimate power. These more subtle types draw on social norms involving obligations to comply, and are termed the legitimate power of reciprocity, equity, and responsibility-dependence.

The *legitimate power of reciprocity* (Gouldner, 1960) suggests that the target should respond in kind for what the agent has done already to benefit the target. For example, the consultant might imply that considerable effort had been expended to develop an acceptable intervention plan, so the consultee should feel obligated to implement the plan as well as possible.

The *legitimate power of equity* (Walster, Walster, & Berscheid, 1978) obligates the target to respond due to a perceived imbalance of expended effort and possible inconvenience incurred by the agent. For instance, a consultant might diplomatically state the idea that, because the consultee did not even try once to implement the intervention, a return trip to the school after 1 week to monitor student progress was unnecessary; in order to compensate the consultant, the consultee might begin the intervention as soon as possible (Erchul & Raven, 1997).

The *legitimate power of responsibility-dependence* is based on a norm that states there is an obligation to help those who cannot help themselves and who are dependent upon others (Berkowitz & Daniels, 1963). A rationale we have presented on occasion to encourage teachers to participate actively in consultation relies on the legitimate power of responsibility-dependence: "I, unfortunately, am not in a position to change the rules and regulations governing special education programs. As a result of her test scores, Sarah cannot be considered to be a student having a learning disability so she will remain in your classroom. I hope I can count on you to help me generate a plan that will meet her educational needs."

Expert Power and Referent Power: Positive Forms

The forms of expert and referent power proposed originally by French and Raven (1959) now are referred to as "positive" forms (Raven, 1992, 1993). As Martin (1978) argued, the positive forms of expert and referent power have great utility in explaining what happens in school consultation. With respect to the positive form of expert power, in order to be effective it is critical for the consultant to be perceived as an expert. The consultant may increase the probability of being accorded expert power by limiting his or her consulting practice to a small number of areas of true expertise, offering recommendations in a confident manner, stating his or her relevant professional training and experience, and mentioning successful past consulting efforts (Erchul, 1992b; Martin, 1978).

The positive form of referent power is a concept that should be familiar to all human service professionals, though it may be more recognizable as "rapport building" or "relationship development." The consultant may be attributed referent power by getting to know a consultee and his or her work setting and demonstrating an understanding of both, pointing out similarities between himself or herself and the consultee (e.g., "You may not be aware of this, but I was a teacher once myself and know the problems you are facing"), engaging in joint decision-making, and describing him- or herself and professional activities in ways that the consultee perceives as favorable (Martin, 1978).

Early Empirical Studies of Positive Expert and Positive Referent Power in School Consultation

According to Erchul and Raven (1997), seven empirical investigations of the positive forms of expert and referent power (French & Raven, 1959) in school consultation were published between 1980 and 1991. Although we shall not review these investigations (termed "Phase I Studies" by Erchul et al., 2008), it may be concluded that in five of these studies, indicators of expert and/or referent power were linked to significant consultation processes and outcomes. In two other studies, no significant relationships were found. Though far from complete, these studies provided initial support for the view that expert and referent power are valued constructs within school consultation.

The Expert–Referent Power Dilemma

Martin (1978) observed that expert and referent power tend to mutually oppose each other. After all, expert power is based on the target's perception that the influencing agent has superior knowledge and thus is different from the target. Referent power, in contrast, grows from mutual identification or a sense of similarity. Recognizing this antagonistic relationship, Martin hypothesized that the most successful consultants are capable of striking a balance between these two power bases. In other words, a consultant should avoid being perceived as "too knowledgeable" (and thus be attributed little or no referent power), and "too similar" (and thus be attributed little or no expert power). It has been suggested that the external consultant is attributed more expert than referent power, and the internal consultant is attributed more referent than expert power (Lippitt & Lippitt, 1986).

A major challenge for the consultant appears to be to develop strategies that reduce the likelihood of expert and referent power undermining each other. The consultant who emphasizes his or her similarity and mutuality with the consultee may find it useful to suggest that he or she is also an expert, but in a gentle, nonthreatening manner. If he or she has been relying heavily on expert power, an occasional reference to common background, mutual goals, and general similarity – without undermining expertise – may be helpful (Erchul & Raven, 1997).

Expert and Referent Power: Negative Forms

Two more recently recognized types of expert and referent power (the "negative" forms) are based on the observation that sometimes the target may do exactly the opposite of what the influencing agent does or desires the target to do (Raven, 1992, 1993). Perhaps this phenomenon exists because the target recognizes the expertise of the agent but distrusts him or her because it is assumed that the agent does not have the target's best interests foremost in mind (i.e., negative expert power). Conversely, maybe the target sees the agent as someone whom he or she dislikes, or someone from whom the target would rather disidentify him- or herself (i.e., negative referent power). Negative influence also can emerge when the target believes that his or her independence, individuality, or sense of personal control is threatened. There may be a strong tendency to avoid doing what the agent requests, or to do the exact opposite. This form of negative influence is called *reactance* (Brehm, 1966; Hughes & Falk, 1981).

Though less commonly seen than their positive forms, the negative forms of expert and referent power are relevant to the practice of school consultation. Perhaps the most relevant application is that school consultants need to be aware of how an overcontrolling attempt at influence or an unpopular personal presentation can lead to nonacceptance by the consultee and to negative influence in the form of active resistance or reactance (Erchul & Raven, 1997).

Informational Power: Direct and Indirect Forms

The direct form of informational power is founded on the information or logical argument that the influencing agent presents directly to the target in order to achieve change. Unlike the other bases of social power, the resulting change in the target stems from the effectiveness of the agent's message rather than from any characteristics of the agent. In order for informational power to produce change in the target, the target must judge the message's content to be very useful and relevant to his or her situation. To clarify further, for both informational power and expert power, the target believes that the recommendation by the agent is the best thing to do. With expert power, however, the target may not really understand why it is best because he or she is relying on his or her faith in the agent's superior knowledge (Raven, 1965, 1992, 1993).

The direct form of informational power has some distinct advantages over other bases of power. First, it is often more comfortable for the target to believe that he or she is doing what the agent asks because it is understood from the agent's presentation that this is the best course of action, instead of being based on faith in the agent's expertise, an obligation to comply, or a concern about the agent rewarding or punishing the target. Second, informational power tends to be more permanent, with no surveillance required, and fewer negative side effects (Raven, 1992, 1993). Third, the direct form of informational power appears to have great potential for the consultant because it does not rest on the consultee's favorable assessment of the consultant (i.e., it is socially independent, unlike the other five power bases; Erchul, 1992b; Parsons & Meyers, 1984). The unique nature of informational power has led to its endorsement by mental health consultation pioneer Gerald Caplan (Erchul, 1993b) and by Raven and Litman-Adizes (1986), who studied doctor–patient interactions.

On the other hand, the direct form of informational power has certain disadvantages. First, it may lead to resistance on the part of the target, depending on the way in which the agent presents it. Second, it may lead to reactance if the target believes that his or her sense of integrity is being violated. For instance, a consultee who is told, "Here are four good reasons why you should change your classroom rules to improve discipline," may respond by doing the exact opposite of what the consultant suggests (Erchul & Raven, 1997). Third, the use of the direct form of informational power may require more time in explanation and depends on the target having background to understand the bases for the recommendation (Raven, 1965). Fourth, there is some evidence that direct use of informational power may also be resisted when a subordinate attempts to influence a superior, or when a female attempts to influence a male (Johnson, 1976; Stein, 1971).

Given these apparent disadvantages of the direct form of informational power, information may be more persuasive if it is presented indirectly. Often, there is a large difference between an agent directly telling a target what he or she wants and why, versus proceeding through the offering of hints and suggestions. Classic social psychological research on the effectiveness of "overheard" communications, when compared to direct communications, illustrates this point (e.g., Walster & Festinger, 1962). Johnson (1976) and Tannen (1994) have noted that women are more likely to use the indirect forms of information, and men are more likely to use direct information. In addition, indirect information seems particularly useful when a person in what is considered a low-power position attempts to influence someone in a superior position (Stein, 1971).

The use of the indirect form of informational power in school consultation is less clear at this time. Although consistent with the psychodynamic elements of Caplan's (1970; Caplan & Caplan, 1993/1999) mental health consultation model, others writing specifically about school consultation do not advocate techniques based on indirect communication (see, for example, Conoley & Conoley, 1992, Chap. 2). Still, the consultant who notes some uneasiness in his or her relationship with a consultee may consider using more subtle, less direct forms of informational influence. For example, in the manner of Caplan's (1970) use of parables, a consultant might say, "I have heard that at a school not far from here, a teacher has been using this method to deal with her classroom problem and has achieved some success. Perhaps you might wish to consider it." Also, given Stein's (1971) major result, a younger consultant may find the use of indirect communication helpful when consulting with a more senior teacher having many years of experience (Erchul & Raven, 1997).

A primary difficulty in the consultant's use of either direct or indirect forms of informational power would seem to be not knowing ahead of time what information the consultee will consider most important and helpful. However, to the extent a consultee can be regarded as a professional "in crisis" and therefore more open to outside influence, this issue may be far less salient. That is, the consultee beset with crisis will tend to be more open to a variety of approaches advocated by the consultant (Caplan, 1989).

Empirical Studies of Raven's (1992, 1993) Social Power Bases Applied to School Consultation

Which social power bases from Raven's expanded model do psychologists and teachers believe will be most *effective* in changing the behavior of a consultee who is described as initially resistant to comply with a consultant's requests? Three studies have addressed this question using the Interpersonal Power Inventory (IPI; Raven, Schwarzwald, & Koslowsky, 1998), a 44-item self-report instrument that measures the 11 social power bases listed in Table 3.1. Erchul, Raven, and Ray (2001) used the IPI to survey 101 school psychologists and found that respondents considered direct informational, positive expert, impersonal reward, and positive referent power to be the four most effective bases when consulting with an initially resistant teacher.

Building on this methodology, Erchul, Raven, and Whichard (2001) polled a national sample of school psychologists and elementary school teachers with consulting experience. In their psychologist subsample, the top four most effective bases were direct informational, positive expert, positive referent, and personal reward power. In their teacher subsample, direct informational, positive expert, legitimate dependence, and positive referent power were perceived as the most effective power bases for a consultant to use when consulting with an initially resistant teacher. It may be concluded that psychologists and teachers similarly acknowledge the effectiveness of direct informational, positive expert, and positive referent power to explain processes and outcomes of school consultation.

Groupings of Social Power Bases: The Soft Versus Harsh Distinction

Analyzed in a slightly different way, these results support the general effectiveness of soft bases over harsh bases (Bass, 1981; Yukl & Falbe, 1991). *Soft* bases are considered to be more subtle, positive, and noncoercive, and typically include positive expert, positive referent, direct informational, legitimate dependence, and personal reward power. *Harsh* bases are more overt, punitive, and "heavy handed," and typically include legitimate reciprocity, impersonal coercive, legitimate equity, impersonal reward, personal coercive, and legitimate position power (Raven et al., 1998). In both Erchul, Raven, and Ray (2001) and Erchul, Raven, and Whichard (2001), respondents indicated the use of soft bases would be more effective than harsh bases when consulting with an initially resistant teacher. To further illustrate this point, direct informational, positive expert, and positive referent power – the top-rated bases relative to perceived effectiveness – are all soft power bases.

Looking at the soft/harsh distinction relative to gender differences, Erchul, Raven, and Wilson (2004) focused only on the psychologists' responses in the Erchul, Raven, and Whichard (2001) dataset. They found female school psychologist consultants perceived soft power bases to be more effective than did male consultants. However, there were no differences between male and female consultants regarding the effectiveness of the 11 individual bases measured by the IPI.

Effectiveness Versus Likelihood of Use of Power Bases

Just because a form of social power is perceived as effective does not mean it will be used often. Impersonal coercion, for example, may be effective but is unlikely to be drawn on if the agent wants to maintain good rapport with the target. Consequently, more recent social power research has asked, which bases from Raven's model do consultants indicate they would be *most likely to use* to influence an initially resistant teacher?

Two studies have examined the likelihood of using specific power bases in consultation. Using a modified IPI, Wilson, Erchul, and Raven (2008) surveyed a national sample of 352 school psychologists and found: (1) school psychology consultants overall were more likely to use soft power bases than harsh bases; (2) female consultants were no more likely to use soft power bases than were male consultants; and (3) when considering the 11 bases measured by the IPI, consultants indicated they were more likely to use direct informational power than the other ten bases and positive expert power more than the remaining nine bases. In a follow-up study, Getty and Erchul (2009) examined consultants' likelihood of using soft power bases (defined through statistical analysis as positive expert, positive referent, legitimate dependence, direct informational, and legitimate position power). In considering consultation with a female teacher: (1) male school psychology consultants were more likely to use expert power than the other four soft bases combined, and (2) female psychologists were less likely to use referent power than the other four soft bases combined.

Relevance of Social Power Base Research Studies for School Consultants

In sum, the reviewed social power base investigations from 2001 through the present (termed "Phase II Studies" by Erchul et al., 2008) have employed the IPI to study the consultant/teacher relationship. Key findings from these studies include: (1) consultants perceive influence strategies that are based on soft power bases as not only more effective but also more likely to be used in practice; (2) teachers view consultant influence strategies that draw on soft bases as more effective than those based on harsh bases; and (3) consultant gender plays an important role in determining which soft power bases a consultant is likely to use.

The significance of the soft/harsh power base distinction for school consultants cannot be underestimated. It is clear – and not surprising – that soft bases are more likely to be used because they provide a means by which social influence can occur in a coordinate, nonhierarchical relationship (Caplan, 1970).

Other Means of Influence

Invoking or Reducing the Power of Third Parties

Another way an influencing agent can effect change in a target is to invoke the power of a third party, either by referring verbally to the third party, or by asking directly for help from the third party (Raven, 1992, 1993). For example, a school consultant could invoke the power of a third party by making reference to another staff member whom the consultee respects (e.g., "I know you think Ms. Anderson is an exemplary teacher. Have you ever noticed what she does to solve these sorts of problems?"). Alternately, the consultant could request assistance from the third party on behalf of the consultee (e.g., "I know that Mr. Benjamin has extensive experience implementing token economy programs in classrooms. Let me see if he would be able to meet with us next time"). It is not recommended that the school principal's legitimate power be invoked because it could irreparably damage the working relationship between the consultant and the teacher (Erchul & Raven, 1997).

The agent also can influence a target by reducing the power of a third party who might block the recommended change. This action may be achieved by undermining the third party's expertise or legitimacy, suggesting that he or she is not a desirable model, or questioning the underlying logic of his or her persuasive appeal (Raven, 1992, 1993). Particularly to the extent school consultation is carried out in an RTI problem-solving team (PST) context (see Chap. 2), the strategy of reducing the power of a third party would appear to be of value. The well-documented finding that the group yields substantial power supports this position (e.g., Ford & Zelditch, 1988; Lewin, 1952). As just one example, a consultant working with a group of teachers may consider exercising expert power to counter a pessimistic teacher's argument that only direct services such as counseling and not indirect services such as consultation can help students with disabilities. Through referent power and personal coercive power, other group members may help to persuade this consultee that indirect services also can be effective (Erchul & Raven, 1997).

Preparatory Devices: Setting the Stage for Social Influence

As the influencing agent evaluates his or her bases of power, the agent may decide that a specific form of power may work in a particular situation, but will require some additional preparation in order to be maximally effective (Raven, 1992, 1993). This preparation may necessitate the use of self-presentational strategies (Jones & Pittman, 1982) or management impression tactics (Schlenker, 1980). In this section, we selectively present what Raven (1992, 1993) has termed *stage-setting devices*. We caution that, although these devices appear to apply to the practice of school consultation, they require further investigation relative to their suitability and effectiveness.

If reward power is to be used, then the agent must mention the availability of rewards to the target. If the agent intends to use personal reward by offering approval or personal coercion by showing disapproval, then the agent may try first to ingratiate him- or herself with the target by complimenting or flattering the target. If legitimate position power is chosen for use, the agent might subtly state that, for example, he or she is the supervisor who shoulders the ultimate responsibility for the job, so the target should comply with forthcoming requests. To prepare for legitimacy based on the reciprocity norm, the agent may do a favor for the target, expecting a later return (Raven, 1992, 1993).

If the influencing agent will be relying on expert power, then some demonstration of his or her superior knowledge may be useful as a stage-setting device. Physicians, attorneys, and other professionals often promote their expertise by displaying their extensive professional libraries, diplomas, awards, etc. Finally, for

Table 3.2 Examples of Preparatory Devices for the Use of Social Power

Preparing the stage or scene:
  Displaying diplomas, library photos with celebrities (expert)
  Wearing laboratory coat, stethoscope, etc. (expert)
  Arranging of podium or desk, chairs (legitimate)
Enhancing or emphasizing power bases:
  References to agent's ability to control rewards; punishments; formal role as supervisor, teacher, doctor, etc. (legitimate)
  Intimidation, presenting fearful image (coercion)
  Ingratiation, via compliments, etc., to increase target's attraction to agent (personal reward, personal coercion, referent power)
  Self-promotion, emphasizing superior knowledge (expert)
  Emphasizing communality of background, identification, goals (referent)
  Doing a favor for target (reciprocity), emphasizing one's dependence upon target (responsibility), telling of one's selfless dedication and sacrifice, reference to some harm which target imposed on agent (equity)
  Making a request that target would not be likely to accept, to induce guilt, in preparation for other request (legitimacy of equity)
  Presenting background information, which can subsequently serve to enhance informational influence
Minimizing target:
  Subtle "put-downs" which decrease target's self-esteem or confidence, so as to increase agent's informational, expert, or legitimate power
Minimizing opposing influencing agents:
  Reducing expertise, reference, legitimacy, etc., of others who may support the target's current position or mode of behavior

Note. From "The bases of power: Origins and recent developments," by B. H. Raven, 1993, *Journal of Social Issues, 49,* p. 238. Copyright © 1993 by The Society for the Psychological Study of Social Issues. Reprinted with permission

referent power, the agent must demonstrate communality with the target. Helping professionals typically lay the groundwork for the exercise of referent power by getting to know their clients, particularly their likes, dislikes, and aspirations – all of which provide a basis for establishing communality. Table 3.2 summarizes Raven's (1992, 1993) preparatory devices.

Given the differential appropriateness of social power bases for the school consultant, we would expect some of these preparatory devices to be used more than others and some not at all. For example, the acknowledged importance of developing and maintaining rapport with consultees suggests that setting the stage for using referent power and personal reward power may be critical. It is also essential that the consultant be perceived as an expert, so he or she might tactfully communicate to the teacher something about his or her experience and training in the area over which consultation will occur. To prepare for legitimacy based on the equity norm, the consultant might first make reference to the long hours that she has logged traveling to various schools in order to study many student problems, so as to help this particular consultee develop possible solutions to a current pressing problem (Erchul & Raven, 1997).

The Mode of Influence

The effectiveness of an influence attempt appears to stem not only from the power base employed, but also from how the influencing agent chooses to deliver it (Raven, 1992, 1993). At one extreme, the agent may attempt to influence using a loud, forceful, threatening, or sarcastic tone. At the other extreme, the agent may use a soft, friendly, or humorous manner. A sophisticated influencing agent may soften a coercive influence attempt by employing a light, humorous delivery. It would seem that a consultant's choice of words, body language, and facial expression can affect the manner in which the consultee responds, both in present compliance and in future interactions with the consultant (Erchul & Raven, 1997; Ng & Bradac, 1993).

Perhaps the high priority placed on establishing and maintaining mutually respectful interpersonal relationships within school consultation (e.g., Meyers, Parsons, & Martin, 1979) make it unlikely that a consultant would try to change a consultee using a harsh or threatening manner. On the other hand, the use of humor, nonthreatening forms of request, and a polite manner have been demonstrated to enhance successful influence, and it is expected the same would hold true within school consultation (Holtgraves, 1992; Holtgraves & Yang, 1990). Therefore, it is important for consultants to look at how an influence attempt is presented, in addition to the social power base it represents (Erchul & Raven, 1997).

A Power/Interaction Model of Interpersonal Influence and Its Application to School Consultation

The complex picture of the many choices and stages in the implementation of social power may be seen in Raven's (1992, 1993) power/interaction model of interpersonal influence, which is displayed in Fig. 3.1. In describing this model, we present the process of influence from motivation to implementation and subsequent readjustment of the influencing agent. It is our approach first to describe each step in a generic way and then to comment on it with specific reference to school consultation.

Before proceeding, however, it is important to note that, when considering social power bases as components of Raven's (1992, 1993) comprehensive model, it is more accurate to refer to the bases as *strategies* (Getty & Erchul, 2009; Wilson et al., 2008) because bases are now being enacted as influence attempts. Therefore, at this juncture, we shall change terminology and use *strategy* in place of *base* where appropriate.

The Motivation to Influence

On the left side of Fig. 3.1, there are a variety of motivational factors for the influencing agent to consider prior to engaging in an influence attempt. These factors then lead the agent to assess the various bases of power and other forms of influence

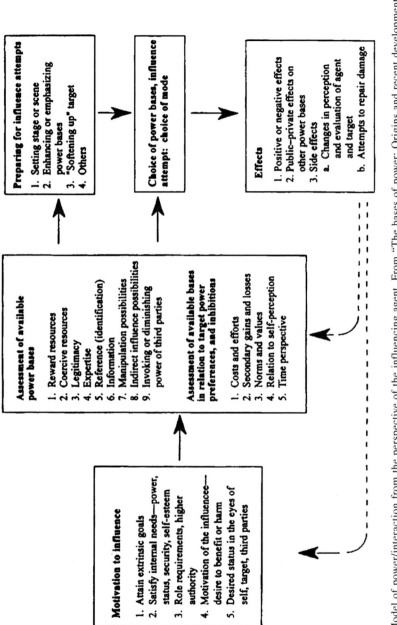

Fig. 3.1 Model of power/interaction from the perspective of the influencing agent. From "The bases of power: Origins and recent developments," by B. H. Raven, 1993, *Journal of Social Issues*, 49, p. 240. Copyright © 1993 by the Society for the Psychological Study of Social Issues. Reprinted with permission

that might be available. For example, the consultant is encouraged to examine what motivates him or her to influence consultees as a part of consultation. Is it ultimately to benefit clients? Is it to make consultees function more competently in their professional roles? Or, less positively, is it mainly for personal gain (e.g., financial, affiliative, status, etc.)?

In the upper middle of the figure, the bases of power and other preparatory devices that might be in the agent's repertoire can be seen. As mentioned previously, the school consultant may find the use of certain power bases and related stage-setting devices more or less likely than others. Influence strategies *least* likely to be utilized by school consultants are those based on impersonal coercion, impersonal reward, and legitimate equity (Wilson et al., 2008).

Assessment of Available Power Bases[3]

Having determined what bases of power might be available, the agent must assess these possible courses of action in terms of their effectiveness in achieving change. What is the likelihood the agent would be successful or unsuccessful using various power bases? For example, the consultant who has not worked with a particular consultee previously may be successful using strategies that are based more on expert power than referent power. A consultant who is already well known to all school staff may believe the reverse to be true.

Assessment of the Available Bases in Relation to Target, Power, Preferences, and Inhibitions

The agent also must examine the cost-benefit ratio of the influence attempt. For example, influence that stems from informational power may require more time and effort to establish than is available. Legitimate power based on dependence (i.e., "I need your help") may lead to loss of respect and may imply an obligation to return the favor. A consultant obviously must weigh these possible risks and benefits. As noted earlier, school psychologists tend to see soft bases as more effective (Erchul, Raven, & Ray, 2001) and more likely to be used than harsh bases (Wilson et al., 2008).

Preparing for the Influence Attempt

In looking at the upper right of Fig. 3.1, it can be seen that the various preparatory or stage-setting devices are introduced at this point. These devices include setting the scene, emphasizing or enhancing the agent's power resources, diminishing the target or opposing influencing agents. As discussed previously, the school consultant is likely to use some of these preparatory devices more than others, and some may not be used at all because of their inappropriate nature.

Choice of Power Bases and Mode in Influence Attempts

The agent chooses not only the power base, but also the power mode (i.e., the manner or tone in which the influence attempt is delivered). As Raven (1992, 1993) observed, the mode of influence at times may be more important than the basis of power. Due to the nature of the school setting and their role within it, consultants are generally restricted in their mode choices, relying mainly on soft, friendly, or humorous approaches. It is unlikely that a school consultant would be seen as effective when using a loud, forceful, or sarcastic manner.

Assessing the Effects of Influence

After the influence attempt, the agent evaluates its effects. Was it successful? Is there some sign that the target has accepted the influence by altering his or her behavior in accordance with the outcome sought by the agent? Has the target internalized the change, or is the change clearly socially dependent? Is surveillance by the agent important for the change to continue, or will the target revert to earlier behavior patterns as soon as the agent is unable to continue to monitor the target's degree of compliance? If the influence strategy was unsuccessful, then the agent may reevaluate power resources, reassess the possibility of future success, and try again.

In assessing the effects of influence, the consultant may ask, "How has the consultee changed?" For instance, if the main goal of the influence strategy was to increase adherence to treatment plan implementation, the consultant obviously will want to monitor the degree of consultee follow-through with this task. Perhaps more importantly, over the span of several consultations with this same consultee, the consultant will want to see whether treatment fidelity becomes internalized or instead consistently requires the consultant's surveillance in order to occur.

Conclusion

With few exceptions, this chapter has presented social influence issues nearly exclusively from the perspective of the influencing agent, or for our purposes, the consultant. It is clear, however, that it also would be valuable to study these issues more extensively from the perspective of the target or consultee (Raven, 1992, 1993). Such an analysis would produce meaningful implications for the school consultant, as others have presented before (e.g., Martin, 1978; Sandoval, Lambert, & Davis, 1977). An effective consultant often will find it advantageous to be open to influence from the consultee, in part because it may strengthen the consultant's power. For example, listening attentively to the consultee may increase the legitimate power of reciprocity (e.g., "I listened to you before, so please hear me out this time"). Being open to the consultee's influence also may increase mutual attraction and result in increased consultee attributions of personal reward and personal coercive power (Erchul & Raven, 1997).

A major point of Chap. 3 is that social influence is a critically important component of school consultation. Just as the chapter opened with the Paradox of School Psychology (Gutkin & Conoley, 1990), we close it with the *Second Paradox of School Psychology*:

> Although school psychologists have the potential to influence and thereby change the behavior of consultees, many are reluctant to recognize and exercise this influence, and as a result the effectiveness of consultation is not maximized. (Erchul et al., 2008, p. 318)

Although a one-on-one relationship between a consultant and consultee is a key component, the practice of school consultation involves much more than this. Because consultation occurs within an organizational context, it is critical for the consultant to understand the structure and function of the consultee's workplace. In Chap. 4, we consider some of the fundamental elements of the school as an organization.

Notes

1. We wish to emphasize that all of us – not just teachers – often require a level of influence beyond basic information in order to change our beliefs, attitudes, and behaviors.
2. This section of Chap. 3 bears the mark of Bertram H. Raven, as it draws from Raven (1992, 1993) and Erchul and Raven (1997). We would like to thank Bert Raven for his insight and support in applying social power and interpersonal influence concepts to school consultation, and credit him for many of the ideas included here.
3. Because of space limitations, we have chosen to omit "manipulation possibilities," "indirect influence possibilities," and "the effects of feedback on the agent," topics that are discussed by Raven (1992, 1993) and included in Fig. 3.1.

Chapter 4
The School as a Setting for Consultation

In the early 1800s, children who were fortunate enough to receive an education did so in one-room schoolhouses. Attendance was sporadic and often depended on the availability of a teacher and the completion of chores around the home or farm. Together with a small number of friends and neighbors, the children who were present each day would be instructed in the fundamentals of reading, writing, and arithmetic using whatever materials were available and at whatever pace was necessary to accommodate their divergent skills. Following the industrial revolution of the late 1800s, it became fashionable to view schools as "factories" and children as "raw materials" who one day would become products capable of meeting the demands of an industrialized society (Cubberley, 1916). Compulsory education, child labor laws, and waves of immigrants entering the United States in the early 1900s produced staggering increases in school enrollments and corresponding increases in state and federal expenditures on public education (Fagan & Wise, 2007).

Today, the American educational system is one of the largest institutions in society employing more than four million teachers, administrators, and support personnel and meeting the needs of more than 44 million children (Apter, 1977; Grant & Snyder, 1986). As with any large organization, public education has come to rely on an extensive bureaucracy as a means of accomplishing its service delivery goals. One-room schoolhouses have been replaced by thousands of elementary and secondary campuses nationwide with vast administrative networks responsible for overseeing their operation. Similarly, a handful of children working with a single teacher for the entire school day has been replaced by regular education classes of 30 or more students; compartmentalized instruction; universal, selected, and targeted intervention programs; and both push-in and pull-out special education services. Within this network of service options, school consultation underlies a variety of alternatives available to teachers in their efforts to accommodate students with special needs.

We believe that an appreciation for schools as organizations and a familiarity with the range of services they offer is crucial in order to enter the service delivery network and to function effectively as a school consultant. Toward these goals, the chapter begins by discussing the characteristics of schools and schooling that have evolved from three very different traditions in organizational thinking: (1) Weber's

W.P. Erchul and B.K. Martens, *School Consultation*, Issues in Clinical Child Psychology, 63
DOI 10.1007/978-1-4419-5747-4_4, © Springer Science+Business Media, LLC 2010

classical theory of bureaucracy; (2) the human relations movement; and (3) organizational behavior theory. Next, we depict the range of services that are offered in a typical school building, and describe a model for eligibility determination, the refer-test-place sequence, which has a longstanding tradition in the American educational system. The chapter concludes by describing the role that school consultation plays in both traditional and RTI services, discussing the utilization of school consultation services from an administrative perspective, and identifying three paradoxes of consultation service delivery. We believe that these paradoxes stem from the dynamic interplay of teaching as an intensive technology and schools as bureaucratic organizations.

Organizational Traditions in the Public School System

Classical Organizational Theory

In response to the often arbitrary and capricious manner in which human service organizations were managed at the turn of the century, Max Weber, a German sociologist, formulated a theory of the efficient, impartial administrative apparatus known as *bureaucracy* (Owens, 1981). A basic tenet of Weber's theory was that if each individual in an organization was trained with the technical expertise to complete one task, administration could assume the function of coordinating these tasks in a rational and impersonal manner. This approach would allow workers to go about their jobs unencumbered by the burdens of decision making, enabling the organization to handle an extensive client base while ensuring uniformity in the services that were provided. Weber's principles for an efficiently run bureaucracy were uniquely suited to the increasingly popular assembly line approach of mass production, and were summarized by Owens (1981) as follows (p. 11):

1. A division of labor based on functional specialization
2. A well-defined hierarchy of authority
3. A system of rules covering the rights and duties of employees
4. A system of procedures for dealing with work situations
5. Impersonality of interpersonal relations
6. Selection and promotion based only on technical competence

By the mid-1900s, Weber's principles of bureaucratic administration had been adopted by a large number of American industries including public education. Because the bureaucratic approach emphasized relationships among job roles rather than people, its application required certain assumptions about the nature of organizations and placed certain restrictions on an organization's ability to adapt to changing circumstances. In many respects, these assumptions have proven to be inconsistent with the business of schools and schooling, and suggest why alternative approaches to service delivery such as school consultation were slow to take root

(M.D. Cohen, March, & Olsen, 1972). First and foremost, bureaucracies are appropriate for organizations with clearly defined goals and objectives. A clear, common goal not only enlists the support of all employees, but provides a criterion by which the organization's success can be measured. Although government policy statements reflect a consensus over the general goals of public education (e.g., the America 2000 initiative, outcome-based education), attempts to implement these policies are often thwarted by a lack of agreement concerning specific educational objectives (Fagan & Wise, 2007; Morison, 1992). Our experience in the schools suggests that pluralistic goals also exist at the district and building levels. For example, regular education teachers may perceive their goal as seeing to it that the majority of children in their classroom master enough of the curriculum to be promoted to the next grade. In order to accomplish this goal, the effective teacher is required to integrate various managerial and instructional practices into a workable system, which is characterized by a group-oriented focus (Gettinger, 1988). Support personnel, in turn, may perceive their goal as encouraging teachers to accommodate a wider diversity of student skills through individualized instruction, whereas school administrators might view both goals as being subordinate to budget accountability.

Second, in order to have a division of labor based on functional specialization, the job to be completed must be capable of being broken down into component tasks. By doing so, each employee has a limited sphere of responsibility, is required to make few decisions throughout the workday that are not dictated by standard operating procedures, and can be replaced by others who have similar skills with no loss of efficiency. *Outside of the classroom*, schools are organized in ways that reflect many of these bureaucratic characteristics, including a graded system of progress through the secondary level, compartmentalized instruction where children change teachers for different content areas, and the use of itinerant substitute teachers who temporarily replace regular teachers as needed. *Inside the classroom,* however, teachers are afforded a great deal of independence and are responsible for dealing with a wide variety of student-related issues (e.g., planning lessons and making presentations, arbitrating student quarrels) (T.B. Gutkin, personal communication, March 22, 1984).

Third, bureaucracies are appropriate for organizations that rely on downward lines of communication between administrators and workers. This "top-down" approach is the way in which changes in procedure are instituted, and it makes lateral communication between departmental units at the same level relatively unimportant. In the public schools, innovative teaching approaches or new curriculum materials are rarely developed and disseminated by teachers during the course of their day-to-day instructional activities. Rather, as noted by Axelrod (1993), university-based educational researchers are typically responsible for promoting teaching practices, publishing companies are responsible for promoting curriculum materials, school boards are responsible for adopting basal series to be used throughout the district, and building principals are responsible for instituting disciplinary procedures. In short, educational innovations tend to occur in a top-down fashion within school districts, reducing the speed and flexibility with which these organizations can adapt to changing circumstances. School consultation is typically initiated by teachers serving on the "front lines" who refer a child to the school's PST. Members of the PST, in turn, rely on the problem solving model and their shared skills and experiences to design and implement an intervention program. As such, school consultation represents an approach to change that occurs in a bottom-up fashion. As with many bureaucratically run organizations, schools may not have adequate mechanisms in place for supporting teachers involvement in or the dissemination of innovative teaching and managerial practices that originate from within (Piersel & Gutkin, 1983).

Related to the issue of vertical information flow, successful school consultation often requires a coordination of efforts and services laterally between various individuals and units within the school building. For example, consider the task of implementing a home-based reinforcement program as a positive behavioral support for a student classified as emotionally disturbed. In a school that adheres to the traditional pull-out approach to service delivery, the student might be placed on a part-time basis in a special education resource room and receive speech as a related service 2 hr a week. Once the child's program is in place, it is unlikely that the speech therapist, resource teacher, and regular classroom teacher will meet regularly to coordinate their respective activities. Successful implementation of the home-based reinforcement program would require that these individuals plus the child's parents meet to establish and review goals for behavior change, that a system be put in place for monitoring the child's behavior in different settings, that reports of behavior be collected at the end of the day and sent home to the parents, and that the parents act on these reports accordingly (e.g., Witt, Hannafin, & Martens, 1983).

The Human Relations Movement

Classical theory focuses on the formal administrative structure of organizations in the absence of individuals. In contrast, the human relations movement grew out of an appreciation for the informal social interactions that arise among individuals despite this formal structure (Owens, 1981). Proponents of the human relations movement believe that members of organizations interact with each other and form alliances based on social psychological variables, and many times these patterns differ from those sanctioned by the formal bureaucratic structure. In order to understand how an organization actually functions, one must look beyond its organizational chart and take into account such issues as organizational climate, group norms, leadership style, and behavioral regularities.

Organizational climate is a term used to describe the informal, social environment of an organization that reflects the values of its members and influences the nature of their interactions and behavior (Halpin, 1966; Tagiuri & Litwin, 1968). Two important determinants of the organizational climate in schools are the principal's leadership style and the group norms of the teaching staff. The relationship of principals' leadership style to the utilization of school consultation services was examined in a study by Bossard and Gutkin (1983). In this study, school consultants were assigned to 10 elementary schools over a 14-week period. At the end of the 14 weeks, the consultant and teaching staff at each school completed the Leader Behavior Description Questionnaire (LBDQ) (Halpin, 1966), which contains two subscales: Consideration and Initiating Structure. According to Halpin:

> Initiating Structure refers to the leader's behavior in delineating the relationship between himself [sic] and members of the work group, and in endeavoring to establish well-defined patterns of organization, channels of communication, and methods of procedure. Consideration refers to behavior indicative of friendship, mutual trust, respect, and warmth in the relationship between the leader and members of his staff. (p. 86)

In addition, the skills of each consultant were rated by experts naive to the purposes of the study, and the utilization of consultation services in each school was calculated as the total number of consultation contacts divided by the number of teachers on staff. Results indicated that differences in consultant skill, principal Consideration, and principal Initiating Structure accounted for 70% of the variance in the number of consultation contacts across the 10 schools. Interestingly, the number of consultation contacts correlated positively with the leadership variable of Consideration ($r = 0.32$) and negatively with the variable of Initiating Structure ($r = -0.35$).

The group norms of teaching staff refer to the often unspoken values and rules for behavior that are adopted in a given school building (Owens, 1981). According to Sarason (1971, 1996), one way of assessing the group norms present in a school is to observe the *behavioral regularities* of teachers and students. Behavioral regularities refer to the ways in which things actually get done versus the ways in which things are supposed to get done. These recurrent patterns of behavior evolve over time based on an interaction between the educational goals of teachers, the physical environment and resources of the school, the leadership style of the principal, and the time constraints under which teachers operate. When examining the behavioral regularities present in a school building, Sarason suggested that the school consultant ask two questions: "What is the rationale for the [observed] regularity?" and "What is the universe of alternatives that could be considered [to achieve the same outcome]?" (p. 64). Asking these questions encourages a suspension of personal values in our attempts to understand organizations, and can represent an important first step in the process of affecting organizational change.

To illustrate, the astute school consultant might observe the following behavioral regularities in a large, suburban elementary school: (1) teachers pack up their belongings and leave the school building immediately after the children leave; (2) during instructional periods, the halls of the school are empty and teachers rarely if ever enter each other's classroom; (3) the principal does all of the talking during faculty meetings and most of her comments are concerned with building procedures, student discipline, and the need to raise standardized test scores; and (4) a large proportion of children (almost 13% of the student population) are receiving special education services. Given these regularities, what might one conclude about the organizational climate of the school? Clearly, the building principal values a smoothly running school and is interested in competing favorably with other buildings in the district. Her behavior during faculty meetings also suggests that she would likely obtain a high score on Halpin's Initiating Structure scale. In response to the principal's bureaucratic management style, teachers concern themselves with their own classrooms, are reluctant to offer informal help to their colleagues, and essentially "punch out" at the end of the school day. When learning problems arise in the classroom, teachers at our hypothetical elementary school are encouraged to "go through the proper channels" by making a referral to the PST.

An interesting arena in which to observe behavioral regularities in service delivery is the multidisciplinary team meeting. As mandated by IDEIA, decisions about a child's eligibility for special education and related services are to be made by a team of professionals in cooperation with the child's parents or legal guardians. As we discuss later in the chapter, after completing an individual evaluation of the student, the evaluation team typically communicates its findings and recommendations to parents during a formal meeting often referred to as a staffing. A number of researchers have examined the behavioral regularities that occur during staffings, and we believe these findings have important implications for school consultants in their attempts to understand the culture of the school. A summary of these behavioral regularities appears below.

1. The average time allotted for meetings was approximately a half hour (Goldstein, Strickland, Turnbull, & Curry, 1980; Pfeiffer, 1981) whereas allowing enough time for the staffing accounted for the most variance in participant satisfaction (Witt, Miller, McIntyre, & Smith, 1984).

2. Parents, social workers, and principals were ranked high in perceived status before the meeting (3rd) and low on actual contributions (9th) after the meeting (Gilliam, 1979).

3. The most influential team members were those with the most knowledge of available placement options in the school (Pfeiffer, 1980).

4. Special education resource teachers assumed primary responsibility for conducting the meeting and developing the student's individualized education plan (IEP) (Goldstein et al., 1980).

5. Satisfaction with the meeting was related to participation and tended to be the highest for the school psychologist and special education teacher (Yoshida, Fenton, Maxwell, & Kaurman, 1978).

6. In all but one instance, students' IEPs were completed prior to the meeting (Goldstein et al., 1980).

7. There was a tendency for the evaluation team to recommend less restrictive placements when such recommendations were based on criterion-referenced rather than norm-referenced assessment data (Goldbaum & Rucker, 1977).

8. When parents were present at meetings, there was a tendency for more school staff to be present and for them to make more recommendations (Singer, Bossard, & Watkins, 1977).

9. Majority vote and resolution by the school psychologist were the most frequently used methods of resolving conflicts (Hyman, Duffey, Caroll, Manni, & Winikur, 1973).
10. Overall parent satisfaction with the meeting was high (Goldstein et al., 1980; Witt et al., 1984).

Behavioral regularities also occur *within* classrooms, and these regularities can be related systematically to different instructional arrangements. By conceptualizing learning as a social process, researchers in this area have identified five *activity segments* that can be used to describe how learning typically occurs in American classrooms; recitation, teacher-directed small groups, seatwork, sharing time, and student-directed small groups (Weinstein, 1991). Activity segments refer to instructional arrangements that contain implicit rules for interaction and which partially dictate teacher and student behavior. According to Weinstein, children who are successful in classrooms are able to discriminate among various activity segments based on physical arrangement or subtle teacher cues, and understand the types of behavior appropriate to each. Characteristics of the three most common activity segments discussed by Weinstein are summarized below (the interested reader is referred to the original article for a complete description and review of supporting research).

Recitation

This activity segment affords teachers the highest degree of control over student interaction and occurs when teachers lecture or present new material to the class as a group. From the teacher's perspective, recitation requires that a certain amount of material be covered while asking for and commenting on responses from students. Students must attend to the material being presented as well as any interactions that occur, are relegated to making brief responses to teacher questions, and must identify when and how to compete for floor holding rights. Observational studies have suggested that teachers who are most effective during recitations call on children randomly to respond, require choral responding, and use alerting statements to introduce a new topic (e.g., "You won't believe what happens next.") (Brophy, 1983; Kounin, 1970).

Teacher-Directed Small Groups

Small-group arrangements are commonly used in the elementary grades for instruction in reading. By dividing the class into groups of children with similar skill levels and meeting with these groups in sequence, teachers are able to balance the practical requirement of maintaining a group-oriented focus while providing more individualized instruction (i.e., more frequent or elaborate prompting, modeling, praise, and feedback). The role of small groups in teachers' efforts to individualize instruction was demonstrated in a study by Allington (1980) who found that teachers tended to correct students' reading errors in ways that promoted comprehension in high-achieving groups, but tended to focus on decoding errors in low-achieving groups.

Seatwork

Independent seatwork in which students sit quietly at their desks reading, answering questions in workbooks, or completing teacher-made worksheets constitutes a significant portion of the school day in both regular and special education class-rooms (Ysseldyke, Christenson, Thurlow, & Bakewell, 1989). Because seatwork activities require students to complete assignments in the absence of teacher direc-tion, behavioral regularities tend to involve cyclical patterns of engagement, off-task behavior, and teacher intervention, as well as attempts to solicit assistance from the teacher or peers (e.g., deVoss, 1979).

Organizational Behavior Theory

Thus far in the chapter, we have depicted the organization of schools as reflecting many of the characteristics of a formal bureaucracy while at the same time sup-porting an informal network of implicit alliances and behavioral regularities. Although schools differ in the balance achieved between these often conflicting perspectives, at the heart of any educational system is the technology used by teachers to accomplish their instructional goals. Organizational behavior theory represents an attempt to examine the relationship between the technology used by an industry and the linkages imposed by this technology among its various depart-mental units (Owens, 1981).

The technology of schooling has been characterized from a number of perspectives including process–product research (e.g., Gettinger, 1988), information-processing models (Doyle, 1985), and direct instruction (Becker, 1988). Common to all of these perspectives is the realization that effective classroom instruction is an inten-sive activity that requires thoughtful planning, systematic execution, and ongoing monitoring of student-related outcomes (e.g., Martens & Kelly, 1993). The intensive technological aspects of instruction are reflected in the fact that teachers are required to perform a variety of operations during the course of the school day, are given a great deal of autonomy in determining what goes on in their classrooms, and receive little by way of direct supervision from principals. As summarized by Sarason (1971, 1996), even though teachers spend almost all of their time in contact with children, the absence of adult contact makes teaching a lonely profession.

To what extent is the intensive technology of teaching appropriate for the often bureaucratic structure of schools? As discussed by Owens (1981), there are three ways to describe the interdependencies between individuals and departments in an organization; sequential coupling, reciprocal coupling, or pooled coupling.

Sequential coupling occurs when each worker is responsible for performing a relatively few number of operations on the product before passing it on to the next individual who in turn makes his or her contribution. Using assembly lines for mass production exemplifies the sequential coupling approach. *Reciprocal coupling* occurs when workers perform a number of operations on the product while passing it back and forth. The process of preparing a manuscript for publication in which the initial draft that is written by the author is edited by the publisher and then returned to the author for revisions would be an example of the reciprocal coupling approach. *Pooled* or *loose coupling* describes organizations in which "members share resources in common but otherwise work independently" (Owens, 1981, p. 29). Schools represent loosely coupled organizations in that teachers share the physical space and resources of their building but function independently in their respective classrooms. Unfortunately, pooled coupling can also be used to describe the relationship between regular education, special education, and related services such as speech and language. In a typical pull-out model of service delivery, each of these entities may be scheduled to work with the child for a portion of the school day with few explicit attempts to coordinate efforts, a situation termed by Giangreco (1989) as "programmatic isolation."

The Service Structure of Public Schools

Available Services

When it comes to the range of services offered in schools, there is no such thing as the typical building. Rather, each school is unique as a function of size, location (e.g., rural, urban), community demographics, amount of parental involvement, number of staff, and administrative priorities. Because a great deal of school consultation occurs with elementary-age children, this section focuses on the types of services one might find in a school housing grades K (kindergarten) through 6. The school we will be describing – let's call it the Bartlett F. Sloane Elementary School – represents a composite of several buildings with which the authors are familiar. Although hypothetical, we believe that Sloane Elementary provides a useful vehicle through which to characterize the diversity of services available in the public school setting.

Sloane Elementary is located in a moderately sized city in the Northeast. It has a total enrollment of 470 students and employs 60 administrators, teachers, and support personnel who receive assistance from 15 volunteer aides. A detailed accounting of Sloane Elementary's demographics is presented in Table 4.1. As shown in the table, approximately equal percentages of Caucasian and African American students attend Sloane, whereas there is a small but significant number of Native American students (almost 5% of the student population). Over half of the students receive free or reduced-price lunch, which often provides a rough indication of parents' socioeconomic status, and no students at Sloane require services

Table 4.1 Demographics of Sloane Elementary School

Enrollment	
By grade:	K (55); 1 (55); 2 (70); 3 (70); 4 (80); 5 (70); 6 (70) – Total: 470
Ethnicity:	Caucasian (47%); Black (48%); Hispanic (0.5%); Native American (4.5%)
Other:	Free lunch (65%); special education (15%); out-of-school suspension (6%)
Teaching and Support Staff	
Regular education:	Pre-K (1); K (3); 1 (4); 2 (4); 3 (4); 4 (4); 5 (4); 6 (4) – Total: 28
Regular education support personnel:	Librarian, instructional specialist, music teachers (2), art teacher, gym teacher, nurse, computer lab teacher
Special education:	Self-contained (5); resources (2) – Total: 7
Special education support personnel:	Speech therapist, adapted physical education teacher, social worker, school psychologists (2), occupation therapist, physical therapist, school counselor

in the English as a Second Language program. The bulk of administration at Sloane is handled by the principal and vice principal with the aid of two secretaries and an attendance monitor. There are four regular education teachers per grade level (including a pre-K classroom), seven special education teachers, and a full complement of support personnel including a librarian (also known as media specialist), instructional specialist, speech therapist, nurse, social worker, psychologist, occupational therapist, and adapted physical education teacher.

Regular Education at Sloane

The four teachers at each grade level are organized into teams, with the role of team leader changing annually. Grade-level teams are responsible for assigning students to classrooms, determining the need for remedial or enrichment programs, adopting supplementary curriculum materials (e.g., supplies for science experiments), and arranging supervision for student teachers from the local university who function as teaching assistants. By virtue of the Adopt-a-School Program, student teachers at Sloane receive a small stipend for training that comes out of monies supplied by local businesses.

Students identified as at-risk for learning and behavior problems receive instructional support through a 3-tiered intervention model similar to that described in Chap. 2. At the universal level, Sloane employs a school-wide PBS program, in which tokens (called "Bartlett Bucks") exchangeable for school supplies, special privileges, and recognition by the principal can be earned throughout the school day for engaging in prosocial behaviors. Sloane also has several Tier 2 programs available to students that involve standard protocols of evidence-based practices. The first of these is the "Read-a-Lot" after-school program, in which small groups of children repeatedly read instructionally matched passages with goal setting, feedback, and reinforcement. Also at Tier 2 is the "Help-a-Friend" peer tutoring program in which students can complete left-over work during an instructional period with the help of a high-achieving peer who is trained to model correct answers, provide feedback, and chart the student's progress. Finally, for students who do not respond to the Tier 1 and Tier 2 programs, Sloane has a PST that meets regularly to design and implement more targeted and individualized Tier 3 interventions.

For those students who have mastered the basic curriculum material and could benefit from opportunities to extend and apply what they have learned, Sloane provides enrichment programs in reading (the School Newsletter), writing (the In-School Mail Delivery System), and math (the School Store). Sloane also participates in a district-wide program designed to expose students to the history and traditions of other cultures, such as that of the Native Americans. Participation in these enrichment programs is dependent on satisfactory progress in all content areas and requires nomination from at least two teachers.

Special Education at Sloane

Four of the five self-contained classrooms at Sloane can generally be distinguished by the teacher-to-student ratio, the presence of a full-time assistant, and the severity of students' disabilities. These characteristics combine to produce a graded hierarchy of restrictiveness with respect to students' placements. Students attend each of these classrooms for the majority of the school day with the exception of specials (e.g., music, art, gym) or mainstreamed subject areas as indicated on their IEPs. The least restrictive self-contained classroom includes 15 children and one teacher, and is devoted almost exclusively to students with learning disabilities or those students who have received more restrictive placements in the past but are transitioning back to regular education. The majority of students with other mild disabilities for whom a self-contained placement is appropriate are served in a second classroom that contains 12 students, one teacher, and one teacher's assistant. Students with multiple disabilities or those who are moderately to severely mentally retarded, attend a classroom containing a total of six students, one teacher, and one teacher's assistant. A similar arrangement is used for students classified as "severely emotionally disturbed." The fifth self-contained classroom at the school is used to house one of the district's two magnet programs for students with autism spectrum disorder. Approximately 15 children between the ages of 4 and 7 years attend the classroom for training in independent living and basic communication skills.

Sloane combines both pull-out and push-in approaches to the delivery of special education resource services. Students receiving resource services are provided assistance and remedial instruction for only a portion of the school day while spending most the day alongside their regular education peers. The two resource teachers at Sloane share one classroom that small groups of eligible students attend for an hour a day (pull-out services). When not instructing students in the resource room, the teachers team teach with their regular education counterparts who have significant numbers of mainstreamed special education students (push-in services). A similar approach to service delivery is taken by the speech therapist who has her own office in the building.

Support Services

The principal at Sloane is a strong advocate of community outreach efforts and as a result, the school offers a number of instructional and counseling groups for both students and parents. In the evenings, the school library and cafeteria double as classrooms for courses offered through the district-wide Adult Education Program (e.g., Beginning through Advanced Guitar and Tai Chi) as well as a 3-week parent training course offered by the school psychologist. Approximately 60 students are involved in one or more counseling groups addressing such issues as social skills training, anger control, or growing up in a single-parent household. These groups are run by the school psychologist and school counselor, who also provide individual counseling to a small number of students as indicated in their IEPs.

Several conclusions can be drawn from the above description of our hypothetical elementary school. First, what goes on inside the school in many ways reflects what goes on outside the school in terms of community demographics, parental values, and the involvement of local businesses. Second, consistent with the notion of schools as loosely coupled organizations, a variety of activities occur in any given school building, and these activities require a coordination of space, materials, and schedules. Third, the majority of services offered in the school can be depicted as falling under one of two administrative units – regular or special education. Although housed in the same facilities, these units maintain separate administrative structures, receive separate lines of funding, and employ their own teaching staff.

Most students who experience difficulties in regular education continue there but with a system of increasingly more intensive supports as needed based on their responsiveness to intervention. Information from these students' cumulative intervention histories is then used to help determine their eligibility for special class placement (Daly, Martens, Barnett, Witt, & Olson, 2007). Students who are unresponsive to interventions in the regular education setting are then evaluated for placement in special education. In determining a student's eligibility for special education services, the evaluation team must identify that a learning or adjustment problem exists, determine under which disability category a student qualifies, make recommendations for programming based on the evaluation data, and assign the student to a special class teacher who is responsible for designing and implementing their special education program. This process is known as the *refer-test-place sequence,* and is described in the following section.

The Refer-Test-Place Sequence

It was suggested earlier in the chapter that one outcome of the bureaucratic structure of schools and the large numbers of children they serve is an emphasis by teachers on group approaches to instruction. As discussed at length in Chap. 10, this emphasis by teachers on group instructional approaches inevitably collides with the diversity of skills and behaviors which students bring to the classroom setting to virtually insure that some children will fail in regular education (Apter, 1977).

Although most students in classrooms across the country will achieve at sufficient levels to be promoted to the next grade, for some children a significant discrepancy develops between their performance and the teachers' performance expectations (Shinn, 1989). At this point, many school districts require teachers in cooperation with a building-level PST to provide increasingly more intensive instructional or behavioral supports to students as described in Chap. 2. If the student's performance does not improve significantly as a result of such intervention efforts, the teacher and PST then refer the child to a building-level evaluation team.

Once a student is formally referred to the evaluation team for additional consideration, district personnel have up to 90 days by law to complete a comprehensive psychoeducational evaluation, communicate their findings and recommendations to the board of education, and arrange appropriate special education services. Parental consent must be obtained before initiating the evaluation which, depending on the nature of the referral, may involve any of the staff members listed in Table 4.1. When conducting the evaluation, IDEIA mandates that tests and assessment procedures be administered in the student's dominant language and be valid for the specific purposes for which they are used. IDEIA also states that no single procedure can be used as the sole criterion for determining a student's eligibility for special services, and students are to be assessed in all areas related to their suspected disability. In actuality, individual psychoeducational evaluations typically include a series of interviews with the child's parents and teachers, a review of the student's permanent school records, systematic and anecdotal observations in the classroom setting, and either the collection of work samples or the administration of curriculum-based assessment probes (e.g., Shinn, 1989). Because of the student-centered focus adopted by many evaluation teams, it is also common practice to administer a battery of standardized, norm-referenced tests to assess the student's functioning relative to others in such areas as general intelligence, adaptive behavior, achievement, language, and social behavior.

After data collection is complete, the evaluation team is responsible for drafting a report that describes the assessment results, summarizes the student's current performance levels, and indicates whether the child is eligible for classification as a child with a disability consistent with state regulations (see Chap. 10 for a complete description of various disability categories). In addition, the report makes recommendations to the receiving special education teacher concerning approximate levels in the curriculum at which to begin instruction, strategies the teacher might find useful in developing the student's IEP, and any related services the student should receive such as speech or physical therapy.

With the evaluation report in hand, one or more members of the building-level team, a designated special education representative, and the child's parents or legal guardians participate in a staffing meeting. During this meeting, the findings and recommendations of the evaluation team are discussed with parents and a decision is made concerning the student's eligibility for special education services. If all parties are in agreement with this decision, the student's IEP is completed or approved by those in attendance by documenting the following information: (1) classification status; (2) annual goals and short-term instructional objectives as well as evaluation criteria and procedures; (3) recommended program, date of initiation, and amount of time per day; (4) placement; and (5) any specialized equipment or related services. The school district is required to provide the agreed upon special education services, usually within 30 days of the receipt of the recommendation. At any point during the proceedings, the child's parents are free to disagree with the actions taken by the school and request an impartial hearing to have their child's case reviewed. In addition, parents may obtain a second opinion of their child's case by seeking an independent evaluation at the school's expense.

The Role of Consultation

RTI models and mandates for prereferral intervention programs have resulted in larger numbers of students with special needs being served in regular education. State education budgets continue to decline, meaning that teachers have to do more with fewer resources, whereas teachers and support personnel alike are expected to make increasing use of evidence-based practices. It is also clear that only a small percentage of children who fail in regular education can ultimately be placed in special education classrooms (probably 7% or less) (e.g., Marston, Muyskens, Lau, & Canter, 2003). These realities of contemporary education have raised the status of consultation to a stand-alone service that is designed to complement the traditional refer-test-place model. Over time, the delivery of school consultation services may actually enhance the effectiveness of special education by reducing the numbers of children who are referred and placed. For example, Gutkin, Henning-Stout, and Piersel (1988) examined the long-term effects of a prereferral intervention model in which school consultation was added as an intermediate step in the referral process. In the 4 years following implementation of the program, outcome data revealed that the percentage of referred children who met their educational objectives, and therefore were not evaluated, increased from 21 to 61%. Interestingly, the percentage of students who were evaluated and deemed eligible for special education placement increased from 69 to 82% during the same time period. These latter data suggest that not only were building-level teams conducting workups on fewer numbers of students, but more of these children were actually recommended for services rather than returned to the regular education classroom following a costly evaluation.

School Consultation from an Administrative Perspective

Factors Influencing the Use of Consultation Services

Numerous school districts across the country now routinely implement prereferral intervention programs as a means of supplementing traditional special education services (Flugum & Reschly, 1994; McDougal, Clonan, & Martens, 2000;

Rosenfield, 1992). As noted by Ponti, Zins, and Graden (1988), these programs represent attempts to view consultation as "an integral part of the educational service delivery system rather than as a separate service provided by individual practitioners" (p. 90). Attempts such as these to institutionalize school consultation practice have met with varying degrees of success as a function of the need to overcome several barriers to innovation at an organizational level. Three of these barriers are particularly common and include support from administration, consistency with traditional services, and documentation of beneficial effects on students.

Because district and building administrators (e.g., principals, vice principals, directors of special education) have authority over resource allocation and make decisions concerning such issues as class schedules and teacher release time, garnering the support of these individuals is crucial for successful school consultation (McDougal et al., 2000). As noted by Piersel and Gutkin (1983), a resistant administrator will in all likelihood ensure the failure of a prereferral intervention model. Given the bureaucratic structure of schools, however, administrators who are merely tolerant of consultation or who offer only moderate levels of support may be equally damning. The greatest barrier to consultation services identified by school consultants themselves is lack of sufficient time (e.g., Costenbader, Swartz, & Petrix, 1992). By lack of time, consultants usually refer to difficulties scheduling uninterrupted meetings with teachers given their busy class schedules, and the challenges of providing consultation services while managing other professional duties (e.g., evaluation caseloads, counseling groups). Inside the classroom, lack of time for teachers may refer to difficulties working individually with a single student while adequately supervising the rest of the class during independent seatwork. Unless the building principal is willing to actively support school consultation by, for example, providing release time for teachers or assigning part-time aides to classrooms, efforts to implement agreed upon intervention programs may actually be viewed as punishing from the teacher's perspective (Piersel & Gutkin, 1983).

In order to ensure that school consultation is being provided in ways that are consistent with and augment traditional services, Ponti et al. (1988) suggest that a needs assessment be conducted prior to program implementation. As discussed in Chap. 5, conducting a needs assessment is part of successful entry into the schools and involves "mapping" the formal and informal services available in the building, identifying key administrative personnel, and evaluating gaps in the service delivery network. Such gaps may refer to high numbers of children who are referred for failure in the regular classroom but are deemed ineligible for special education, a lack of continuity or duplication of effort in the refer-test-place process, or effective services that are underutilized because school staff are unaware of their existence. McDougal et al. (2000) suggest that consultation services also be evaluated formatively throughout implementation using such means as focus groups, roundtable meetings, surveys, and direct observation. Information collected from these sources can be used to revise the way consultation services are delivered (e.g., computerized referral forms) or to arrange additional staff training in key areas (e.g., instructional interventions).

Finally, school consultation may be viewed as incompatible with more sequentially coupled special education services because its utilization and effectiveness is more difficult to document (Piersel & Gutkin, 1983). Funds for special education are typically allocated based on the number of students with disabilities in a given district. As the number of these students increases, the district can be expected to receive a corresponding increase in state and federal funds. Consultation services, on the other hand, may be directed toward children in both regular and special education classrooms, typically involve multiple contacts with any given teacher, and often have no formal relationship to district funding. For example, in New York State there is a small amount of money available to schools under the category of Educationally Related Support Services (ERSS). These funds were used in the past to obtain additional services for regular education students such as social skills training or counseling. In recent years, several districts have required support personnel to document the amount of time they spend in consultation activities, enabling a portion of these funds to be used to support prereferral intervention services.

The Three Paradoxes of School Consultation

We conclude this chapter with a discussion of three paradoxes that continue to pervade the delivery of school consultation services. A paradox is defined as a statement that is seemingly absurd or contradictory, yet is in fact true. The dynamic tension between schools as bureaucracies and teaching as an intensive technology often places the school consultant in situations that call for seemingly contradictory actions in their attempts to deliver services. Understanding consultation from the perspective of both administrators and teachers can be helpful in resolving these situations to the mutual satisfaction of all parties involved.

Paradox 1: Although Teachers Are Frequently Exposed to Innovative Educational Practices, Change Occurs Slowly in Schools

Educational innovations are typically developed by individuals outside the school setting, adopted by district administrators, and passed on to building principals for dissemination downward to teachers. Teaching is an intensive technology, however, and teachers maintain high levels of autonomy over what goes on in their classrooms. As a result, many innovations that are supposedly adopted in schools using a top-down model fail to be implemented at the level of the classroom (Sarason, 1971, 1996). This means that attempts to implement a prereferral intervention model that have administrative backing but do not involve teachers and support personnel as planning team members will probably not succeed (McDougal et al., 2000). Similarly, informal attempts by individual support personnel to implement school consultation services are likely to run counter to the generally accepted model of top-down change. As an innovation developed from within the school, consultation services in this case must be disseminated upward through the administrative hierarchy before they receive organizational approval. Although bureaucracies are well suited for moving information downward from administrators to workers, they often have few mechanisms in place for going in the reverse direction. As a result, "grass-roots" attempts to implement school consultation services in the absence of administrative approval may also be likely to fail.

Paradox 2: Most Teachers Want to Be Involved in Responding to Children's Learning and Adjustment Problems, but Schools Are Run in Ways That Limit This Involvement

In a survey of 171 teachers from 12 public and parochial schools, Gutkin (1980) found that 96% of the respondents judged the involvement of teachers in developing intervention programs for difficult-to-teach students as being "quite" or "very" important. Our own experiences in the schools have suggested that most teachers are indeed genuinely invested in the welfare of their students.

Despite their high levels of commitment, teachers come in contact with a large number of students during their career and are typically held accountable for the achievement of groups rather than individuals. In contrast, school consultation often requires teachers to provide more intensive and individualized instruction to meet the needs of at-risk students. Tension occurs when teachers desire to make these accommodations, but are expected to do so in the absence of building-level supports or against the group-focused values of building administrators.

In an era of tiered service delivery models and evidence-based practices, this tension may play out in several ways. On the one hand, teachers may be quick to support universal or even standard protocol interventions because (a) these are often implemented by support personnel, and (b) require few if any changes in teachers' instructional practices. On the other hand, these same teachers may be resistant to implementing individualized, Tier 3 interventions because these do affect their day-to-day activities and, if effective, will become the child's baseline level of instruction for the foreseeable future. Schools with substantial personnel or financial resources have attempted to overcome this resistance by hiring PST aides and volunteers to implement targeted interventions several times per week. In such schools, teachers may actually be enthusiastic about Tier 3 interventions because these too may be implemented by someone else. Ironically, however, as responsibility for plan implementation shifts away from the teacher, opportunities to broaden teachers' instructional practices thereby allowing them to accommodate a wider range of students are lost.

Paradox 3: For School Consultation to Become a Stand-Alone Service Delivery Option, One Must Decrease the Bureaucratic Nature of Schools or Increase the Bureaucratic Nature of School Consultation

In several ways, the principles of school consultation are at odds with those of classical organizational theory. First, as will be discussed in Chap. 6, consultation was originally conceived as a voluntary, collaborative, and confidential relationship between coequal professionals in which the consultee maintained the right to reject consultant suggestions. These core characteristics were appropriate when consultation was essentially a "grass-roots" movement provided by individual professionals (i.e., an intensive technology). Now that consultation has become a mandated, stand-alone service provided by building-level teams (i.e., a sequential technology), the core characteristics of voluntary participation, the right to reject consultant suggestions, and confidentiality may no longer apply (Martens & DiGennaro, 2008). Second, when teachers change their behavior as a function of the consultant's problem solving, social influence, and professional support activities, this tacitly increases the number of individuals to whom the teacher is required to report. Third, during the course of their interactions with teachers, it is not uncommon for school consultants to arrange alternative service delivery configurations such as that described in the home-based reinforcement example. The exception principle of classical theory states that when the same or a similar problem arises repeatedly, solutions to this problem should be established as standard operating procedures (Owens, 1981). Because each child presents a unique set of circumstances to the teacher and consultant, it may be difficult to establish a standard set of routines in meeting their individual needs. In schools characterized by high levels of principal Consideration (Halpin, 1966) and group norms that promote creative professional behavior, teachers may be more willing to deviate from "standard operating procedures." By contrast, principals who strive to initiate a bureaucratic structure in their schools may take a dim view of such activities, unless they can be shown to facilitate the traditional special education model. In these schools, providing consultation services in a more sequentially coupled fashion by developing standard procedures for accepting consultation referrals, a standard pool of effective intervention options, and a standard set of measures for evaluating outcomes are likely to be consistent with the prevailing organizational climate (McDougal et al., 2000).

In this chapter, we attempted to describe the operation of schools from an organizational perspective and to provide the reader with an appreciation for the range of services that are offered. In Chap. 5, we begin discussion of our integrated model of school consultation by analyzing the historical antecedents of consultation as a service delivery approach and describing the principles associated with the two major consultation models – mental health consultation (Caplan, 1970; Caplan & Caplan, 1993/1999) and behavioral consultation (Bergan, 1977; Bergan & Kratochwill, 1990).

Part II
Consultation Processes and Outcomes

Chapter 5
Bases of an Integrated Model of School Consultation

In this chapter, we present the underlying bases of the integrated model of school consultation, which is described in detail in Chap. 6. Bases associated with community mental health are the concepts of population-oriented prevention, crisis, and social support as well as Gerald Caplan's model of mental health consultation (Caplan, 1970; Caplan & Caplan, 1993/1999). Bases associated with behavioral psychology are problem solving, behavior modification in applied settings, and John R. Bergan's model of behavioral consultation (Bergan, 1977; Bergan & Kratochwill, 1990). Another important foundation is social influence, particularly as revealed through social power bases. Finally, we address the issue of laying the groundwork for successful entry into school and classroom settings. After reading this chapter, one should understand the bases of and rationale for the integrated model of school consultation presented in Chap. 6.

Community Mental Health and Mental Health Consultation Bases

After World War II, mental health professionals explored new ways of promoting mental health and preventing mental illness in the public at large, a perspective known as the community or preventive approach. This approach – later legitimized by federal legislation and popularized during the community mental health movement – was founded on the concepts of epidemiological strategies, a primary prevention orientation, and community-wide social support systems (Schulberg & Killilea, 1982).

One of the key originators of the preventive approach was child and community psychiatrist Gerald Caplan (1917–2008). Particularly influential among his approximately 180 publications are Caplan (1961, 1963, 1964, 1970, 1986, 1989) and Caplan and Caplan (1980, 1993/1999). His early professional career in Israel (1948–1952) and later work at Harvard University (1952–1977) saw the development of models and techniques that were integral to the community mental health movement (Erchul & Schulte, 1993). In this opening section, we describe four models commonly

W.P. Erchul and B.K. Martens, *School Consultation*, Issues in Clinical Child Psychology, 83
DOI 10.1007/978-1-4419-5747-4_5, © Springer Science+Business Media, LLC 2010

associated with Caplan: population-oriented prevention, crisis, support systems, and mental health consultation.

Population-Oriented Preventive Model

For many years, the traditional practice of psychiatry concerned itself with the long-term psychoanalysis of individual patients. In the 1940s, therefore, it was a radical departure for Gerald Caplan to advocate for a population-oriented approach that viewed prevention as the ultimate goal (cf. Caplan & Bowlby, 1948). Interestingly, the basis for the population-oriented preventive model is not found within psychiatry, but rather within the field of public health. While a Harvard faculty member in the early 1950s, Caplan attended lectures on conceptual models within public health and epidemiology presented by faculty colleagues. Caplan specifically credits Hugh R. Leavell (e.g., Clark & Leavell, 1958) with the conceptual development of primary, secondary, and tertiary prevention within public health practice (Erchul, 1993b). Caplan (1961, 1964) later developed a new model of prevention in the mental health field that incorporated this now familiar typology of prevention.

Primary prevention relates to decreasing the incidence (i.e., rate of occurrence over time, or new cases) of a disorder by defeating the harmful factors before they produce the disorder in the population. Within public health, primary prevention may be accomplished through interventions that target health promotion, such as education, or specific protection, such as vaccination (Clark & Leavell, 1958). In adapting this concept, Caplan (1964) noted that the primary prevention of mental disorders may result from social action (including attempts to increase physical, psychosocial, and sociocultural supplies to the population) and interpersonal action (including attempts to maximize the mental health professional's benefit to the population). In Caplan's (1986) model – the "recurrent themes model of primary prevention" – past risk factors (biopsychosocial hazards) interact with intermediate variables (competence, reactions to crisis, and social supports) to produce outcomes of good or poor mental health. Interventions intended to achieve primary prevention include community social action, consultation, collaboration, education, crisis intervention, and support systems intervention.

Secondary prevention refers to actions intended to decrease the prevalence of a disorder, with prevalence signifying the percentage of the population that has the disorder at a given time. Its aim is to reduce the rate of old and new cases, generally accomplished by shortening the duration of the disorder (Caplan, 1964). Secondary prevention efforts typically focus on an at-risk group – a segment of the population that may be very likely to develop a particular disorder under certain conditions. (Primary prevention efforts, in contrast, focus on the entire population.) As an example, children of recently divorced parents may be considered an at-risk group for behavioral and emotional problems. Other examples of secondary prevention efforts are the Head Start program and the Primary Mental Health Project (Cowen & Hightower, 1990).

Tertiary prevention refers to attempts to decrease the extent of impairment in the population currently afflicted (Caplan, 1964) or increase the degree of ongoing role-functioning in the population that already has recovered (Caplan, 1989). Tertiary prevention may be achieved through rehabilitation or disability limitation efforts (Clark & Leavell, 1958). The purpose of tertiary prevention is to return individuals with disorders to their highest level of adaptive, productive functioning as soon as possible (Caplan, 1964). An example of tertiary prevention would be teaching social skills to a child with attention-deficit/hyperactivity disorder whose excessive motor activity has been managed through stimulant medication.

A key update regarding this prevention typology is in order. The current terms that describe levels of prevention within public health are *universal, selective,* and *indicated* prevention (Gordon, 1983, 1987). These terms bear some resemblance to, though are not identical to, primary, secondary, and tertiary prevention, respectively. They also roughly correspond to Tier 1, Tier 2, and Tier 3 interventions as described in Chap. 2, but again, are not synonymous with them. Because the Committee on Prevention of Mental Disorders of the Institute of Medicine has dropped the original public health terms and has now adopted *universal, selective,* and *indicated* prevention as part of its overall model of intervention, these terms are both preferred and in common use today (Mrazek & Haggerty, 1994). Greater integration of these terms (and the concepts behind them) with tiered systems of intervention in schools is likely to be seen in the future (e.g., Ikeda, Neessen, & Witt, 2008).

Crisis Model

A crisis is a short period of psychological upset that occurs when a person encounters significant life problems that cannot be escaped and are not easily solved with his or her usual problem-solving strategies (Caplan, 1974). A crisis may be developmental, arising from the physiological and psychological changes that are part of normal growth (cf. Erikson, 1959), or it may be situational, arising from changes in a person's environment, social role, or health status. When a person's customary problem-solving responses do not resolve the crisis, he or she becomes upset and distressed at both the continuation of the stressor and the inability to deal with it successfully. Typical patterns of functioning are disrupted, and negative emotions that can include fear, anxiety, frustration, or guilt are experienced. The upset and tension become an impetus for the person to mobilize internal and external resources. He or she is more likely to seek the help of others, and is more suggestible and receptive to new approaches to solve the problem. If these approaches turn out to be helpful, the tension and upset subside and psychological equilibrium returns. However, if the problem continues, "major disorganization of the individual" (Caplan, 1964, p. 41) results.

How one resolves a crisis has future implications. If, during a crisis, a person learns appropriate and adaptive coping strategies, then these strategies are available for later use. For example, assisting a recently transferred teacher to mobilize new sources of social support, rather than to reinforce her belief that she will be returning shortly to her former school, can help her cope adaptively with the present and leave her better prepared for the future. Conversely, if a person learns and later uses strategies that are ineffective or maladaptive, he or she is left more vulnerable to psychopathology. Every crisis, therefore, "presents both an opportunity for psychological growth and danger of psychological deterioration. It is a way station on a path leading away from or toward mental disorder" (Caplan, 1964, p. 53).

Support Systems Model

The fundamental premise of the support systems model is that social support plays an important health-promoting function and can reduce the risk of both physical and mental illness (Caplan, 1986). Caplan (1974) defined social support as "an enduring pattern of continuous or intermittent ties that play a significant part in maintaining the psychological and physical integrity of the individual over time" (p. 7). Social support, such as that offered by family members, friends, and community institutions, helps the individual to: mobilize psychological resources and master emotional burdens; learn to distinguish safe from dangerous situations; share tasks; and provide various resources such as money, materials, or skills (Caplan, 1974).

The simple premise underlying the support systems model has profound implications. For universal prevention efforts, it suggests that increasing the social supports available to a population can decrease the incidence of physical and psychological disorders. For secondary and tertiary prevention efforts, it suggests that individuals who are provided with social support in stressful situations will be more likely to experience positive outcomes. In other words, high stress in the presence of high social support does not increase susceptibility to mental illness and generally appears to enhance mental health outcomes (Caplan, 1989; Cohen & Wills, 1985).

In our integrated model of school consultation, we find it useful to distinguish between emotional and instrumental support. *Emotional support* refers to "the provision of aid which reflects concern for a person's emotional reactions to an event" (Tardy, 1994, p. 72). Within consultation, emotional support may be evidenced by a consultant serving as an empathetic and active listener, promoting the functioning of natural helpers in an organization, or convening support groups or mutual help groups for consultees facing a common problem (Caplan, 1986). By comparison, *instrumental support* refers to helping another to solve a problem (Sarason & Sarason, 1986). In offering instrumental support, the consultant may provide consultees with feedback, training, and materials that address problem-solving aspects of consultation. Sharing tasks within consultation is another way a consultant can exhibit instrumental support.

Caplan's Model of Mental Health Consultation

Mental health consultation (including Gerald Caplan's specific model) has been hailed as "a major, if not the major technique and focus of community psychology, community psychiatry, and community mental health" (Mannino & Shore, 1971, p. 1). To some degree, all consultation approaches are based on Caplan's mental health model and all consultants can benefit from understanding it (Erchul, 2009). This model is described in detail in Caplan (1963, 1964, 1970), Caplan and Caplan (1993/1999), and Erchul (1993a); interested readers are encouraged to seek out these references for a more comprehensive description. Here we present some underlying assumptions of Caplan's model, define his four types of consultation, and examine key issues related to the model's consultee-centeredness.

Fundamental Assumptions

Brown, Pryzwansky, and Schulte (2006) have explicated five major assumptions of Caplan's model. Because the model is sometimes misinterpreted as being narrowly intrapsychic in nature, and these assumptions are not always explicit in Caplan's writings, they are listed here.

1. *Both intrapsychic and environmental factors are important in explaining and changing behavior.* This approach clearly focuses on intrapsychic variables that are important in behavior change to a greater extent than any other model of consultation. However, much less publicized is the fact that Caplan promoted a strong environmental focus through a major emphasis on making social institutions (such as schools) function more effectively by improving their ability to deal with the mental health problems of their clients. Astor, Pitner, and Duncan (1998) clearly illustrated the importance of environmental factors within Caplanian consultation with teachers concerning school violence prevention issues.
2. *More than technical expertise is important in designing effective interventions.* A consultee's decision to adopt an intervention technique is not based solely on its effectiveness. It is influenced by many factors, including elements of the consultee's professional role and organizational culture.
3. *Learning and generalization occur when consultees retain responsibility for action.* The direct involvement of a consultant in problem resolution will diminish the consultee's feelings of ownership over problems and solutions generated to resolve them, and thus is not recommended.
4. *Mental health consultation is a supplement to other problem-solving mechanisms within an organization.* There are several ways of addressing client difficulties within an organization and, for many types of problems, procedures other than consultation are more appropriate. For example, skill deficiencies in consultees are handled better through supervision because consultants are unlikely to understand the skills involved in professions except their own.
5. *Consultee attitudes and affect are important in consultation, but cannot be dealt with directly.* Instead of focusing on consultee affect, the Caplanian consultant develops hypotheses about the types of personal issues that are interfering with the consultee's functioning and then intervenes indirectly by using the work problem as a metaphor for the consultee's problem (Brown et al., 2006).

The Four Types of Mental Health Consultation

Caplan (1970; Caplan & Caplan, 1993/1999) distinguished among four types of consultation based on two major considerations: (1) whether the content focus of consultation is difficulty with a particular client versus an administrative difficulty, and (2) whether the central purpose of consultation is provision of information in the consultant's area of specialty versus improvement of the consultee's problem-solving capacity.

Client-centered case consultation is perhaps the most familiar type of consultation performed by mental health professionals. A consultee encounters difficulty with a client for whom he or she has responsibility and seeks a consultant who will evaluate the client, arrive at a diagnosis, and offer recommendations concerning how the consultee might modify his or her treatment of the client. Often, the assessment, diagnosis, and recommendations are summarized in a written report. The consultee then uses the information provided in the report to develop and implement a plan for dealing with the client, with minimal subsequent involvement of the consultant. The primary goal of client-centered case consultation is to develop a plan for dealing with the client's difficulties; education or skill development for the consultee is a secondary focus.

Consultee-centered case consultation is the type of consultation that is most closely associated with Gerald Caplan. Consultee-centered case consultation is concerned with difficulties a consultee faces with a particular client for whom he or she has responsibility in the work setting. The primary goal of consultee-centered case consultation is remediation of the "shortcomings in the consultee's professional functioning that are responsible for difficulties with the present case" (Caplan, 1970, p. 125). Client improvement is a secondary goal.

Program-centered administrative consultation is similar to client-centered case consultation. In both types, the consultant is regarded as a specialist who is contracted to study a problem and to provide recommendations for dealing with the problem. In client-centered case consultation, however, the consultant's assessment, diagnosis, and recommendations deal with the problems of a particular client; in program-centered administrative consultation, the consultant considers the problems surrounding the development of a new program or some aspect of organizational functioning.

Consultee-centered administrative consultation is a fourth type of consultation specified by Caplan. Its goal is to improve the professional functioning of members of an administrative staff. Although consultee-centered administrative consultation may assume different forms, it is generally based on a rather broadly conceptualized role for the consultant. For example, the consultant does not limit consultation to problems brought to his or her attention by consultees, but instead takes an active role in identifying and assessing organizational problems. The consultant may work globally to improve the overall health of the organization, perhaps by having consultees consider the development of system-wide policies that promote the mental health of staff members and their clients.

The Consultant–Consultee Relationship

In establishing relationships with consultees, the Caplanian consultant works to establish a *coordinate, nonhierarchical relationship*, in which professional issues and concerns can be discussed openly. Ideally, it should be a supportive relationship of mutual respect, in which there is no power differential between parties. Social influence is clearly important within this relationship, but Caplan stated that a consultant's influence should never be based on coercion (Erchul, 1993b).

Consultees must learn to view themselves as active participants who can educate the consultant about their professional role and its constraints, so that the consultant may be most helpful. It is also important that the consultant deal directly with confidentiality issues, specifically assuring consultees that their actions will not be discussed with others without their consent. Consultees also must understand that they retain complete freedom to accept or reject the consultant's advice (Caplan, 1970). Also, unlike mental health collaboration, wherein responsibilities for outcomes are shared between parties (Caplan, Caplan, & Erchul, 1994), consultees must understand that they alone retain full responsibility for consultation outcomes.

Sources of Consultee Difficulty

Caplan (1970; Caplan & Caplan, 1993/1999) identified four major sources of consultee difficulty: lack of knowledge, lack of skill, lack of self-confidence, and lack of objectivity. Although the first three sources mentioned are relatively straightforward, lack of objectivity is more complex in nature. This type of difficulty occurs when consultees lose their usual professional distance when working with clients and then cannot apply their skills effectively to resolve a current work problem. Lack of objectivity may also be regarded as stemming from consultees' faulty perceptions and incorrect attributions surrounding the present situation. Caplan noted that, when supervisory and administrative mechanisms are functioning well in an organization (and lack of knowledge and lack of skill can be ruled out as explanations), most instances of consultee ineffectiveness will be attributable to lack of objectivity (Erchul, 1993b).

Caplan delineated five major types of consultee lack of objectivity: direct personal involvement, simple identification, transference, characterological distortion, and theme interference. Again, somewhat more complex than the rest is the last one mentioned, theme interference. A *theme* is a representation of an unsolved problem or prior defeat that the consultee has experienced that influences his or her expectations regarding a current work difficulty. For example, suppose a teacher unconsciously harbors the theme, "Boys from single-parent homes are always behavior problems in the classroom." This theme may interfere with the teacher's ability to objectively view a new student named Tom, who lives with his mother, a divorced single parent. The teacher may conclude erroneously that Tom either is, or has great potential to become, a disruptive student. The consultant may try to restore the teacher's objectivity by indicating through indirect confrontation that not all boys who live with one parent have behavior problems (Erchul & Conoley, 1991).

Although the preceding example illustrates the method of *theme interference reduction,* consultee themes may be addressed through other verbally mediated psychodynamic techniques, including the verbal focus on the client and the parable. Still other methods are the nonverbal focus on the case and nonverbal focus on the consultation relationship. These techniques can be used alone or in combination to invalidate the interfering theme and thus improve the consultee's objectivity and problem-solving capacity with respect to the present case (Caplan, 1970).

How the Mental Health Consultant Offers Support to Consultees

Caplan regarded consultation as part of a support system (Erchul, 1993b), so it is important to see how the consultant acts as a supporter. The provision of *instrumental support* is apparent in mental health consultation when the consultant supplies information and resources the consultee needs. In instances of consultee lack of skill, the consultant is to support the consultee in understanding the issues involved in the case, and perhaps engage in limited supervision of consultee skill development. Also, guiding the consultee through the problem-solving process of consultation provides evidence of instrumental support.

It is somewhat more difficult to understand how the Caplanian consultant offers *emotional support,* as he or she is not to address consultee affect in a direct manner. Generally speaking, however, the indirect methods associated with Caplan's model provide emotional support to consultees by permitting them to experience and express intense feelings about an issue without the consultant using insight-giving psychotherapy to illuminate their inner conflicts (Caplan, 1993b). In other words, mental health consultation offers a safe, nonjudgmental arena for consultees to discuss their professional problems. Along these lines, we believe that the principal vehicle for providing emotional support in mental health consultation is the coordinate, nonhierarchical relationship. Though a challenge for most consultants to establish and maintain (Erchul, 1993c), this relationship of coordinate interdependence is essential for the success of mental health consultation. A final, specific way in which the mental health consultant provides emotional support concerns instances of a consultee's lack of confidence. Here, the consultant is to provide nonspecific ego support (i.e., basic support and encouragement) until other sources of support can be located within the host organization (Caplan, 1970).

Our presentation thus far has concentrated almost exclusively on issues concerning how the mental health consultant works with consultees, yet another strength of Caplan's model is its emphasis on understanding the organizational context, in which consultation occurs and the entry process itself. We shall consider some of these ideas near the end of this chapter.

Behavioral Psychology and Behavioral Consultation Bases

A second set of influences on the practice of school consultation comes from behavioral psychology. As we have seen, the theoretical basis of mental health consultation is psychodynamic and system-based, and draws from traditions of psychiatric practice. In contrast, a behavioral approach to consultation is based on operant and classical conditioning, observational learning/modeling, and, increasingly, behavioral ecology and cognitive-behavioral perspectives (Vernberg & Reppucci, 1986). Drawing from its laboratory research traditions, the approach is known for its emphasis on quantification, specificity, and empirical validation. At the core of behavioral approaches is the assumption that both normal and abnormal behavior is developed and maintained by the same learning principles. In this section, we present three important behavioral psychology bases of our integrated model of school consultation: D'Zurilla and Goldfried's (1971) problem-solving model, Tharp and Wetzel's (1969) application of behavior modification in natural settings, and Bergan's (1977; Bergan & Kratochwill, 1990) model of behavioral consultation.

Problem-Solving Model

Although all models of psychological consultation have problem-solving components (Zins & Erchul, 2002), behavioral consultation, more than other models, makes these components explicit to consultees. A classic exposition of problem solving involving the use of behavior modification procedures is found in D'Zurilla and Goldfried (1971). They described problem solving as a process that makes many potentially effective alternatives available to individuals, and increases the probability of selecting the most effective one. D'Zurilla and Goldfried's model assumes that people behave ineffectively because of a learning or skill deficit, and therefore overall effectiveness can be increased by teaching general problem-solving skills that can be applied across situations.

D'Zurilla and Goldfried's (1971) problem-solving model proposes five stages of effective problem solving. First, during *general orientation,* individuals develop attitudes that include: accepting the fact that problems do occur in life, recognizing these problems when they occur, and inhibiting the tendency to act impulsively or to do nothing. Second, in *problem definition and formulation,* individuals define all aspects of the problem in operational terms and identify relevant aspects of the situation. Third, during *generation of alternatives,* individuals attempt "brainstorming" and later combine various alternatives. Fourth, in *decision making,* individuals predict the outcomes likely to be achieved by each available option. Finally, during *verification,* individuals assess the effectiveness of their efforts by comparing actual outcomes to predicted outcomes.

Interestingly, when a consultant subscribes to the notion of consultation exclusively as a problem-solving process, he or she assumes that effective consultants must be process (but not necessarily content) experts. However, with few noteworthy exceptions (e.g., Schein, 1969), the view that a consultant can succeed having only process skills is not prevalent in the consultation literature. In sum, although heuristically useful, D'Zurilla and Goldfried's (1971) model fails to address critical issues a school consultant needs to know. It does not address, for example, the specifics of problem solving, the basis for selecting effective intervention alternatives, or even how one implements the model in the "real world."

Application of Behavior Modification in Natural Settings

Tharp and Wetzel (1969) presented a comprehensive method of applying principles of behavior modification in human service settings such as schools and residential treatment centers. Their method of consultation is a logical extension of the assumptions of a behavioral approach to therapy. Importantly, they formalized the role of direct care providers (such as parents and teachers) as behavior change agents in natural settings.

Tharp and Wetzel (1969) noted three key participants: (1) *consultant,* who is anyone with knowledge and expertise in behavior analysis; (2) *mediator,* who is anyone who controls reinforcers for client behavior and can administer them contingently; and (3) *target,* who is anyone with a problem. Although their triadic models developed independently, we wish to point out the similarities between Caplan's (1964, 1970) use of the terms "consultee" and "client," and Tharp and Wetzel's (1969) terms *mediator* and *target.*

Tharp and Wetzel's pioneering efforts resulted in other attempts to train staff in principles of behavior modification at various institutions (see, for example, Reppucci & Saunders, 1974). Of interest is that the training usually was conducted by university-based personnel who were not staff members and who generally left the setting after the demonstration project grant funds expired. Although these highly financed training efforts enjoyed short-term success, their positive effects often faded after the trainers departed.

Regrettably, a direct translation of behavior theory developed in the laboratory to natural settings (as Tharp and Wetzel attempted) cannot be entirely successful because of factors left unaccounted for in the theory. These missing factors include the constraints of the host organization, verbal messages consultants must deliver in order to be effective, ways of handling problems associated with modifying staff behavior, and the limited resources typically available in most schools and agencies. Fortunately, others writing about school consultation have addressed these topics, at least to some degree.

Bergan's Model of Behavioral Consultation

Further refinement of principles advanced by D'Zurilla and Goldfried (1971), Tharp and Wetzel (1969), and others resulted in John R. Bergan's (1977; Bergan & Kratochwill, 1990) model of behavioral consultation. This model combines strategies and tactics of behavior analysis with a structured problem-solving approach, uses behavioral technology to develop intervention plans, and employs the technology of behavior analysis to evaluate treatment outcomes.

Fundamental Assumptions

Bergan (1977) listed seven key features that underlie his consultation model:

1. The consultee is an active participant in the process in terms of designing the plan to solve the problem, implementing the plan, and evaluating its effectiveness.
2. The model can develop problem-solving skills in the client by having the consultant involve him or her in the same capacity as the consultee. The extent of the client's involvement is dependent upon his or her developmental level, the nature of the problem, and the consultee's views pertaining to how much responsibility the client should assume.
3. The model provides a knowledge link between the consultant and consultee. Consultants supply a medium through which knowledge producers can communicate information to knowledge consumers.
4. Behavioral consultation attempts to link decision making to empirical evidence. Decisions relating to the course of action to pursue are based on direct observations of the client's behavior and scientific findings regarding behavior change.
5. The model defines problems presented in consultation as residing outside the character of the client. In contrast, the use of a label such as "learning disabled" or "emotionally disturbed" does not facilitate understanding of the client's current behavior or specify goals that might be attained in consultation.
6. The model stresses the role of environmental factors in controlling behavior. As such, respondent, operant, and modeling procedures are used frequently in behavioral consultation. Research findings indicate that it is possible to bring about marked changes in behavior by altering environmental conditions.
7. Behavioral consultation focuses its evaluation on goal attainment and plan effectiveness rather than on the client's characteristics. This approach emphasizes what has been accomplished in consultation rather than what is wrong with the client (Bergan, 1977).

Bergan's (1977) behavioral consultation model adheres to a four-stage problem-solving process derived from D'Zurilla and Goldfried (1971), a process that maximizes the chances of generating an effective solution. The four stages of the model include three separate interviews, each of which contains specific objectives that the consultant is expected to achieve. In the sections that follow, we summarize the nature of each stage of behavioral consultation: problem identification, problem analysis, plan implementation, and problem evaluation.

Problem Identification

This first stage involves the specification of the problem to be resolved as a result of consultation. Problem identification is accomplished through a *problem identification interview* (PII) between the consultant and consultee. The PII represents a critical point within behavioral consultation because it creates expectations for the use of a behavioral perspective on the client's problems and stresses the role of current environmental events as being mainly responsible for the problem behavior. Specific objectives associated with the PII are:

1. Assess the scope of consultee concerns
2. Prioritize problem components or identify a target problem area
3. Define the target problem in overtly observable behavioral terms
4. Estimate the frequency, intensity, or duration of the problem behavior
5. Identify tentative goals for change
6. Tentatively identify environmental conditions surrounding the problem behavior as antecedents, sequences, and consequences
7. Establish data collection procedures and responsibilities
8. Schedule the next interview (Bergan, 1977; Bergan & Kratochwill, 1990; Martens, 1993a)

Problem Analysis

During the second stage of behavioral consultation, the problem is examined further and a plan is designed to solve it. The *problem analysis interview* (PAI) has six objectives:

1. Determine the adequacy of baseline (i.e., preintervention) data
2. Establish goals for change
3. Analyze environmental conditions surrounding the problem behavior as antecedents, sequences, and consequences
4. Design and implement an intervention plan
5. Reaffirm data collection procedures
6. Schedule the next interview (Bergan, 1977; Bergan & Kratochwill, 1990; Martens, 1993a)

Plan Implementation

This third stage does not involve a formal interview, but instead assumes that the consultant and consultee will meet through a series of brief contacts. During plan implementation, the consultant helps to ensure that the consultee is implementing the intervention plan as agreed and that the probability of the plan succeeding is maximized. There are three objectives associated with plan implementation:

1. Determine whether consultee has requisite skills to implement the intervention plan
2. Monitor data collection and overall plan operations
3. Determine need for plan revisions (Bergan, 1977; Bergan & Kratochwill, 1990)

Problem Evaluation

The fourth and final stage of behavior consultation is problem evaluation, which entails the determination of problem solution and plan effectiveness. Problem evaluation is accomplished through the *problem evaluation interview* (PEI), which has four objectives:

1. Determine whether intervention goals were met
2. Evaluate plan effectiveness
3. Discuss continuation, modification, or termination of the plan
4. Terminate consultation or schedule additional meetings to recycle through the problem-solving process (Bergan, 1977; Bergan & Kratochwill, 1990; Martens, 1993a)

Updates to the Original Interview Series

Although the preceding section describes the recognized steps and consultant tasks contained in behavioral consultation interviews, it is worth noting that several individuals have introduced additional stages and/or consultant tasks to Bergan's (1977) model. For example, acknowledging the importance of the working alliance between consultant and consultee to promote cooperation and decrease resistance, Kratochwill, Elliott, and Stoiber (2002) proposed an initial stage they labeled, "Establishing a Consultant–Consultee Relationship." Similarly, recognizing that few interventions developed in consultation will succeed unless implemented with integrity (Noell, 2008), Wilkinson (2006) advanced the Treatment Monitoring Interview (TMI), which occurs between the plan implementation stage and the PEI.

Verbal Behavior of the Behavioral Consultant

As Gutkin and Curtis (1982) noted, "At its most basic level, consultation is an interpersonal exchange. As such, the consultant's success is going to hinge largely on his or her communication and relationship skills" (p. 822). Given the many objectives associated with the conduct of behavioral consultation, it is especially important that behavioral consultants communicate clearly and effectively. To evaluate behavioral consultants' interviewing effectiveness, Bergan and Tombari (1975) developed the Consultation Analysis Record (CAR).

Despite its development about 35 years ago, the CAR remains the only coding system designed specifically for quantifying verbal interactions occurring during school consultation (see Martens, Erchul, & Witt, 1992, for three other systems that have been applied to study school consultation). Coding using the CAR proceeds in two steps. First, transcribed interviews are divided into independent clauses or "thought units" (the basic unit of analysis) that are then numbered consecutively. Second, each clause/thought unit is coded according to four categories:

1. *Message source* refers to whether the consultant or consultee is speaking.
2. *Message content* refers to the topic under discussion, and contains the subcategories of background environment, behavior setting, behavior, individual characteristics, observation, plan, and other.

3. *Message process* refers to the function served by the independent clause, and contains the subcategories of specification, evaluation, inference, summarization, and validation.
4. *Message control* refers to how the speaker influences the verbal behavior of the other through greater use of elicitors (clauses that request information) than emitters (clauses that present information).

Space does not allow for a detailed description of the CAR and its categories and subcategories. Therefore, we suggest consulting Bergan (1977), Bergan and Tombari (1975, 1976), or Bergan and Kratochwill (1990) for additional information.

Behavioral Consultation Research Using the CAR

Researchers have used the CAR primarily to obtain indices of consultant effectiveness that subsequently are related to indices of consultation outcome (Martens, 1993a). A sampling of important findings from classic research using the CAR includes: the best predictor of problem resolution is the consultant's skill in having the consultee define the problem in behavioral terms (Bergan & Tombari, 1975, 1976); the consultant's use of behavioral cues – as contrasted with medical model cues – leads to higher teacher–consultee expectations with respect to their ability to teach a client who has academic problems (Tombari & Bergan, 1978); and the odds are 14 times higher that a teacher-consultee will identify resources and a means to carry out an intervention plan if the consultant asks instead of tells the consultee (Bergan & Neumann, 1980). Though clearly dated, these results inform the actions of behavioral consultants even today (Martens & DiGennaro, 2008). Some additional research on behavior consultation is presented in Chap. 6.

Interpersonal Influence and Social Power Bases

To provide a summary of the interpersonal influence and social power bases of our integrated model of school consultation, we return to some major principles presented in Chap. 3. In many cases, merely supplying needed knowledge to consultees will prove inadequate relative to having them change behaviors and/or solve problems. Therefore, consultants must use their content expertise along with strategic communication and dyadic social influence to establish a cooperative relationship that ultimately will facilitate positive outcomes in consultation. Operationalizing this approach requires an understanding of social influence.

Raven's (1992, 1993) power-interaction model of interpersonal influence provides a clear foundation for this approach. In applying this model, the consultant must carefully examine his or her available power bases and determine the advisability of their use in a specific instance. Although at one time only expert and referent power were believed to be relevant to the work of the school-based consultant (Martin, 1978), more recently it has been shown that school psychologists and teachers view positive expert, positive referent, and direct informational power bases specifically, and *soft* bases generally, as effective in influencing teachers in consultation (Erchul, Raven, & Ray, 2001; Erchul, Raven, & Whichard, 2001). Moreover, school consultants are most likely to *use* influence strategies that draw on the soft bases of direct informational, positive expert, legitimate dependence, and positive referent power (Wilson, Erchul, & Raven, 2008). Other means of influence may be exercised, such as invoking or reducing the power of third parties, selecting an effective mode of influence, or using preparatory devices to set the stage for social influence. When applying principles of interpersonal influence, the consultant must maintain an ethical focus, which is achieved in part by making consultees more powerful and influential.

Summary of the Bases of an Integrated Model of School Consultation

This chapter has presented many bases that underlie the integrated model of school consultation. In summary, these foundational areas are population-oriented prevention, crisis, social support, Caplan's mental health consultation model, problem solving, behavior modification in applied settings, Bergan's behavioral consultation model, interpersonal influence, and social power bases. As a prelude to Chap. 6, we proceed by explaining what the consultant must typically do to enter the school and/or classroom in order to conduct consultation.

Achieving Entry in School Consultation: Entering the Service Delivery Network

The reader may recall from Chap. 1 that we believe the integrated model of school consultation is not only highly appropriate for, but also in fact intended for, the internal consultant. Given this emphasis, one might question the need for a presentation of entry issues because the internal consultant is "already part of the system." We would disagree, as negotiating one's role within an organization is an important task for any consultant.

Entry into an organization may be considered a four-step process (Gallessich, 1982). First, an organization's needs are explored and the match between these needs and the consultant's skills are assessed. Second, assuming a good match, the consultant and the host institution proceed to negotiate a contract. As the third step, the consultant makes *physical entry* into the organization. Finally, the consultant interacts directly with consultees and eventually achieves *psychological entry*, signifying that consultees trust and have confidence in the consultant. Others (Brown et al., 2006) have referred to physical entry as *formal entry* and psychological entry as *informal acceptance*. Although the external consultant must pass through all four of Gallessich's entry steps, the internal consultant generally can bypass several of these steps.

The reader also may recall from Chap. 1 that the integrated model of school consultation is not an organization development model. Notwithstanding, it is necessary that the consultant understand the school as an organization along the lines presented in Chap. 4. Following a brief presentation of selected aspects of assessing a school's functioning, we consider critical issues of contracting and entry within school consultation.

Assessing the School as an Organization: Some General Considerations

Getting to "Know the Territory"

In beginning his work as a school consultant in the early 1960s, renowned community psychologist Ira Iscoe was instructed by one of Gerald Caplan's staff members, Charlotte Owens, to "know the territory" (Iscoe, 1993, p. 92). By this she meant that Iscoe should take the time to study what goes on each day in the school and attempt to understand its organizational atmosphere, as well as to explore the neighborhood in which the school is located. Such study will lead to the uncovering of regular patterns and insights as well as the generation of hypotheses that ultimately will facilitate the consultant's work.

In our experience as school consultants, we have gained an understanding of "the territory" by obtaining answers to questions such as these:

1. What leadership style (e.g., authoritarian, authoritative, democratic, laissez-faire) does the principal exhibit? What are the effects of this style on school staff?
2. Who exerts social influence in the school? How is it displayed? Besides the influence that stems from status or position (e.g., formal legitimate power), who exerts influence that draws on less formal power bases (e.g., soft power bases)?
3. Who functions as a "gatekeeper," controlling access to school staff and resources?
4. Where is the school located? What are salient characteristics of the immediate neighborhood?
5. What is the makeup of the students attending the school with respect to socio-economic status, racial–ethnic composition, percentage of regular education versus special education enrollment, etc.?
6. What is the school's physical layout? How do aspects of the physical structure affect the staff's efficiency and morale as well as students' academic achievement and emotional adjustment?
7. How is the typical school day structured? When do periods begin and end? Do teachers have planning periods during which consultation might occur?
8. What are the school's culture and norms? Are these unusual or different from those of other schools? Do all staff participate in the school's culture and norms? How are those who "deviate" treated by others?

9. What is the school's organizational climate? Are staff members generally satisfied or is there evidence of widespread professional burnout? Are staff members' conversations warm, forced, task-oriented, etc.?
10. What are the school's hidden agendas, if any? Is it possible that you will be set up as a scapegoat and blamed for others' errors?
11. Are there any taboo or embarrassing topics that you should avoid discussing?
12. What is the history of the school, particularly with respect to its prior use of consultants? Have previous consultants been welcomed and successful in their work?
13. Does the principal understand and completely support your professional mission?
14. What changes does the school anticipate making, and how are they likely to affect your work as a consultant?

In all cases, the descriptive information contained in answers to these questions must be carefully analyzed with respect to the implications for the school, administration, staff, students, and, most importantly, your role as consultant.

The careful assessment of any organization can be a lengthy and complex endeavor, and a school presents no exception. With particular relevance to the external consultant, some writers (Marks, 1995; Meyers, Proctor, Graybill, & Meyers, 2009) have comprehensively discussed critical issues regarding the organizational assessment of schools and achieving entry into them. Also, several classic references from the organizational psychology literature include Bennis (1969), Blake and Mouton (1976), French and Bell (1978), and Levinson (1972). The interested reader may wish to refer to these sources for further information.

Assessing a School's Readiness for Change

How does one determine whether a school is prepared and receptive to take on a planned change effort, such as an innovative service delivered via consultation? Although numerous approaches have been advanced in the literature (e.g., Curtis, Castillo, & Cohen, 2008; Ervin & Schaughency, 2008), one noted framework is the A VICTORY model (Bennett, 1984; Davis & Salasin, 1975; Maher & Bennett, 1984).

A VICTORY is an acronym representing *A*bility, *V*alues, *I*dea, *C*ircumstances, *T*iming, *O*bligation, *R*esistance, and *Y*ield. The consultant can systematically assess the organizational context of the school by asking key questions related to each A VICTORY factor. The example below concerns the introduction of an RTI/multitiered intervention program (see Chap. 2), an effort that brings together teachers, students, parents, and school support staff to plan, implement, and evaluate academic and behavioral interventions for students. As a matter of systems change, launching RTI involves a significant reallocation of existing resources (Reschly & Bergstrom, 2009).

Are adequate human, technological, informational, physical, and financial resources available to the school to support this multitiered intervention program (Ability)? Are the values behind the program (i.e., RTI) consonant with those of the school community (Value)? Does the school community accurately perceive the purposes, goals, and activities associated with this new approach to school-based educational and psychological service delivery (Idea)? What is the nature of factors pressing for or detracting from the integration of this program with other elements already in place in the school (Circumstances)? Does the introduction of multitiered interventions synchronize with other important events occurring in the school (Timing)? What is the perceived need on the part of the school community for adopting an RTI-based approach (Obligation)? Does anyone demonstrate any overt or covert resistance to implementing RTI (Resistance)? What rewards and benefits are expected by the school community as a result of instituting this program (Yield)?

A VICTORY is useful for the consultant in helping a school assess its readiness for implementing contemplated changes. It should be noted, however, that assessment using A VICTORY can lead to the conclusion that bringing about changes through a consultative effort would be ill-advised at the present time. This situation may force a consultant to abandon the effort altogether (cf. Conoley & Conoley, 1992, Chap. 4).

Negotiating the Contract

Contracting is a critical skill within consultation, and it involves a more formal process for the external consultant. Assuming that the external consultant and the school agree that there is a good fit between the consultant's qualifications and the school's needs, a contract is prepared. A contract is usually a written agreement between the consultant and the host institution that specifies the relevant parameters and nature of the consultation (Caplan, 1970). Although agreements of this sort can be verbal, the use of a written agreement is recommended to avoid possible later misunderstandings. If the agreement initially is only verbal, it is advisable that the consultant follow up with a letter that explicitly states what has been agreed to by both parties (Kirby, 1985).

Although the length and coverage of contracts will vary, all consultation contracts or letters of agreement should use precise language and cover the following issues:

1. General goals of consultation
2. Tentative time frame
3. Consultant's responsibilities, including services to be provided, methods to be used, time to be committed to the organization, and evaluation of the degree to which goals are achieved
4. Organization's responsibilities, including nature and extent of staff contributions to consultation, and fees to be paid to consultant
5. Consultant's boundaries, including: the contact person to whom the consultant is to be responsible; people to whom the consultant is to have (or not have) access; consultant's access to departments, meetings, and documents; conditions for bringing in other consultants or trainees; confidentiality rules regarding all information
6. Arrangements for periodic review and evaluation of the consultant's work, and explication of either party to terminate the contract if consultation progress is unsatisfactory (Gallessich, 1982, pp. 272–273)

Achieving School-Level (Physical) Entry

After the terms of the contract have been agreed upon, the external consultant has official sanction to enter the school and to begin exploring issues of concern. The internal consultant, of course, is already physically housed at the school but must attend to many of the same entry issues described below.

In the early phase of physical entry, the consultant's assessment of the school may continue along the lines of refining initial answers to the 14 "know the territory" questions posed earlier as well as A VICTORY. Although it is important for the consultant to proceed in this task-oriented manner, it is equally important for the consultant to develop his or her relationship with the consultee institution and with individual consultees (Caplan, 1970).

Building Relationships with the Host School

Central to the consultant's success in establishing relationships with a host organization is building channels of communication. Caplan (1970) advocated "finding key members of the communication network who have easy access to significant groups of line workers and also to the authority system, and then building relationships of trust and respect with them so that they will act as communication bridges between the consultant and the staff of the institution" (p. 51). As consultants, we often have involved school counselors and special education lead teachers in this capacity.

There are several predictable obstacles to developing effective communication during entry, particularly for the external consultant (Caplan, 1970). First, the consultant can expect ambivalent feelings from school staff who, on one hand, may welcome the consultant's expertise and assistance but who, on the other hand, may feel threatened by the consultant's impending attempts to "change the system." Second, mental health professionals who work as consultants are likely to conjure up anxiety-provoking fantasies in consultees, who believe the consultant will psychoanalyze or otherwise judge them. For both obstacles, Caplan (1970) has instructed consultants to dissipate these inaccurate, stereotypical thoughts principally by interacting with as many people in the setting as possible, and especially with those individuals who are influential in molding the opinions of others. Suspicion of the consultant subsides when all can see that he or she is a person worthy of trust and respect (Caplan, 1970).

Addressing Confidentiality Issues

During formal entry, the consultant's commitment to confidentiality concerns should be made explicit to the head administrator, generally the principal. This administrator needs to understand the limits of what he or she will learn from the consultant about specific staff members. The consultant can share general impressions, organizational issues, or specific problems that seem to be common among the staff. Most administrators accept the limits of what the consultant can report. Perhaps most importantly, the school consultant must tell the principal that he or she is not a "spy" who is there for the benefit of the administration (Conoley & Conoley, 1982; Sarason, Levine, Goldenberg, Cherlin, & Bennett, 1966).

Obtaining the Sanction of the Principal and Other Administrators

It is critical that the school consultant acquire the support of the building principal, keep him or her informed of ongoing activities, and solicit feedback about the nature of services being rendered (Caplan, 1964). Stated alternately, "effective and sustained innovations require sanction and access from the top administrator of the host organization" (Kelly, 1993, p. 77). Within schools, other layers of the bureaucracy to keep informed include vice principal(s) and other educational supervisors (Caplan, 1970). Although this point may be self-evident to seasoned consultants who operate in the private sector, failure to obtain proper sanction has led to the downfall of many change efforts in public education (cf. Sarason, 1982, 1996).

Achieving Classroom-Level (Psychological) Entry

After accomplishing physical entry, the consultant then meets with teachers and other staff members with whom he or she will work directly. Although the consultant may be introduced to the school initially in a large group context, such as a school faculty meeting, eventually he or she will meet face-to-face with individual consultees. When meeting consultees, the consultant needs to display interpersonal skills expected in many other helping relationships (e.g., active listening, rapport building).

Additionally, the consultant must address aspects of *role structuring* during this stage of consultation.

Role structuring has four major components (Brown et al., 2006). First, the consultant must discuss and/or negotiate the roles that each party will assume. This action models open communication and helps to avoid later misunderstandings. For example, a consultee initially may believe that it is the consultant's job to solve the problem alone, when the consultant thinks that the two will be working together to jointly solve the problem. To avoid misunderstanding, the consultant should indicate to the consultee the general nature of the consulting relationship. This often takes the form of explaining how he or she "usually works" with consultees. For instance, if describing Caplan's (1970) coordinate, nonhierarchical relationship, one could use the terms "egalitarian" or "cooperative partnership," or say, "we will work together." Although the specific elements of roles may be negotiated, the point here is that both parties must understand and agree on the basic parameters of the relationship early on (Zins & Erchul, 2002).

Second, the consultant is to establish an agreement for action. Again, a common consultee misperception is that the consultant will do all the work, including implement the intervention. Assuming that it is consultation rather than mental health collaboration (Caplan et al., 1994) that will take place, however, it is generally the consultee who will be implementing the intervention. It is extremely important that the consultant convey this point clearly. Third, the consultant is to emphasize the short-term nature of consultation, and prepare the consultee for eventual termination of the process (Brown et al., 2006).

Finally, the consultant is to address confidentiality and its limits (Brown et al., 2006). The consultee must be assured that his or her interactions with the consultant will be completely confidential or be warned of the limits of confidentiality. Assuming the consultant has previously negotiated this point with the principal, he or she might say to a consultee, "I will regard everything you say as strictly confidential, unless what you say concerns a law that has been, or will be, broken." In school consultation, perhaps the most likely reason for breaking confidence is suspected or documented child abuse or neglect.

To avoid a breach of confidentiality, the consultant should not report even the consultee's *successes* without permission. However, it is generally safe to comment on shared, public knowledge about a consultee. If a breach of confidence is made unknowingly, it is recommended that the consultant go immediately to the injured party and apologize. It is important to act nondefensively in this situation, should it arise (Conoley & Conoley, 1982).

Beyond the separate components listed above, accomplishing entry in consultation ultimately means having established a safe and comfortable atmosphere in which consultees are free to openly discuss key issues of professional concern. The establishment of this atmosphere is critical to the consultant's success in achieving the problem-solving, social influence, and support and development tasks of consultation. We examine these tasks and the integrated model of school consultation in Chap. 6.

Chapter 6
Model Description and Application

In Chap. 5, we traced the evolution of two prominent consultation models, mental health consultation and behavioral consultation, and discussed the assumptions and principles underlying each. An approach to strategic communication based on Raven's social power and interpersonal influence models (Erchul & Raven, 1997) was reviewed briefly, followed by a discussion of issues (e.g., the 14 "know the territory" questions, the A VICTORY model) that should be addressed in order to gain successful entry into the service delivery network of schools. In this chapter, we discuss research findings that point to the limitations inherent in relying on any one consultation model as a means of delivering comprehensive services in the schools. Based on these limitations, we present an integrated model of school consultation that we believe is particularly appropriate for use by internal consultants (e.g., school psychologists) and that combines the elements of social influence and professional support within a problem-solving context. Each of these elements (problem solving, social influence, professional support) is discussed as a component task of the school consultation process, which begins after the consultant has a basic understanding of schools and classrooms and has successfully entered the service delivery network. The chapter concludes by considering the outcomes of successful school consultation in terms of improving the learning and adjustment of children as clients and improving the professional functioning of teachers as consultees.

A Critical Appraisal of Consultation Models

Mental Health Consultation

The concepts and methods of mental health consultation began with Gerald Caplan's efforts during the late 1940s to provide psychological services to large numbers of immigrant children in Israel. Caplan believed that if direct care staff were able to deal more effectively with children's adjustment problems on a daily basis, then more severe disorders could be prevented resulting in fewer institutional placements

(Caplan, 1993b). As noted in Chap. 5, this preventive focus became the hallmark of Caplan's mental health consultation model and was instrumental in the widespread establishment of community mental health centers in the United States.

As a prevention model, mental health consultation is based on the assumption that periods of psychological upset or crisis force individuals to mobilize the resources available to them and therefore represent opportunities for personal and professional growth. Support (either emotional or instrumental) provided by community professionals during these times can serve a preventive function by lessening the impact of the crisis and helping the individual resolve their problem. Consistent with this view, Caplan's early efforts were aimed at helping direct care providers (e.g., visiting nurses, clergy, welfare workers) to address the psychological problems of their clients that emerged during their regular professional duties. Because many of these early consultees were highly trained and well supervised, Caplan found that their need for consultative assistance often resulted from lack of objectivity rather than lack of knowledge or skill (Caplan, 1993b). Given this fact and being true to his psychodynamic training, Caplan's model of mental health consultation emphasized consultees' perceptions, attributions, and beliefs as barriers to effective functioning.

Although mental health consultation has played a major role in community psychology and psychiatry (Erchul, 1993a; Mannino & Shore, 1971), its contributions to research and practice in school consultation have been more limited. Several reasons likely exist for the lack of emphasis on mental health consultation in the schools. First, as we noted in Chap. 1, the community mental health movement in general and consultation in particular emerged during a time of discontent with traditional approaches to psychotherapy (Hersch, 1968). Included in these criticisms were the disease model of abnormal behavior, the inefficiency of long-term psychotherapy, the unreliability of clinical diagnosis, and the lack of specificity with respect to therapeutic goals, processes, and outcomes (Albee, 1968; Eysenck, 1952; Hobbs, 1964; Szasz, 1960). Because the support strategies of mental health consultation are rooted in a psychodynamic model, in many ways these are inconsistent with the historical antecedents of consultation as a service delivery approach. Second, the processes and outcomes of mental health consultation have not been well operationalized and therefore may be difficult to teach and implement with integrity (Costenbader et al., 1992). Perhaps related to this issue, mental health consultation enjoys only limited empirical support (Gresham & Kendell, 1987; Gutkin & Curtis, 1990; Medway, 1979). Third, Caplan himself has suggested that in many cases, consultee ineffectiveness is likely to result from lack of knowledge or skill rather than lack of objectivity (Erchul, 1993b), and there is some research to support this observation when consulting with teachers (Gutkin, 1981). Rather than emphasizing psychodynamic techniques such as theme interference reduction, this finding would suggest the importance of enhancing consultee skills through strategies such as modeling, coaching, and performance feedback (e.g., Noell, Witt, Gilbertson, Ranier, & Freeland, 1997).

In summary, Caplan's model of mental health consultation has not been used widely in schools because of its psychodynamic approach, lack of specificity, and limited empirical support. As a precursor to all other consultation approaches, however, we believe that mental health consultation holds strong conceptual relevance for school consultants by virtue of (1) the model's preventive focus in which periods of crisis are viewed as opportunities for personal and professional growth when individuals are given the appropriate supports; (2) emphasis on consultee perceptions, attributions, and beliefs when developing intervention plans; and (3) the position that social institutions can serve a preventive function by dealing more successfully with client problems on a day-to-day basis. With respect to the first point, we find it useful to view consultees as individuals who are undergoing crises at the time they seek consultative assistance. The crisis model helps to explain why consultees are likely to seek out others for assistance, be more open to influence, and be more willing to try new behaviors. It also offers a reason to believe that short-term interventions that are developed within a consultative relationship can have significant and long-lasting effects (Caplan, 1964). The essence of the crisis model for school consultation then is that, during times of stress, consultees are receptive to high levels of support and influence to help them overcome presenting problems.

Behavioral Consultation

As discussed in Chap. 5, the historical roots of behavioral consultation include the problem-solving approach of D'Zurilla and Goldfried (1971) as well as efforts in the 1960s and early 1970s to apply behavioral treatment principles in human service settings (e.g., Reppucci & Saunders, 1974). A key feature of these early efforts was the involvement of direct care providers as principal change agents in the intervention process. As early as 1969, Tharp and Wetzel described a consultative model for implementing contingency management techniques that required at least three individuals: (1) the behavioral consultant or anyone with knowledge of behavior analysis and intervention; (2) the target client or anyone who exhibited problem behavior; and (3) the mediator or anyone who was in direct contact with the client and was therefore in a position to control reinforcers. During the 1970s, researchers attempted to formalize the behavioral consultation approach by describing a four-stage problem-solving process to be enacted over the course of three interviews, specifying the goals and objectives to be accomplished at each stage, and developing a coding scheme to assess the effectiveness of consultants' interviewing tactics (Bergan, 1977; Bergan & Tombari, 1975).

The behavioral approach continues to enjoy widespread popularity today among school consultation researchers and practitioners. For example, more consultation outcome studies published between 1985 and 1995 were concerned with behavioral consultation than any other model (Sheridan, Welch, & Orme, 1996). This model is the most frequently addressed in preservice training programs for school psychologists, and is reported to be the most widely used by practitioners in the schools (Costenbader et al., 1992). Behavioral consultation has also been adopted as a basis for prereferral intervention programs or collaborative efforts between referring teachers and school-based consulting teams to provide behavioral and instructional supports to students before considering their eligibility for special education (Fuchs, Fuchs, & Bahr, 1990; Graden, Casey, & Christenson, 1985; McDougal, Clonan, & Martens, 2000; Sheridan & Kratochwill, 1992).

Although a variety of historical factors have pointed toward a behavioral-ecological approach to school consultation, we believe that two features of the behavioral consultation model itself have contributed to its popularity. First, the goals and strategies of behavioral consultation have been clearly specified, leading to standard interviewing protocols, competency-based training programs, and measures of consultant effectiveness (D. Fuchs & L.S. Fuchs, 1989; Kratochwill, VanSomeren, & Sheridan, 1989; McDougall, Reschly, & Corkery, 1988). Second, the problem-solving objectives of behavioral consultation are based on the principles of applied behavior analysis (e.g., defining target behaviors, specifying performance goals, conducting functional assessments, specifying treatment procedures, evaluating outcomes). As will be discussed in Chap. 8, behavior analytic approaches to instruction and management are effective, empirically validated, and uniquely suited for use by school personnel.

To summarize then, the principal features of behavioral consultation as a service delivery model include: (1) its reliance on a systematic problem-solving process with clearly specified interviewing objectives and tactics; and (2) its use of a behavior analytic approach to intervention, the effectiveness of which has been supported by empirical research. Because it emphasizes problem solving and maintains a strong client-centered focus, behavioral consultation has been viewed as an effective professional practice in the schools (Mannino & Shore, 1975; Medway, 1979; Sheridan et al., 1996). It may seem somewhat paradoxical, therefore, that prior to the 1997 and 2004 amendments to IDEA, behavioral consultation services were frequently underutilized by teachers. For example, Martens, Peterson, Witt, and Cirone (1986) found that consultation with a specialist was rated by teachers as being among the least effective and most difficult to use methods of responding to children's learning and adjustment problems. Consistent with these perceptions, Ysseldyke, Pianta, Christenson, Wang, and Algozzine (1983) reported that when generating ideas for ways to accommodate children with special needs, teachers ranked consultation with the school psychologist fifth behind speaking with the principal. When consultation did occur, only half of the intervention plans that consultees agreed to implement were actually completed (Happe, 1982).

Now that behavioral consultation is the vehicle through which many mandated services are provided in schools (e.g., positive behavioral supports, response-to-intervention eligibility determination), teacher involvement in the consultation process has become more commonplace. School consultants, however, face different kinds of challenges, namely that of using the consultation process to help support personnel design effective, evidence-based intervention plans and to help teachers implement these plans with integrity over time. In the past, intervention choices were often driven by considerations such as teacher skill, familiarity with the procedure, acceptability, or perceived ease of use rather than effectiveness. Given the amendments included in IDEA 1997 and IDEIA 2004 as well as passage of NCLB, consulting teams are expected to rely primarily, if not solely, on evidence-based interventions and procedures for selecting these interventions (Martens & DiGennaro, 2008). Similarly, numerous studies have suggested that even after teachers are trained in the specifics of plan implementation, plan use drops to near zero levels almost immediately in the absence of additional support (DiGennaro, Martens, & Kleinmann, 2007; Noell et al., 1997).

We believe that many behavior analytic strategies that are central to effective school-based intervention may be underutilized by school personnel for primarily three reasons. First, more recent advances in behavioral assessment techniques that can be used to inform treatment selection did not exist when behavioral consultation was first developed (e.g., functional analysis and assessment; Hanley, Iwata, & McCord, 2003; Sterling-Turner, Robinson, & Wilczynski, 2001). As a result, school consultants may not be skilled in the use of these strategies.

Second, teachers are not typically trained in behavior analytic principles, strategies, or instructional programs. In a survey conducted by Begeny and Martens (2006), 110 preservice teachers were asked to report on the amount of coursework and applied training they had received in empirically supported, behavioral instruction practices. Regardless of their preparation program (elementary, secondary, or special education), most teachers in the sample reported little or no training in 22 of the 26 items (e.g., curriculum-based measurement, prompting, generalization, error correction, peer tutoring). As noted before, in order to design and implement school-based interventions, the teacher and consultant must first engage in a series of face-to-face meetings or interviews (Gutkin & Curtis, 1982; Witt, 1990). Interventions that are suggested during these interviews typically require some change in teacher behavior as a means of accommodating the student. These changes may require teachers to learn new performance monitoring skills (e.g., momentary time sampling, curriculum-based assessment), alter their instructional or managerial practices (e.g., provide student feedback through public posting), or make use of existing resources in different ways (e.g., assign high-achieving students as peer tutors). Without prior exposure or training in these strategies, teachers may not understand their importance, agree with their use, or be willing to put forth the effort to implement them over time.

Third, the behavioral consultation model implicitly adopts what is known as an empirical–rational approach for promoting changes in consultee behavior. As noted in Chap. 4, an *empirical–rational approach* is based on the assumption that if data are presented showing evidence-based practices to be superior, then teachers as rational consumers will adopt these practices because it is in their best interest to do so (Chin & Benne, 1969; Owens, 1981). It is assumed (albeit incorrectly) that no other efforts to promote intervention use by teachers are needed. Although information about a plan's effectiveness can influence teacher perceptions (Von Brock & Elliott, 1987), the relationship between treatment acceptability, use, and outcome is more complicated (Martens & McIntyre, 2009). In general, research has shown that: (a) initial *commitment* to a plan has little to do with *adherence* to a plan, (b) perceived acceptability is a weak predictor of implementation integrity, but (c) implementation integrity is a strong predictor of treatment outcome (DiGennaro et al., 2007; Gresham, Gansle, Noell, & Cohen, 1993; Happe, 1982; Sterling-Turner & Watson, 2002). Equally as important, recent research has demonstrated effective strategies for promoting the integrity with which teachers implement agreed-upon plans, and we draw on this research to inform our integrated model.

The Consultative Relationship

A widely held assumption in the conceptual literature is that consultation involves a collaborative, nonhierarchical relationship between coequal professionals (Conoley & Conoley, 1992; Gutkin & Curtis, 1990). Within this collaborative relationship, the consultant and consultee are perceived as having coordinate status and as contributing equally to the problem-solving process. In the absence of empirical support, however, this perspective has been termed by some as the collaborative *myth* of consultation (Witt, 1990). Indeed, several investigations involving relational control (discussed in Chap. 3) have suggested that consultation may be more accurately described as a cooperative relationship, in which the consultant leads and the consultee follows. *Relational control* refers to the manner in which influence is exerted by one person and accepted, rejected, or evaded by another person during a verbal exchange (Erchul, 1987). In an initial study examining the relational control aspects of school-based behavioral consultation, Erchul coded the verbal statements of eight consultant–consultee dyads during problem identification, analysis, and evaluation interviews. Results indicated that consultants made significantly more bids for control during all three interviews, that consultants who had high dominance scores were judged as more effective by consultees, and that consultees who had high domineeringness scores were judged by consultants as less likely to collect baseline data.

In a follow-up study, Erchul and Chewning (1990) used the relational coding scheme developed by Folger and Puck (1976) to analyze consultant–consultee interactions in 30 sets of interviews. Within the Folger and Puck scheme, requests are coded as dominant or submissive and affiliative or hostile, whereas responses to these requests are coded as accepted, rejected, or evaded. Results of this study indicated that the number of requests made by consultants far outnumbered that of consultees (more than six to one), and that the majority (94%) of consultee responses involved acceptance of these bids. It was also found that the number of consultant requests decreased during the final problem evaluation interview (PEI), whereas requests coded as instructions or orders occurred most frequently during the intermediate problem analysis interview (PAI). On the basis of these latter findings, the authors concluded that consultees became more equal in status with the consultant by the time the PEI occurred, but that "a mixture of persuasion and negotiation" (p. 15) was used by the consultant during problem analysis to ensure plan implementation. More recent behavioral consultation research has found consultant influence to be particularly important to intervention selection during the PAI (Erchul et al., 2009).

An Integrated Model of School Consultation

We believe that the client-centered, problem-solving focus of behavioral consultation makes this approach particularly well suited for addressing school-based learning and adjustment problems. Because consultation is an *indirect service model,* however, behavioral consultants typically have limited contact with children and must rely on teachers to carry out recommended intervention plans. This means that achieving the service delivery goals of behavioral consultation (i.e., accommodating special needs students in regular education classrooms) depends in large measure on the consultant or consulting team's ability to influence the consultee (Erchul & Martens, 2002; Gutkin & Conoley, 1990). Mental health consultation, with its consultee-centered, preventive focus, is based on the premise that efforts to support and influence consultees during times of stress can lessen the severity of the crisis while expanding the person's resources for dealing with similar problems in the future. Research has suggested that consultees indeed look to consultants to control the relationship, and are likely to follow the consultant's lead during consultative interviews (Erchul, Covington, Hughes, & Meyers, 1995; Erchul et al., 2009; Martens, Erchul, & Witt, 1992). However, because the influence strategies of mental health consultation are psychodynamic in origin, there is little documented empirical support for their effectiveness. As discussed in Chap. 3, influence strategies have received considerable attention in social psychological research, and many of these seem applicable to school consultation.

By drawing on the strengths of both the behavioral and mental health consultation models, taking into account the findings from relational communication research (Erchul, 1987; Erchul & Chewning, 1990), incorporating the principles of social power and influence from the social psychological literature (Chap. 3), and recognizing the importance of implementation support, we have developed an integrated model of school consultation depicted in Fig. 6.1. In our model, school consultation is defined as a process for providing psychological and educational services, in which a specialist (consultant) works cooperatively with a caregiver (consultee) to improve the learning and adjustment of a student (client) or group of students. During face-to-face interactions, the consultant helps the consultee through the mechanisms of systematic problem solving, social influence, and professional support. In turn, the consultee helps the client through selecting and implementing effective school-based interventions. In all cases, school consultation serves a remedial function and has the potential to serve a preventive function (Erchul & Martens, 2002).

As shown in the middle portion of Fig. 6.1, the school consultation process is seen as involving three interrelated tasks; problem solving, social influence, and support and development. These tasks are considered to be interrelated because the problem-solving objectives of school consultation can only be accomplished through a social influence process between the consultant and consultee, the goals of which are to assist the consultee in expanding his or her repertoire of professional skills. For example, a school consultant might suggest a cover-copy-compare intervention with progress charting (Skinner, McLaughlin, & Logan, 1997) as a means of improving a student's performance in spelling (a problem-solving issue). In the absence of prior experience with these procedures, however, a teacher may be resistant to trying them in his or her classroom. In response to the teacher's resistance, the consultant might offer to assume the responsibility for training the student and charting progress initially while the teacher observes in order to: (1) encourage the teacher to take over implementation via the principle of reciprocity (a social influence issue) and

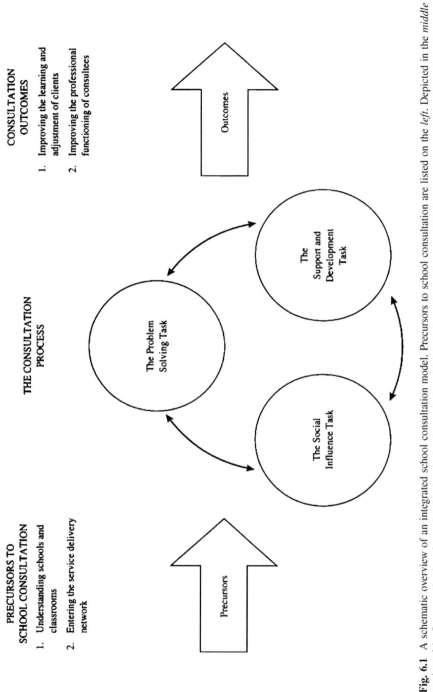

Fig. 6.1 A schematic overview of an integrated school consultation model. Precursors to school consultation are listed on the *left*. Depicted in the *middle* portion of the figure are the three interrelated tasks of school consultation which include problem solving, social influence, and consultee support and development. Outcomes of the school consultation process are listed on the *right*

Table 6.1 Core Characteristics of School Consultation

Triadic alignment between the consultant, consultee, and client
Consultant–consultee relationship characterized by cooperation and teamwork
Voluntary participation by the consultee
Right of the consultee to reject consultant suggestions
Active involvement of the consultee in problem solving and plan implementation
Confidentiality of information shared during the consultative interviews
Focus on professional, work-related issues
Pursuit of problem solving, social influence, and professional development goals
Emphasis on behavior analytic approaches to instruction and management
Systematic evaluation of incntervention outcomes

Note. Adapted from Erchul (1993c), Gutkin and Curtis (1990), and Martens (1993a)

(2) train the teacher and provide performance feedback concerning the specifics of implementation (a support and development issue). In another case, a school consultant might use informational power to convince a teacher of the merits of using listening passage preview (e.g., Chard, Vaughn, & Tyler, 2002) prior to small-group reading instruction (a social influence issue). Due to time constraints, however, the teacher may be reluctant to provide such help. If individual assistance could be provided by a part-time peer tutor (a support and development issue), the teacher might be more willing to implement the agreed upon program (a problem solving issue).

In addition to being interrelated, the three tasks of school consultation must be accomplished within a professional, consultative relationship that can be described by a set of *core characteristics*. These core characteristics derive from the historical antecedents of consultation as a service delivery model, and delineate the boundaries of the consultative relationship. For example, school consultation is intended to be voluntary and work related in focus (Conoley & Conoley, 1992; Gutkin & Curtis, 1982). This means that professional activities that are not voluntary or work related would fall outside the definition of school consultation (e.g., earning continuing education credits to meet employment requirements, seeking counseling for personal adjustment problems). The core characteristics of school consultation are presented in Table 6.1, and components of the integrated model are discussed in turn below.

Precursors to School Consultation

Consultation is only one of a variety of tiered, alternative services available to teachers in the school setting. Because of this, we believe that school consultants must have an understanding of schools as organizations and teachers as professionals within that organization before attempting to offer consultation services. Toward this goal, the sequentially coupled and intensive technological aspects of schooling as well as the traditional refer-test-place model of special education were discussed at length in Chap. 4. Chapter 5 discussed several approaches for achieving successful entry into the service delivery network, and the characteristics of teachers as professionals are addressed in Chap. 9.

Perhaps, equally important to successful school consultation is being aware of the expectations that teachers bring to the consultative relationship and the problem-solving activities they engage in before seeking assistance from others. The crisis model of mental health consultation suggests that teachers enter into a consultative relationship after attempts to resolve a problem on their own have failed (Caplan, 1963). We believe that the scope and persistence of these problem-solving activities are related to the skills that teachers bring to the consultative relationship, their experiences with consulting teams in the past, and characteristics of schools in which teachers work. For example, consider a teacher who seeks help from her school's prereferral intervention team for a child with problem behavior. In a tiered service-delivery model, her school may recommend that the child participate in a small-group "tootling" program, in which brief, anecdotal reports of positive peer behavior (i.e., tootles) are reinforced at the end of the day by the school psychologist (a Tier 2 intervention; Cihak, Kirk, & Boon, 2009). Moreover, aides assigned to the intervention team may be responsible for conducting observational probes in order to monitor improvements in the child's behavior. Although the intervention may prove effective, ultimately the teacher may not be required to change the way she interacts with the student. As a result, the teacher may be less willing in the future to implement a more intensive and individualized Tier 3 program if asked to do so by the intervention team.

Before seeking consultative assistance, teachers often attempt a number of interventions on their own reflecting their instructional and managerial skills, attributions for classroom behavior problems, and role perceptions as a teacher. Ysseldyke et al. (1983) asked 105 teachers from nine states to describe the interventions attempted and individuals consulted when devising strategies for classroom problems. Results indicated that teachers most often responded to classroom problems by altering their teaching methods (e.g., using small group instruction) or using contingency management procedures (e.g., manipulating reinforcers). Interestingly, most of the interventions reported were implemented for unspecified periods of time, and the effects of these procedures were rarely evaluated. Only 13% of the interventions resulted from conferences with other building professionals, suggesting that teachers viewed themselves as assuming primary responsibility for the development of intervention strategies.

In terms of attributions, research has shown that teachers tend to perceive factors within the child or the child's home as the primary causes of classroom behavior problems (e.g., Martens, Kelly, & Diskin, 1996). McKee and Witt (1990) have suggested that within-student problem attributions may present barriers to school consultation that is typically aimed at changing some aspect of the instructional environment. Teachers who attribute classroom problems to low student ability may not see the value in significantly altering their own instructional or managerial practices as a means of accommodating a range of student skill levels. Providing feedback about teachers' instructional practices during consultation has been shown to focus attention on these variables, alter teacher attributions, and affect the types of school-based interventions that are selected (Aldrich & Martens, 1993).

The Problem-Solving Task

All psychoeducational services can be viewed as solutions to problems or attempts to reduce the discrepancy between observed and desired student behavior (Reynolds, Gutkin, Elliott, & Witt, 1984; Shinn, 1989). In accordance with this view, the first task of school consultation as a service delivery approach is to achieve the problem-solving objectives of behavioral consultation listed in Chap. 5. These objectives are revisited below and research is presented documenting their importance to successful problem resolution.

The Problem Identification Interview

The primary goals of the Problem Identification Interview (PII) are threefold: (1) to identify a target behavior and define it in overtly observable terms; (2) to obtain tentative estimates of how often the behavior occurs and under what conditions; and (3) to begin ongoing data collection for use in evaluating treatment outcomes. The importance of successful problem identification in line with the objectives stated above cannot be overestimated. For example, Lambert (1976) found that teachers rarely described children's problems in specific terms and would likely need "considerable support for gathering more precise information about the nature of children's problems before interventions can be considered" (p. 515). McDougall et al. (1988) evaluated the effectiveness of a 1-day training workshop on consultants' interviewing skills. Participants in the workshop were asked to submit audiotaped interviews before and after training which were subsequently scored for the number of PII objectives met. Consistent with the findings by Lambert (1976), the number of subjects meeting each PII objective at baseline ranged from only 5.9 to 47.1%. After training, between 58.8 and 94.1% of the participants completed the same interviewing objectives. Finally, in the often-cited study by Bergan and Tombari (1976), approximately 60% of the variance in plan implementation was accounted for by merely identifying the problem. Equally as interesting, consultant interviewing tactics were found in the study to have their greatest impact on problem resolution during the initial interview.

The Problem Analysis Interview

During the PAI, the consultant and consultee are responsible for (1) using the baseline data that are collected to establish goals for behavior change; (2) conducting a functional assessment to generate hypotheses about why problem behavior is occurring; and (3) designing and implementing an intervention plan. Perhaps, the most critical goal of the PAI is to identify factors that contribute to problem behavior as antecedents and consequences by conducting a functional assessment. This goal is typically accomplished by first asking the consultee to describe classroom events and conditions that occur before the target behavior (e.g., unstructured free-time, assigning math seatwork), consequences that result from engaging in the target behavior (e.g., attention from peers, being sent to the office), or interventions for the target behavior that were tried previously but failed (e.g., moving the child's location in the classroom, time-out). After interviewing the consultee, additional information about the scope of problem behavior and its possible reinforcing functions can be obtained by having the teacher complete one or more behavior rating scales (e.g., Questions About Behavioral Function; Paclawskyj, Matson, Rush, Smalls, & Vollmer, 2000). In addition, either the teacher or consultant may find it useful to record occurrences of problem behavior across different times and instructional conditions (i.e., a scatterplot analysis; Touchette, MacDonald, & Langer, 1985) and to conduct sequential observations of behavior and its consequences during those times when it occurs the most (Martens, DiGennaro, Reed, Szczech, & Rosenthal, 2008). Given the importance of functional assessment in designing school-based interventions, various assessment strategies for both behavior and academic problems are discussed in more detail in Chap. 7. Determining possible reasons for why these problems are occurring can enable school consultants to develop interventions that teach new skills or that counteract, eliminate, or weaken the consequences supporting problem behavior (Martens, Witt, Daly, & Vollmer, 1999).

The Problem Evaluation Interview

The primary focus of the PEI is to determine if the goals established during the PAI were met and if the intervention plan was sufficiently effective to warrant its continuation. The former objective (goal attainment) requires that the frequency, intensity, or duration of the target behavior during intervention be compared to the goal established at baseline. Although a variety of statistical methods are available for making this comparison, the most common strategy used in consultation is to display the data in a time-series figure or graph and evaluate the degree of change based on visual inspection (Bergan & Kratochwill, 1990).

Beyond evaluating changes in the target behavior, at least two other issues should be addressed in order to conclude that a plan was effective. First, it must be determined that the plan was implemented by the consultee in the manner intended (i.e., treatment integrity). Second, one must be confident that the plan was responsible for improvements in student behavior before suggesting that the plan be continued or attempted again in the future (i.e., internal validity). Toward this latter goal, several authors have described the design and implementation of school-based interventions as a problem-solving process that closely resembles *single-case experimental research* (Barlow, Hayes, & Nelson, 1984; Gresham, 1985). Given the logistical similarities between the two activities, we agree with Hayes (1981) that it is desirable to incorporate naturally occurring experimental design elements into consultation casework whenever possible. For example, a teacher and consultant may decide to have two students in a classroom self-monitor the amount of work they complete accurately each day and record this information in a folder. Staggering the procedure's introduction so that the second student begins self-monitoring several days after improvements have been observed in the first student would be consistent with a multiple baseline design across subjects. Implementing the plan in this way would allow one to conclude with greater confidence that self-monitoring rather than some other chance event in the classroom was in fact responsible for improved student performance.

Interviewing Tactics

Bergan and Tombari (1975) originally proposed that consultants should direct the interviewing process by (1) asking questions about children's behavior problems and the conditions surrounding these problems; (2) paraphrasing information provided by the consultee; and (3) soliciting confirmation from the consultee as to the accuracy of these summary statements. Early research by Bergan and Tombari (1976) indicated that consultants who controlled the dialog with questions, stayed on a topic of conversation that concerned child behavior, and summarized and validated consultee statements engaged in a higher number of initial consultative interviews during an academic year. In a subsequent study, Tombari and Bergan (1978) examined the effects of verbal cues provided by the consultant (i.e., medical model versus behavioral) on consultee behavior. Sixty student–teachers participated in a PII, during which they were separated from the consultant by an opaque screen. Results indicated that consultant verbal cues that were classified as behavioral produced significantly more consultee statements about behavior or conditions surrounding behavior, higher expectations for problem resolution, and more behaviorally specific definitions of the child's problem.

Martens, Deery, and Gherardi (1991) compared two types of consultant summarization statements for their effects on consultee verbal behavior during the PII. As part of the study, consultants were instructed to alternate between statements summarizing consultee affect (e.g., "You seem frustrated with Austin") and message content (e.g., "So you estimate that Austin gets out of his seat every 5 min") using a counterbalanced ABCBC design. Consultee agreement was found to occur significantly more often during conditions of reflected content, with consultee statements about themselves and their emotions occurring significantly more often during conditions of reflected affect. Application of lag sequential analysis to the response sequences revealed an immediate dependency between consultee agreement and consultant summarization statements. Findings from these and other studies have suggested that consultants who function as effective problem solvers indeed tend to conduct interviews by asking questions about the child's behavior and surrounding events and by summarizing and expressing agreement with statements made by the consultee (Curtis & Zins, 1988; Martens et al., 1992; McDougall et al., 1988).

The Social Influence Task

We believe that strategically influencing consultee perceptions in order to promote changes in consultee behavior constitutes the second task of the school consultation process. That is, in addition to problem solving, effective school consultation also involves a social influence task (Erchul, 1993c; Erchul & Raven, 1997; Gutkin & Conoley, 1990; Martens, 1993a; Martens et al., 1996). Although social influence has received little attention in the consultation literature, its importance was anticipated by a number of authors. Following attempts to promote the use of behavioral technology in a state institution, Reppucci and Saunders (1974) concluded that the ability to modify staff behavior was ultimately critical to program success. Tharp and Wetzel (1969) anticipated the importance of influencing third-party adults as treatment agents by suggesting that consultee behavior might be controlled by sources of social reinforcement other than the consultant (e.g., supervising teachers, principals). These authors went on to suggest that such individuals might be recruited to promote consultees' adherence to treatment plans (i.e., invoking third-party influence), and that social psychological role theory might be useful in identifying the types of treatment plans which consultees would be likely to implement. Martin (1978) provided one of the first discussions of social power applied to school consultation, suggesting that effective consultants were able to maximize both positive expert and positive referent power bases.

Martens et al. (1996) examined the effects of two sequential-request strategies, foot-in-the-door (FITD) and door-in-the-face (DITF), on teachers' ratings of treatment acceptability and implementation of a classroom intervention. Both the FITD (Freedman & Fraser, 1966) and DITF (Cialdini et al., 1975) techniques represent compliance-gaining strategies, in which making an initial request is expected to increase the chances that a person will comply with a second request. In the case of FITD, the initial request is small or trivial, such as answering a question over the phone, and individuals agree to its performance. When asked to comply with a second, larger request (e.g., participating in a 2-hr survey), these individuals are more likely to agree, presumably to maintain consistency in their self-perceptions. In the case of DITF, the initial request is large (e.g., donating 2 hr a week for 2 years), and individuals typically do not agree to its performance. However, when asked to comply with a second, smaller request (e.g., donating 2 hr for a field trip), these individuals are more likely to agree, presumably because a concession has been made and they feel compelled to make a concession also.

In the Martens et al. study, 61 teachers were randomly assigned to one of three experimental conditions, in which they complied with a small initial request, failed to comply with a large initial request, or received no initial request. Teachers then rated the acceptability of a classroom intervention (i.e., a fixed-interval schedule of verbal praise) that they were asked to implement for 1 hr on each of two consecutive school days. Results showed the mean acceptability ratings for the DITF condition to be significantly lower than the Control condition, but neither differed significantly from the FITD condition. Moreover, fewer teachers in the DITF condition implemented the classroom intervention than controls. It was concluded from the study that school consultants should be cautious when attempting to use the DITF procedure because any favorable perceptions that are produced by conceding one's position must overshadow the negative perceptions created from making what may have been an unreasonable request in the first place.

As discussed in Chap. 3, the most comprehensive treatise on social power and influence applied to school consultation can be found in an article by Erchul and Raven (1997). These authors expanded on Martin's (1978) argument by describing how all six social power bases, as currently conceptualized (Raven, 1992, 1993), might be applied to the school consultation process. A basic premise of this argument is that the indirect service model of school consultation often requires consultants to alter the attitudes and behaviors of consultees in order to benefit clients (Gutkin & Conoley, 1990). For example, a teacher may be resistant to taking part in a home-based reinforcement program because of the belief that children should not be given special privileges for behavior that is expected of them anyway. Discussing the program as a means of helping the child become more responsible (a trait the teacher values) or as a way to recruit support for schooling at home (a view consistent with the teacher's attributions for student failure) may go far in reducing such resistance.

Because school consultation involves aspects of relational control (Erchul, 1987), we believe changes in consultee behavior can be encouraged in a noncoercive fashion by using the strategic communication approaches described in Chap. 3. Rather than repeating that discussion here, presented in Table 6.2 are examples of how each of French and Raven's social influence tactics is believed to effect behavior change from the perspective of the consultee. A skilled consultant is able to use these tactics as needed during the interview process, thereby accomplishing both problem-solving

Table 6.2 Examples of Social Influence Strategies from Chap. 3

Influence strategy	Example
Coercive	I will look bad if I didn't do what the CT asked when she checks (Personal and Impersonal)
Reward	I will look good if I did what the CT asked when she checks (Personal and Impersonal)
Legitimate	I feel obligated to do what the CT asks
Position	As a CE, I am expected to do what a CT asks
Reciprocity	The CT has contributed a lot so I should contribute too
Equity	I feel guilty for causing the CT more work and should make up for it
Responsibility	I have a responsibility to help children by doing what the CT asks
Positive expert	The CT knows the best thing to do because she is an expert
Negative expert	The CT is trying to boss me around with her expertise, so I will do what I want
Positive referent	Because the CT and I are alike, it makes sense to do what she asks
Negative referent	Because the CT and I are different, it doesn't make sense to do what she asks
Informational	What the CT suggests really seems like the best thing to do (Direct and Indirect)
Third parties	Mrs. Jones down the hall has done this, so I should do it too
Mode of influence	When the CT uses harsh or threatening language versus friendly or humorous language
Preparatory devices	When the CT emphasizes intimidation to aid coercion, flattery to aid reward, communality to aid referent, self-promotion to aid expert, and CT role and time spent to aid legitimate

Note. CT = consultant; CE = consultee

and social influence goals. As an example, consider the school consultant who, after listening to a teacher's initial description of a child's failure to work independently, summarizes the main points of what was said, and adds, "When I volunteered in a classroom several years ago, I also remember feeling very drained by children who asked for constant attention." Such a statement not only serves the problem-solving function of encouraging additional description from the teacher (Martens et al., 1991), but can be instrumental in helping the consultant establish a referent power base. Additional examples of the various and often multiple functions served by consultant statements can be found in the consultation case transcripts presented in Chap. 11.

The Support and Development Task

In keeping with the conceptual underpinnings of Caplan's mental health model, we believe the third task of school consultation is to support consultee efforts in dealing with crises that arise during their normal professional duties while facilitating the development of consultee skills. Although mental health consultation focuses on providing emotional support to consultees, any attempts at supporting teachers' efforts are likely to be viewed as beneficial. Evidence of this was provided in a series of experimental studies that showed individuals who experienced distress from a problem-solving task tended to view messages of emotional and instrumental support as being equally helpful (Tardy, 1994). That is, subjects under stress perceived any support attempt by another as emotionally supportive, even if it was clearly instrumental in nature.

Supporting the consultee's efforts as a teacher and an intervention agent is consistent with what has been termed an empowerment philosophy of helping (Witt & Martens, 1988). An *empowerment philosophy* is based on the assumption that consultees are skilled individuals who can become more capable of resolving their own problems by knowing what resources are available to them and how to make use of these resources (Dunst & Trivette, 1987). For example, our experience in the schools has suggested that many classroom teachers are unaware of the programs and services available in their own building for responding to children's learning and adjustment problems. One of the first assignments for our consultation practicum students, therefore, is to "map out" the various services which are offered in the building in which they are placed. As discussed in Chap. 5, similar organizational mapping activities have been recommended for consultants in their efforts to gain entry into the service delivery network. Beyond entry, however, sharing this information with teachers through inservice education, team meetings, or even memos distributed in mailboxes can serve a supportive function by promoting their access to existing resources.

Equally important to accomplishing the preventive goals of school consultation is helping consultees develop their professional skills within a problem-solving context. As noted earlier, school consultation typically requires teachers to engage in more direct, evidence-based approaches to instruction (e.g., word list training, passage previewing and repeated readings), more systematic strategies for monitoring student progress (e.g., curriculum-based measurement, time sampling), or more structured forms of classroom management (e.g., self-monitoring and charting, time-out) (Martens, Witt, et al., 1999). As such, intervention programs that are developed during consultation require teachers to learn new skills and make what are often significant changes in the way they interact with students. In the absence of prior training in these skills, teachers must rely on their interactions with the consultant to learn why a given procedure is relevant for the child's problem, how to implement it correctly, and how to collect and interpret data concerning treatment outcome.

Noell et al. (2000) observed that school consultants rarely have formal administrative authority over teachers whose behavior they are attempting to change. Thus, the extent to which teachers actually follow through in implementing agreed-upon plans may depend largely on the consultant's interpersonal influence and implementation support skills (Erchul & Martens, 2002). Until recently, however, efforts to promote intervention use by teachers have relied primarily on verbal instruction from the consultant prior to implementation (Bergan & Kratochwill, 1990). Our experiences in the schools suggest that we as consultants typically *underestimate* the amount of training and support that teachers require to successfully change their behavior (Martens & Ardoin, 2002). Consistent with this notion, Joyce and Showers (1981) reviewed effective strategies for in-service training and concluded that verbal instruction alone is not likely to promote maintenance of behavior change unless it is followed by demonstration, practice, feedback, and in vivo application. More recent research (e.g., DiGennaro et al., 2007; Noell et al., 2000) has suggested that performance feedback together with reinforcement for correct implementation should be standards of practice when supporting teachers' implementation efforts. Described below are several strategies that have been shown to be effective in supporting teachers' use of school-based interventions and developing their intervention skills.

Implementation Protocols and Other Mediational Cues

One simple but often overlooked way to train consultees in how to use an intervention plan and to promote its use after training has ended is to provide them with checklists or scripts detailing the steps required to carry out the plan. For example, Ehrhardt, Barnett, Lentz, Stollar, and Reifin (1996) developed intervention scripts collaboratively with caregivers for use in responding to behavior problems exhibited by four preschoolers. The scripts detailed in step-by-step fashion what each caregiver was supposed to do in order to implement the intervention and contained a place to indicate when each step had been completed. Results suggested that the scripts were effective at increasing implementation integrity and these levels were maintained at follow-up.

In a similar study, Hiralall and Martens (1998) developed a scripted protocol for use by four teachers in implementing a direct instruction sequence. The protocol was used during a structured art activity and required teachers to engage in a multistep instructional sequence involving requests for eye contact, instruction, modeling, praise, and redirection. Not only did all four teachers increase their use of instructional statements, modeling, and praise with use of the protocol, but two teachers maintained these levels at 1-month follow-up. Implementation protocols appear to be effective at promoting intervention use by teachers, are easy to develop, can be used to monitor treatment integrity, and can be use in conjunction with performance feedback (e.g., Witt, Noell, La Fleur, & Mortenson, 1997).

In addition to their informational value, protocols may promote intervention use through their mere presence by cueing teachers that it is time to implement the procedure. This strategy, referred to by Stokes and Baer (1977) as *programming common stimuli*, can be a simple yet effective means of promoting the generalization of behavior change from training to nontraining settings by having common stimuli or cues present in both settings. As an example, Scheeler, Bruno, Grubb, and Seavey (2009) attempted to promote the generalization of complete learning trials (i.e., presentation of an antecedent, a student response, and feedback) by preservice teachers from their student teaching sites to their first classroom assignments following graduation. Teachers were first trained to a 90% mastery criterion in their student teaching sites through use of a bug-in-the-ear device. Each teacher then selected a common stimulus from the training site that would be visibly displayed in the generalization site (e.g., lesson materials, the bug-in-the-ear device). Results suggested that the high levels of complete learning trials reached during training were maintained in the generalization setting through use of the common stimulus procedure.

Social Influence Strategies

As noted in Chap. 3, social influence strategies that are viewed as most effective by school psychologists include direct informational and positive expert power (Erchul, Raven, & Ray, 2001). We believe that several other social influence strategies hold particular promise for school consultants. As professionals-in-training who are external to a school building, our practicum students are often cast in a "one-down" position relative to full-time staff members. At the same time, teachers who spend most of their time during the day talking with children often like to connect and interact professionally with other adults as observed by Sarason (1996). Under these circumstances, our students have realized some success in promoting consultee behavior change by: (1) assuming the bulk of responsibility for material development and plan implementation initially and then gradually reducing their involvement over time (i.e., the legitimate power of reciprocity), (2) praising teachers for participating in meetings and following through with assigned responsibilities (i.e., personal reward power), (3) highlighting similarities with teachers in terms of educational values or past teaching experiences (i.e., positive referent power), and (4) highlighting the successful use of similar interventions by other teaching staff (i.e., invoking the influence of third parties).

Setting Goals for Teacher Behavior

In behavioral consultation, tentative goals for student behavior change are established during the PII to determine if teachers harbor unreasonable expectations, whereas formal goals are set during the PAI to assess treatment outcome (Bergan & Kratochwill, 1990). Interestingly, the same level of goal specificity is not required with respect to changes in teacher behavior, which ultimately mediate student improvement. We believe that setting explicit standards for consultee behavior represents an important but largely untapped method for supporting plan implementation. This potential was illustrated in a study by Martens, Hiralall, and Bradley (1997). Baseline observations revealed generally low but variable levels of appropriate behavior by two kindergarten students with emotional disturbance as well as low rates of teacher praise (approximately three times in a 30 min period). This information was shared with the teacher who established a goal for herself of six praise statements every 30 min. Each morning thereafter, the teacher was given a brief feedback note prompting her as to which behaviors to praise in each student and stating whether or not she had met her goal the previous day. As a function of the goal setting plus feedback intervention, the average number of praise statements delivered by the teacher to each student increased to over 14 in a 30 min period, and mean levels of appropriate student behavior increased to over 80% of the intervals observed.

Performance Feedback and Reinforcement

Noell and his colleagues (Noell et al., 1997, 2000; Witt et al. 1997) conducted a series of investigations examining the effectiveness of performance feedback at increasing intervention use by teachers. Each of the studies employed a similar approach to staggering when feedback began for each teacher, sequence of consultation activities, and method for monitoring teacher implementation. The intervention plan was first described to the teacher, materials needed to implement the plan were provided, and use of the plan was modeled by the consultant who coached the teacher through implementation during one session in the classroom. After this initial training, the teacher implemented the plan independently, received a performance feedback package, and again implemented the plan independently (i.e., a maintenance phase). The performance feedback package consisted of graphs depicting levels of student behavior and teacher implementation (i.e., percentage of steps completed), discussion of implementation errors, and praise for implementing the intervention as planned.

A consistent pattern of findings emerged across the studies. Although teachers initially implemented all intervention steps, implementation dropped considerably within several weeks. Implementation levels increased dramatically with introduction of performance feedback, but maintenance after feedback ended was variable. Because the start of each condition was staggered across teachers, some teachers received performance feedback during a large number of sessions before moving to the maintenance phase. Interestingly, these teachers tended to show greater maintenance, suggesting that performance feedback may have helped them master the skills required for correct implementation and perhaps reinforced their use.

In addition to performance feedback, research both by Noell and others has suggested that social positive reinforcement in the form of praise from the consultant or even the principal (Gillat & Sulzer-Azaroff, 1994) can be effective at increasing teachers' implementation efforts. More recent research has shown that social negative reinforcement in the form of avoiding meetings with the consultant to rehearse missed steps may also be effective and perceived as an acceptable means of support by teachers (DiGennaro, Martens, & McIntyre, 2005; DiGennaro et al., 2007). DiGennaro et al. (2005) evaluated the effects of performance feedback together with a directed rehearsal/meeting cancelation contingency on the behavior of four elementary teachers and their students' off-task behavior. Similar to Noell et al. (1997), teachers were initially trained in how to implement an intervention through instruction, modeling, coaching, and corrective feedback. After reaching 100% accuracy on two occasions, the teachers' implementation dropped to between 0 and 25% when the consultant withdrew assistance. The teachers were then given daily written feedback about their accuracy (i.e., performance feedback) and told that they could avoid subsequent meetings with the consultant to rehearse missed steps if their accuracy was 100%. Using a multiple baseline design across teachers, integrity increased to 100% for three of the four teachers following the performance feedback/negative reinforcement package. Integrity was maintained at high levels when feedback was faded to once a week and then once every 2 weeks, and moderate decreases in students' problem behavior were also observed.

Outcomes of School Consultation

In order to achieve the goals of school consultation, the consultant and consultee must engage in separate yet complementary activities following each meeting. These activities constitute outcomes of the school consultation process and are depicted in the right-hand portion of Fig. 6.1.

The preventive aspects of school consultation occur when the consultee's professional skills are enhanced as a result of the consultant's support and influence attempts during times of crisis, and when the consultee is able to successfully apply the systematic problem solving process in other situations. With respect to the former issue, Gutkin and Hickman (1988) found that increasing consultees' perceptions of control and self-efficacy over presenting problems resulted in an increased willingness to engage in consultation. Although it is a common belief that consultation serves a primary prevention function (e.g., Meyers, Parsons, & Martin, 1979), others are skeptical that this in fact is the case (e.g., Gutkin & Curtis, 1982; Trickett, 1993). We and others (e.g., Zins, 1995) believe that school consultation is more often provided in the service of secondary and tertiary prevention and that data attesting to its primary preventive function are limited.

Following completion of the PII and PAI, the consultee is expected to assist in the collection of baseline data and assume primary responsibility for implementing the agreed upon plan. As will be discussed in Chap. 8, data-based decision making in conjunction with a behavior analytic approach to instruction and management has been shown to be an effective means of accommodating special needs students.

With respect to changing client behavior then, the outcomes of school consultation are likely to involve changes in teachers' instructional practices, the systematic evaluation of treatment options (e.g., Jones et al., 2009), or full implementation of a school-based intervention plan. Whereas the consultee maintains primary responsibility for plan implementation, Gresham (1989) has suggested that consultants should be responsible for monitoring treatment integrity, or the extent to which treatment is implemented in the manner intended. By assessing treatment integrity, consultants can recommend changes in treatment procedures that help consultees incorporate suggested interventions into their professional repertoires. In addition to monitoring treatment integrity, the consultant can also play a principal role in the evaluation of treatment outcome. This role involves helping the consultee determine (1) if the goals established for behavior change were achieved, partially achieved, or not achieved; and (2) if the changes observed in student behavior were a function of the treatment procedure or resulted merely from chance (Martens & McIntyre, 2009). Based on these determinations, the decision can be made to continue with an intervention plan or recycle through aspects of the consultation process as necessary. In either event, the consultant is responsible for providing ongoing support to the consultee until a mutual decision is reached to terminate the relationship (Gutkin & Curtis, 1990). It should be clear from the foregoing discussion that the systematic evaluation of treatment outcomes is central to the consultation process. Accordingly, a variety of behavioral assessment methods that can be used to monitor treatment outcome including direct, systematic observation, behavior rating scales and checklists, and curriculum-based measures of student performance are discussed in Chap. 7.

Chapter 7
Assessment in School Consultation

As discussed in Chap. 6, our integrated model of school consultation involves three interrelated tasks; problem-solving, social influence, and support and development. Of these, the problem-solving task is the primary vehicle through which school-based interventions are designed, implemented, and evaluated. As such, problem solving (or the general problem-solving model described in Chap. 2) forms the basis of school consultation as a method of service delivery.

Accomplishing the problem-solving task requires that the consultant or consulting team address specific objectives over the course of the three interviews (i.e., the PII, PAI, and PEI). Although these objectives were listed in Chap. 5, it is important to recognize that each interview contains objectives related to the assessment of client (i.e., student) behavior. During the PII, consultants are required to begin identifying conditions that may be contributing to problem behavior as antecedents and consequences and to establish procedures for data collection. A more thorough assessment of behavioral function is conducted during the PAI to support hypotheses about why problem behavior is occurring and to select conceptually relevant interventions. Finally, a primary goal of the consultant during the PEI is to evaluate treatment outcomes relative to consultee goals that were established in the PII as well as baseline levels of client performance.

In describing their behavioral consultation model, Bergan and Kratochwill (1990) acknowledged the importance of behavioral assessment and proposed several strategies that reflected the "state-of-the-science" at the time for addressing the assessment goals noted above. Although a thorough discussion of these strategies is beyond the scope of the present chapter, three characteristics are noteworthy. First, the primary means of analyzing conditions surrounding problem behavior or deficits in client skills was to elicit consultee verbal reports during the PAI. Second, direct observation of client behavior in the natural environment by consultees, teacher aides, or even clients themselves was viewed as the most relevant strategy for collecting both baseline and outcome data. Third, depending on the specifics of each case, additional strategies for measuring client performance might be considered, including standardized tests, curriculum-based measurement (CBM) probes, and review of student work samples. Of these supplemental strategies, standardized tests were seen as the least useful because they measured broad psychological constructs rather than specific skills or behaviors. Student work samples represented a convenient albeit informal way

W.P. Erchul and B.K. Martens, *School Consultation*, Issues in Clinical Child Psychology, DOI 10.1007/978-1-4419-5747-4_7, © Springer Science+Business Media, LLC 2010 to measure academic performance, whereas CBM, still in its infancy, was recognized as "an important step in problem identification, analysis, and evaluation" (p. 95).

Conducting a PAI and observing client behavior in the natural environment continue to be staples of the behavioral consultation process today. With respect to the former method, it should come as no surprise that the quality of information gained from the PAI will partly be a function of the consultant's interviewing skills. Put another way, consultants who are more knowledgeable about the situational determinants of children's academic and behavior problems are likely to conduct a more thorough interview. To aid readers in the development of questions to ask during the PAI, we present several conceptual models for understanding the situational determinants of children's behavior in Chap. 8. With respect to the latter method, a variety of observation codes have been reported in the literature for assessing children's classroom behavior (Volpe, DiPerna, Hintze, & Shapiro, 2005). Typically, these schemes allow observers to record several categories of student behavior as well as instructionally relevant categories of teacher behavior (Luiselli, Reed, & Martens, 2010). Children's behavior within these categories is recorded using one of several strategies including event recording, percentage recording, interval recording, and time sampling (e.g., Miltenberger, 2008). *Event recording* simply involves tallying the frequency or rate of behavior or timing the duration or latency to initiate a behavior during each observation period. *Percentage recording* involves tallying the number of times a behavior occurred as a percentage of the opportunities presented for it to occur (e.g., percent correct, percent steps completed). *Interval recording* refers to a set of procedures for observing behavior in which occurrence or nonoccurrence is recorded during brief, consecutive intervals (e.g., 15 s). The resulting data are summarized as the percentage of intervals in which behavior occurred during any part of an interval (partial interval recording), during an entire interval (whole interval recording), or the instant the interval ends (time sampling).

Beyond the PAI and direct observation, there have been a number of advances in behavioral assessment over the past two decades. Several of these advances are particularly relevant to school consultation and have occurred in the areas of functional behavior assessment, systematic formative evaluation, CBM, and brief experimental analysis (Ardoin et al., 2004; Martens & DiGennaro, 2008; Martens & Gertz, 2009). The first two approaches were mandated by IDEIA as the basis for positive behavior support and SLD determination in a response-to-intervention model, whereas brief experimental analysis is considered by many to represent "best practice" in instructional intervention (e.g., Jones et al., 2009). As anticipated by Bergan and Kratochwill (1990), many school districts across the country now routinely collect grade-level norms using CBM probes as a basis for systematic formative evaluation.

In this era of high-stakes, team-based service delivery, the practice of relying entirely on consultee verbal report to conduct a functional behavior assessment is not likely to be a defensible professional practice (Drasgow & Yell, 2001; Martens & DiGennaro, 2008). Similarly, given that data from a child's cumulative intervention history can be used for eligibility determination, these data should be collected using formal measures with known psychometric properties. Although consultation remains an indirect service model, it has become increasingly clear that consulting teams need to supplement information gained from the interview process with more direct assessment data (Martens & DiGennaro, 2008).

The goal of this chapter is to familiarize school consultants with behavioral assessment strategies that can be used to design and evaluate interventions for children's learning and behavior problems. Toward this goal, the chapter begins by describing "best practices" in functional behavior assessment and presents a 6-step assessment sequence that can be used by school consultants. Next, CBM is described as a reliable and valid approach for measuring children's academic skills. A downward extension of CBM for early reading skills, *Dynamic Indicators of Basic Early Literacy Skills* (DIBELS; Good & Kaminski, 2002) is also described, and the use of both measures to monitor student progress in a response-to-intervention model is discussed. The chapter concludes with an overview of the strategies involved in conducting a brief experimental analysis of intervention options, including repeated measurement, visual inspection of graphed data, and demonstration of experimental control.

Functional Behavior Assessment

Functional behavior assessment refers to a set of procedures for describing behavior and the events surrounding its occurrence in the natural environment (Witt, Daly, & Noell, 2000). As a means of informing decisions about intervention alternatives, functional behavior assessment is based on three assumptions. First, many problem behaviors are learned (i.e., reinforced) in the situations in which they occur. This reinforcement occurs as adults and children interact on a daily basis during various activities in the classroom setting. Sometimes, the reinforcement of problem behavior is obvious (e.g., "You seem upset, come sit with me.") and other times less obvious (e.g., "If you won't work, then go to the office!"). Understanding these sources of reinforcement can help treatment agents decide how teacher–student interactions need to change in order to promote more desired classroom behavior.

Second, in our experience, children's problem behavior never occurs all the time and is rarely unpredictable. Rather, over time patterns develop in the ways that teachers and students interact, and these patterns can be identified to reveal potential sources of reinforcement. Although these patterns may be as varied and unique as individuals themselves, there are only four broad categories of reinforcing stimuli for problem behavior (Hanley, Iwata, & McCord, 2003). *Social positive reinforcement* involves the contingent presentation of desired items, attention, or activities that increase problem behavior. Although the intention behind such actions might be to calm children down or distract them with another activity, problem behavior may be maintained or actually increase as a result. *Social negative reinforcement* involves allowing children to escape or avoid unpleasant tasks contingent on problem behavior. Escape motivated problem behavior often occurs when children are assigned work that is too difficult or too easy for their skill level, engage in disruptive behavior as a result, and then are not held accountable for the work (Martens & Witt, 2004; Weeks &

Gaylord-Ross, 1981). As the name indicates, both social positive and social negative reinforcement are socially mediated, meaning that someone else in the child's environment is responsible for their occurrence. In contrast, *automatic reinforcement* results from simply engaging in the behavior itself and does not require interaction with others. Automatic positive reinforcement occurs when engaging in problem behavior produces sensory stimulation or arousal (e.g., hand flapping by a child with autism spectrum disorder) (Miltenberger, 2008). Automatic negative reinforcement occurs when problem behavior is soothing or reduces pain, such as going to the bathroom or when a child with an inner ear infection repeatedly tugs on her ear during a seatwork activity.

A third assumption of functional behavior assessment is that once the potential reinforcement maintaining problem behavior has been identified, steps can be taken to eliminate, reverse, or weaken such reinforcement thereby increasing desired behavior (Martens, Witt, Daly, & Vollmer, 1999). In principle, functional behavior assessment can allow treatment agents to design interventions that are more strategic, individualized, and potentially more effective when dealing with children's problem behavior. This latter assumption is the primary reason why functional assessment techniques have become so popular in research and mandated by IDEIA as a basis for designing positive behavioral supports.

What constitutes "best practices" in functional behavior assessment? First of all, the data are fairly clear concerning what does not constitute a functional behavior assessment. As readers will recall, IDEA 1997 was the legislation in which the mandate for functional behavior assessment first appeared. As such, one might expect a "settling in" period as school districts adopted practices to comply with the law. This is exactly what Drasgow and Yell (2001) found in their review of 14 due process hearings held at the state level in the 3 years following the enactment of IDEA 1997. In these hearings, parents contested the school districts' appropriate implementation of the functional behavior assessment mandate. In 11 cases, school districts failed to conduct an assessment when required by law. In 3 cases, the hearing officer determined that the assessment team abbreviated the process by obtaining too few data using informal methods (e.g., a handwritten, fill in the blank sheet) and therefore conducted an inadequate functional behavior assessment.

The functional behavior assessment mandate has now been on the books for more than 10 years. A considerable amount of research, prescriptive models, and legal writings have appeared on the topic during this time (e.g., Daly, Martens, Skinner, & Noell, 2009; Drasgow & Yell, 2001; McDougal, Chafouleas, & Waterman, 2006; Miltenberger, 2008; Sterling-Turner, Robinson, & Wilczynski, 2001; Witt et al., 2000). In general, these authors are in agreement that a comprehensive functional behavior assessment should involve at a minimum three sets of activities: (a) indirect assessment methods including interviews with direct-care providers (e.g., the PII and PAI), review of records, and informant report scales about behavioral function; (b) direct assessment methods involving systematic observation of antecedents (e.g., events, times, and situations) that occasion problem behavior and consequences for both its occurrence and nonoccurrence; and (c) hypothesis generation

Table 7.1 A 6-Step Functional Assessment Sequence

Indirect Assessment Phase
Step 1: Conduct a PII and PAI with the consultee (i.e., teacher, parent, or caregiver) who is requesting assistance and who has had an opportunity to observe the child
Step 2: Have the consultee complete a behavior rating scale or checklist to corroborate descriptions of problem behavior from the interview
Step 3: Have the consultee complete a questionnaire about behavioral function
Direct Assessment Phase
Step 4: Observe the problem behavior during times and/or activities suggested in the PII and PAI
Step 5: Observe the consequences for problem behavior using sequential recording during those times and activities when it occurs the most
Step 6: Based on patterns in the descriptive assessment data, hypothesize the potential functions of problem behavior

about potential maintaining variables based on patterns in the resulting data (Daly, Martens et al., 2009).

Based on a series of case studies and recent research reflecting "best practices" in functional behavior assessment (Eckert, Martens, & DiGennaro, 2005; Martens & Ardoin, 2010; Martens, DiGennaro, Reed, Szczech, & Rosenthal, 2008; Reed & Martens, 2008a), a 6-step functional assessment sequence is presented in Table 7.1.

Indirect Assessment Phase

As shown in the table, the indirect assessment phase of a functional behavior assessment begins by conducting a PII and PAI as described in Chap. 5. Although teachers and other consultees can often provide a considerable amount of information during the interview process, this information will depend on the interviewing skills of the consultant, the teacher's ability to recall prior events, and the extent to which the teacher is aware of or has had the opportunity to observe the child's behavior. One way to corroborate (i.e., increase one's confidence in) descriptions of the target behavior elicited during the PII is to have the consultee complete a behavior rating scale or checklist. These scales prompt consultee responses by providing information about a wider range of problem behaviors and domains than typically queried during the PII and are more reliable than semi-structured interviews. When items endorsed by the consultee as occurring often are consistent with those identified in the PII, the consultant or team can be more confident that an important problem behavior has been targeted. The final step using indirect assessment methods is to have the consultee complete a questionnaire about behavioral function. One such scale is the *Motivation Assessment Scale* or MAS (Durand & Crimmins, 1988). The MAS is a 16-item questionnaire that asks caregivers to rate the frequency with which problem behavior seems to occur for various reasons using a 7-point scale (0 = never, 6 = always; Sample item: Does the behavior occur following a request to perform a difficult task?). Items on the MAS are combined into four subscales representing possible sources of reinforcement (sensory stimulation, escape, attention, access to tangibles). Another scale which has been shown to yield consistently reliable scores is the *Questions About Behavioral Function* or QABF (Paclawskyj, Matson, Rush, Smalls, & Vollmer, 2000). Similar to the MAS, the QABF contains 25 items rated on a 4 point scale (0 = never, 3 = often; Sample item: Engages in the behavior to get attention). Responses are also grouped by possible reinforcing function, and these include attention, escape, nonsocial, physical, and tangible.

Direct Assessment Phase

Once the indirect assessments have been completed, the consultant or consulting team moves to the direct assessment phase which involves direct observation of client behavior. This phase is actually similar to the collection of baseline data that typically occurs in behavioral consultation. Specifically, systematic observation procedures are used to record occurrences of behavior during times and conditions suggested in the PII (Bergan & Kratochwill, 1990). When used as part of a functional behavior assessment, however, samples of behavior are collected across a broader array of antecedent conditions. These samples are brief (e.g., 15 min) and might involve different times of the day (e.g., morning, after lunch), different content areas (e.g., math, reading, social studies), or different instructional arrangements (e.g., independent seatwork, small-group instruction) as suggested by the interview (e.g., Eckert et al., 2005). These behavioral samples may be collected by the consultant, an aide assigned to the consulting team, or the teacher, depending on available resources. Known in general as a *scatterplot analysis* (Touchette, MacDonald, & Langer, 1985), these data can help confirm when problem behavior is most likely to occur, lead to the development of hypotheses concerning aspects of these situations that may be problematic (e.g., assignment of frustrational-level work), and indicate the most efficient times to observe consequences for problem behavior.

The second set of data collected during this phase also requires direct, systematic observation but involves the sequential recording of behavior and its consequences. *Sequential recording* is an observational strategy that is uniquely suited to functional behavior assessment and which involves the scoring of a target, problem behavior or its absence during brief intervals (e.g., 15 s) (Martens et al., 2008). Also during each interval, the observer records whether each of several consequences was delivered to the child following problem behavior by adults or peers in the classroom setting. Typically, these consequences are defined prior to conducting the observations and are selected to represent the broad categories of reinforcement described earlier in the chapter (i.e., social positive, social negative, and automatic reinforcement) (e.g., Anderson & Long, 2002; McKerchar & Thompson, 2004). Once the data have been collected, the consulting team can identify those consequences that frequently follow problem behavior by calculating the conditional probability of their occurrence (e.g., Lalli, Browder, Mace, & Brown, 1993). For example, Lalli et al. found that teacher attention was a frequent consequence for problem behavior in three students with severe mental retardation (i.e., the conditional probability of attention given problem behavior ranged from approximately 0.20–0.52). In contrast, escape via discontinuation of a task and access to preferred tangible items never followed problem behavior for two of the students. Given this pattern of consequences, problem behavior for all three students was hypothesized to serve an attention function.

Also using sequential recordings of behavior and its consequences, Martens et al. (2008) described a technique known as *contingency space analysis* for identifying events that are contingent on problem behavior. From an operant perspective, consequences are said to be contingent on behavior if they occur more often following behavior than in its absence (Gibbon, Berryman, & Thompson, 1974). From a child's perspective, these consequences consistently follow problem behavior, and engaging in problem behavior is a reliable way to obtain them. A contingency space analysis is conducted in three steps. First, consequences are recorded following both the presence and absence of problem behavior during brief intervals (i.e., sequential observations). Second, for each consequence, two conditional probabilities are computed: (a) the probability of the consequence occurring given behavior and (b) the probability of the consequence occurring given the absence of behavior. Third, when plotted together in coordinate space, the two probability values indicate the degree to which a consequence is contingent on problem behavior (plotted along the y-axis) or its absence (plotted along the x-axis) [the reader is referred to Martens et al. (2008), for a detailed discussion of contingency space analysis]. Those consequences shown to be contingent on problem behavior are likely candidates as potential maintaining variables.

The final step of the direct assessment phase is to hypothesize potential functions of problem behavior given patterns in the data that were collected. As an example, consider a teacher who reports in a PAI that she typically sends a child out of the room to the hallway for 5 min contingent on aggressive outbursts. When asked to complete the *Child Behavior Checklist* (Achenbach & Rescorla, 2001), the teacher rates the child in the clinical range on the Aggressive Behavior and Attention Problems subscales. Thus, aggression is confirmed as the behavior of primary concern. When completing the QABF in relation to the problem behavior of aggression, the teacher gives high ratings to items comprising the "escape" subscale. Scatterplot recordings of aggressive behavior at different times in the day suggest that it occurs more often during core academic content areas but rarely during specials, lunch, or in the hallway. Sequential observations during language arts (when aggression occurs the most) reveals the following pattern in teacher–student interactions: (a) a 0.90 probability of removal from either the activity area or the classroom (i.e., escape) given aggression, and a 0.05 probability of escape given no aggression; and (b) a 0.80 probability of teacher attention given aggression and a 0.10 probability of attention given no aggression. Taken together, these indirect and direct assessment data are consistent in suggesting that aggression is most likely maintained by negative reinforcement in the form of escape and may possibly be maintained by positive reinforcement in the form of teacher attention.

The assessment model summarized in Table 7.1 and described above can be used by consultants in a variety of settings to supplement information obtained from a PAI. It represents a sequenced, multimethod approach to functional behavior assessment that is consistent with "best practices" and can aid in the development of effective, individualized treatments for children's behavior problems. Because it requires time and personnel resources beyond that of the PAI, however, functional behavior assessment is perhaps best suited for use in developing more intensive targeted interventions at Tier 3 of a response-to-intervention model.

Systematic Formative Evaluation

A key feature of any school-based intervention program should be efforts to systematically monitor its effects on student performance. Fuchs and Fuchs (1986a) first referred to the ongoing evaluation of program outcomes that lead to revisions in program procedures as *systematic formative evaluation.* Systematic formative evaluation is based on the assumption that outcomes of school-based intervention programs cannot be predicted with certainty, but instead represent hypotheses that must be tested empirically (Kavale, 1990; Ysseldyke & Marston, 1990). This view can be contrasted with an ability–training approach, in which academic failure is attributed to deficits in one or more inferred mental processes within the child (i.e., student aptitudes). Standardized tests are typically used to diagnose these process deficits, and it is believed on the basis of theory that certain instructional programs can be used to remediate certain underlying deficits. Once the appropriate aptitude X treatment interaction has been identified, program effectiveness is assumed. Currently, there is no empirical support for an aptitude X treatment interaction approach to school-based intervention (Reschly, 2004). Reasons for this lack of support include poor psychometric properties of many existing aptitude measures as well as uncertainty over the extent to which various instructional programs actually address the aptitudes being targeted.

Although federal law requires that IEPs for children receiving special services be reviewed at least annually, monthly or even weekly monitoring of progress has been shown to significantly increase student achievement. In their now frequently cited article, Fuchs and Fuchs (1986a) conducted a meta-analysis of the effects of systematic formative evaluation on student achievement. For purposes of the study, evaluation was defined as twice-weekly monitoring of student progress using CBM probes, depicting these data in a figure or graph, and using data-evaluation rules to guide decision making. Results indicated that monitoring progress and graphing the data were associated with an average *ES* of 0.70 regardless of the instructional procedure used. Using data evaluation rules increased the average *ES* to 0.91. These findings indicate that students' achievement test scores improved by nearly one standard deviation over controls simply as a function of how the instructional program was monitored. Fuchs, Fuchs, Hamlett, and Allinder (1991) compared the effects of weekly progress monitoring on students' achievement in spelling. Teachers who monitored student progress, graphed the results, and decided when to change instruction based on explicit rules averaged 2.7 instructional adjustments over an 18-week period. Teachers in the control group averaged only.17 changes in instruction during the same time period. Not surprisingly, the students of teachers who frequently monitored progress learned three times more spelling words by the end of the study.

To be useful in evaluating intervention outcomes, measures of student performance must have certain characteristics. When monitoring academic performance, measures must be directly related to the skills taught, sensitive to short-term improvements, capable of repeated administration, and time and cost efficient in addition to being reliable and valid (Fuchs & Fuchs, 1986b; Shinn, 1989). CBM is now widely recognized as one method of assessing children's academic performance that has these characteristics (Ardoin et al., 2004). CBM probes are brief samples of production-type responses that are obtained using standard sets of grade-level material (Hintze & Christ, 2004). Administered in standardized format, CBM probes involve 1 min of passage reading, 2 min of spelling from dictation, 2 min of math computation, and 3 min of writing from a story starter. Different materials are selected at each grade level and scored for fluency, or the number of correct responses in the time allocated (e.g., correctly read words per minute). Not only are these measures psychometrically sound, but they have been shown to be useful for academic screening, progress monitoring, and instructional decision making (Hintze & Christ, 2004; Shinn, 2002).

More recently, CBM has emerged as the assessment strategy of choice for monitoring both level and slope of academic improvement in a response-to-intervention model (Ardoin et al., 2004; Fuchs & Fuchs, 1998). With this approach, children at each grade level are tested three times a year (e.g., fall, winter, and spring) to develop school-wide CBM norms. Those children who perform significantly below their grade-level peers during these universal screenings are considered to be at-risk for reading problems (i.e., a discrepancy in performance level). Children deemed at risk then receive a standard protocol intervention at Tier 2 and if necessary, a targeted intervention at Tier 3. At the end of each intervention period, the children are retested with grade-level CBM probes to evaluate their individual rates of progress in relation to the progress made by their typical peers (i.e., a discrepancy in rate of improvement). Students who after receiving Tier 2 and Tier 3 interventions continue to perform below their peers in terms of level and rate of progress are considered eligible for classification as SLD in what is known as a *dual discrepancy model* (Burns & Senesac, 2005; Fuchs & Fuchs, 1998) or *dual discrepancy approach* (Burns & Gibbons, 2008).

Good and Kaminski (2002) developed a downward extension of CBM for assessing children's early literacy skills known as DIBELS. As with CBM, DIBELS probes also involve brief fluency measures of production-type responses. DIBELS probes, however, involve performance on early literacy tasks shown to be predictive of later reading competence. Included among these tasks are phonological awareness (e.g., phonemic segmentation fluency), decoding (e.g., nonsense word fluency), and oral reading fluency. A notable feature of DIBELS is the use of performance benchmarks at the beginning, middle, and end of each grade for use in universal screening. For example, a child whose nonsense word fluency is below 29 correct letter sequences per min at the end of first grade would be considered deficient in the development of this skill.

Brief Experimental Analysis

Thus far in the chapter, we have described a variety of behavioral assessment strategies (e.g., systematic observation, behavior rating scales, CBM probes) and models (functional behavior assessment, systematic formative evaluation) that can be used by school consultants to supplement the interview process. Consistent with a problem-solving model, the ultimate goal of these strategies is to help consultants design or select effective interventions for children's learning and behavior problems.

Often times following a thorough discussion of the variables influencing problem behavior and/or when armed with data from a comprehensive functional behavior assessment, consulting teams may identify more than one relevant treatment. In such cases, it may ultimately be time and resource efficient to conduct a brief experimental analysis of treatment options (Martens, Eckert, Bradley, & Ardoin, 1999). *Brief experimental analysis* involves the use of single-case experimental design elements to rapidly compare effects of two or more interventions on a child's behavior (Martens & Gertz, 2009). As such, brief experimental analysis combines the strategies of behavioral assessment discussed earlier with the tactics of experimental analysis into a tool for assessing treatment outcomes. By combining these strategies and tactics, brief experimental analysis allows school consultants to make evidence-based decisions about treatment efficacy prior to full implementation by the consultee.

In practice, a brief experimental analysis involves the collection of one or a small number of "probe" measures of child performance at baseline and under rapidly alternating treatment conditions. The resulting data are graphed in time-series format and examined for clear, visible changes in level across the conditions being evaluated. Once a change is observed, it is common to repeat evaluation of the most effective condition by implementing a brief return to baseline followed by reinstatement of that condition. The treatment evaluation can also be repeated by returning to a previous, ineffective condition rather than baseline as long as reinstatement of the effective condition produces a clear, immediate change in behavior. Figure 7.1 shows the type of data that might be collected in a brief experimental analysis of a child's oral reading fluency. For this analysis, the consultant assembled six grade-level CBM passages equated for difficulty. Following each intervention, the child was assessed on the trained passage associated with that condition using the dependent measure of words read correctly per minute (WCPM). In this example, three interventions believed to improve oral reading rate were compared and included contingent reinforcement, listening passage preview, and repeated readings. Contingent

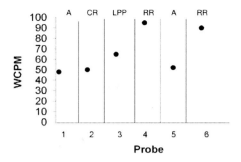

Fig. 7.1 Sample data from a brief experimental analysis (A = baseline; CR = contingent reinforcement; LPP = listening passage preview; RR = reported reading)

reinforcement consisted of allowing the child to choose a prize if she read more WCPM than in the baseline probe. Listening passage preview involved having an adult read the story to the child prior to the child's reading in order to model unknown words. Repeated reading involved having the child practice reading the passage three times with corrective feedback before reading the story a fourth time to assess increases in reading rate (e.g., Martens et al., 2007).

As shown in the figure, the child's oral reading rate at baseline was just below 50 WCPM. The reinforcement condition produced no visible change in performance, whereas a small increase was observed following listening passage preview. In contrast to these two conditions, the child's WCPM nearly doubled from baseline during the repeated reading condition. Reading level dropped following a second baseline probe, and again increased with reinstatement of repeated reading. Data such as these would provide a consulting team with strong evidence to suggest repeated reading as the intervention of choice for this client. Confidence in this intervention could be increased further by conducting a more extended analysis of repeated reading in conjunction with systematic formative evaluation.

Generally speaking, three conditions must be met in order to conduct a brief experimental analysis (Martens, Eckert et al., 1999). First, the consultant or consulting team must be able to collect repeated measures of child behavior or performance under different treatment conditions. Because they are sensitive to short-term instructional changes and capable of being administered repeatedly, CBM probes and systematic observations using event or interval recording are well suited for use in a brief experimental analysis. Second, the interventions being compared must be sufficiently specified to determine when they are being implemented or not and must be capable of producing rapid changes in child behavior. With respect to this latter requirement, some school-based interventions may be slower to take effect (e.g., cognitive behavior modification), involve a gradual learning curve (e.g., small group social skills training), or have effects that cannot be quickly "turned off" (e.g., stimulant medication). It would be difficult to compare such procedures in a brief experimental analysis when significant changes in behavior are expected to result from the first "dose." Conversely, many of the behavior analytic strategies listed in Chap. 8 (e.g., differential reinforcement, time-out, listening passage preview, repeated readings) satisfy these requirements. It is not surprising then that brief experimental analysis has typically been used to evaluate these and other school-based behavioral interventions. Third, the consulting team must adopt a strategy for comparing child behavior under treatment and no-treatment (i.e., baseline) conditions and this comparison must be repeated to increase confidence in the results. Along these lines, several authors have noted that single case experimental designs share many of the same requirements as empirical clinical practice and therefore may be useful in a brief experimental analysis (Hayes, 1981; Martens et al.). To date, the design elements most commonly used in brief experimental analyses have included a brief return to baseline or a previously ineffective condition (i.e., a mini-withdrawal) and the sequential application of increasingly more intensive or intrusive conditions.

Although conducting a brief experimental analysis can be strategically demanding, it represents a powerful assessment technique because of its reliance on the demonstration of experimental control. Experimental control is achieved "when one observes clear, immediate changes in behavior between adjacent conditions that are replicated with the treatment and person being evaluated" (Martens & Gertz, 2009, p. 92). In order to demonstrate experimental control, one must manipulate an independent variable (i.e., introduction and removal of an instructional strategy) while observing changes in a dependent variable (i.e., child performance) under controlled conditions (Johnston & Pennypacker, 1980). If the instructional strategy is effective and if those effects are replicated with the child in question (i.e., experimental control is demonstrated), one can conclude with confidence that instruction caused the desired change. The demonstration of experimental control, therefore, allows for a level of confidence in treatment decisions that is qualitatively different from the use of descriptive assessment strategies (Martens & Eckert, 2000).

To date, brief experimental analysis has been used to evaluate interventions for a variety of behaviors including oral reading fluency (Daly, Martens, Hamler, Dool, & Eckert, 1999; Jones et al., 2009), on- and off-task behavior (Harding, Wacker, Cooper, Millard, & Jensen-Kovalan, 1994; Kern, Childs, Dunlap, Clarke, & Falk, 1994), phoneme blending and segmenting (Daly, Johnson, & LeClair, 2009), and letter writing (Burns, Ganuza, & London, 2009). For example, Burns et al. used a brief experimental analysis followed by an extended analysis to identify an effective intervention to improve a 2nd grade student's letter formation. Using a brief analysis with mini-withdrawals, three interventions were compared for their effects on the percentage of correctly formed letters scored from story starters. The interventions included contingent reinforcement, use of large-boxed graph paper underneath the student's writing paper, and modeling and practice via a cover-copy-compare procedure (e.g., Skinner, McLaughlin, & Logan, 1997). Of the three procedures, cover-copy-compare was shown to be the most effective intervention. Using a multiple baseline design across letter sets, a subsequent extended analysis was conducted confirming the effectiveness of the cover-copy-compare intervention.

Jones et al. (2009) showed how DIBELS screening, brief experimental analysis, extended experimental analysis, and progress monitoring could be combined within a response-to-intervention model. In this study, problem identification consisted of fall and winter DIBELS benchmarking combined with weekly CBM baseline assessments while students received their typical Tier 2 program. Problem analysis consisted of a brief experimental analysis with a mini-withdrawal comparing contingent reward, repeated reading, listening passage preview plus phrase drill error correction, and easier materials. Treatment design consisted of an extended analysis of the most effective intervention package conducted over a 2- or 5-week period. Finally, progress monitoring consisted of weekly pretraining CBM probes that were compared to an aimline (i.e., aspirational performance trajectory) to evaluate slope of improvement. Either repeated reading or phrase drill error correction was identified as the most effective intervention for each of the six participants during the brief experimental analysis. Although additional components were needed during the extended analysis to consistently achieve mastery levels, all but two children showed progress monitoring data that met or exceeded the aim line.

As illustrated by the Jones et al. (2009) study, conducting a brief experimental analysis of school-based interventions reflects the basic tenets of the problem-solving model discussed in Chap. 2 and combines elements of behavioral assessment, systematic formative evaluation, evidence-based practice, and response-to-intervention. As such, brief experimental analysis represents a rigorous approach to treatment design that, in principle, can be used to evaluate interventions at all levels of a tiered service delivery model. Because Tier 3 (targeted) interventions tend to be more individualized, require more resources to implement, and are more intensive, the additional time and effort required to conduct a brief experimental analysis may be more justified at this level. Continuing our focus on effective intervention, in Chap. 8 we discuss the relative efficacy of various intervention alternatives and discuss ways of conceptualizing children's learning and behavior problems that can be used to guide treatment design.

Chapter 8
Selecting Effective School-Based Interventions

A primary goal of school consultation is to help teachers select, implement, and evaluate intervention programs for children's learning and adjustment problems. Accomplishing this goal requires that school consultants go beyond assessment and diagnosis of problems and participate in the treatment process. From our experiences as school consultants and from supervising psychologists-in-training, we realize that being involved in treatment decisions can be both rewarding and challenging. The rewards come from helping a teacher successfully implement an intervention program and seeing dramatic improvements in children's behavior as a result. The challenging aspects of treatment stem from making what are often difficult decisions about program alternatives, tailoring programs to individual case needs, and soliciting judgments of program effectiveness from teachers, parents, and other school personnel.

Although a variety of bases exist for the practice of psychology, we agree with recommendations by the American Psychological Association (APA; Task Force on Promotion and Dissemination of Psychological Procedures, 1995) that, wherever possible, school consultants should use *empirically validated treatments*. The US Department of Education adopted a similar position in the NCLB Act of 2001 by "promoting schoolwide reform and ensuring the access of children to effective, scientifically based instructional strategies and challenging academic content" (Section 1,001. Statement of Purpose, [9], p. 1,440). According to APA criteria, "empirically validated" refers to those treatments whose efficacy has been demonstrated in at least two studies employing randomized group designs or in a series of studies employing replicated single case designs (e.g., ABAB withdrawal). At the heart of both the APA and NCLB recommendations is the requirement that treatment agents base their decisions on *empirical data* gathered through the *scientific method*. Empirical data refers to information about treatment effectiveness that is derived from valid, real world measures collected across a variety of cases. The scientific method, in turn, refers to the use of strategies for ruling out competing explanations when evaluating treatment efficacy (e.g., random assignment to groups, within-subject replication). We believe that together, these principles can minimize the challenging aspects of school-based intervention by (1) increasing one's confidence that a chosen treatment will have the intended effect, and (2) providing a tangible basis for treatment decisions thereby maximizing the accountability of one's professional

W.P. Erchul and B.K. Martens, *School Consultation*, Issues in Clinical Child Psychology,   141
DOI 10.1007/978-1-4419-5747-4_8, © Springer Science+Business Media, LLC 2010

activities (Martens & Eckert, 2000). Finally, data-based decision making is also in keeping with the Ethical Standards of the American Psychological Association, which state that "Psychologists' work is based upon established scientific and professional knowledge of the discipline" (Standard 2.04 Bases for Scientific and Professional Judgments, 2002).

This chapter begins by summarizing research on evidence-based practices in the schools, and in so doing highlights the contributions of applied behavior analysis (ABA) to school-based intervention. Next, we describe several conceptual models, rooted in the principles of ABA, which we have found useful in understanding why children's behavior and academic problems occur and how to relate these causes to treatment. The chapter concludes with a discussion of four key considerations in designing and implementing any school-based intervention program, namely conceptual relevance, treatment strength, treatment integrity, and treatment acceptability.

Effectiveness of Intervention Alternatives

Results from Meta-Analytic Reviews

Teachers and educational support personnel are constantly bombarded with new procedures for instruction and management in what some have called "a never ending cycle of fad, excitement, adoption, poor outcome, disenchantment, [and] new fad" (Delmolino & Romanczyk, 1995, p. 27). For example, during the 1990s, we witnessed the popularization and subsequent criticism of such approaches as facilitated communication for training individuals with autism and whole language instruction for teaching reading. If we add to this list the literally hundreds of treatment approaches that have appeared in the psychological literature (Lipsey & Wilson, 1993), the potential difficulties in selecting an intervention program for any reported problem become clear. Meta-analytic reviews of psychological, educational, and behavioral treatment studies have aided in treatment selection by examining the effectiveness of a wide variety of available procedures (e.g., Kavale, 1990). Consistent with a data-based approach to service delivery, we believe that school consultants should be aware of these findings in order to select intervention programs that have the greatest likelihood of success.

As discussed in Chap. 1, *meta-analysis* is a quantitative approach for summarizing the effects of treatment across large numbers of original research studies (Smith & Glass, 1977). Two meta-analytic reviews have attempted to summarize the effects of a wide range of interventions on educationally relevant outcomes, and therefore seem particularly useful for school consultants (Kavale, 1990; Lipsey & Wilson, 1993). Although a detailed discussion of these reviews would be beyond the scope of the chapter, for comparison purposes the *ES* statistics for 10 common approaches to school-based intervention are presented in Table 8.1. (The interested reader is referred to the original sources for a description of the sampling procedures and the

Table 8.1 Effect Sizes of 10 Common Approaches to School-Based Intervention

Intervention	Mean effect size in standard deviation units
Positive reinforcement procedures	1.17
Instructional cues, student participation, and feedback	0.97
Peer tutoring	0.59
Stimulant medication	0.58
Cognitive behavioral modification	0.47
Cooperative learning	0.30
Modality-based instruction	0.14
Diet intervention	0.12
Perceptual-motor training	0.08
Special class placement	−0.12

number of studies included in each calculation.) These approaches were selected because they span the range of interventions being used in schools today, including behavior analysis, psychopharmacology, ability training, diet intervention, and special education placement. As shown in Table 8.1, the first two behavior analytic procedures are extremely effective (*ES* near 1.0), stimulant medication and peer tutoring are moderately effective (*ES* near 0.60), and the two variations of ability training (i.e., modality-based instruction and perceptual-motor training) are patently ineffective (*ES* approaching 0). What is not obvious from Table 8.1 is that, regardless of the approach taken, most school-based interventions are likely to be more variable in their effects than beneficial (Kavale, 1990). For example, whereas the average *ES* for special class placement in the review by Kavale was −0.12, the standard deviation for this approach was 0.65! The implications of these data for school consultants should be clear. First, whenever possible, we should base our intervention efforts on approaches that have been shown to be effective (i.e., evidence-based practices) and avoid those shown to be ineffective. Second, these findings also suggest that intervention programs need to be tailored to the individual needs of the client and consultee, and that the outcomes of these programs should be systematically evaluated because they cannot be predicted with certainty (Ysseldyke & Marston, 1990). As discussed in Chap. 7, achieving these goals requires that school consultants supplement interview information with more direct assessment data, particularly when conducting a functional behavior assessment. In the next section, we describe several conceptual models that can help school consultants link functional assessment data to effective treatments based on the hypothesized causes of children's problems.

The Role of ABA in School-Based Intervention

ABA refers to "a set of strategies for selecting, implementing, and evaluating intervention programs based on the lawful principles of behavior" (Martens, Witt, Daly, & Vollmer, 1999, p. 638). A fundamental assumption of behavior analysis applied to school-based intervention is that most teaching and management activities require adult–child interaction, and it is through these interactions that children acquire new skills, are encouraged to engage in certain behaviors, or are discouraged from engaging in other behaviors. The possible ways that teachers can influence children's behavior through their interactions are described by basic behavioral principles (e.g., positive reinforcement), whereas intervention programs designed to invoke these principles refer to behavioral procedures (e.g., point systems for positive reinforcement, overcorrection for punishment, graduated guidance to establish stimulus control). Depending on the type and severity of client problems and consultee skill level, more elaborate or structured programs may be necessary to produce desired changes in student behavior.

We believe that a behavior analytic approach is uniquely suited for use by school consultants for a number of reasons. First, a great deal of research has accumulated over the past 30 years demonstrating the effectiveness of behavioral procedures for teaching new skills and responding to children's learning and adjustment problems (Daly, Martens, Skinner, & Noell, 2009; Neef, Iwata, Horner, Lerman, Martens, & Sainato, 2004). As noted above, behavioral procedures are associated with larger average effect sizes when compared with alternative approaches to school-based intervention. Second, most behavioral procedures were designed for use by direct-care providers in homes, schools, residential facilities, and other child-related settings. These procedures can be clearly specified and often require little in the way of extra materials or expenditures for implementation. Third, because behavioral procedures promote learning by manipulating events that immediately precede or follow behavior, they are capable of producing relatively rapid changes in performance. This is an important consideration for any school-based intervention program given the limited time available for instruction in a typical school day.

Conceptual Models of Children's Learning and Behavior Problems

Academic Intervention Models

A focus on what we can observe children *do* (i.e., performance) rather than on what we infer they *know* (i.e., ability) is a hallmark of the ABA approach to instructional intervention (Luiselli, Reed, & Martens, 2010). For example, we saw in Chap. 7 that CBM probes measure children's academic performance in terms of percent correct or number correct per min on tasks involving production-type responses (e.g., reading a passage aloud, writing answers to computation problems). One benefit of using direct, rate-based measures of academic responding is that such measures are sensitive to short-term instructional changes and can be used to monitor children's progress over time. Put another way, direct measures of academic responding allow us to determine how children's performance varies with and is controlled by teachers' instructional practices. In general, these instructional practices can be grouped into two broad categories: *antecedents* that provide information about what to do before responding (e.g., modeling and prompting) and *consequences* that provide information about the correctness of responding (e.g., feedback and reinforcement). The notion of control over responding by instructional stimuli, or *stimulus control*, is the central concept underlying all behavioral approaches to instruction (Daly, Martens, Barnett, Witt, & Olson, 2007).

Whereas stimulus control involves bringing an academic response under the control of specific instructional stimuli (e.g., saying "cat" to the printed letters c-a-t), stimulus generalization involves increasing the range of instructional stimuli that control academic responding (Luiselli et al., 2010). To develop stimulus control, teachers must call learners' attention to cues which signal when a correct response will be reinforced (e.g., the "+" operation sign on a math computation problem) and then differentially reinforce correct responding in the presence of those stimuli (e.g., adding to get the correct answer; Lannie & Martens, 2008; Wolery, Bailey, & Sugai, 1988). To promote stimulus generalization, teachers must differentially reinforce correct responding in the presence of stimuli that differ from those used in training but that contain the same critical elements.

The astute reader will notice two important implications of the principles of stimulus control and stimulus generalization for understanding children's learning problems. First, stimulus control develops gradually over time by requiring students to actively respond and requiring teachers to actively and systematically program for student responding by varying instruction. Second, these principles "represent an instructional sequence in which accurate and fluent responding is first brought under control of key instructional stimuli, strengthened through practice in the presence of these stimuli, and then systematically programmed to occur when these stimuli are varied or occur in different contexts" (Luiselli et al., 2010, p. 1690). Taken together, these implications suggest that academic performance problems can be viewed as deficits in the development of stimulus control or stimulus generalization, which can be overcome by more direct or intensive instruction.

The notion that stimulus control develops gradually over time through active responding is related to another useful model of learning and instruction known as the *instructional hierarchy* (IH; Haring, Lovitt, Eaton, & Hansen, 1978). The IH describes different levels of proficiency in performing a new skill (i.e., a learning hierarchy), each of which is associated with specific instructional procedures that promote mastery at that level (i.e., an instructional hierarchy; Martens & Witt, 2004). The first stage, *acquisition*, refers to a learner's initial attempts to perform a new skill that usually occur with varying degrees of accuracy. The goal at this stage is to increase the accuracy of responding in the presence of key stimuli, and is best promoted by modeling, prompting, and corrective feedback from the instructor. The second stage, *fluency*, refers to increasing the proficiency or speed with which an already acquired skill can be performed. Thus, once a skill can be performed correctly, the focus of instruction shifts to increasing the rate of correct responding. Fluency is best promoted through frequent, brief practice opportunities with reinforcement (e.g., a "beat your score contingency," charting progress) to maintain the learner's motivation. The third stage, *maintenance*, involves fluent performance of a skill but under more demanding practice conditions. Maintenance-level activities require that practice conditions be engineered to promote retention in the absence of practice, endurance over longer work intervals, and stability in the face of distraction

(Johnson & Layng, 1996). The fourth stage, *generalization*, involves the performance of a skill at times or in situations that differ from training. Although conceptually related to maintenance, generalization activities require the learner to respond rapidly to target cues or stimuli in contexts that were not previously trained (e.g., fluent reading with comprehension from newspaper articles versus grade-level readers). The final stage of the instructional hierarchy is termed *adaptation* and involves arranging situations that require modifications in the way the skill itself is performed. Adaptation-level responding represents skill mastery and is associated with creativity.

Although the IH describes how performance of a particular skill improves over time, children's academic problems often involve multiple skill deficits. For example, consider the results of a DIBELS (Good & Kaminski, 2002) screening assessment for a first grader with significant reading problems presented in Table 8.2. For each subtest, the consultant recorded fluency in terms of correct responses per min as well as accuracy in terms of the percentage of correct responses. As shown in the table, the student exhibits low accuracy for sounding out nonsense words (acquisition), is below the fluency benchmark for phoneme segmentation (fluency), and has difficulty transferring gains in oral reading from one first-grade passage to a second passage with a high percentage of word overlap (generalization). Instructional programming for this student will likely need to address deficits in all three skill areas (i.e., nonsense words, phoneme segmentation, oral reading fluency) using instructional techniques that are appropriate to the student's proficiency level in each skill (i.e., acquisition, fluency, generalization). We have found that a *skill area X proficiency level matrix* can be a useful tool for summarizing assessment data about students' academic responding based on the IH.

When seeking consultative assistance, classroom teachers are often concerned with overcoming learning deficits that occur in the early stages of the IH, particularly acquisition. Providing information about how to perform a behavior, or *prompting*, has been shown to be an effective means of promoting the acquisition of a wide range of educationally relevant skills. Prompts refer to any type of assistance provided after a direction is given that increases the likelihood of a correct response. Prompts can vary in their degree of intrusiveness from brief verbal statements or gestures to modeling or pictures to partial or full physical manipulation. The strategic use of prompts is an integral part of errorless learning procedures, the most common of which being prompt and test, prompt and fade, most-to-least prompting, least-to-most prompting, graduated guidance, and time delay prompting (Wolery et al., 1988).

The prompt and test procedure requires a series of prompted trials followed by test trials to assess mastery of a skill. The prompt and fade procedure requires

Table 8.2 A Skill Area X Proficiency Level Matrix in Reading

DIBELS subtest	Benchmark	Fluency	Accuracy (%)	Stage
Letter naming	37	45	98	Established
Phonemes	35	25	85	Fluency
Nonsense words	50	9	50	Acquisition
ORF (1st)	40	25	88	Fluency
ORF (1st HWO)	40	18	80	Generalization

teachers to prompt correct behavior on initial trials, then gradually withdraw the prompt until the behavior can be performed independently. Most-to-least and least-to-most prompting both require sequences of progressively less (or more) intrusive prompts to promote independence. Graduated guidance requires that a teacher remain in close proximity to a child and provide assistance as necessary, whereas time delay prompting calls for progressively longer intervals between the initial direction and the prompt. As the interval increases, the child begins to anticipate the correct response and produces it independently before the prompt is given. These errorless learning procedures have not only been shown to facilitate acquisition but they are also efficient (i.e., require fewer learning trials), promote positive interactions between teachers and students, reduce the opportunities for students to practice errors, and decrease a child's motivation to escape the learning situation by engaging in disruptive or acting out behaviors (Wolery et al., 1988).

The IH and its underlying concepts of stimulus control and stimulus generalization can provide useful models for linking assessment information to effective interventions for children's academic problems. Daly, Witt, Martens, and Dool (1997) proposed a framework that does this directly by relating observed deficits in academic responding (e.g., low accuracy in the target skills) to hypothesized deficits in instruction (e.g., insufficient modeling, prompting, and error correction to establish stimulus control) to potentially relevant evidence-based interventions (e.g., passage previewing, cover-copy-compare). This model summarizes various "gaps" in a child's instructional history by proposing five reasons why children may respond incorrectly to curricular demands in their current classroom; (a) *they don't want to do it* (i.e., correct responding is not reinforced), (b) *they have not spent enough time doing it* (i.e., there were not enough practice opportunities to strengthen stimulus control), (c) *they have not had enough help to do it* (i.e., stimulus control was never established through modeling, prompting, and error correction), (d) *they have not had to do it that way before* (i.e., curricular materials were not varied to program for stimulus generalization), and (e) *it's too hard* (i.e., curricular materials are too difficult) (Luiselli et al., 2010). Instructional interventions that have been shown to be effective for responding to children's academic problems are listed in Table 8.3 (adapted from Martens, 1996).

Behavioral Intervention Models

Similar to the models described above for academic interventions, ABA approaches to classroom behavior problems also involve relating those problems to events surrounding their occurrence. A basic tenet of ABA is that children's classroom behavior, like many forms of behavior, represents *free operant responding* (Daly, Martens, Skinner, & Noell, 2009). This means that "at any moment in the classroom, children are free [to choose] to engage in a variety of alternative behaviors" (Martens, 1992, p. 131). Given these choices, what might predict whether a child will sit quietly and complete work or turn around and disrupt a peer? A considerable amount of both

Table 8.3 Instructional Interventions for Academic Problems

Matching instructional materials to the student's skill level (instructional match)
Modeling and prompting procedures
Cover–copy–compare
Taped words
Discussion of key words
Listening passage preview
Passage preview
Error correction
Word supply
Sentence repeat
Word drill
Phrase drill
Phonic drill
Drill and reinforcement
Response cards
Repeated readings

basic and applied research on free operant responding has shown that choices in behavior can be predicted by the relative amount of reinforcement available for each alternative (e.g., Davison & McCarthy, 1988; Reed, Critchfield, & Martens, 2006). When choosing between nearly identical behaviors and reinforcers, relative rates of responding have been shown to match relative rates of reinforcement or what is known as *the matching law* (Herrnstein, 1961, 1970). When choices involve behaviors that differ in terms of effort and/or reinforcers that differ in terms of quality or immediacy, the matching relation still holds but is biased to favor one behavior over another (Reed & Martens, 2008b).

How might the matching law help school consultants conceptualize and treat classroom behavior problems? First, when we observe behavior problems occurring, it is reasonable to assume that they are being reinforced (perhaps even unwittingly) by teachers or peers in the classroom setting. Although the specific ways in which problem behavior might be reinforced are unique to each child and classroom, categories of reinforcing stimuli are relatively small in number. As discussed in Chap. 7, these categories include *social positive reinforcement* in the form of desired tangible items, attention, or activities, *social negative reinforcement* in the form of escape or avoidance of unpleasant or boring tasks, and *automatic positive and negative reinforcement* in the form of stimulation or relief. Second, many reinforcers for children's classroom behavior are under teacher control, particularly in the elementary grades (Martens, 1992). Thus, teachers often play a role in reinforcing the very problem behaviors they seek help with during consultation. Conversely, teachers can play an equally significant role in reducing problem behavior by manipulating those same reinforcers. Third, when we observe behavior problems occurring frequently, the matching law would suggest that more reinforcement is available for problem vs. appropriate behavior. Intervening in this case involves helping teachers achieve greater consistency in encouraging desired or appropriate behavior while discouraging undesired or inappropriate behavior. This strategy, known as *differential reinforcement*, involves both reinforcement and extinction components and has been shown to be effective for a wide range of problem behaviors (Cataldo, Kahng, DeLeon, Martens, Friman, & Cataldo, 2007; Martens et al., 1999).

Not only do the types of reinforcement potentially maintaining problem behavior differ for each child but children also differ in their preferences for reinforcer [AU1] *dimensions* (Daly, Martens et al., 2009; Neef & Noone Lutz, 2001). These dimensions involve the quality, rate, and delay of reinforcement as well as the response effort required to earn reinforcement. Quality refers to children's preferences for different reinforcing stimuli [e.g., time coloring (low quality) vs. playing video games (high quality)], rate refers to how often tokens or points exchangeable for back-up reinforcers are delivered (e.g., every 1 or 5 min), and delay refers to when the tokens or points can be exchanged (e.g., immediately after a work period, the next day, the end of the week). These three reinforcer dimensions interact with response effort, or how difficult it is to earn reinforcement by engaging in desired or problem behavior, to influence children's choices in behavior. For example, Neef and Noone Lutz assessed the preferences of two students with ADHD for the four reinforcer dimensions just described, and then used this information in designing interventions to reduce classroom disruption. During the reinforcer dimension assessment, each student was able to work math problems from two sets on a computer, each set associated with a different combination of reinforcer dimensions (e.g., low effort/high quality vs. high effort/low quality reinforcers). Based on the relative number of problems chosen, both students preferred lower effort problems, whereas one student also preferred more immediate reinforcement and the other higher quality reinforcement. When the preferred reinforcer dimensions were incorporated into a differential reinforcement program for each student, disruptive behaviors decreased to near zero levels.

In our experience, the classroom environment of children who exhibit frequent behavior problems is often characterized by low rate and low quality reinforcers for work completion (e.g., "Children are just expected to get their work done!") together with high effort tasks (e.g.,. frustration-level material). On the other hand, social reinforcers for problem behavior occur more frequently and are easier to obtain. Under these circumstances, it is little wonder that children choose to engage in problem behavior, foregoing the less preferred consequences for engaging in more difficult academic tasks.

As with ABA approaches to instruction, a variety of procedures can be used to differentially reinforce desired classroom behavior and these procedures differ in the degree of structure they place on the nature and frequency of teacher–student interactions. For example, verbal praise and behavior contracts are both procedures that are designed to invoke the principle of positive reinforcement to increase behavior. Verbal praise requires teachers to reward children whenever possible by stating the desired behavior together with some form of positive evaluation. Behavior contracts require the teacher and child to specify in writing the desired behavior and its required level of performance as well as any consequences that will be given for failing to meet, meeting, or exceeding the performance criterion. Although both procedures can be effective at increasing desired student behavior, some consultees may require the extra guidance and structure of behavior contracts in order to successfully change the way they respond to children. Although a review of these interventions would be beyond the scope of the chapter, Table 8.4 presents a listing of procedures that have been used successfully in responding to children's classroom behavior problems. In general, procedures for increasing desired behavior rely on social positive reinforcement, whereas procedures for decreasing undesired behavior rely on differential reinforcement, type I punishment (presenting something aversive), or type II punishment (withdrawing something positive).

When selecting among the procedures in Table 8.4, it is important to keep the following points in mind. First, whenever possible, it is better to select less intrusive, less structured interventions over those that require more time, energy, and resources or those that constrain teacher–student interactions. Not only is this practice consistent with IDEIA's least restrictive environment mandate, but less complicated procedures can also be implemented more quickly and teachers are more likely to use them for extended periods of time. Second, procedures that reinforce appropriate behavior should be emphasized over those that punish inappropriate behavior. Consistently administered reinforcement encourages children to choose certain behaviors over others and these choices extend through time. Punishment, on the other hand, merely informs children about what not to do, leaving the choice of what to do up to the child's discretion. Third, the overall quality of teacher–student interactions should be taken into consideration before suggesting any school-based intervention. Are the teacher's instructional practices based on an adopted curriculum? Is the difficulty of assigned work appropriate for students' skill levels? Are interactions between the teacher and students generally positive and enjoyable or tense and punitive? Without a foundation of positive teacher–student interactions and instructionally matched materials, many school-based interventions may not have their intended effects or may be too much for teachers to handle given their regular duties. For example, the effectiveness of timeout as a behavior reduction technique is based

Table 8.4 Behavioral Interventions for Classroom Problems

Procedures for increasing desired behavior
Goal setting and feedback
Verbal praise
Self-monitoring (self-reinforcement, self-charting, public posting)
Point systems and token economies
Behavioral contracts
Group contingencies (dependent, independent, interdependent)
Home-based reinforcement
Procedures for decreasing undesired behavior
Verbal reprimands
Ignoring
Response cost
Time-out (contingent observation, exclusionary, isolation)
Overcorrection (positive practice, restitutional)
Differential reinforcement of other behavior (DRO), alternative behavior (DRA), or low rates of responding (DRL)

on a discrepancy between the reinforcing properties of time-in (i.e., time spent in ongoing classroom activities) and time-out (i.e., time spent being excluded from such activities) (Cataldo et al., 2007). If students do not find ongoing classroom activities enjoyable, then time away from these activities contingent on misbehavior is not likely to be perceived as aversive.

Limitations of ABA Approaches to School-Based Intervention

Despite the effectiveness of ABA approaches on average, their use requires teachers to establish clear goals and objectives for student achievement and to define problem behaviors in operational terms (Kazdin, 1994). Oftentimes, however, teachers describe children's behavior problems in vague or general terms (e.g., the child is "lazy" or "poorly motivated"). Researchers have found that teachers also experience difficulty when writing students' individual educational goals, with such goals frequently stated in terms that are either too vague (e.g., "will improve") or too specific (e.g., "will make the long-e sound") to allow for systematic progress monitoring (Shinn, 1989).

ABA approaches require changes in the frequency and type of teacher–student interactions, and as such are only effective at times and in settings when these changes occur. One implication of this is that, in order to be effective, behavioral interventions must be adopted by teachers and implemented as planned on an ongoing basis. Although issues surrounding program implementation are discussed in the following section, the use of any procedure over time may be difficult if it: (1) requires frequent, individual contacts with students; (2) is used in classrooms with high student-to-teacher ratios; or (3) is used by teachers who experience difficulty managing their regular classroom duties. Another implication here is that improvements in behavior that result from intervention are not likely to generalize unless they are explicitly programmed. Generalization programming can be time consuming, and is typically viewed as being less important than initial program implementation. For example, in a review of behavioral treatment studies, Stokes and Baer (1977) found that the most common approach to generalization programming was to implement treatment and *hope* that generalization occurred. Lundervold and Bourland (1988) reported that only 2% of the treatment studies they reviewed programmed for the generalization of treatment effects.

Implementation Issues

A number of factors are likely to influence the effectiveness of any school-based intervention effort. These factors include selecting an intervention that is appropriate for a given problem and which teachers find acceptable, taking steps to maximize treatment strength, and helping teachers implement treatment in the intended fashion. Research in each of these areas is reviewed in the following sections. Because these and other issues that are negotiated during consultation are specific to each case, we believe school consultants should have an appreciation for teachers' roles and responsibilities in schools, their reasons for seeking consultative assistance, and their expectations for receiving such assistance. These issues are the focus of Chap. 9.

Conceptual Relevance

According to Yeaton and Sechrest (1981), *conceptual relevance* refers to the appropriateness of treatment for a given problem. In psychology, determinations of conceptual relevance are typically based on a theoretical relationship between the active treatment components and the causes of the problem. For example, if irrational means-end thinking is seen as the cause of poor social relationships, then insight-oriented therapy, which uses confrontation to challenge such thinking, would have conceptual relevance.

A key assumption of the behavior analytic approach is that classroom behavior problems are caused, or at least maintained, by the basic behavioral principles operating during teacher–student interactions. These possible causes for problem behavior are listed in Table 8.5 along with the behavioral principle underlying each. Because the active treatment components of behavioral interventions can also be specified in terms of basic behavioral principles, the conceptual relevance of these interventions can be determined empirically by conducting a *functional assessment* (Martens & DiGennaro, 2008). As was discussed in Chap. 7, the goal of a functional assessment is to develop hypotheses about why problem behavior is occurring based on a careful examination of the conditions surrounding its occurrence (Martens, Witt et al., 1999). Once these hypotheses are made, interventions can be designed to counteract, eliminate, or weaken the variables believed to be maintaining the problem behavior.

Table 8.5 Why Classroom Behavior problems Occur

Cause	Behavioral Principle
The child has not learned a more appropriate behavior that leads to the same consequence	Skill deficit
More appropriate behaviors are ignored	Extinction
More appropriate behaviors lead to undesired consequences	Punishment
The problem behavior is followed by desired sensory, edible, tangible, social, or activity consequences	Positive reinforcement
The problem behavior allows the child to stop or avoid undesired situations	Negative reinforcement
The problem behavior occurs when it is likely to be reinforced	Stimulus control
The problem behavior occurs when it is initiated by other individuals	Prompting
The problem behavior occurs because the child observed someone else doing it	Modeling

Treatment Strength

Although classroom behavior problems are often maintained by one or more of the principles described in Table 8.5, these principles operate in ways that are unique to each case. One implication of these findings is that a given treatment procedure will not be universally strong for all children, and that interventions need to be tailored to the individual needs of each case. Yeaton and Sechrest (1981) define *treatment strength* as the likelihood prior to implementation that treatment will have the intended effects. As discussed at the beginning of the chapter, one importance indicator of treatment strength is effect size. From a theoretical perspective, treatments will be associated with larger effect sizes if they contain larger amounts of the active treatment component. Thus, if the goal of treatment is to promote self-disclosure through questioning, reflection, and support, then treatment approaches that contain relatively more questions, reflective statements, and supportive comments would be considered "stronger." Similarly, if the goal of treatment is to increase desired behavior using a point system, then the intervention program would be strengthened by delivering points on a more frequent schedule or by arranging more desirable backup reinforcers. In general, reinforcement-based procedures can be strengthened by optimizing the reinforcer dimensions of quality, rate, delay, and response effort.

There are several dimensions of treatment strength that can be applied to almost any psychological intervention, and these should also be considered when implementing school-based procedures (Gresham, 1991). First, intervention programs tend to be stronger if they are implemented for longer periods of time or with greater intensity (e.g., continuously throughout the school day versus 1 hr in the morning). Second, interventions are likely to be stronger if the procedures for their implementation and the responsibilities of participants are clearly specified. Third, treatment programs produce greater effects if they are implemented or assisted by individuals with special expertise and experience in using the procedure. These latter two points are particularly relevant to school consultation because they emphasize the importance of communicating program requirements clearly to teachers and supporting teachers' implementation efforts using the strategies described in Chap. 6.

Treatment Acceptability

Because teachers maintain primary responsibility for implementing school-based intervention programs, whether they agree with these programs in principle or view them as acceptable is likely to influence program success (Reimers, Wacker, & Koeppl, 1987; Witt & Elliott, 1985). *Treatment acceptability* refers to judgments by teachers about whether treatment is fair, reasonable, or intrusive, appropriate for a given problem, and consistent with notions of what treatment should be (Kazdin, 1980). Research in this area has demonstrated that both preservice and experienced teachers view treatment acceptability as a multifactor construct that includes such considerations as appropriateness, potential risk to the target child, time and skill required for implementation, and effects on other children in the classroom (Witt & Martens, 1983). Acceptability has also been shown to differ by virtue of the procedure being recommended, with procedures that reinforce desired behavior being viewed more favorably than those that punish undesired behavior (Witt, Martens, & Elliott, 1984). Finally, a number of variables other than type of treatment have been examined for their effects on acceptability ratings including problem severity and type (Elliott, Witt, Galvin, & Peterson, 1984; Kazdin, 1980); status of the rater (Witt & Robbins, 1985); the way the intervention is described (Witt, Moe, Gutkin, & Andrews, 1984); gender and race of the teacher (Elliott, Turco, & Gresham, 1987); the student's disability (Epstein, Matson, Repp, & Helsel, 1986); and years of teaching experience (Witt et al., 1984).

These findings provide a number of directions for tailoring suggested intervention alternatives to teachers' preferences. Although teachers' preferences should be taken into consideration during plan development, we do not believe that judgments of acceptability should be used as the sole criterion for program selection. First, treatment acceptability is not an outcome variable in the consultation process but rather a predictor of more important outcomes such as treatment integrity and effectiveness. As a predictor variable, pretreatment ratings of acceptability have a generally weak correlation with actual plan implementation (Martens & McIntyre, 2009; Reimers, Wacker, Cooper, & DeRaad, 1992; Sterling-Turner & Watson, 2002). Second, a defining feature of the school consultation model presented in this book is that change is difficult and that many of us resist change even when it may be in the best interest of the children for whom we have responsibility. Thus, when faced with consultee resistance to a suggested intervention, one approach is to work together with the consultee to develop an equally effective but more acceptable intervention program. An alternative approach, which was discussed at length in Chap. 3, is to attempt to reduce consultee resistance by strategically altering teachers' attitudes and perceptions.

Treatment Integrity

Many times, the realities of classroom instruction require teachers to alter an intervention program as discussed during the problem analysis interview. The extent to which a plan is implemented as intended is referred to as *treatment integrity* (McIntyre, Gresham, DiGennaro, & Reed, 2007). Because most behavioral interventions were designed for use by direct care providers rather than expert clinicians, one might expect that adherence to treatment guidelines is routinely assessed, but such has not been the case. In a review of behavioral intervention studies published between 1968 and 1980, Peterson, Homer, and Wonderlich (1982) found that only 20% of the studies sampled provided data concerning treatment integrity. In a review of treatment studies addressing behavior problems in children, Gresham et al. (1993a) found that only 15.8% of studies between the years 1980 and 1990 reported treatment integrity data.

Although several authors have argued for the need to assess treatment integrity in research, this practice is even more important when treatment plans are being implemented within an indirect service model like school consultation (Martens & McIntyre, 2009). During consultation, plans are developed primarily through a series of brief, face-to-face meetings between the consultant and consultee. Oftentimes, these meetings may be insufficient for communicating clearly the various procedural details of an intervention, particularly if the intervention requires activities with which teachers have had little or no prior experience. Moreover, when teachers knowingly deviate from a plan as discussed, they often do so for good reason. Assessing treatment integrity can help identify those aspects of a plan that were difficult to implement, focus efforts to revise the plan, and ultimately lead to greater acceptance and use of the plan over time.

Treatment integrity can be discussed from two perspectives as it relates to school consultation. On the one hand, it is meaningful to talk about the integrity of the consultation process, or the extent to which the various interviewing objectives are successfully addressed during the PII, PAI, and PEI. In a study by Fuchs and Fuchs (1989), consultation services were provided to 24 teachers of difficult-to-teach students in four schools. Evaluation of consultation integrity revealed that the interviewing process occurred as planned in more than 80% of the cases. This high degree of process integrity, however, was attributed to the consultants' use of standard interviewing protocols. In the absence of such protocols and prior to training in the consultation process, McDougall, Reschly, and Corkery (1988) found that only between 6 and 47% of consultants met any single PII objective. On the other hand, it is also meaningful to talk about the integrity of the intervention process itself. Although minor deviations from treatment protocols are to be expected, there comes a point when changes in the treatment procedure are so extensive that the treatment principle is sacrificed. For example, suppose the decision is made to implement a program whereby a child earns one point for each in-class assignment completed correctly, and these points are to be exchanged for special privileges at the end of each day. After 2 weeks of implementation, you discover that the teacher's busy schedule has precluded time at the end of the day for exchanging points, and that the child is completing less work than ever. Without the opportunity to exchange what are essentially meaningless points for desired privileges, the principle of positive reinforcement never occurred when the teacher deviated from the plan. In the absence of the support strategies discussed in Chap. 6, one can generally assume that teachers' implementation integrity will be low, thereby decreasing the effectiveness of school-based interventions.

Part III
Key Participants in Consultation

Chapter 9
Teachers as Consultees

Although the school consultant may assist many different consultees – including administrators, counselors, and parents – he or she is most likely to consult with teachers (Costenbader, Swartz, & Petrix, 1992). Furthermore, given the fact that most school consultation occurs in elementary schools (Alpert & Yammer, 1983; Gresham & Kendell, 1987), it is reasonable to assume that the consultant's most frequent consultee will be an elementary schoolteacher. For this reason, in Chap. 9, we shall focus to a large extent on characteristics of teachers who have been assigned to kindergarten through grade 6 classrooms as well as aspects of consultation that occur at these grade levels. Chapter topics that pertain to the general enterprise of teaching are the complexity of classroom teaching; rewards and challenges of teaching; and teacher recruitment and retention issues. Other topics regarding teachers and consultation are: why teachers seek consultation; teacher expectations for consultation; how teachers view and respond to student problems prior to consultation; and characteristics that differentiate teachers who participate in consultation from those who do not. The final section of Chap. 9 presents potential strategies to maximize the effectiveness of consultation with teachers (e.g., adapting consultation methods to fit teachers' daily schedules; working with problem-solving teams (PSTs) as in RTI; and enhancing knowledge and skill transfer back to the classroom). A major point of this chapter is that, although most teachers today are dedicated and want to help students to succeed, often they are not assisted sufficiently in their efforts to do so. Therefore, it is incumbent upon the school consultant to offer support to teachers via consultation so that they may work effectively within the constraints of their role.

Perspectives on Teachers and Teaching

The Complexity of Classroom Teaching

To say the work of a classroom teacher is complex is both accepted fact and gross understatement. Furthermore, for students, the difference between being taught by an effective teacher and less-than-effective teacher can result in a full grade level of

W.P. Erchul and B.K. Martens, *School Consultation*, Issues in Clinical Child Psychology,   159
DOI 10.1007/978-1-4419-5747-4_9, © Springer Science+Business Media, LLC 2010

achievement in one school year! (Hanushek, 1992). Though it is not possible in this chapter to include a detailed description of what goes on in an elementary school classroom (see Good & Brophy, 2000), consider briefly what an effective teacher accommodates on a regular basis:

1. *Multidimensionality.* A multitude of diverse tasks and events happen in the classroom, and a teacher is expected to keep track of them. For example, student work is assigned, monitored, collected, and assessed; records are kept; and schedules are followed. Furthermore, a single teacher behavior can produce very different consequences. For instance, allowing a boy with an articulation disorder the opportunity to give a lengthy oral response may increase his motivation to succeed, but decrease the interest and motivation of the rest of the class.
2. *Simultaneity.* There are many events that occur at the same time in classrooms. During direct instruction, for example, an elementary teacher often simultaneously presents content, monitors student comprehension, and manages student behavior.
3. *Immediacy.* The rate at which classroom events unfold is extremely quick. One indicator of this rapid pace is that an elementary teacher may participate every day in as many as 1,000 face-to-face exchanges with students (Jackson, 1968).
4. *Unpredictable and public classroom climate.* Unanticipated events occur regularly in classrooms, often prompting teachers to respond quickly and decisively. Also, how a teacher treats a particular student is usually witnessed by many other students; given this public atmosphere, students often can infer how the teacher feels toward their classmates.
5. *History.* As the school year progresses, a class develops certain norms and common understandings. Occurrences early in the school year also may influence classroom functioning later in the year. For example, a particular boy's severe outbursts of disruptive behavior that occurred when school first began now may cue students to stop whatever they are doing and return to their seats so the teacher can act more swiftly and efficiently to place the boy in time-out (Doyle, 1985).

Good and Brophy (2000) argued incisively that, because teaching is complex, teachers often lack a full awareness of their behavior and, even if aware of their behavior, they may be unaware of its effects. Major obstacles to greater teacher awareness include the rapid pace of classroom events, preservice training that often fails to equip teachers with specific teaching techniques and skills for analyzing classroom behavior, and lack of a consistent means (e.g., mentoring) to provide teachers with corrective feedback. Unfortunately, many classroom problems can result when teachers lack insight into their professional actions, such as unintentional teacher domination of classroom communication, lowered emphasis on the meaning of concepts presented in instruction, overuse of factual questions, fewer attempts to motivate students, and an overreliance on repetitive seatwork (Good & Brophy, 2000). It would seem that a consultant with an appropriate background could offer valuable assistance with many of these issues.

The Rewards of Teaching

In 1964, Lortie (1975) undertook his classic sociological study of teachers in Dade County, Florida. Using survey and interview methodologies, his major interest was to examine patterns of outlooks and feelings that are unique to teachers and that distinguish the teaching profession from others. In 1984, Cohn and Kottkamp (1993) replicated and expanded on Lortie's original research. This section of the chapter draws on the conceptualizations and findings of these investigators. Although we recognize the datedness of both studies, to our knowledge there has not been a more recent published replication of either.

The rewards associated with the work of teaching may be categorized as extrinsic, ancillary, and intrinsic or psychic (Lortie, 1975). *Extrinsic rewards* relate to the "earnings" associated with teaching and may be defined more specifically as salary, status, and power or influence over others. In both the 1964 and 1984 samples, only about 14% of teacher respondents indicated that, of all possible extrinsic rewards, they derived the most satisfaction from their earned salary. Extrinsic rewards viewed as much more important to both groups were the respect received from others and the opportunity to wield some influence. Although there were some differences, about one-third of each group endorsed each of these responses as a major basis of their job satisfaction. Interestingly, in a trend that appears to run counter to that observed in the larger US society, almost 28% of the 1984 sample claimed they derived *no satisfaction* from any extrinsic rewards associated with teaching (Cohn & Kottkamp, 1993).

Ancillary rewards are objective characteristics of the work situation that some teachers may regard as rewarding but others may not. For example, the rather flexible work schedule of teaching, which includes holidays and summers off, may serve as an ancillary reward for a mother with school-age children but may not be perceived as rewarding by an unmarried male. Across the 20-year period spanning the two research efforts, there was an interesting trend relative to ancillary rewards: whereas in 1964, only 23% of respondents felt that the work schedule of teaching was a significant positive feature, and by 1984 over 35% of respondents saw it this way.

Intrinsic or psychic rewards consist of entirely subjective evaluations of the work situation that teachers find rewarding. By far the most common intrinsic reward mentioned by teachers is the satisfaction stemming from the realization that they have successfully instructed a student or group of students. In both samples, 86% of respondents indicated that this outcome was their most satisfying psychic reward. The next most pleasing psychic reward, mentioned by about 7% in both groups, was the opportunity to associate with students and to develop relationships with them.

Across the three types of work rewards, intrinsic or psychic rewards are easily the most important to teachers. In the 1964 sample, about 76% of respondents chose psychic rewards as most important, compared with about 12% each for extrinsic and ancillary. In the 1984 sample, the percentage of respondents selecting psychic rewards as most important dropped slightly to about 70%, and ancillary rewards had increased to about 18% (Cohn & Kottkamp, 1993; Lortie, 1975).

Major Challenges Facing Teachers Today

A study of the rewards of teaching, however, necessarily gives way to a presentation of less positive aspects of this occupational role. In addition to problems of the bureaucratic structure of schools and schooling discussed in Chap. 4, we present four other significant challenges for teachers identified by Cohn and Kottkamp (1993) and commented on by others since then.

The Decline and Dearth of Extrinsic Rewards

A teacher's salary may be best viewed as both substance and symbol. Taking salary as substance, it is useful to consider the following:

1. Classroom teacher salaries are 12–14% lower than the salaries of nonteachers in 16 comparable occupations (Allegretto, Corcoran, & Mishel, 2004).
2. The 2000 US census data revealed the average annual earnings of teachers to be approximately $38,000 versus about $60,000 for nonteachers in comparable occupational roles (Taylor, 2008).
3. The 1999 salary of the modal teacher (someone with about 16 years of experience) was $40,574. Engineers with comparable experience earned an average of $68,294; computer systems analysts, $66,782. Thus, the earnings gap that develops over time between teachers and other professionals is huge (Gursky, 2000/2001).

Taking salary as a symbol, it is important to note that salary and social status are tied closely together in contemporary US society. Unfortunately for teachers, lower salaries suggest lower social status (Cohn & Kottkamp, 1993).

Students as Less Motivated and More Difficult to Teach

Teachers interviewed by Cohn and Kottkamp expressed great surprise and even shock at students' attitudes toward school and learning. Some teachers had been threatened by students, and others were appalled by the widespread student apathy. Nearly all respondents attributed student motivational problems to changes in the family structure, particularly the aspects related to divorce and single-parenting, as well as the loss of parent–child quality time in dual-earner families. Teachers also believed that student drug use (particularly cocaine) and the materialism inherent in US culture contributed to problems in motivating students.

Updating this list of student-related concerns voiced by Cohn and Kottkamp's teachers, we would add the growing problem of school violence (Jimerson & Furlong, 2006), and student-on-teacher assaults in particular. For example, during the 1999–2000 academic year, over 300,000 elementary and secondary schoolteachers in the US were threatened with injury by a student, and 135,000 were physically attacked (DeVoe, Peter, Noonan, Snyder, & Baum, 2005).

Parents as Unsupportive

Although some of Cohn and Kottkamp's respondents who taught in suburban school systems praised parents for their support, the majority instead cited parents for their failure to provide it. Teachers apparently view the concept of parental support bimodally, seeing problems with parents who show either too little interest or involvement or, on the other hand, too much interest or involvement. In the first case, teachers noted a lack of support with respect to parents' failures to attend scheduled school meetings, to monitor completion of homework, to take an interest in children's report cards, and to take notice of other critical school events. Parental reactions to teacher telephone calls reporting discipline problems also shocked many teachers; whereas parents previously would have generally "backed up" teachers' disciplinary actions, teachers could no longer count on them to do so. In the second case, teachers characterized many parents who displayed too much interest or involvement as unsupportive. For example, some overinvolved parents were said to make excuses for their children, attempt to get them out of work, or even lie for them. Wealthy parents allegedly were able to exercise their influence to change grades, classes, programs, and school policies.

Though the described parent/teacher relational dynamics are still valid today, it has been proposed that recent school reform (e.g., the decentralization of school operations, NCLB) has changed power relations between parents and teachers. For example, teachers still enjoy parents' involvement in school activities but also feel greater pressure because empowered parents now tend to scrutinize teachers' work more intently (Addi-Raccah & Arviv-Elyashiv, 2008).

Increased Vulnerability

In Cohn and Kottkamp's sample of teachers, 93% saw themselves as more vulnerable professionally at that time than in the past. For 51% of the group, this increased vulnerability was connected to the possibility of personal liability in lawsuits over student rights and welfare. Some elementary schoolteachers, for instance, were fearful of groundless accusations of student molestation and abuse. Another major source of vulnerability was the school system's expectation that they be held accountable for student acquisition of basic skills as reflected in standardized test scores. Of course, today's reality is that under NCLB, teachers *are* accountable for student achievement, and a recent national poll indicated that 67% of the general public supports replacing teachers at schools that fail to meet student achievement standards for five consecutive years (Howell, West, & Peterson, 2007).

From this discussion, it may be concluded that teachers tend to view their work to be more difficult and less rewarding than it was previously. In particular, the last three challenges illustrate the decline of psychic rewards for teachers. Knowing that psychic rewards hold the greatest importance for teachers (Cohn & Kottkamp, 1993; Lortie, 1975), this situation is very serious indeed. Facing these challenges without adequate support is likely to increase stress, which can result in burnout, which in turn, may lead one to decide to abandon the teaching profession altogether.

Teacher Recruitment, Attrition, and Retention

The demand for teachers currently is high and shortages are apparent in much of the US, especially in inner cities and rural communities (Guarino, Santibañez, & Daley, 2006). Although figures have varied somewhat over time, annual teacher turnover rates have been reported as 12.4% for public schoolteachers and 18.9% for private schoolteachers, with turnover defined as a mixture of leaving the teaching profession altogether and migrating to another school (Ingersoll, 2001). Attrition has been shown to follow a *U*-shaped curve with respect to age, with predictable departures of younger (i.e., within the first 5 years) and older (i.e., nearing retirement age) teachers (Guarino et al., 2006). Moreover, the cost of replacing teachers who leave is quite expensive, estimated at 30% of a departing teacher's salary, which, for the year 2000, was estimated at about $2.2 billion in the US (Borman & Dowling, 2008).

It is clear that recruitment and retention of quality teachers is a significant problem and one that is expected to grow (Darling-Hammond, Berry, Haselkorn, & Fideler, 1999). Strategies implemented by school systems to address this problem have included: (1) mounting aggressive outreach programs that target university teacher education programs; (2) offering financial incentives such as signing bonuses, low-interest mortgages, housing allowances, and day care subsidies; (3) establishing policies that allow retired teachers to return to teaching without losing full pension benefits; (4) making full use of nontraditional/alternative teacher certification programs to "grow" and retain teaching staffs; (5) increasing administrative and mentoring support; and (6) providing teachers with greater influence, autonomy, and/or control over their daily work (Guarino et al., 2006; Supply and Demand: The Teacher Shortage, 2001).

Implications for the School Consultant

From these selected perspectives on teachers and teaching, one is led to conclude that many teachers need and deserve support in their professional role beyond that provided already by our nation's school systems. Key factors underlying this conclusion include: teaching is a complex activity, the salary is not sufficient compensation for the demands of the job, the status associated with teaching is lower than that for other occupations requiring similar education, preservice training is said to fall short in providing specific and pragmatic classroom strategies, quality mentoring experiences are not always available, students and parents today appear to be less cooperative and more problematic, teachers perceive themselves as more vulnerable to lawsuits than before, educational reforms assume that it is teachers who are to blame for lower student achievement and thus must be held accountable, and adequate teaching resources and physical facilities often are unavailable. To this list we add other factors raised in Chap. 4, including Paradox 2 of school consultation: Most teachers want to be involved in responding to children's learning and adjustment problems, but schools are run in ways that limit this involvement.

Taken together, these factors constrain what teachers are able to accomplish in their professional role. *The experienced school consultant thus recognizes that a realistic goal is to help consultees function better within the constraints of their role rather than to expect that his or her assistance somehow will allow consultees to overcome these constraints.* We advocate this as a realistic goal of school consultation primarily because truly overcoming these constraints would require massive changes in the culture of schools (Sarason, 1996; Wyner, 1991), the culture of teaching (Ost, 1991), and certain trends in contemporary US culture (e.g., low teacher salaries despite the high importance placed on public education). Attempts at school reform, including those that direct extensive resources to individual schools (e.g., Scott, 2001), have demonstrated how changes along these lines can be made. These types of activities, however, are still fairly rare.

Perspectives on Teachers and School Consultation

Stepping back from these larger, societal issues regarding teachers and teaching, we now examine various aspects of school consultation from the teacher's standpoint.

Three Views on Why Teachers Seek Consultation

Although a teacher may acknowledge a work-related problem in approaching a consultant, the specific reasons why there is a need for assistance may not be apparent "on the surface." Assuming teacher participation in consultation is generally voluntary rather than forced (cf. Harris & Cancelli, 1991), we offer three different though overlapping perspectives on this issue.

The first view comes from the behavioral approach to consultation, presented in Chaps. 5 and 6. The behavioral perspective, very much embedded within a problem-solving tradition (Bergan, 1995), regards consultee difficulties as arising from a lack of knowledge and/or skills. Along these lines, as consultants we have found that teachers may readily acknowledge their current problems as stemming from a failure to understand the classroom situation or an inability to do what it takes to solve the problem at hand. Accordingly, the focus of behavioral consultation often involves the direct, explicit remediation of knowledge or skill deficits in the consultee and/or client. The major approaches to intervention within behavioral consultation thus tend to involve education and skill development for consultees, and these approaches plus a variety of behavioral interventions for clients (Bergan, 1977; Bergan & Kratochwill, 1990; Martens & DiGennaro, 2008).

A second view regarding why teachers seek consultation takes the behavioral view and adds other possibilities to it. Within his model of mental health consultation, Caplan (1963, 1970; Caplan & Caplan, 1993/1999) posited four sources of consultee difficulty: lack of knowledge, lack of skill, lack of self-confidence, and lack of objectivity. To the extent that supervisory and administrative mechanisms are functioning poorly in schools, Caplan agreed with the behavioral view and asserted that most teacher difficulties probably result from a lack of knowledge and/or skill (Erchul, 1993b). He then added that a consultee's low self-confidence also may explain impaired work performance under the described organizational conditions. However, when supervision and administration practices are functioning well in an organization, Caplan (1970) stated that a lack of objectivity is more likely to explain consultees' work difficulties. In contrast to knowledge or skill deficits, highly trained and competent consultees rarely have the insight that lowered objectivity is hindering their effectiveness.

When a loss of objectivity is the hypothesized source of the problem, consultees may harbor unconscious themes or irrational assumptions (Caplan, 1963, 1970). While implementing mental health consultation with elementary schoolteachers, Robinson and Falconer (1972) discovered these irrational assumptions held by their teachers:

1. The teacher who is competent and working to capacity can do the job without help.
2. A good teacher should be able to work with any and every child.
3. The teacher must be friendly at all times.
4. The teacher next year will blame me if the student has not learned all he is supposed to know.
5. If I fail in a particular area, I will be revealed as the failure I always feared I was.

The question of whether teachers display a greater number of problems related to a lack of skills, knowledge, confidence, or objectivity has not been answered satisfactorily, nor do we believe that it is a critical question for most consultants. In the only empirical study, Gutkin (1981) examined daily logs from ten advanced school psychology graduate student consultants in order to determine the relative distribution of consultation cases into the four categories. In reviewing 171 consultation cases, Gutkin found that 38, 27, 27, and 7% of the cases resulted from a lack of consultee knowledge, skill, confidence, and objectivity, respectively. Although these findings suggest that objectivity rarely is viewed as the source of teachers' difficulties, Gutkin's consultants, trained in behavioral consultation, were simply more likely to attribute consultee problems to knowledge or skill deficits than to lowered objectivity (Conoley & Wright, 1993). To the individual consultant, then, the relative distribution of cases into the four categories is less important than an understanding of which reasons are most relevant to the case he or she is currently handling. The school consultant also must be alert to the strong possibility that more than one reason may best explain teacher difficulties.

Accepting the validity of the first two perspectives, but also acknowledging the literature on teachers and teaching reviewed earlier, as well as the content of Chap. 4, we present a third perspective. Increasingly, we believe that many teachers approach consultants due to a *lack of support* from the schools and society. This perspective recognizes the value of skills, knowledge, confidence, and objectivity as explanations for individual consultee problems, but it also places this issue into a larger sociological

and career path context that directly acknowledges the occupational role of "teacher."
As Darling-Hammond et al. (1999) noted:

> What has been lacking in most districts, states, and at the national level is a framework for
> policy that creates a coherent infrastructure of recruitment, preparation, and *support
> programs* [emphasis added] that connect all aspects of the teacher's career continuum
> into a teacher development system that is linked to national and local education goals
> (pp. 184–185).

Also undergirding our third perspective is an historical characterization of teaching
as a lonely profession, with teachers expressing feelings of isolation in their work
(Jackson, 1968; Sarason, 1996). Thus, an elementary teacher who spends most of
his or her day interacting with young children may have a strong desire to speak
with a caring, supportive adult. Teacher isolation is another indicator of the clear
value of supporting teachers through consultation services.

Teacher Expectations for Consultation

In examining teachers' expectations for consultation, we rely on a sampling of
research that has documented teacher perceptions of school consultation. Some
of this literature was presented earlier in Chap. 3, including investigations by Erchul
(1987), Fuchs, Fuchs, Bahr, Fernstrom and Stecker (1990b), Erchul et al. (2009),
and Erchul, Raven, and Whichard (2001). Here we present results from five additional
studies relevant to this topic.

Gutkin (1980) surveyed 171 teachers from 12 different schools in order to
understand their perceptions of consultation following the provision of consultative
services to them by advanced school psychology graduate students over a 14-week
period. Important results were: (1) 88% of teachers believed it was desirable to have
a psychological consultant available at school, and only 4% viewed it as undesir-
able; (2) 69% felt consultation services were more effective than traditional assessment services offered by the psychologist, and only 4% indicated consultation was
less effective; and (3) 81% of teachers agreed that working with a consultant would
result in an improvement of their professional skills, and only 6% disagreed with
the likelihood of this outcome. These robust findings indicate clear teacher support
for school-based consultation services. Importantly, Gutkin also noted that these
results do not vary as a function of the demographic characteristics of the schools
or communities from which he sampled teacher opinions.

In a follow-up investigation, Gutkin (1986) polled 191 teachers from 24 schools
with respect to their reactions to consultation services that were provided by graduate
student consultants. Stepwise regression analyses were conducted to predict teachers'
perceptions of several key outcomes, including the utility of the ideas and programs
generated as a result of consultation, improvement in their professional skills, and
overall consultant effectiveness. The utility of ideas and programs developed in
consultation was best predicted by a model comprised of the following entry of variables: consultant knowledge and application of psychological principles, consultant

communication skills, consultant interest, and enthusiasm ($R^2 = 0.48$). The best models for predicting both teachers' improvement in professional skills and consultant effectiveness were composed of variables having the following order of entry: consultant knowledge and application of psychological principles, consultant communication skills, and teacher understanding of the consultation process (R^2s = 0.52 and 0.64, respectively).

Using a similar method of data collection, Hughes, Grossman, and Barker (1990) investigated how elementary schoolteachers' self-efficacy and outcome expectations affect their participation in and evaluation of consultation. *Self-efficacy* refers to a person's confidence that he or she can accomplish a specific task or solve a given problem; *outcome expectancy* refers to an individual's estimate that a particular behavior or activity (e.g., consultation) will lead to certain outcomes (Bandura, 1977). Hughes et al.'s major results were: (1) a significant negative correlation existed between self-efficacy and outcome expectancy ($r = -0.37$), suggesting that teachers with higher self-efficacy scores have lower expectations that consultation can really help them; (2) a trend was found between self-efficacy and teacher reported change in their professional performance ($r = -0.44$, $p = 0.11$), suggesting that teachers with high self-efficacy are less likely to report changing their approach to handling classroom problems following consultation; and (3) a significant correlation was found between teacher outcome expectancy and teacher evaluation of consultation ($r = 0.42$), suggesting that teachers having high positive expectations for consultation perceive the consultant as more effective.

Investigating relationships between processes and outcomes of school consultation, Erchul, Hughes, Meyers, Hickman, and Braden (1992) used an interpersonal perspective in which consultee and consultant perceptions on the same issues were compared and then correlated with several outcome measures. Sixty-one advanced graduate students engaged in problem-solving consultation with one consultee each, after which perceptions of the process were obtained from both parties. Key findings were: (1) a variable based on the extent to which, within a particular dyad, the consultant understood the consultee's role and vice versa was significantly related to consultee perceptions of both the beneficial nature of consultation ($r = 0.38$) and consultant effectiveness ($r = 0.45$); and (2) the degree to which consultant and consultee saw themselves as a "team" was significantly related to consultee perceptions of the beneficial nature of consultation ($r = 0.56$), growth in consultee competence ($r = 0.42$), client improvement ($r = 0.34$), and consultant effectiveness ($r = 0.57$). Given these findings, Erchul et al. reasoned that more favorable outcomes in consultation result from consultants and consultees agreeing on their respective roles and seeing their actions as stemming from teamwork.

In a recent analog experimental study using videotaped consultation vignettes, Tysinger, Tysinger, and Diamanduros (2009) gathered teacher perceptions of *collaborative-directive* versus *collaborative-nondirective* consultation approaches. These researchers operationalized *collaboration* as the consultant being "receptive to consultee input throughout" (p. 324), and *directiveness* in ways similar to Erchul (1987) and Erchul and Chewning (1990). Consistent with studies cited in Chap. 3, Tysinger et al.'s 202 teacher respondents rated the collaborative-directive consultant as more effective than the collaborative-nondirective consultant. Moreover, teachers perceived the intervention developed in the collaborative-directive consultation condition as significantly more acceptable than the same intervention developed in the collaborative-nondirective condition. The authors noted, "consultees appear to respond positively to the increased consultant input of the collaborative-directive consultation" (p. 329).

Results of these five studies of teacher perceptions of consultation suggest several conclusions regarding teacher expectations for consultation. In general, teachers look forward to consultation, viewing it as more effective than traditional psychological assessment and capable of enhancing their professional skills. However, teachers who have a high degree of self-efficacy may have lower expectations regarding the beneficial nature of consultation, and may see themselves as not changing their usual approach to solving classroom problems following consultation. Teacher expectations regarding the usefulness of ideas produced in consultation, the probability his or her skills will be upgraded, and the effectiveness of the consultant seem to be linked to a perception of the consultant as a skilled communicator who understands psychological principles and knows how to apply them. Also, the extent to which consultant and teacher see themselves as a team appears to enhance teacher perceptions of similar outcomes in consultation. Finally, teachers rate consultants who exhibit a collaborative-directive style as more effective than those who exhibit a collaborative-nondirective style. Interventions generated within collaborative-directive consultation are also viewed as more acceptable than those generated within collaborative-nondirective consultation.

What Teachers Do Before Seeking Consultation

This issue may be recast as the question, "How do teachers view and respond to student problems?" Research findings indicate that teachers prefer to take an active role in attempting to resolve problems before a consultant is called for assistance. For example, most elementary teachers (96%) want to be involved in responding to children's learning and adjustment problems (Gutkin, 1980), and they often attempt two or three types of interventions on their own before asking for help (Ysseldyke et al., 1983). Furthermore, of the interventions that might be implemented in the classroom, teachers rate as highest those that they direct themselves (Algozzine, Ysseldyke, Christenson, & Thurlow, 1983).

Despite elementary teachers' strong interest in intervening, research suggests that they typically do not assess student problems well or intervene in a systematic way on their own. For example, in studying teacher responses to prereferral intervention cases, Ysseldyke et al. (1983) noted that teachers tend to use interventions that are not related to the original reasons for referral, implement interventions for an unspecified time period, and employ few evaluation measures that document behavior change. Also, Algozzine et al. (1983) had 174 elementary teachers rate 40 intervention choices for each of three student problems: immaturity, perceptual difficulties, and unmanageability. One key result was that the type of student problem was unrelated to teachers' choice of intervention, leading Algozzine et al. to two conclusions: (1) detailed assessment data apparently have little value in teachers' intervention planning, and (2) the selection of interventions by teachers may be the result of an unsystematic process.

From this discussion, it may be seen that before requesting consultation, a teacher typically has tried several interventions that have been unsuccessful for various reasons. When the teacher then approaches a consultant, he or she is often very frustrated because of the lack of prior success and possibly because the problem has gotten even worse. Though a lack of knowledge or skills may account for the teacher's inability to resolve the problem, his or her rising frustration level may result in a failure to see the problem with reasonable objectivity. A consultant therefore needs to be aware of how the history of a problem may constitute a crisis (Caplan, 1964) for the teacher and perhaps focus initial attention on the support and development task rather than rush into the problem-solving task.

Factors that Distinguish Teachers Who Participate in Consultation from Those Who Do Not

Consultation may be of benefit to many teachers but, in most cases, teachers first need to seek out the service. Along these lines, Stenger, Tollefson, and Fine (1992) sought to determine which variables differentiate elementary teachers who have engaged in consultation from those who have not. Stenger et al. surveyed a randomly selected group of 500 female, predominantly white elementary schoolteachers and obtained 352 usable questionnaires. Of this number, 186 teachers had consulted with a psychologist within the past 10 months, and 166 others had not. A stepwise discriminant function analysis was conducted to determine the variables that offered the greatest degree of discrimination between the two groups. A single discriminant function, correctly classifying 73% of the sample, contained five significant predictor variables.

In order, the variables that distinguished the users of consultation from the nonusers were:

1. The perception that the psychologist offers help on a regular basis at the teacher's school (standardized canonical coefficient=0.75).
2. The perception of themselves as having good problem-solving skills (0.60).
3. The perception that the psychologist has had training in problem-solving skills (0.28).
4. The teachers having fewer years of teaching experience (0.20).
5. The perception that the entry-level training required for the psychologist is higher than that required for a teaching position (0.12).

These results suggest that teachers will be more likely to engage in consultation with psychologists whom they see as available, knowledgeable, and competent in problem solving. Interestingly, the finding that teachers with good problem-solving skills are more likely to use consultation runs counter to what Hughes et al. (1990; reviewed earlier) found. Stenger et al. (1992) attributed this discrepancy to the different definitions of problem solving used in the two studies, specifically that self-efficacy cannot be equated with problem solving.

Increasing the Effectiveness of Consultation with Teachers

Adapting Consultation to the Teacher's Schedule: The 15-Min Consultation

As noted in Chap. 4, another constraint that teachers (and many psychologists) operate under is having limited time for consultation. The school day is tightly structured, suggesting that before school and after school as well as during recess, lunch, and teacher planning periods (if available) are the times that consultation can occur. Unfortunately, these occasions often do not provide extended blocks of time (e.g., 30 or more minutes) that are usually needed to explore problems in a thorough manner. Another drawback to meeting during one of these times is that a teacher may want to be doing something other than consultation.

Assuming that consultation should provide an opportunity for unhurried, systematic reflection (Caplan, Caplan, & Erchul, 1995), there is no simple solution to this vexing problem. However, one response to time constraints in schools is the "15-min consultation," so named because it is assumed that no single contact with a consultee will exceed about 15 min (Brown, Pryzwansky, & Schulte, 2006). Steps that a consultant would follow in the first meeting are:

1. Help teacher prioritize the issues of concern, and have him or her identify an important issue that could be addressed given the limitation of time.
2. Inform teacher about the advantages and disadvantages of this approach to consultation as well as other consultation models that could be used (see trade-offs below).
3. Determine whether teacher has a hypothesis regarding the problem, and ask what interventions have been tried already.
4. Advance alternative (perhaps competing) hypotheses, and emphasize that different hypotheses usually result in different interventions.
5. Agree on follow-up responsibilities and the time of the next meeting or contact.

After the first session, Brown et al. (2006) suggested that telephone contacts be used in conjunction with face-to-face meetings, and that a classroom observation take place, particularly if there is a clear reason to do so. E-mail communication may also be feasible, depending on the specific context. Interventions developed over the course of subsequent "15-min consultations" appear to be devised by the consultant, rather than through the joint efforts of both parties (cf. Erchul et al., 2009).

Evaluation of outcomes remains an important goal, although it may be based on more expedient measures (e.g., brief classroom observations). To illustrate the approach, Brown et al. provided a case study in which a psychologist consults with a teacher across six sessions, each ranging in length from 5 to 20 min.

Brown et al. (2006) have noted definite trade-offs associated with the 15-min consultation. On the negative side, a teacher may distort or misrepresent problems that, given the time frame, the consultant is unable to assess or verify further. When a consultant acts on incomplete information and then is wrong in setting the course for consultation, the teacher may find the consultant to be unhelpful and perhaps the consultant's credibility with other potential consultees will suffer. The brief time available also tends to preclude the implementation of a complex intervention, which may be needed. Finally, a quick approach to school consultation unfortunately encourages a view that a consultant is omniscient and thus minimizes the consultee's active participation (Brown et al., 2006).

More positively, the 15-min consultation tends to fit a teacher's schedule better and thus reduces one predictable source of resistance to consultation. Administrators and school boards may like it because precious classroom instruction time does not have to be sacrificed for the sake of perhaps only one student. In principle, a consultant could work with greater numbers of teachers using this approach as opposed to using a more in-depth consultation model for the same amount of time. Also, it is arguable that brief contacts spread out over an extended period of time may benefit consultees and clients more than would a focused and intense problem-solving period (Brown et al., 2006).

We believe that the 15-min consultation has merit and deserves further study. At present, its greatest strength is its guiding assumption that teachers are extremely busy and do not have the time that consultants usually prefer to devote to consultation. However, instead of leaving important elements out of consultation due to time constraints, we prefer to address them across an extended period, using several brief contacts. For example, a behavioral consultant may consider achieving all of the goals of the Problem Identification Interview (Bergan & Kratochwill, 1990) across two or three short meetings with a teacher rather than in a single, longer session (which may not be an option for either party anyway).

Consulting as Part of a Prereferral Intervention/ Problem-Solving Team

As mentioned in Chap. 2, provisions of IDEIA 2004 require that teachers implement some type of intervention for students who are experiencing difficulties in their classroom before more intensive intervention (as in a higher RTI tier) or referral for special education is undertaken. Since the 1980s, these prereferral interventions have been commonly observed in schools (Burns & Symington, 2002; Carter & Sugai, 1989). Moreover, one vehicle that has evolved for carrying out the prereferral intervention process is the *prereferral intervention team* or PIT (Truscott, Cohen,

Sams, Sanborn, & Frank, 2005). As mentioned in Chap. 2, PITs are evolving into problem-solving teams (PSTs) under the RTI provisions of IDEIA 2004.

A PIT is usually comprised of a group of multidisciplinary professionals (school psychologist, special education teacher, general education teacher, administrator, school counselor, etc.) who convene to help regular education teachers to develop interventions for their students. Or, as summarized by McDougal, Clonan, and Martens (2000):

> Prereferral intervention is a consultation-based approach for providing behavioral and/or instructional support to students experiencing problems before considering their eligibility for special class placement.... As such, prereferral intervention services involve consultation between a referring teacher and a team of consultants toward the common goals of specifying the referral problem in behavioral terms, analyzing maintaining variables, and designing, implementing, and evaluating one or more intervention plans (p. 150).

In North Carolina, the current version of the state's regulations concerning exceptional children's services requires that "two scientific, research-based interventions …including progress monitoring documentation" (p. 70) occur prior to formal referral for several types of disabilities. The affected categories are Emotional Disability, Intellectual Disability, Specific Learning Disability, and Other Health Impairment (North Carolina Department of Public Instruction, 2007). It is clear that prereferral intervention delivered via consultation is mainly how these scientific, research-based interventions are selected, implemented, and evaluated.

Numerous examples of prereferral intervention programs have been reported in the consultation literature (e.g., Fuchs, Fuchs & Bahr, 1990; Graden, Casey, & Christenson, 1985; Gravois, Groff, & Rosenfield, 2009; Gutkin, Henning-Stout, & Piersel, 1988; McDougal et al., 2000; Rosenfield & Gravois, 1999). As noted, a PIT typically consists of a school psychologist, an instructional specialist or special education teacher, one or more support personnel (e.g., a social worker or language specialist), a regular education teacher, and a school administrator. Other common characteristics of PITs are that they: (1) adhere to the four-stage problem-solving process of the behavioral consultation model; (2) have regularly scheduled meetings to discuss cases; (3) make use of some type of recording form, checklist, protocol, or manual to guide team interactions; and (4) use both direct (e.g., classroom observation, curriculum-based assessment) and indirect (e.g., teacher report) measures to evaluate the consultation process and intervention outcomes. At an organizational level, successful prereferral intervention programs tend to have the active support of key administrators, commitment to provide needed resources (e.g., funds for release time, training by external consultants, part-time teacher assistants), a planning team of consultants internal to the district, and a process for conducting formative evaluations (McDougal et al., 2000).

Prereferral intervention programs such as those listed above have been shown to be effective in responding to children's problems and in decreasing the number of students ultimately referred for special education placement. For example, after evaluating their School-Based Intervention Team (SBIT) Project, McDougal et al. (2000) found that: (1) consultation objectives were either met or partially met during 90.5% of observed team meetings, (2) teachers rated children's problems as significantly less severe after participating in the SBIT process, (3) children referred for classroom behavior problems showed a 20% increase in time on-task over baseline following intervention, (4) children referred for reading problems gained an average 3.7 words per week, and (5) referrals to special education decreased by 36%. In addition, Burns and Symington's (2002) meta-analysis of PIT outcomes revealed an *ES* of 1.15 for student outcomes, an *ES* of 0.90 for system outcomes, and an *ES* of 1.10 across all 57 outcomes. The authors, however, noted that university-led PITs were more successful than practitioner-led PITs (*ES*s = 1.32 and 0.54, respectively).

As one might suspect, the dynamics of consulting with teachers as part of a team are likely to differ from those of one-on-one consultation. For instance, each team member can expect fewer opportunities to participate in discussion simply as a result of having more people present. Beyond this, however, mandates for PIT/PST-based consultation may call into question several of the core characteristics of consultation described in Chaps. 1 and 6 (Goldstein & Martens, 2000). First, school consultation was initially conceived of as involving a collaborative relationship between co-equal professionals (Gutkin & Curtis, 1982). Subsequent research on relational communication has depicted school-based, problem-solving consultation more as a cooperative relationship in which the consultant leads and the consultee follows toward the mutual goal of intervention selection and implementation (e.g., Erchul et al., 2009). Second, with federal mandates for prereferral intervention and the introduction of RTI, consultation has become a stand-alone educational service regulated by state law. One result of such mandates is that all members of the intervention team, including the referring teacher, are held to higher levels of accountability with respect to intervention integrity and outcome (Martens & DiGennaro, 2008). Whereas teachers may have been free to reject consultants' suggestions when consultation was delivered informally, doing so following mandated team consultation that incorporates research-based interventions may be tantamount to denying children access to an appropriate education. Third, school consultants have historically relied on teachers' verbal reports as a basis for intervention design (Witt, 1997). Higher levels of accountability and the need to demonstrate beneficial outcomes for children have made it increasingly more common for intervention teams to supplement teacher verbal reports with more direct assessment data (e.g., classroom observation), particularly when conducting a functional assessment as described in Chap. 7.

Increasing Knowledge/Skill Transfer and Maintenance

Despite the best intentions of all involved parties, why do changes in teacher behavior not always generalize beyond the face-to-face meetings with the school consultant? Goldstein and Martens (2000) have suggested three reasons. First, many consultants erroneously assume an *empirical–rational* approach to change will be effective when it generally is not (see discussion in Chap. 3). Second, even in behavioral consultation – the most widely used and researched model of school consultation – often a naive "train and hope" model of generalization (Stokes & Baer, 1977) is relied upon.

Third, it is often difficult for a consultant to adequately understand the contingencies under which teachers operate to harness these contingencies to optimize follow through efforts.

Chapter 6 specified the importance of four components relative to the support and development task of school consultation: social influence; goal setting; modeling, coaching, and performance feedback; and implementation protocols (Goldstein & Martens, 2000). We continue by offering some strategies from the staff development literature.

The school consultant may benefit from knowing what makes staff development activities result in having teachers transfer a high level of knowledge and skill back to the classroom. The research program of Bruce Joyce and Beverly Showers is instructive in this regard (see Joyce & Showers, 2002; Showers, 1990). Joyce and Showers have documented the odds of achieving knowledge and skill transfer can be increased through training activities designed to help teachers accomplish these objectives: (1) to understand fully the theoretical basis of the innovation and what it is supposed to accomplish; (2) to observe demonstrations of the innovation through the use of both live and taped models; (3) to take advantage of opportunities to practice new skills in the training setting; and (4) to participate in peer coaching teams in which teachers provide instrumental and expressive support to each other in the implementation of the innovation in the classroom (Showers, 1990).

With respect to the last objective, Joyce and Showers (1988; cited in Showers, 1990) reasoned that teachers' difficulty in transferring technology back to the classroom could be attributed to characteristics of the school setting, particularly the isolation that many teachers face. To combat this isolation and enhance the quality and frequency of teachers' implementation attempts, they organized groups in which teachers coached one another in the use of new classroom strategies through collegial interaction. In these mutual help teams, teachers shared curriculum materials, observed one another using the new strategies, and provided peer–professional feedback. A controlled study of peer coaching study teams showed that, after 1 year, 80% of the teachers who participated in peer coaching had transferred the new teaching strategies into their active repertoire, compared to only 10% of the teachers who had undergone the same theory–demonstration–practice training sequence but had not participated in peer coaching activities (Showers, 1990).

Taken together, findings from the literatures on the generalization of gain in psychotherapy (Goldstein & Martens, 2000) and staff development (Showers, 1990) present several implications for the effective practice of school consultation. First, within consultation, there is a need to set performance goals for consultees just as is commonly done for clients. Establishing explicit performance goals for consultees may enable them to become more effective change agents. Second, in our experience, many school consultants do not conduct – or even attempt to conduct – the modeling, coaching, and performance feedback activities deemed critical for knowledge and skill transfer and maintenance. These same consultants then wonder why their teachers have not implemented a classroom intervention with integrity and/or demonstrable results. Finally, the peer coaching activity, seen as integral to the success of staff development efforts, argues convincingly for a goal of consultation to provide a support system for consultees (Erchul, 1993b) as well as for the greater use of group consultation with teachers (Babinski & Rogers, 1998; Caplan & Caplan, 1993/1999).

Providing Consultative Support to Teachers

School consultation usually results in additional teacher responsibilities or demands, which we know are already considerable. Therefore, a major task of the consultant is to offer support and assistance to teachers during the consultation process. As a way of making some of the more abstract concepts of this chapter more concrete, we conclude Chap. 9 by listing a dozen pragmatic ways consultative support may be offered to teachers:

1. Listen attentively to teacher frustrations with classroom problems.
2. Provide a "sounding board" for teacher ideas.
3. Compliment teacher actions when successful.
4. Offer encouragement when teacher efforts are less than successful.
5. Instruct teachers about how to assess classroom problems in a systematic manner.
6. Help identify and, whenever possible, take an active role in recruiting additional resources or seeking alternative solutions that may be available elsewhere in the school.
7. Help teachers help themselves, as in peer coaching.
8. Make school-based consultation available to a greater number of consultees.
9. Inform teachers of the best available treatment technologies.
10. Guide teachers through the problem-solving process of consultation.
11. Assist teachers in systematic treatment implementation and evaluation.
12. Help teachers make assessment information relevant for intervention.

Exactly how the consultant should perform these activities is not firmly established, as specific behavioral markers of the optimal consultant/consultee relationship continue to defy easy identification (e.g., Busse, Kratochwill, & Elliott, 1999). Notwithstanding, the transcribed case study presented in Chap. 11 shows how some of these actions have been taken. Before considering this case, Chap. 10 examines a variety of issues germane to a greater understanding of child and adolescent clients, considered more specifically as students in classrooms.

Chapter 10
Students as Clients

Each September, millions of children across the country return to their classrooms ready to begin another year of public schooling. The majority of these children will be successful in learning the material presented to them, will earn passing marks from their teacher, and will be promoted to the next grade level. For a certain proportion of children, however (approximately 11% nationwide; Reschly, 1988), the year at school will be a markedly different experience. Some of these children will lack the skills needed to tackle grade-level material, and as a result will struggle with even routine classroom assignments. Others will be unaccustomed to waiting patiently for the teacher's attention or working quietly in their seat, and as a result will engage in behavior that disrupts others.

For nearly 35 years now, American schools have been committed to providing a free, appropriate, public education (FAPE) to those students who find it difficult to succeed in the regular education system (Telzrow, 1999). This commitment has been the direct result of federal legislation mandating services in the schools and has increased the range of opportunities for school consultants to work alongside teachers in meeting the needs of exceptional students. This chapter begins with an overview of federal legislation governing service delivery in the schools and identifies the implications of these mandates for school consultation services. Next, educational approaches to classifying students with disabilities are discussed, including the rationale underlying ability grouping, characteristics and examples of state diagnostic criteria, and the relationship of educational classification schemes to the *Diagnostic and Statistical Manual of Mental Disorders Fourth Edition – Text Revision* (*DSM-IV-TR*) of the American Psychiatric Association (2000). In order to highlight the limitations of educational approaches to classification, issues surrounding the identification of children as learning disabled and emotionally disturbed are discussed in detail. Following this presentation, we consider the characteristics of regular education classrooms that limit the degree to which students with special needs can be accommodated in the mainstream. The chapter concludes with a description of variables in the instructional environment that have been shown to influence student achievement, and that therefore represent important considerations for the school consultant.

W.P. Erchul and B.K. Martens, *School Consultation*, Issues in Clinical Child Psychology,
DOI 10.1007/978-1-4419-5747-4_10, © Springer Science+Business Media, LLC 2010

Legislation Governing Service Delivery in the Schools

Without question, the two pieces of legislation that have had the greatest impact on the types of services delivered to children in schools have been *Public Law (P.L.) 94-142 The Individuals with Disabilities Education Act* (IDEA; formerly the Education for All Handicapped Children Act of 1975) and *Section 504 of the Vocational Rehabilitation Act*. IDEA was passed by the 94th Congress and signed into law by President Ford on November 29, 1975. The intent of IDEA was to make law the decisions and mandates that had been reached in a number of court cases heard prior to 1975. The majority of these cases involved class action suits against defendant school districts that were brought on the basis of (1) unequal access to public education by students with disabilities; (2) minority overrepresentation in special classrooms offering inferior educational opportunities; and (3) inappropriate uses of standardized tests to make student placement decisions (e.g., administering intelligence measures in English to Spanish-speaking students). Stemming from the decisions in these cases, IDEA guarantees to all students between ages 3 and 21 a free, appropriate public education, which includes special education and related services needed to meet their unique needs. *Free* means that education is to be provided at public expense and the appropriateness of this education is to be agreed upon and documented in writing by the student's *individualized education program* or IEP.

Beyond guaranteeing the right to a free appropriate education, IDEA contains a number of protections involving the process that is due a student being considered for special education placement. Included in these *due process requirements* is the need to obtain parental consent before evaluating a student for possible classification, the parents' right to obtain an independent evaluation at the school's expense, and the use of evaluation instruments that are reliable and valid for the purposes intended. With respect to the child's IEP, the law mandates that it be developed by a team of qualified professionals, which include the child's parent or guardian; that it contains statements about the child's present levels of functioning, annual goals, and criteria for evaluating progress; and that it be reviewed at least annually. Finally, with respect to the services provided, IDEA mandates that school districts make available a continuum of alternative placements and services to meet the needs of students with disabilities. The law states further that students with disabilities receive their education in the *least restrictive environment* and alongside typical peers to the maximum extent appropriate.

In the spring of 1997, IDEA was amended by Congress and signed into law by President Clinton on June 4th to reflect a number of changes in the way that students with disabilities were evaluated. Telzrow (1999) summarized these changes, which included: (a) elimination of the term "serious" from the category of emotional disturbance, (b) participation by students with disabilities in district-wide assessments with appropriate accommodations, (c) inclusion of parents as evaluation team members, (d) inclusion of a regular education teacher as an evaluation team member for students placed at least part-time in regular education, and (e) use of existing data where appropriate during reevaluations.

In response to increased concern over school violence, the IDEA 1997 Amendments also made provisions for students with disabilities who exhibit severe problem behavior or who violate school rules. Specifically, IDEA 1997 required that "if a student with disabilities exhibits problem behaviors that impede his or her learning or the learning of others, then the student's IEP team shall consider strategies, including positive behavioral interventions, strategies, and supports to address that behavior" (Drasgow & Yell, 2001, p. 240). Positive behavior support (PBS) refers to procedures that teach and/or reinforce appropriate behavior instead of relying on punishment to reduce inappropriate behavior. IDEA 1997 stipulated further that positive behavioral interventions were to be based on a functional assessment as described in Chap. 7. Functional assessments were also required when a student with a disability accumulated 10 school days of suspension, was removed from school in a manner that constituted a change of placement, or was placed in an interim alternative education setting for a weapons or drug offense (Drasgow & Yell, 2001).

As described in Chap. 2, the current reauthorization of IDEA is the *Individuals with Disabilities Education Improvement Act of 2004* (IDEIA 2004). Two important additions to how services are provided in schools were contained in IDEIA 2004. First, in determining whether a child has a specific learning disability, a local education agency may use "*a process that determines if a child responds to scientific, research-based intervention*" (i.e., the RTI model) in addition to the IQ-Achievement discrepancy model. Second, the definition of PBS was refined and expanded to promote a tiered service delivery approach consisting of primary/universal, secondary/selected, and tertiary/targeted interventions.

Using somewhat different wording, the right to a FAPE with due process requirements was also guaranteed by Section 504 of the Vocational Rehabilitation Act of 1973. Section 504 is a civil rights statute that states:

> No otherwise qualified handicapped individual in the United States shall, solely by reason of his [sic] handicap, be excluded from the participation in, be denied the benefits of, or be subjected to discrimination under any program or activity receiving Federal financial assistance.

Section 504 in general and IDEA in particular have had far-reaching implications for the delivery of services in the schools. For example, with the mandate for multidisciplinary teams to evaluate students' eligibility for special education, individually administered tests of achievement and intelligence became increasingly popular as diagnostic tools. Because school psychologists often administered these tests, they found themselves cast in the role of gatekeeper for entry into special education with corresponding increases in caseloads. As controversy heightened over the use of intelligence tests to classify children with mental retardation (particularly children from minority and other underrepresented groups), the years following passage of IDEA saw "a veritable epidemic" of students classified with learning disabilities (Reschly, 1988, p. 460).

IDEA also has had important implications for the role of support personnel (e.g., psychologists, psychiatrists, reading specialists, social workers) in configuring educational programs for students with special needs. First, by mandating a continuum of services, IDEA introduced the concept of the resource room. A *resource room* is a classroom in which children with disabilities can receive special education services for only a portion of the school day while spending the majority of their instructional time in the regular classroom setting. In contrast to previous policies of "place or not place," children needing special services could now receive those services on a part-time basis. In keeping with the least restrictive environment mandate, two arrangements emerged for providing part-time special education services including the *pull-out program* in which students with mild disabilities received remedial instruction in a resource room and the *push-in program* in which students with more severe disabilities received instruction in a regular classroom.

An important implication of these arrangements was that regular classroom teachers who had been trained to teach relatively homogenous groups of typical children were now required by law to accommodate students with special needs for a portion of the school day. Second, in order to help regular education teachers accommodate a more diverse student population, the instructional and managerial strategies used by special education teachers were to be shared with their regular education counterparts. This sharing of instructional technology was to be accomplished through mandated personnel development programs and the delivery of consultative services by special education resource teachers. Thus, IDEA provided an important impetus for school consultation through what has become known as the *teacher consultant model*. In New York State, consultant teacher services refer to "direct and/or indirect services, as defined in this subdivision, provided to a student with a disability in the student's regular education classes and/or to such student's regular education teachers" (New York Regulations of the Commissioner of Education [NYRCE], 2009, 200.1[m]).

Building on the impetus of the original 1975 version of IDEA, the 1997 and 2004 reauthorizations attempted to advance the continuum of school-based service delivery by incorporating research on functional assessment, brief experimental analysis, systematic formative evaluation, and school-wide reinforcement programs. In so doing, IDEIA 2004 consolidated the role of school consultation in two ways; (a) as a stand-alone service for students with behavior problems via functional assessment and PBS, and (b) as an alternative approach to eligibility determination for students with academic problems via RTI.

Educational Approaches to Classification

As discussed in Chap. 4, in order to receive special education and related services in the schools, students must be (a) unresponsive to increasingly more intensive, evidence-based interventions provided in their regular education setting; and (b) deemed eligible by a team of professionals based on a comprehensive psychoeducational evaluation. Completing the evaluation and arranging for appropriate services can take up to 60 days from the receipt of parental consent to conduct the evaluation and can include, but is not limited to, a physical examination, a psychological evaluation, a social history, and assessments in other areas required to determine the child's need for special education programming. An important outcome of this evaluation that renders children eligible for special services is being classified with a disability under one or more of the conditions specified in IDEIA 2004 and interpreted with respect to regulations developed by each state's education agency. Because obtaining a disability classification plays such an important role in the types of school-based services children receive, we believe that school consultants should be aware of the rationale behind educational classification systems, the various disabilities and criteria contained in state regulations, and the ways in which school-based practitioners translate these criteria into practice.

Rationale for Classifying Special Needs Students

We began the chapter by observing that children who enter school each year represent a diverse population in terms of skills and behaviors. As with most measured characteristics of individuals, student abilities can be viewed as continuous variables that tend to be normally distributed in the general population. This suggests that student achievement levels will range incrementally from about three standard deviations above the mean to about three standard deviations below the mean, with the majority of children who enter school (i.e., the 68% found between plus/minus one standard deviation from the mean) performing in the average range. This also suggests that children who have adjacent scores on a test of intelligence or achievement are best viewed as differing quantitatively rather than qualitatively with respect to the characteristic being measured (Reschly, 1988). This position, known as a *dimensional model* of student ability, has been supported by research showing that low achieving students differ from those with high incidence or mild disabilities by degree of underachievement but not the presence of physical symptoms, biological anomalies, or even intelligence–achievement discrepancies (Luiselli, Reed, & Martens, 2010).

Just as students are likely to enter school with a range of abilities, teachers also are likely to bring a range of instructional and managerial practices to the classroom. These practices are developed through formal training in teacher preparation programs and evolve as a function of experience and informal contacts with other faculty. Teachers' instructional and managerial practices are also determined in part by the practical constraints of moving large numbers of students through a basal curriculum. A *basal curriculum* is a hierarchical sequence of academic skills and corresponding instructional materials that are organized by learning objectives. These learning objectives are linked from year to year, with mastery being synonymous with academic achievement and failure having cumulative effects as students advance through the grade levels.

Interestingly, research into the nature of teachers' instructional practices has shown that these practices are consistent across schools, differ little between regular and special education classrooms, and have changed little over time (Good, 1983; Sirotnik, 1983; Ysseldyke, Christenson, Thurlow, & Bakewell, 1989). Together, these findings suggest that the range of teachers' instructional practices is likely to be narrower than the range of student abilities these practices are intended to accommodate. As early as 1977, Steven Apter described this situation as the *"One Right Model"* of public education. Specifically, Apter suggested that the bureaucratic structure of schools produces a certain rigidity of educational programming in which teachers focus their efforts on the average students in the classroom. Because the majority of children in classrooms are by definition average, this approach enables schools to educate most children most of the time. However, the "One Right Model" also ensures that some children will not succeed in regular education because their skills and behaviors fall outside the acceptable range of the regular classroom teacher. For these children, a discrepancy exists between their performance and the teacher's performance expectations (Shinn, 1989). Consistent with the belief that it is easier to teach 10 children who are similar than 10 children who are different, special education was developed as a solution for students who failed in regular education. Special education is expensive, however, costing approximately twice as much per pupil as regular education (Reschly, 1988). Some system was required therefore to identify those students most in need of the additional expenditures associated with special education services. This system was mandated by IDEA and translated into the various disabilities and classification criteria specified in state regulations.

Overview of Childhood Disabilities

The two major approaches for classifying childhood psychopathology in use today are individual state's regulations for students with disabilities and the *DSM-IV-TR*. Although similarities exist between the two systems, they were developed to fulfill somewhat different functions. Regulations for students with disabilities were developed by state education agencies primarily to serve an administrative function by (1) assisting in the identification of students who are eligible for special services, placements, or resources; and (2) providing a system for calculating the amount of state and federal aid received by schools from one year to the next. Evidence that these guidelines were designed to meet administrative rather than diagnostic goals can be found in Section 200.6, subsection (a) (3) of the NYRCE (2009), which states that, "Students with disabilities placed together for purposes of special education shall be grouped by similarity of individual needs." This suggests that a student's educational needs rather than disability was intended as the basis for determining placement.

Disability labels, definitions, and criteria for classification are likely to vary from state to state (e.g., Epstein, Cullinan, & Sabatino, 1977), although, in all cases, the language used must be in accord with IDEIA. For comparison purposes, the disabilities specified in the regulations for the states of North Carolina and New York are listed in Table 10.1. Although it would be beyond the scope of the chapter to list the classification criteria under each condition, several common features are noted

Table 10.1 Disabilities Specified in the Special Education Regulations for North Carolina and New York State and the DSM-IV-TR

North Carolina	New York State	DSM-IV-TR
Autism spectrum disorder	Autism	Autistic disorder; pervasive developmental disorder
Emotional disability	Emotional disturbance	Conduct disorder; oppositional defiant disorder; certain mood disorders
Deafness and deaf-blindness	Deafness and deaf-blindness	Axis III general medical condition (eye and ear, nose, and throat)
Hearing impairment	Hearing impairment	Axis III general medical condition (ear, nose, and throat)
Intellectual disability	Mental retardation	Mental retardation; Axis III general medical condition (congenital abnormalities)
Multiple disabilities	Multiple disabilities	Various comorbid diagnoses
Orthopedic impairment	Orthopedic impairment	Motor skills disorder; Axis III general medical condition (musculoskeletal)
Other health impairment	Other health impairment	Axis III general medical condition; attention-deficit/hyperactivity disorder
Developmental delay	N/A	Various diagnoses, including disorder of infancy, childhood, or adolescence not otherwise specified
Specific learning disability	Learning disability	Learning disorders
Speech or language impairment	Speech or language impairment	Communication disorders
Traumatic brain injury	Traumatic brain injury	Axis III general medical condition (nervous system)
Visual impairment	Visual impairment/blindness	Axis III general medical condition (eye)

below, and the definitions for two conditions, Learning Disability and Emotional Disturbance, are discussed in detail in subsequent sections.

One common element found in both states' classification criteria is that the language used to describe the various disabilities often suggests a medical model rather than an ecological view of childhood disabilities (Gresham & Gansle, 1992). For example, *specific learning disability* is a term used in North Carolina for "*a disorder in one or more of the basic psychological processes involved in understanding or in using language, spoken or written, that may manifest itself in the impaired ability to listen, think, speak, read, write, spell, or to do mathematical calculations, including conditions such as perceptual disabilities, brain injury, minimal brain dysfunction, dyslexia, and developmental aphasia*" (North Carolina Department of Public Instruction [NCDPI], Policies Governing Services for Children with Disabilities, 2007, NC 1500-2.4, p. 4).

Second, the criteria for classifying children as disabled differ in specificity across conditions, and these differences tend to reflect current standards of practice and training. For some years now, individually administered tests of intelligence and adaptive behavior have been the standards of practice in diagnosing mental retardation

(Grossman, 1983; Witt & Martens, 1984). Accordingly, the New York State regulations define the condition of *mental retardation* based on assessment in these two areas. In contrast, the criteria for *emotional disturbance* in New York State are much less precise, containing such language as "an inability to build or maintain satisfactory interpersonal relationships with peers and teachers" and "inappropriate types of behavior or feelings under normal circumstances." Gresham (1985) observed that psychologists working in the schools are often inadequately trained to assess children's social–emotional functioning, and suggested that this may contribute to the lack of precision in state definitions.

Third, state regulations concerning the identification of students with disabilities often contain exclusionary criteria. Ostensibly, these *exclusionary criteria* were designed to prevent certain groups of children who might be served by other means from entering the special education system (e.g., students for whom English is a second language, children placed as juvenile delinquents by the courts) (Forness & Knitzer, 1992). In actual practice, however, these exclusions imply a hierarchy of causes for certain disorders that may be difficult to tease out during a typical psychoeducational evaluation. For example, students classified with a learning disability in both North Carolina and New York State cannot have learning problems that result primarily from visual, hearing, or motor disabilities, mental retardation, emotional disturbance, or environmental, cultural, or economic influences. Research has shown that children with learning disabilities often exhibit social skill deficits and other problem behaviors (e.g., Gresham & Reschly, 1986). Although a comprehensive assessment could describe a student's current levels of academic and socioemotional functioning, it would be difficult to conclude that a causal relationship existed between the two areas.

With its multiaxial classification approach, the *DSM-IV-TR* system was designed to aid in the diagnosis of psychopathology while organizing a wide range of information about client functioning. Evidence of this can be found in the descriptions of Axis II disorders (personality disorders and mental retardation) that include key diagnostic features, subtypes and/or specifiers, procedures for recording the diagnosis, associated diagnostic features and related disorders, and criteria for rendering a differential diagnosis. *DSM-IV-TR* also provides epidemiological summaries of the various disorder types including prevalence, culture, age, and gender features, course of the disorder, and familial patterns. Together with the requirement by the Joint Council on Accreditation of Hospitals that individuals receive a *DSM* diagnosis upon institutionalization, the *DSM* system serves an administrative function by (1) helping to forecast incidence rates in populations served and (2) creating a system of accountability for third-party reimbursements to health care providers.

DSM-IV-TR classifies childhood disorders under the Axis I category of *Disorders Usually First Diagnosed in Infancy, Childhood, or Adolescence* as well as the Axis II disorder of *Mental Retardation*. Presented in Table 10.1 is a list of childhood disorders contained in these sections of *DSM-IV-TR* as well as relevant medical conditions listed on Axis III. As shown in the table, several of the more general disorder labels overlap with the disabilities specified in state regulations. State education agency regulations, however, do not include the subcategories that are listed under each disorder label in the *DSM* taxonomy. Thus, a child classified with an autism spectrum disorder according to the North Carolina regulations might be diagnosed in *DSM-IV-TR* with a pervasive developmental disorder (Rett's disorder, childhood disintegrative disorder, Asperger's disorder), a feeding disorder of infancy or early childhood, or autistic disorder. The lack of specificity evident in state regulations is consistent with their administrative function of determining eligibility for special services rather than providing a comprehensive system of clinical diagnosis as in *DSM-IV-TR*.

The majority of children (upwards of 85%) who receive special education services in the schools are classified with mild or high incidence disorders (Reschly, 2004). Prevalence rates of children with mild disorders indicate that classification as learning disabled is the most common (4.7% of the student population), followed by speech impaired (2.9%), mildly mentally retarded (1.3%), and emotionally disturbed (1%) (Reschly, 1988). Because school consultants are likely to be involved with students who at some point may be considered for classification as learning disabled or emotionally disturbed, we believe it is important to understand the characteristics of these children and the issues involved in determining their eligibility for special services.

Students Classified as Learning Disabled

The definition of specific learning disabled (SLD) contained in the 2007 North Carolina special education regulations reads as follows:

> [SLD] Means a disorder in one or more of the basic psychological processes involved in understanding or in using language, spoken or written, that may manifest itself in the impaired ability to listen, think, speak, read, write, spell, or to do mathematical calculations, including conditions such as perceptual disabilities, brain injury, minimal brain dysfunction, dyslexia, and developmental aphasia. Specific learning disability does not include learning problems that are primarily the result of visual, hearing, or motor disabilities, of mental retardation, of serious emotional disturbance, or of environmental, cultural, or economic disadvantage.

This definition is consistent with that of most states in conceptualizing SLD as a processing deficit that is manifested as low achievement in one or more basic academic skills. In a review of the literature on SLD, Merrell and Shinn (1990) identified five competing views of the SLD construct, including processing deficit models, ability–achievement discrepancy models, low academic achievement models, social policy models, and social skill deficit models. To identify those variables most predictive of SLD classification, Merrell and Shinn compared children referred and classified as SLD to a matched group of children who were referred but not classified. Results of a discriminant function analysis revealed that the most critical determinant in the decision to classify a child as SLD was low academic achievement in the areas of reading and written language. Surprisingly, only 37.5% of the children in the SLD group actually met the discrepancy criterion for classification in their state.

In practice, federal and state regulations allow evaluation teams to determine children's eligibility for classification as learning disabled in one of two ways. First, students may be classified with a learning disability if a significant discrepancy exists between the student's intellectual ability and achievement level (i.e., the IQ–ACH discrepancy model). Making this determination requires the administration of standardized, norm-referenced tests of intelligence and achievement by evaluation team members. The scores on these tests are used to determine if a child is achieving significantly below grade level in relation to same-age peers and whether this level of achievement is discrepant from the child's measured intelligence (e.g., Reynolds, 1981). Although widely used in the schools, the discrepancy model of SLD identification has been criticized on a number of grounds (e.g., Gresham, 2009; Vaughn & Fuchs, 2003). Specifically, researchers have found that (a) constant score differences do not indicate reliable discrepancies, (b) IQ–ACH discrepancy does not differentiate students with SLD from their low achieving peers, (c) some measures of intelligence (e.g., processing speed) are more apt to be related to and not discrepant from achievement, and (d) IQ–ACH discrepancy does not inform instruction.

Although low academic achievement is often predictive of SLD classification, many students who experience failure in the local curriculum are deemed ineligible for special education services. One reason for this inconsistency has to do with the degree of content overlap between the student's curriculum materials and the items contained on standardized achievement tests, or what is known as *curriculum content validity* (Fuchs & Fuchs, 1986b; Jenkins & Pany, 1978). Numerous studies have examined the degree of overlap between standardized, norm-referenced achievement tests and commercially available basal reading curricula (e.g., Armbruster, Stevens, & Rosenshine, 1977; Bell, Lentz, & Graden, 1992; Good & Salvia, 1988; Jenkins & Pany, 1978; Shapiro & Derr, 1987; Webster, McInnis, & Craver, 1986). In the majority of these studies, overlap was assessed by comparing word lists from the basal readers with word lists from the word recognition subtests of standardized instruments. Different numbers of exact word matches were found across tests when compared to a single reading program and across reading programs when compared to a single test, leading to conclusions of curriculum bias.

Jenkins and Pany (1978) concluded that these differences could significantly affect a child's eligibility for special education services depending upon which test was administered in conjunction with what program. Shapiro and Derr (1987) found that the majority of grade equivalent scores obtained by a hypothetical student who had mastered all words taught in a curriculum fell below expected grade levels regardless of the test administered. These results suggest that scores on standardized tests may not accurately reflect what a student has learned. Curriculum bias also appears to exist for standardized measures of reading decoding (Martens, Steele, Massie, & Diskin, 1995). These authors compared four basal reading programs to the phonetic analysis subtests of three standardized achievement tests and found that: (1) programs differed in the number and sequence of phonics skills taught; (2) percentile and grade equivalent scores differed across programs at each grade level for a given test; and (3) the proportion of grade equivalent scores falling at or above expected grade levels differed across tests for a given program (range of 29–71%).

The second approach to determining children's eligibility for SLD classification requires evaluation teams to "utilize a process that determines a student's response to scientific research-based intervention" (NCDPI, 2007, NC 1503-2.5, p. 71). Here, PSTs may refer a student for special education because of chronic failure in the regular education curriculum *and* following documented failure to make adequate progress when provided with evidence-based Tier 1, Tier 2, and Tier 3 interventions. With this approach, a key determinant in the decision to classify a child as learning disabled is the school's success in accommodating the student's needs with a tiered model of prereferral interventions. The potential role that such intervention efforts can play in reducing the numbers of children subsequently placed in special education was highlighted in a study by Rosenfield (1992). During the year prior to establishing school-based consultation teams to assist teachers in the development of instructional interventions, 73% of children who were referred were later placed in special education. This percentage declined steadily following implementation of the project, with only 6% of children referred to the instructional consultation teams receiving placements in year four.

Students Classified as Emotionally Disturbed

According to the New York State Regulations (2009), emotional disturbance (ED) means:

> a condition exhibiting one or more of the following characteristics over a long period of time and to a marked degree that adversely affects a student's educational performance: (i) an inability to learn that cannot be explained by intellectual, sensory, or health factors; (ii) an inability to build or maintain satisfactory interpersonal relationships with peers and teachers; (iii) inappropriate types of behavior or feelings under normal circumstances; (iv) a generally pervasive mood of unhappiness or depression; or (v) a tendency to develop physical symptoms or fears associated with personal or school problems. The term includes schizophrenia. The term does not apply to students who are socially maladjusted, unless it is determined that they have an emotional disturbance.

The majority of children referred for classification as ED are male (approximately 67%), and these children tend to be referred for disruptive, acting-out behaviors. Whereas SLD makes up approximately 48% of all students with mild handicaps, ED constitutes only about 10% (Reschly, 1988), and there is evidence to suggest that students with ED may actually be underidentified in the schools (Brandenburg, Friedman, & Silver, 1990). Despite the least restrictive environment mandate of IDEIA, students with behavioral or emotional problems tend to be overrepresented in self-contained placements (US Department of Education, 1987), and children classified as ED are particularly at risk for segregated schooling.

Due in part to the imprecise language contained in state definitions, psychologists working in the schools evaluate children for ED classification using a wide range of assessment instruments (Gresham, 1985). For example, best practices in the assessment of children with attention deficit hyperactivity disorder call for a multimethod approach that includes parent and teacher interviews, reviews of school records, behavior rating scales, and systematic classroom observations (DuPaul, 1992). By comparison, when psychologists were asked to identify the instruments they used most commonly with adolescents, between 51 and 84% of respondents reported frequently or almost always using projective measures such as the Rorschach or Human Figure Drawings (Archer, Maruish, Imhof, & Piotrowski, 1992). Less than 20% of those surveyed reported using behavior rating scales such as the Conners or Child Behavior Checklist. After reviewing evidence concerning the use of figure drawings, Motta, Little, and Tobin (1993) concluded that "figure drawings should not be used as personality test instruments in that they do not provide valid descriptions of personality, behavior, or social–emotional functioning" (p. 165).

To aid in the identification of children as ED, the Workgroup on Definition of the National Mental Health and Special Education Coalition proposed an alternative definition to that contained in many state regulations and which is consistent with RTI models of LD classification (Forness & Knitzer, 1992). Children are classified as ED under this definition if their behavior in school differs so much from age-appropriate norms that it adversely affects academic performance. In addition, behavior that is judged to be inappropriate must be more than temporary, exhibited in two different settings, and unresponsive to interventions in the regular education setting. The first requirement, determining if behavior differs significantly from age-appropriate norms, is consistent with Ullmann and Krasner's (1969) interactional perspective on deviance known as *social labeling*. From a social labeling perspective, behavior is judged to be deviant based on an interaction of behavior, the tolerance level of an observer, and the context in which the behavior occurs. For example, frequent out-of-seat behavior is likely to be viewed as abnormal in a traditionally structured class-room where the teacher demands quiet seatwork. The same behavior, however, may well be within tolerable limits for a teacher who emphasizes cooperative learning and organizes his or her classroom into work stations. Instead of viewing behavioral and emotional problems as being intrinsic to the child, social labeling suggests that behavior is abnormal if it is judged as such by significant adults in the child's environment. Because these judgments are based implicitly or explicitly on comparisons to other children, social labeling argues in favor of using structured informant reports when making decisions about ED classification (Martens, 1993c).

Consistent with IDEIA, state regulations also include program standards for behavioral interventions, and these interventions are often developed for children classified with ED. For example, NYRCE (2009) states that, "in the case of a student whose behavior impedes his or her learning or that of others, the [PST] shall consider strategies, including positive behavioral interventions and supports and other strategies to address that behavior." (200.22[b]). At a minimum, positive behavioral supports involve the collection of baseline measures of behavior, evidence-based interventions for increasing desired, decreasing undesired, or teaching more adaptive behavior, and evaluation of treatment outcomes. In the following section, we consider the constraints present in regular education that limit a teachers' ability to accommodate difficult-to-teach students. We then discuss those variables in both regular and special education classrooms that have been shown to influence student achievement.

A Contextual Model of Student Achievement

As noted earlier, some children fail under the "One Right Model" of regular education because their behavior or achievement levels are not being adequately addressed by the instructional practices of the classroom teacher. This does not mean that students who fail automatically require special education placements, nor does it mean that classroom teachers are unwilling to assist children with special needs. Rather, this means that the range of instructional and managerial techniques used by the teacher is narrower than the range of skills and behaviors exhibited by the students. For students with behavioral problems, the usual incentives (e.g., teacher approval, written feedback) and disciplinary actions (e.g., stern looks, visits with the principal) may be insufficient to bring about compliance with classroom rules. Appropriate behaviors must be taught more explicitly and encouraged with stronger and more frequently delivered reinforcers (Martens & Witt, 2004). Students with achievement problems may have insufficient opportunities for active responding in curricular materials, inadequate amounts of prompting and feedback, instructional demands that do not promote mastery of curricular objectives, or grade-level material that is too difficult (Daly, Witt, Martens, & Dool, 1997). Teachers must provide more elaborate help in the form of prompts and models, more opportunities to respond in the form of drill and reinforcement, or curriculum materials that are matched to the student's skill level. In both of these cases, efforts to accommodate students' needs are synonymous with more explicit, evidence-based practices for promoting learning. These practices form the basis of prereferral interventions that are implemented by teachers in regular classroom settings. *When working with classroom teachers to develop and implement intervention programs, we believe that school consultants should be aware of the variables that constrain a teacher's ability to accommodate diverse learners.* These constraints are inherent in regular education classrooms, and successful accommodation efforts may require that they be partially overcome through the infusion of additional resources or the introduction of new knowledge and skills.

Variables Limiting Individualized Instruction

It is probably the case that all students could benefit from individualized instruction. Why is it then that individualized education programs are reserved for Tier 3 interventions or placement in special education, and regular classroom teachers find it difficult to accommodate special needs students? One way to answer these questions might be to consider for a moment the characteristics of a typical regular education classroom and the ways in which these constrain teachers' instructional and managerial activities. First, regular education teachers must conform to daily or weekly schedules of content instruction, lunch and recess, and special activities such as music, art, and gym. For example, during a 6-hr school day, students may be scheduled to spend an hour at lunch, 30 min at recess, and an hour each at both music and gym. This leaves approximately 3 1/2 hr of *allocated time* for instruction in the basic content areas (e.g., reading, arithmetic), not taking into account time spent preparing materials or transitioning from one task to the next (e.g., Gettinger, 1986; Ysseldyke et al., 1989). The same periods of allocated time are scheduled for all students in the classroom regardless of skill level, and teachers usually have little freedom to alter the schedule by, for example, doubling the amount of time spent on reading at the expense of math. This can pose a problem for students who may be doing well in one subject, but are struggling and therefore could benefit from increased instructional time in another subject.

Second, regular education teachers are required to adopt a basal curriculum, which is consistent with the school district's *scope and sequence charts*. School district scope and sequence charts specify the grade level at which various learning objectives are to be introduced, instructed, and mastered in each content area. Because these learning objectives are linked from year to year, it is important for students to master the curriculum material in the correct sequence and at the specified rate. This means that regardless of a given student's ability, teachers must focus the majority of their efforts on material contained in the curriculum and must limit the time spent on each lesson so students can be instructed in most or all of the objectives at their grade level. Because of the need to move students along in the curriculum, teachers may be limited in the amount of time they can spend helping low achievers acquire the skills introduced in one unit before moving on to the next unit.

Third, it is not uncommon to encounter student to teacher ratios of 30:1 or higher in many regular education classrooms. As the number of students in a classroom increases, it becomes more difficult for teachers to set ambitious goals for classwide achievement, to actively engage each student in the learning process, and to monitor student progress and adjust instruction accordingly. Research in both psychology and education has shown that an effective sequence of academic instruction involves gaining students' attention, specifying the goals of what you want them to do, providing them with enough assistance until they can do it correctly, having them do it correctly a number of times while providing feedback, and reinforcing effort (Martens & Witt, 2004). In order to effectively manage large classrooms, however, teachers must often rely on group instructional techniques. Although many components of effective instruction can be implemented at a group level, students with different abilities will require differing amounts of alerting, assistance, feedback, and reinforcement to maximize learning.

Variables Related to Student Achievement

Given that regular education teachers are often constrained in their attempts to individualize instruction, school-based interventions must involve effective and efficient educational practices. Interestingly, research in this area has shown that the same set of variables leads to increased student achievement in both regular and special education classrooms (Daly, Martens, Barnett, Witt, & Olson, 2007; Reschly, 2004).

This research has also called into question the assumption that achievement is primarily a function of within-student characteristics. As early as 1989, Christenson and Ysseldyke argued that an *ecological perspective*, which acknowledges a variety of influences on student achievement (both intrinsic and situational), is necessary to design effective school-based interventions. Key assumptions of this ecological perspective, known as the Student Learning in Context (SLIC) model, are that (1) learning involves an interaction between student skills, the instructional environment, and the demands of the curriculum; (2) instructional interventions are subordinate to the curriculum and must facilitate movement through the curriculum; (3) changes to instruction are best viewed as hypotheses that must be tested empirically; and (4) the effects of these changes should be evaluated as frequently as possible on the basis of student performance on actual curriculum materials.

With respect to the first assumption, a number of teacher variables has been shown to influence student achievement, including clearly communicated goals and expectations for student progress, detailed lesson plans and briskly paced instructional presentations, rules for behavior that are consistently reinforced and trained at the beginning of the school year, and procedures for evaluating student performance that are sensitive to short-term gains (Cataldo, Kahng, DeLeon, Martens, Friman, & Cataldo, 2007). Also related to student achievement is the degree of correspondence between the difficulty level of the curriculum materials and the student's skill level, or what is referred to as *instructional match*. In order to benefit from instruction, students must be able to complete assigned tasks with a high degree of accuracy and minimal errors (Martens & Witt, 2004). When modifying students' instructional programs, it may be necessary to adjust their placement in the curriculum sequence downward until they consistently exhibit a high proportion of correct responses (e.g., 80% or above) or meet benchmarks for fluency given the grade level of the curriculum material.

With respect to the second assumption, the majority of students who are low achieving or have a mild disability are capable of pursuing the same curriculum as their regular achieving peers with adequate supports. What distinguishes these groups of students, however, is the level at which they are placed in the curriculum and their rate of progress as a function of programming effectiveness (i.e., the presence of a dual discrepancy; Burns & Senesac, 2005). For example, Shinn (1986) assessed the reading performance of 505 students with mild disabilities between the grades of 1 through 6 who had been placed in special education. The students were tested at three points during the school year using passages sampled from their curriculum materials. Similar data were collected on approximately 9,000 regular education students at the same intervals. Although the number of words read correctly by the students in special education increased significantly at each time of testing, their performance became significantly more discrepant from regular education peers as the year progressed. These findings indicated that while the students in special education were improving in reading, their counterparts in regular education were improving at a much higher rate. Given that many of the constraints present in typical classrooms are relaxed in special education, one has to wonder why special education programming is not more effective. Kavale (1990) suggested that special education students may not achieve at higher rates because their teachers do not set ambitious goals and expectations for learning. In the absence of ambitious goals, special education may ultimately serve a maintenance rather than a remediation function.

Finally, as discussed in Chap. 8, the available evidence suggests that school-based interventions are likely to be extremely variable in their effects on children, and that we cannot predict the outcomes of these interventions with certainty (Kavale, 1990). This means that decisions about intervention effectiveness can only be made by systematically evaluating program outcomes. This also means that one cannot predict with certainty whether a student with special needs will require a special education placement until prereferral interventions are tried and evaluated in the regular classroom setting.

In the following chapter, we consider many of the issues and concepts presented thus far in this book via a case study example. The transcribed consultation sessions comprising the case as well as our retrospective analysis represent attempts to demonstrate the integrated model of consultation "in action."

Chapter 11
Consultation Case Study

From our earlier chapters, one can see that the school consultant's effectiveness depends a great deal on his or her strategic interpersonal communication (Daly & Wiemann, 1994). We therefore consider the study of messages that are exchanged in consultation to be an extremely important means for learning how to consult. The strength of this belief leads us to devote an entire chapter to a single example of school consultation. Seeing many of the concepts discussed thus far carried out may enable readers to incorporate more readily aspects of the contemporary practice of school consultation into their daily work.

Chapter 11 contains a set of two interviews (PII and PAI) between a psychologist-consultant and a first grade teacher-consultee. They discuss a 6-year-old girl ("Tamara") who has been diagnosed with ADHD and who exhibits academic and behavioral difficulties, with early literacy skill deficits in particular. English is Tamara's native language. The described client-centered case consultation is taken from Lehigh University's Project PASS (Promoting Academic Success for Students; DuPaul et al., 2006; Jitendra et al., 2007).

Project PASS investigated the effectiveness of academic interventions for students with ADHD designed via a data-based decision-making teacher consultation model termed Intensive Data-based Academic Intervention (IDAI) consultation. Prior to the formal start of consultation, IDAI consultants provide teachers with descriptive and treatment information about ADHD in a 30 min session, which also offers the opportunity for rapport building and basic contracting for the consultation relationship. The PII then occurs in much the same way described by Bergan and Kratochwill (1990). Following the IDAI PII, a functional academic assessment of the classroom is conducted (Daly, Witt, Martens, & Dool, 1997), student work products are reviewed, and curriculum-based assessment data are collected in reading and/or math. Then, within the IDAI PAI, the consultant proposes several research-based academic interventions and consequently has the teacher select the intervention(s) seen as most appropriate to his/her classroom and the student's needs (DuPaul et al., 2006; Jitendra et al., 2007).

A disclaimer offered at the outset is that the consultant in the featured case was not explicitly trained in the integrated model of school consultation described in this book. She does, however, display many consultant behaviors that are central to this

W.P. Erchul and B.K. Martens, *School Consultation*, Issues in Clinical Child Psychology,   193
DOI 10.1007/978-1-4419-5747-4_11, © Springer Science+Business Media, LLC 2010

model, and, more importantly, behaviors that are highly relevant to the contemporary practice of school consultation. For comparison purposes, it may be useful to review a different, more consultee-centered, case study found in Chap. 9 of previous editions of this book (Erchul & Martens, 1997, 2002).

After each interview transcript, we comment on the consultant's approach relative to key aspects of the integrated model. Each consultant message is numbered for easy reference. Borrowing from Caplan's (1970, p. 192) suggestion, the reader initially may wish to read both transcripts back-to-back in order to gain a perspective on the consultation. Transcripts then may be reread separately, this time incorporating the comments. Following the two interview transcripts, selected case outcome data are presented for further consideration and discussion.

Problem Identification Interview: February 18

CONSULTANT: (1) Mainly what we will be talking about today are the primary academic concerns for Tamara.

TEACHER: OK.

CONSULTANT: (2) What would you say her primary problem is in, reading or math?

TEACHER: Definitely reading.

CONSULTANT: (3) OK, what specifically about reading?

TEACHER: She is below grade level, she is lacking in the basic skills.

CONSULTANT: (4) Basic skills, meaning like letter-sound correspondence, or?

TEACHER: Right. Tracking letter sounds as far as beginning to end, and consistency in remembering words that she has already learned.

CONSULTANT: (5) Sight words or just regular words?

TEACHER: Sight words.

CONSULTANT: (6) OK.

TEACHER: She's having a lot of difficulty just in that consistency. She may know the word one minute and then later not have a clue.

CONSULTANT: (7) OK. Are you doing any decoding yet?

TEACHER: We have been doing a lot of decoding, pretty much all year.

CONSULTANT: (8) OK.

TEACHER: Our new reading series is very phonics based. There's a lot of phonemic skills as far as blending words together, sounding them out into their individual sounds, diagraphs, and phonemes. It's all pretty much done phonetically with the exception of those sight words.

CONSULTANT: (9) OK. Does she know all her letters?

TEACHER: Yes. If you ask her, she can tell you letter sounds. She can tell you individual sounds, but as far as blending the sounds together to make a word, she is still having a lot of difficulty.

CONSULTANT:	(10) Now when you say blending the letter sounds, you don't necessarily mean letter blends, like sounding out "cat," right?
TEACHER:	Right. Just the three or four letter words she has some difficulty with. And we have done things like the *ch, gh, sh, qu, wh* sounds and the *ck, all,* and *ill* words. We are getting ready now to go into long vowels.
CONSULTANT:	(11) OK.
TEACHER:	We have done the *ar.* We started on the *ir, er,* and *ur.* Probably in another 3–4 weeks, we will be starting long vowels and she just really is not ready for that.
CONSULTANT:	(12) OK. Would you say that it is primarily a skill deficit or a performance deficit on her part?
TEACHER:	Definitely a skill deficit.
CONSULTANT:	(13) OK. On a scale of 1–5 with 5 being the most severe, how would you rate her academic difficulties in reading?
TEACHER:	I would say she is a 4½ or 5.
CONSULTANT:	(14) OK. And when does she seem to have the most academic difficulty? Is it in large group, small group, or independent work?
TEACHER:	I think it is probably large group and some independent work. Because when it comes to doing it independently, she doesn't have the background or skill-base.
CONSULTANT:	(15) OK. And how about the least difficulty? In small group?
TEACHER:	She does pretty well in small group and individually if you pull her out. She does go to reading support where she does OK, but she is still the lowest.
CONSULTANT:	(16) Right.
TEACHER:	And she has difficulty as far as keeping her attention and having her interact and that type of thing. She does much better in a small group than in a whole group situation.
CONSULTANT:	(17) OK. How often does she go to reading support?
TEACHER:	She goes to reading support every day.
CONSULTANT:	(18) But she still has reading with you every day, too?
TEACHER:	Right. She has 30 minutes of reading support every morning and then she is with the rest of the group.
CONSULTANT:	(19) Do you notice any particular antecedent conditions, those that occur most frequently before you recognize her academic difficulties or before she demonstrates that she is having trouble? Is it when you pose a question to her or give an example or anything else along those lines?
TEACHER:	I don't think there is any one thing. She has a very difficult time as far as paying attention in large groups. Tamara will play with her shoes, her pants, or anything that she might have at that moment. The challenge is getting her attention and keeping her attention focused on one thing.

CONSULTANT: (20) OK. So, if you ask her more questions more frequently, does that tend to keep her attention?

TEACHER: It does if you stay on her. She can if I ask her a question and then I repeat it one or two times. She just has a lot of problems paying attention at first.

CONSULTANT: (21) OK. So if you ask her a question, what would be her typical response? Would it be that she just hasn't heard you, does she ask you to repeat it?

TEACHER: Usually she will just look at me and then she will guess what she thinks that she is supposed to be answering.

CONSULTANT: (22) OK. And she normally gets the correct answer, you said, when you ask her again?

TEACHER: After it's repeated, she usually does, yeah.

CONSULTANT: (23) OK. Do you always repeat the question or do you sometimes just skip her if she isn't paying attention? What is your typical response when things like that happen?

TEACHER: Well, today she was not paying attention when we were reading. So when I got to her I waited because I wasn't sure if she didn't know the word or if she didn't know where we were, so I just skipped her. Usually if it's an activity or something we are doing on the rug, I'll repeat it for her and give her the opportunity to at least try.

CONSULTANT: (24) OK. And there is no particular time of day?

TEACHER: No.

CONSULTANT: (25) Or maybe a different setting? It's just all the time?

TEACHER: Yes.

CONSULTANT: (26) Does she have any off-task or disruptive behaviors?

TEACHER: She is not disruptive to the rest of the classroom per se. She can be disruptive to the people who are sitting around her. Like today, she was sitting on the rug next to a little boy, and the entire time they were sitting there, picking things off the rug, playing with whatever he found in his pocket and whatever she had to play with. It is more that she is distracted and she may or may not have an accomplice.

CONSULTANT: (27) OK. Are there children in the class who, even if she tries to bring them off-task with her, are very resistant to that? Or is everyone pretty much following her?

TEACHER: I have a very social bunch this year, so I would say that she wouldn't have any trouble finding somebody else to talk to.

CONSULTANT: (28) OK. Based on her current performance in reading, what do you think would be a reasonable goal or goals to set? You can pick as many as you want.

TEACHER: Right now, I think just trying to get her to know her sight words. They all have a sight word book to take home and she consistently forgets it, and that is not helping her at all. She should be reading that book every night. I just went back with her last week to the first four or five stories that we read back in September and she is just now mastering those words. So, basically that is a whole half a year behind.

CONSULTANT: (29) Right.

TEACHER: If we could just get her to master those words in the book, even if it means going back to the beginning and starting there and working our way up. The words that we are learning now, she really doesn't know anything about them.

CONSULTANT: (30) Do you know how many sight words they have in their books now?

TEACHER: It's usually about 6 or 8. This week's story has 8.

CONSULTANT: (31) OK.

TEACHER: And those are just words that they just have to know by sight, they don't have to be able to spell them. They just have to know how to read them.

CONSULTANT: (32) OK. Um so you don't know exactly or an approximate of how many to date they have in their books?

TEACHER: No, I couldn't say.

CONSULTANT: (33) I was just looking for relative to how many words they have, what do you think would be reasonable for us to pick? Say they have 100 words in their book, how many do you think would be reasonable for her to know? All 100? Maybe 75? Or a percentage of those words?

TEACHER: I think at least 50% of what's already in their book would be a good start. And like I said, she's not consistent.

CONSULTANT: (34) Right.

TEACHER: She doesn't have the consistency where she says a specific word this week but next week she may not have any idea what that word is.

CONSULTANT: (35) OK. So, 50%. Is that the only goal that you want to pick for her?

TEACHER: I'd like to see her…because she does try and that's one good thing. She's not one of those children who just gives up and says, "I can't do it." She does try and she does sometimes ask other children for help. I would like to see her…because actually we've started spelling.

CONSULTANT: (36) Uh huh.

TEACHER: We've done 4 or 5 weeks of spelling now and she only gets half of the words. The normal amount is 10 words per student and she's been getting only 5.

CONSULTANT: (37) Uh huh.

TEACHER: But every other week she's gotten them all correct, even the first week where I wanted all students to try all 10, she got them all right.

CONSULTANT: (38) OK.
TEACHER: So, that type of performance is possible. I want to see her put that
              more into the reading part, you know.
CONSULTANT: (39) Right!
TEACHER: If she can spell the words, she should be able to relate the sounds
              and learn them together, so I'd like to see her trying more blending
              of the sounds together.
CONSULTANT: (40) OK.
TEACHER: Because the words that we're doing in spelling, they are ones she
              can sound out. They are words that have short *u* sounds, like *pu* and
              mu. Those are the types of words she can sound out.
CONSULTANT: (41) Uh huh.
TEACHER: If she can write them out, she should be able to consistently
              sound them out, and read the word "map," for example.
CONSULTANT: (42) OK. I hear what you're saying, I understand what you're say-
              ing. I'm just trying to think of a way to quantify that. Is there
              anything that you do…
TEACHER: [interrupts] One thing we do that's pretty much daily is they all
              have letter cards in their desks and we build words.
CONSULTANT: (43) Uh huh.
TEACHER: We build the words and a lot of times Tamara will just sit there.
              She doesn't try or she might try one word and not try another. I'd
              like to see her consistently work on trying to build those words
              instead of thinking, "Oh, I can't do it."
CONSULTANT: (44) Uh huh.
TEACHER: Or just waiting for the next student to do it, because she can do it
              if she tries. I have seen her do it. It's just a matter of getting her
              to consistently try and to build those words and to sound them
              out.
CONSULTANT: (45) Do you think that's more of a skill problem or a motivational
              problem?
TEACHER: Well, I think she's not motivated because she feels like she
              doesn't know it, so she doesn't even try.
CONSULTANT: (46) OK. Are you familiar with the DIBELS (Good & Kaminski,
              2002)?
TEACHER: A little bit.
CONSULTANT: (47) OK. I'm trying to think of tasks that I would be able to come
              in and measure her on. I would think that she would be able to do
              letter-sound correspondence by pointing to a picture that starts
              with a particular sound. Do you think she would be able to point
              to those?
TEACHER: I think she would have some trouble doing it.
CONSULTANT: (48) OK. I'd have to take a look to see what's been done so far
              because I know our data collectors have already been out to
              observe her in the classroom to see how she did on the DIBELS

measures. If she is below what they consider benchmark, which is where she should be by kindergarten for those skills, then we could make that level her quantitative goal.

TEACHER: Right.

CONSULTANT: (49) And then we could build interventions to address that goal, although some things might be similar to what you're already doing, like building the letters and things like that. So I'll look into that and we could put temporarily, if it's OK with you, meeting the benchmarks on the DIBELS subtests as a goal.

TEACHER: Yeah, that's fine. Next year we will be using the DIBELS for kindergarten and first grade.

CONSULTANT: (50) I would think that what our data collectors have done with her should reflect what you're saying is problematic for her. OK, as far as these two goals, how would you like to see them prioritized? Which would be #1 and #2?

TEACHER: I think the sight words are our main priority right now. If she becomes more familiar with those, it might help in other areas.

CONSULTANT: (51) OK. I know you've already been involved with the Project for a while now but, just so you know, I will come out to watch a reading class. I'll observe how she is in the class and get a feel for how things generally go in your classroom. I don't know if you know your lesson plans yet for next week, but when might be a good time for me to come out and do that? It would be about a 10 minute observation.

TEACHER: OK. We usually start at about 9:25, so if you picked a day then I could just make sure that I started that activity when you came in.

CONSULTANT: (52) OK. What about next Tuesday?

TEACHER: As of right now, I don't think I have anything then. That should be fine. I don't think there's any assemblies or anything next week.

CONSULTANT: (53) Well, they sometimes creep up, so if that happens it's not a problem. OK, the 25th at 9:25. All right, I know you already told me this already but, what do you actually expect the students to do during this lesson time? Are they primarily listening to what you're saying, or do they manipulate objects when you start building words, or...?

TEACHER: [interrupts] Well, when they're on the rug it's pretty much a conversational type thing.

CONSULTANT: (54) OK.

TEACHER: When we start, there may or may not be sentences on the board but if the sentences are up, there is usually a blank they have to fill in. Today we were talking about things you might do on a hot day, like where you might go or what you might do in the water. If they raise their hand, I let them talk and they say the sentence and fill it in.

CONSULTANT: (55) Uh huh.

TEACHER: So we do that, then we listen to the poem or story, then we do a little bit more discussion about the story or poem. Then we'll pull out words from the story or the poem and that is that's where the phonemic awareness will come into play as far as what's the beginning sound, or the blend, or whatever the particular skill is.

CONSULTANT: (56) So there aren't any permanent products or any actual work samples that they produce during this time?

TEACHER: No.

CONSULTANT: (57) OK. What is your main objective? What are you expecting them to learn and do as a result of this lesson?

TEACHER: Listening, interacting, being able to verbalize what they hear. They need to listen to the word that I say to be able to tell me what the beginning sound is.

CONSULTANT: (58) OK. I'm assuming how you assess that they have mastered the content of the lesson is just by their responses?

TEACHER: Yes.

CONSULTANT: (59) OK. Does Tamara have any permanent products that she's already completed on these types of activities with the letter-sound identification, the blends, and so on? Does she have any worksheets or anything I could take a look at?

TEACHER: Yes, this is her journal. You can see this is done pretty much independently. They copy the work sentences off the board and try to fill in the last word or whatever. We also use it to do word families and that type thing.

CONSULTANT: (60) Uh huh.

TEACHER: Now they're pretty much writing their own sentences. They brainstorm on the board and then write their own things.

CONSULTANT: (61) OK. So does she normally finish her work?

TEACHER: Yeah, she does finish it most of the time.

CONSULTANT: (62) OK. Do you currently collect any type of assessment data like when they have tests and quizzes?

TEACHER: No, not really, but one thing we have done this year is the *LeapFrog* stuff.

CONSULTANT: (63) Uh huh.

TEACHER: And on the *LeapFrog*, they've done assessments. I can print hers out for you next week if you'd like.

CONSULTANT: (64) Yes, thank you.

TEACHER: They are given three assessments. The first assessment is letter-sound recognition, then letter recognition in both capital and lower case, and the third one is a combination of rhyming words that involve beginning sounds and ending sounds. Those are the three assessments I believe she has completed.

CONSULTANT: (65) OK.

TEACHER: So I can print out her record for you.

CONSULTANT:	(66) OK.
TEACHER:	And you can get an idea of what she does and doesn't know. Like this plus and minus, she either knows her sight words or she doesn't know them.
CONSULTANT:	(67) OK.
TEACHER:	And she's a consistent "doesn't know them."
CONSULTANT:	(68) OK, and that's for each story?
TEACHER:	Right, for each story.
CONSULTANT:	(69) OK.
TEACHER:	And it goes all the way back to the first story. Last week she just read these three so, since the very beginning of the school year, she has only successfully read the sight words for the first five stories.
CONSULTANT:	(70) OK. How do you arrive at their grades in reading other than based on their sight word performance? Do they have reading tests just on the stories?
TEACHER:	That's what they've been getting, reading tests on the stories.
CONSULTANT:	(71) OK. So you're not testing any straightforward phonics skills necessarily?
TEACHER:	Right, we're not doing that.
CONSULTANT:	(72) OK. By way of summary, I want to make sure that I touched on all of these points. So we will primarily be focusing on her sight words and then secondary to that, the DIBELS benchmarks: letter-sound correspondence, reading segmentation, all those types of skills.
TEACHER:	Uh huh.
CONSULTANT:	(73) There isn't any antecedent event that necessarily comes before her academic difficulties. It's just really a lack of attention that you're finding with her answering your questions and then a skill deficit on top of that complicating the situation?
TEACHER:	Right. Her attention is really a main problem, a main concern.
CONSULTANT:	(74) Uh huh. If you had to make a judgment, do you think she would be more likely to be paying attention if she understood it and had those academic skills? Or do you think that attention is a huge part of the reason why she doesn't have those skills?
TEACHER:	Yeah, I think she has some of the academic problems because of the attention problem.
CONSULTANT:	(75) OK. As far as progress monitoring, depending on what we decide to do as far as her intervention for the sight words goes, I may just check in with you when you do these checks because it looks like you're already staying on top of how many of the sight words she knows. But we'll have to see.
TEACHER:	Maybe some of the DIBELS subtests may be easier for her. If we focus on some of the DIBELS, maybe we'll find that'll help her with the sight words. Maybe then we'd want to flip-flop, depending on what you find and what you come back with next week.

CONSULTANT: (76) OK. We can definitely talk about that but I will be doing the
               DIBELS subtests with her for progress monitoring regardless to see
               if she's reaching benchmark on that.
TEACHER: OK.
CONSULTANT: (77) The next time that we actually sit down to talk, it will be to
               talk about interventions, taking into account what we've found.
               And that will be a couple weeks from now. But remember that I'll
               be back on Tuesday to observe, right?
TEACHER: Yes, Tuesday at about 9:25.
CONSULTANT: (78) Great, I'll see you then.

An Analysis of the First Interview

1–11. The consultant begins this PII by jumping right into the problem-solving task.
An external consultant would have been more likely to give a role-structuring statement as described in Chap. 6. Given the nature of the Project PASS IDAI consultation,
however, we can assume the consultant and teacher met previously to address entry
issues. In messages 1–11, the consultant quickly moves from broad to specific topics
in examining Tamara's reading problems. Note also that the consultant uses several
closed-ended "either-or" questions to help define the problem here. Although this
may be appropriate given the narrow academic scope of project PASS, consultants
typically rely on more open-ended questions early in the PII to assess the scope of
consultee concerns.

1, 33, 49, 72, 75, 76, 77. The consultant's use of the words *we* and *us* may be
viewed as attempts to develop both rapport and positive referent power (Erchul &
Raven, 1997), thereby contributing to both the support and development task and
social influence task of school consultation.

2, 3, 5, 7, 9, 10, 19, 21, 27, 28, 33, 47, 48, 49, 50, 57, 70, 72, 77. These selected
statements contain either the consultant's comments on, or her modeling of, the
problem-solving process. As such, the statements exemplify the development portion
of the support and development task as well as the problem-solving task. To the
extent the statements reflect an advanced understanding of reading skills, assessment
techniques, etc., the consultant's positive expert power (Erchul & Raven, 1997)
may have been enhanced.

12, 45. Because of the implications for later intervention selection, it is critical to
assess early on if a described client problem represents a skills deficit ("can't do")
versus a performance deficit ("won't do") (Witt, Daly, & Noell, 2000).

14–15. Effective school consultation requires one to carefully examine presenting
problems with respect to setting issues. With these two questions, the consultant
begins a longer interview segment (i.e., functional assessment) that focuses on variables
in the immediate classroom setting that may be affecting Tamara's performance.

19–25. Here, the consultant addresses the problem-solving task by asking pointed
questions related to antecedent conditions (message 19), Tamara's response to an

identified antecedent condition (messages 20–22), the teacher's typical response to Tamara (message 23), and regular behavioral patterns (messages 24 and 25). The consultant's skillful use of questions and control of topics provide evidence of addressing the social influence task.

28–35. Having at least tentatively identified Tamara's reading problem, the consultant works with the teacher to establish goals for her. The goal specified for Tamara in this interview segment is for her to identify at least 50% of the words in her sight word book.

36–41. In the teacher message that precedes consultant message 36, the teacher tries twice to state another goal for Tamara (i.e., "I'd like to see her…"). The consultant unfortunately seems initially unresponsive to pick up on the teacher's hesitancy to generate another goal. In retrospect, deeper probing here may have facilitated the teacher's thinking along these lines, thereby broadening the conceptualization of Tamara's academic problems.

42. The consultant's explicit statement of encouragement and understanding of the teacher's situation illustrates the support aspect of the support and development task. Although this statement represents the consultant's only "pure" message of social support found in this PII, her friendly yet professional demeanor throughout appeared to project a clear sense of caring and concern for the teacher's classroom problem.

46–49. As presented in Chaps. 2 and 7, direct assessment of client performance is expected in the modern practice of school consultation. This is particularly true when addressing academic problems and using systematic formative evaluation to monitor student progress. In message 47, the consultant refers to the Initial Sounds Fluency subtest of the Dynamic Indicators of Early Literacy Skills (DIBELS; Good & Kaminski, 2002). It also bears mentioning that Project PASS utilizes data collectors besides the consultant to gather information related to client and teacher behaviors and perceptions.

50. When multiple goals are generated, it is advisable to prioritize them in order to proceed efficiently (Bergan, 1977).

51–58. In addition to assessing client performance using standardized measures, it is important for the consultant to observe the client in the setting(s) in which the identified problem occurs. This observation often takes place between the PII and PAI and can be used to supplement the initial functional assessment information obtained from the PII. It can also provide an opportunity for the consultant to observe instructional variables related to student performance as discussed in Chap. 8. The teacher may have perceived the consultant's plan to observe as also serving a supportive function, knowing that additional insights would be shared during the PAI.

59–69. The consultant is attempting to find already completed permanent products to serve as baseline data against which to evaluate Tamara's progress following intervention implementation. Although from context it is difficult to specify which *LeapFrog* product was being used in the classroom, it might have been the Phonemic Awareness Series or Interactive Decodable Series (www.leapfrogschool.com).

72–76. The consultant effectively summarizes and validates key content discussed during the PII.

77. The day and time of the next meeting between consultant and teacher is verified before the interview concludes. Though seemingly a minor objective, it is an important one to address to emphasize that school consultation is a continuing process requiring full participation of all parties.

Overall, this consultant's interviewing style appeared to emphasize questions (i.e., specification elicitors) and brief acknowledgments of consultee responses in the form of "OK" or "Right!" (i.e., positive validation emitters; Bergan & Tombari, 1975). Compared to a prototypical PII, the consultant used relatively fewer summarization statements (at 10, 22, 35, 42, 72, and 73), but these appeared to be effective (particularly at 72 and 73) given the consultee's agreement.

Problem Analysis Interview: March 4

CONSULTANT: (1) OK, today we're going to review some standardized reading measures that we have for Tamara, review academic goals set for her, talk about interventions and see if there are any that you think would work well in the classroom, talk about a plan to put those into action, and determine when you would actually be able to implement them.

TEACHER: OK.

CONSULTANT: (2) As far as reading goes, on the DIBELS subtest of Initial Sounds Fluency (Good & Kaminski, 2002), the test administrator says, "point to the picture that starts with the sound *b*" and Tamara would then point to the ball. Phoneme Segmentation Fluency, a second subtest, is when I say a word and she sounds it out for me. Letter Naming Fluency, a third subtest, is simply naming letters, and at kindergarten a child should be able to name 60 letters in a minute. Finally, Nonsense Word Fluency has fake words, which you sound out by using basic phonics rules. She was at frustrational levels on Phoneme Segmentation, Letter Naming, and Nonsense Word Fluency, which means she is below where she should be by kindergarten. She was instructional on Initial Sounds Fluency, and that was fine.

As far as achievement on the Woodcock-Johnson III (Woodcock, McGrew, & Mather, 2001) goes, she was a little bit low on just about everything except for Word Attack Skills, where she was about where she should be, at 1.4, which corresponds to the fourth month of first grade. On everything else she was in late kindergarten but still in the kindergarten range. On Letter-Word Identification, she was at the first month of first grade.

TEACHER: OK.

CONSULTANT: (3) When I came into observe, there were about equal rates of her being on-task and off-task during reading. The day I was here I did not get to see any permanent products from her because you and your class were doing rug time. I did, though, go over these materials that you had given me and highlighted what she had missed, the letter identification, for example.

TEACHER: Uh huh.

CONSULTANT: (4) We had discussed her goals of knowing 50% of her sight words, and obviously none of these assessment measures tapped into that. But that is a reasonable goal. And then we had discussed her reaching benchmark on all the DIBELS subtests, and there are data that clearly indicate she needs with help with that. So there is definitely a discrepancy with where she should be with reading achievement levels.

TEACHER: Right.

CONSULTANT: (5) OK, when I observed her, it wasn't super-structured, hands-on time, it was a lot of question asking instead. Was that typical of how she normally behaves?

TEACHER: Yes.

CONSULTANT: (6) OK, and we had discussed behaviorally that she gets distracted easily and can be…

TEACHER: [interrupts] She is easily distracted and off-task.

CONSULTANT: (7) Our goals are fine: recognizing 50% of sight words and hitting the DIBELS benchmarks. What I have come up with is basically an intervention menu, and the first several interventions speak more to the benchmarks for the phonological awareness and not the sight words. There is actually only one suggestion for the sight words and we will get to that one in a few minutes.

The first intervention is the *Elkonin Cards* (Blachman, Ball, Black & Tangel, 2000), in which the student is presented with a picture card and at the top there is a picture of say, a sun, and then there are letter tiles underneath the word, including "s," "u," and "n." As the teacher, you would model how to sound out the word. As you are sounding each letter out, you would drag the letter tile into the box because at the bottom, all the separate letter boxes are connected to make the word.

TEACHER: OK.

CONSULTANT: (8) Does that make sense? So you would say "*ss-uh-nn*" as you are dragging out the letters, and you would model that for the student. The student would repeat it and she would eventually do it on her own. You would typically do four or five cards a day. There is a whole packet of different *Elkonin Cards* with the pictures and they are all CVC (consonant-vowel-consonant) words.

TEACHER: OK.

CONSULTANT: (9) It has all the basic letter/sound correspondences, and that is the *Elkonin Card* activity.

Let's Fish (Blachman et al., 2000) is a little bit different. It involves picture cards that are face down and then the student has a little fishing pole or they can just pickup a card with their fingers. When they pick it up, they have to identify the picture – and then you can do this any way you want – it can either be having them identify the initial sound or initial phoneme, or ending sounds, or middle sounds. That is the idea of *Let's Fish*.

TEACHER: Do they just identify the sound, or like if it is "sun," do they have to say "*sss*" and it is the letter "*s*"?

CONSULTANT: (10) You can do it any way you want.

TEACHER: Oh, OK.

CONSULTANT: (11) It certainly wouldn't hurt to have them identify the letter as well as the sound.

TEACHER: OK.

CONSULTANT: (12) Next, *Save the Rabbit* (Blachman et al., 2000) is very similar to the game Hangman, but using a rabbit instead of a hangman. The complete rabbit is drawn first and then you would erase away parts of it for incorrect responses rather than add parts as in Hangman. The student would have five to ten letters to pick from to complete an easy three-letter CVC word.

TEACHER: Uh huh.

CONSULTANT: (13) We can use *sun* again as an example. The given letters might be "a" "m" "s" "n" "u" and "i," so they would only have a certain number of letters to pick from rather than being confused with all the letters in the alphabet.

TEACHER: Right.

CONSULTANT: (14) If they pick a letter that is not in the word, then you would take away the letter so they cannot pick it anymore. Then you would erase part of the rabbit, just like in Hangman.

TEACHER: Right.

CONSULTANT: (15) I think it's just more of a fun way for them to go about it. Again, they have to identify what the word is and what each of the sounds is in the word.

TEACHER: Uh huh.

CONSULTANT: (16) OK, then *Sound Bingo* (Blachman et al., 2000) is just like traditional Bingo except that the bingo card consists of letters and pictures. You can do this one any way you want, too. Maybe you want to have a cutout bingo card and you show the child the picture or you can say the picture that starts with the letter "s" or the sound "*s*." Does that make sense?

TEACHER: Yeah.

CONSULTANT: (17) So that is *Sound Bingo*, and that is all of them for phonological awareness.

TEACHER: OK.

CONSULTANT:	(18) Do any of those interventions sound feasible? Or interesting?
TEACHER:	Yes, some of them do. How often would she need to be doing these activities?
CONSULTANT:	(19) I would recommend that you do at least one of them twice a week.
TEACHER:	Twice a week?
CONSULTANT:	(20) Uh huh, at least that often.
TEACHER:	OK. I do have a parent assistant that comes in on Thursday mornings.
CONSULTANT:	(21) OK.
TEACHER:	And I have another assistant who comes in Friday afternoons. Even though it is math time, I can take the last few minutes before she goes to a special class and just have her do one of these activities for five or ten minutes and she really wouldn't be missing anything.
CONSULTANT:	(22) Great!
TEACHER:	So I know we have these two times a week, as long as there is nothing else, like we shouldn't be having anymore snow days or anything.
CONSULTANT:	(23) Right! (laughs)
TEACHER:	So as long as everything else is fine, I know during those two days we can definitely put in some time.
CONSULTANT:	(24) That would be good. The other thing to keep in mind is if there are multiple ideas here that you like, feel free to use any of them you want. However, we will have to set up a plan to consistently implement at least one of them on those two days each week. So, this is not to say because you pick *Let's Fish* you can't do the *Elkonin Cards* at some other time. It is just that we'll need to regularly monitor one specific intervention. With that said, is there one that looks more interesting? Or, if you tell me none of them do, that's fine, I can go back to the drawing board.
TEACHER:	No, I like the *Elkonin Cards* but I don't have any of those…
CONSULTANT:	(25) (Interrupts) I would provide all of those materials for you.
TEACHER:	OK, I kind of like that because she does have difficulty taking the single sounds and remembering them. The reading specialist teacher says Tamara can give you each sound but has difficulty blending the sounds together to make the word. She might say "*ss*," "*uh*," and "*nn*" but then when she goes back she might bring the "*nn*" back to the beginning of the word.
CONSULTANT:	(26) OK.
TEACHER:	So I think that moving the tiles around would actually do a lot of good for her.

CONSULTANT: (27) Good. OK, then we will mark that one down. Can you determine any constraints in resources that you would have to implement the intervention?

TEACHER: I think that the only problem I would have would be the time factor.

CONSULTANT: (28) Uh huh.

TEACHER: But as long as my assistants come in, I'll have the time because they can work with her.

CONSULTANT: (29) Right.

TEACHER: That would really be the only problem. If the assistants weren't coming in, then I suppose I could have another child if we had free time maybe play the *Let's Fish* game with her.

CONSULTANT: (30) Uh huh.

TEACHER: And there are also a lot of other assistants available in the building, and if I knew in advance that one wasn't coming, maybe I could speak to the two people who are in charge of assigning the assistants.

CONSULTANT: (31) OK, that all sounds good. So, as far as the materials go, I will get you the *Elkonin Cards*.

TEACHER: OK.

CONSULTANT: (32) Do you have letter tiles or anything like that?

TEACHER: I do have some little letters somewhere in that giant box (*points to and retrieves box*).

CONSULTANT: (33) OK.

TEACHER: Here they are, they came with the *Leapfrog* series. What do you think of these little cards?

CONSULTANT: (34) Perfect, perfect. The boxes on the *Elkonin Cards* might be a little small for those but that doesn't matter.

TEACHER: Right.

CONSULTANT: (35) They don't have to fit exactly into that box.

TEACHER: Right.

CONSULTANT: (36) Those tiles would be absolutely perfect for that.

TEACHER: OK.

CONSULTANT: (37) I wish I had all of these resources at my disposal! (laughs) I am always amazed when I go into classrooms and see all of that neat stuff teachers have and I am like, "wow!"

TEACHER: Sometimes it is too much, though. They give you all this stuff and you are like, "what am I going to do with all of this?"

CONSULTANT: (38) (laughs) OK, so, two times a week, Thursday and Friday.

TEACHER: Uh huh.

CONSULTANT: (39) And what times on Thursdays and Fridays? Do you know?

TEACHER: Thursdays it would be in the mornings, and Fridays it would be in the afternoon.

CONSULTANT: (40) OK, as far as a starting date, if you wanted to start this week, I think I can get you everything by then (*checks schedule*). Yes, I have to be up here tomorrow for a meeting at Sloane Elementary, so I may just pop in and drop it off to you. It is not going to take an extensive explanation.

TEACHER: That's fine.

CONSULTANT: (41) The other thing is that I will type up a list of instructions of exactly how it should be done so if there are any questions you can fall back on those or you can always e-mail or call me.

TEACHER: Sure, that's fine.

CONSULTANT: (42) Oh, back to the sight words, I almost forgot. This particular strategy, the folding in drill, has been very effective with teachers who have used it for both sight words and multiplication facts (e.g., Browder & Shear, 1996; Neef, Iwata, & Page, 1977). It is essentially a flashcard drill, but it is building more on things they know and blending in what they don't know, so they are coming away not as frustrated because they didn't know any of the words. For example, Tamara would have seven sight words that she knows and three sight words that she doesn't know. They would be presented in this sequential order: unknown word, known word, unknown, known, known, unknown, known, known, known, known. Every time, you'd basically present the first card, second card, then go back to the first card, second card, third card, first card, second card, third card, fourth card, and so on.

TEACHER: OK.

CONSULTANT: (43) So she is always getting that repeated practice through each of the initial presentation. You would go through all ten cards, shuffle them again, and repeat that two more times. Essentially she is seeing all of the words at least six times in one five to ten minute drill.

TEACHER: Right.

CONSULTANT: (44) As far as I can find, that is the most effective strategy for learning sight words. Does that seem like something that would be possible to do with her?

TEACHER: Yeah, I know she has been working with flashcards and this might actually be a little bit easier. We can just pull out seven cards she knows, then take three cards she doesn't know. With her it's consistency that is the problem, and if you are doing it that way, she is seeing it over and over again and that might help with the consistency.

CONSULTANT   (45) Right. Something I forget to mention is that once she knows the word after it has been presented three times, then that word becomes a known word. If she doesn't know it, then it just transfers to the next day as an unknown word.

TEACHER   Right.

CONSULTANT   (46) Do you have a list of her sight words? What I am thinking is that if I could get a copy of the list, I could make up her flashcards.

TEACHER: OK.

CONSULTANT: (47) You would have a copy of them so you could have a consistent running list of the words she knows and doesn't know. Then, if you could find five minutes to do it with her at least once or twice a week, you would be able to be more on top of it than letting one teacher do it one day and another teacher do it another day. She'd get more consistent feedback on it and practice with it. Does that sound feasible?

TEACHER: Yeah, I should be able to do that. Let me see if I have the list here. (*Leaves to get list.*) OK, she gets a modified list, with five rather than all ten of the words. And also what happens is they get words, then they get them used in sentences, and in the sentences are other words that they either already have mastered or words that are in the story.

CONSULTANT: (48) OK, let me ask you this – and by all means feel free to say "no" – would you mind if I took this list with me tonight to make up her flashcards? Because I will be back here tomorrow, I can get this list back to you regardless of whether the flashcards are made.

TEACHER: Sure, that's fine.

CONSULTANT: (49) Whether I will have her flashcards made by tomorrow, that's a different story, but that would be less work on your part, for me to go through this list and type it up. I can do all that without a problem.

TEACHER: Sure.

CONSULTANT: (50) As long as you don't mind that I take her word list home. (laughs) I mean I don't want her to be without it if she has homework tonight!

TEACHER: No, I have all of the lists in here.

CONSULTANT: (51) OK, I will come up with flashcards for those words. All right, moving on, can you speculate when you would have time to do the folding in drill with her?

TEACHER: I can try and get it in first thing in the morning.

CONSULTANT: (52) OK.

TEACHER: It is a little hectic sometimes, but I am sure we could pick a few minutes and do it.

CONSULTANT: (53) How about we shoot for two mornings a week?

TEACHER: OK.

CONSULTANT: (54) And then hopefully it will get done. If not, once a week would be OK. It's just one of those things, like the more practice she gets with it, the faster the skill will be acquired.

TEACHER: Right.

CONSULTANT: (55) OK, I'll put tomorrow down as the start date, but I might not necessarily have the flashcards to you depending on what comes up between here and my way home and when I get back to my office.

TEACHER: Uh huh.

CONSULTANT: (56) If there are any anticipated problems for that I am assuming it will be time again.

TEACHER: Uh huh.

CONSULTANT: (57) OK, the skills to be measured will be 50% of her sight words and the DIBELS benchmarks. For the sight words what I am going to say initially is, if you want, I can go through the entire list and figure out which words are known and which words are unknown.

TEACHER: OK.

CONSULTANT: (58) Then I can generate a list for you and, as unknown words become known words, I can check in with you every week when I am here to do her DIBELS. From your records, I'll be able to see which words she has learned that week.

TEACHER: OK.

CONSULTANT: (59) Obviously, we could track her sight words that way, if that sounds OK.

TEACHER: OK.

CONSULTANT: (60) In terms of the frequency of data collection, I will be here once a week to do her progress monitoring, so I will check in with you then.

Just to recap, Tamara's two goals are going to be reaching the benchmarks on all the DIBELS subtests and knowing 50% of her sight words from her word book. The interventions we are going to do are the *Elkonin Cards* for the phonological awareness, and the folding in drill for her sight words. You will be responsible for tracking which words become known words when you do this activity with her, and I will come in to do the DIBELS subtests with her and track her progress through that. As far as phonological awareness goes, she will do the *Elkonin Cards* twice a week with the assistants when they come in on Thursdays and Fridays. You will also do the folding in drill with her twice a week in the mornings when she comes in.

OK, the next thing I need to mention, but what we won't schedule right now because it is another four weeks away, is the Problem Evaluation Interview.

TEACHER: OK.

CONSULTANT: (61) Basically at that time we'll just sit down again and talk about how things are going, if anything needs to be changed, if she is progressing, and so on. Also, I think I've already explained treatment integrity, for which I will type up a list of instructions for both the *Elkonin Cards* and the folding in drill. Because they are evidence-based interventions, they have specific procedures that need to be followed.

TEACHER: Uh huh.

CONSULTANT: (62) So, I will come out and observe each intervention three or four times by the end of the school year to assess how things are

	going and if those specific steps that I have laid out for you are being followed.
TEACHER:	OK.
CONSULTANT:	(63) The last thing that we need to go over is her current progress on these target behaviors. What I'm asking is on a day-to-day basis, how often does she demonstrate that she knows 50% of her sight words? Would you say "never," "sometimes," "often," or "very often"?
TEACHER:	50%?
CONSULTANT:	(64) Uh huh.
TEACHER:	I would have to say "never" for that.
CONSULTANT:	65) That makes sense, as obviously nothing has started yet. But the basic idea behind this is when I check in with you in a couple of weeks, she will know some of those words.
TEACHER:	Right, right.
CONSULTANT:	(66) That is basically the whole point. You seemed to be looking at me like, "Why are you asking me this?" It wouldn't be a goal, obviously, if she was showing good progress already! OK, the benchmarks on the DIBELS might be a little more difficult for you to take a stab at, considering that you don't have the same method of measurement, but as far as demonstrating phonological awareness, would you say "never," "sometimes," "often," or "very often"?
TEACHER:	I would probably have to say "sometimes."
CONSULTANT:	(67) OK.
TEACHER:	Some skills she can do, other skills she can't.
CONSULTANT:	(68) OK, that is really it. Do you have any questions, comments, or concerns?
TEACHER:	No, I'm fine.
CONSULTANT:	(69) OK.

An Analysis of the Second Interview

1. The consultant opens with a comprehensive preview of what content will be addressed in the PAI.

1, 4, 6, 7, 13, 24, 27, 59, 60, 61. The use of *we* or *our* in these consultant messages suggests further development of rapport and positive referent power (Erchul & Raven, 1997), thereby addressing both the support portion of the support and development task and the social influence task of school consultation.

1, 4, 7, 18, 24, 27, 41, 42, 44, 51, 57–62. These statements reflect either the consultant's comments on, or her modeling of, the problem-solving process. As such, these messages represent the development portion of the support and development task as well as the problem solving task.

2–3. The consultant quickly reviews Tamara's DIBELS subtest and Woodcock-Johnson III Tests of Achievement subtest scores.

4. This message is a restatement of goals generated in the PII, with the conclusion reached that a discrepancy exists with respect to Tamara's current versus desired performance.

5. The consultant checks to see whether the classroom observation allowed her to see a representative sample of Tamara's behavior.

7–17. The consultant presents a menu of four evidence-based interventions: *Elkonin Cards* (messages 7–9), *Let's Fish* (messages 9–11), *Save the Rabbit* (messages 12–15), and *Sound Bingo* (messages 16–17). A consequence of presenting these interventions to the teacher may have been to bolster the consultant's positive expert power (Erchul & Raven, 1997).

10, 11, 19, 20, 44, 69. These messages offer professional guidance and/or information and thus may have enhanced both the consultant's positive expert power and the teacher's professional development (i.e., support and development task).

18, 24. In messages 7–17, the teacher has been given a forced choice intervention menu from which it is expected she will select at least one intervention. Now, with these three questions, the consultant addresses perhaps the most important social influence task of the PAI: How do I get commitment from the teacher to implement an evidence-based intervention?

19–23. The consultant fields questions regarding the expected frequency of implementation, which leads the teacher to identify other staff (i.e., a parent assistant) who may be able to help.

25. The teacher selects the *Elkonin Cards* but quickly adds she does not have the necessary materials. The consultant wisely jumps in to say that she can provide everything that is needed, thereby addressing the support and development task.

25, 31, 41, 46, 48, 58. These messages, in which the consultant offers to do something or provide materials related to intervention implementation, may well represent influence strategies drawing on legitimate reciprocity and/or legitimate equity (Erchul & Raven, 1997). That is, the teacher may feel obligated to faithfully carry out the agreed-on interventions because the consultant has done so much in advance to facilitate her efforts.

27–30. The consultant asks whether there will be any constraints to the teacher's implementation of the intervention. Interestingly, the teacher's answer (i.e., her limited time) causes her to reflect further and come up with two possible solutions: use teaching assistants and/or another child. This message exchange illustrates the behavioral consultation research finding that when a consultant asks (instead of tells) a teacher what to do regarding implementing an intervention, the odds are 14 times higher the teacher will identify needed resources and methods to carry out the intervention (Bergan & Neumann, 1980). By the consultant serving as a "sounding board" rather than an expert, the teacher in this case appeared to retain responsibility for the problem *and* its solution.

31–41. This interview segment describes the procedures to follow to implement the *Elkonin Cards* intervention. Specific topics addressed are: the materials needed and who will supply them (messages 31–37), frequency of implementation (message

38), days and times of implementation (message 39), starting date (message 40), and detailed instructions for implementation (message 41). If there was a reason to believe that the teacher was not skilled enough to use the *Elkonin Cards*, it is assumed that the consultant would have trained her before proceeding further.

36–37. The consultant expresses approval over the teacher's tiles and then her classroom supplies (i.e., "neat stuff") more generally. These statements may be interpreted as examples of building rapport and personal reward power (Erchul & Raven, 1997).

42–56. In this interview segment, the consultant essentially repeats the same steps found in messages 31–41 but for the folding in/interspersal activity. With respect to the social influence task, it should be noted that here the teacher is not given a choice of interventions as was the case for the preceding interventions that targeted DIBELS benchmarks. Rather, there is a strong suggestion that she will commit to the folding in activity because it is the only evidence-based intervention the consultant presents to increase Tamara's sight word vocabulary. Consistent with the instructional hierarchy as a conceptual model of academic intervention presented in Chap. 8, the consultant describes the folding in procedure as providing repeated practice of previously unknown words, thereby promoting retention. Teacher attributions of positive expert power to the consultant may have facilitated the apparent commitment to the folding in activity.

48, 50. These statements represent what Caplan (1970, pp. 96–97) referred to as "onedownsmanship," as they have the consultant deferring to the teacher by not wanting to inconvenience her by temporarily removing Tamara's sight word list from the classroom.

57–68. The last portion of the interview offers a comprehensive summary of key PAI content (particularly within message 60) and what will need to be done during the next stage, intervention implementation. These topics include: specific skills to be measured (message 57), method of measurement (messages 57–59), frequency of data collection (message 60), treatment integrity issues (messages 61–63), and progress to target behavior ratings (messages 63–68).

Problem Evaluation Interview: April 9

Although a Problem Evaluation Interview was held, it was not audiotaped, so a transcript is unavailable. We consequently finish this consultation case presentation by providing some data collected as a part of the consultation.

Child Measures

1. Woodcock-Johnson III Word Attack Skills (Woodcock et al., 2001):

    – Raw scores: pretreatment=4; posttreatment=4.
    – Percentile rankings: pretreatment=52; posttreatment=28.
    – Standard scores: pretreatment=101; posttreatment=91.

2. Woodcock-Johnson III Letter-Word Identification (Woodcock et al., 2001):
   - Raw scores: pretreatment = 18; posttreatment = 20.
   - Percentile rankings: pretreatment = 28; posttreatment = 17.
   - Standard scores: pretreatment = 91; posttreatment = 86.

3. Though they were collected, Tamara's DIBELS (Good & Kaminski, 2002) subtest scores were not available. One of the agreed upon intervention goals was for Tamara to reach benchmarks on the DIBELS subtests. At pretest, she performed in the frustrational range on Phoneme Segmentation, Letter Naming, and Nonsense Word Fluency. Because these subtests were directly related to skills trained in the *Let's Fish, Save the Rabbit,* and *Sound Bingo* interventions, it is reasonable to assume that they would have been sensitive to improvement as generalization probes.

Teacher/Consultation Case Measures

1. Teacher-rated Student Progress-to-Target Behavior: Posttreatment rating *minus* Pretreatment rating = 1. (Potential range of ratings is 0–3, with *never* to *very often* as scale anchors). For a Project PASS sample of consultation cases on this measure, Erchul et al. (2009) reported M = 1.11 and SD = 0.45. The teacher's rating corresponds roughly to the sample mean.
2. Consultant Observations of Teacher's Treatment Integrity: Four observations across time indicated 100% treatment integrity. For a Project PASS sample of consultation cases on this measure, Erchul et al. (2009) reported M = 92.55 and SD = 15.99.
3. Postconsultation BIRS-T Intervention Acceptability (Elliott & Von Brock Treuting, 1991): Raw score = 71 (Potential range of scores is 15–90, with higher scores suggesting greater acceptability.) For a Project PASS sample of consultation cases on this measure, Erchul et al. (2009) reported M = 70.43 and SD = 7.07. The teacher's intervention acceptability rating nearly equals the sample mean.
4. Postconsultation BIRS-T Intervention Effectiveness (Elliott & Von Brock Treuting, 1991): Raw score = 33. (Potential range of scores is 7–42, with higher scores suggesting greater effectiveness.) For a Project PASS sample of consultation cases on this measure, Erchul et al. (2009) reported M = 28.10 and SD = 4.57. The teacher's rating is slightly higher than the sample mean.

Conclusion

Unfortunately, not every school consultation produces an unqualified success. The consultant in this case carried out established practices of problem-solving consultation with a high degree of process integrity, supplemented interview information with direct client assessment data, and recommended evidence-based interventions, which the teacher faithfully implemented and judged as essentially acceptable and effective. Although the teacher noted some progress toward Tamara's target behaviors over time and Woodcock-Johnson III subtest scores revealed raw score increases, Tamara simply lost ground relative to her peers. Specifically, the W-J III percentile rankings and standard score equivalents showed a slight decrease from pretreatment to posttreatment. Relative to teacher/consultation case data, however, the reported measures fell at or above average levels reported by Project PASS across 20 cases (Erchul et al., 2009).

Acknowledgment We wish to thank Dr. George DuPaul (Principal Investigator) and Dr. Asha Jitendra (Co-Principal Investigator) of Project PASS for allowing us to include this case in Chap. 11. Project PASS was supported by the National Institute of Mental Health, Grant R01-MH62941. We are also grateful to Erin Barbato, Megan Bennett, and Courtney Fox for transcribing the interviews.

Chapter 12
Epilog: The Effective Practice of School Consultation

In the 1970s, P.L. 94-142/IDEA wrote into law many of the remedies handed down in previous court cases regarding special education services. The major provisions of IDEA were to guarantee children: (a) the right to a free, appropriate public education; (b) assessment in all areas related to their suspected disability using nondiscriminatory practices; (c) long-term goals and short-term objectives specified in an individualized education program (IEP); (d) due process protections in all matters of identification, evaluation, and placement; (e) access to related services; and (f) education in the least restrictive environment.

At the time, IDEA created what many considered a paradigm shift in special education. First, by requiring that children be diagnosed with a disability in order to receive services, IDEA established the refer-test-place sequence discussed in Chap. 4 as the primary means of eligibility determination. Second, by mandating that most services be provided by or in consultation with special education teachers, IDEA placed responsibility for accommodating students with special needs on these professionals. Third, IDEA required that children who were diagnosed with a disability be educated alongside their typical peers to the maximum extent deemed appropriate. Although not a mandate for mainstreaming/inclusion per se, the least restrictive environment clause established the notion of a continuum of services ranging in intensity from assistance by a consulting teacher to part-time resource room attendance to full-time, special class placement.

In the 30-plus years since IDEA was passed, the American education system has faced repeated cuts in federal and state budgets, increasing numbers of children diagnosed with high-incidence disabilities (e.g., SLD), and rising costs of special education. These developments have led to disenchantment with the refer-test-place sequence and special education as the primary vehicles for school-based service delivery. The former has been characterized as a costly, wait-to-fail model that delays services and reduces their effectiveness (e.g., Vaughn & Fuchs, 2003), whereas the latter has been criticized for relying on an outdated and ineffective aptitude × treatment interaction (ATI) model that results in low exit rates and inadequate educational outcomes (Kavale, 1990; Reschly, 2004).

As discussed in Chap. 2, the general problem-solving model of school consultation emerged in response to these mounting criticisms. Central to this model are a focus

W.P. Erchul and B.K. Martens, *School Consultation*, Issues in Clinical Child Psychology,   217
DOI 10.1007/978-1-4419-5747-4_12, © Springer Science+Business Media, LLC 2010

on children's skills rather than abilities, a tiered system of early intervention using evidence-based practices, and systematic formative evaluation of treatment outcomes. Although it began as a grass-roots movement by researchers interested more in intervention than diagnosis, school consultation has now become a mandated, stand alone service in the schools with the passage of NCLB and IDEIA 2004 (Martens & DiGennaro, 2008). Just as the original IDEA created a paradigm shift in school-based services during the 1970s and 1980s, these two pieces of legislation mark a paradigm shift occurring today (Reschly, 2008). We believe this paradigm shift has implications for the future of school consultation practice and research in three important ways.

First, the primary responsibility for accommodating students with special needs appears to have shifted from special to regular education. Along these lines, many schools have adopted some version of a tiered service delivery model, the goals of which are to (a) provide early identification and treatment for at-risk students and (b) balance the cost of services with the level of intensity required to bring about desired outcomes. Although tiered delivery systems are also intended to provide a continuum of services, most of these services are now provided by or in consultation with *regular* education teachers. In order to avoid the problem of programmatic isolation which plagued poorly coordinated special education services, school consultants and consulting teams will need to become more familiar with regular education practices. This means selecting intervention materials and designing intervention programs in ways that produce generalized outcomes in the regular education curriculum. This also means developing small and large-group instructional practices that will be effective and practical for teachers to use as Tier 1 and Tier 2 interventions.

Second, more schools across the country will likely adopt some version of an RTI model to determine the eligibility of students exhibiting both academic (i.e., SLD) and behavior (i.e., ED) problems. Because systematic formative evaluation plays such a central role in problem solving, the success of these efforts will depend in large part on the collection and management of assessment data from students' cumulative intervention histories (Daly et al., 2007). In order to be useful for high-stakes RTI decision making, these data will have to allow school professionals to compare children to each other and to themselves over time in a dual-discrepancy model/approach. To enable both kinds of comparisons (i.e., inter- and intra-subject), consulting teams will need to adopt measures that meet the criteria from two different assessment traditions. From the perspective of classical test theory, these measures must be reliable and valid. That is, they must yield consistent scores across parallel samples and predict performance on more global indices of performance. From the perspective of domain sampling theory, these measures must directly assess educationally meaningful or clinically relevant behaviors, be capable of repeated administration, be sensitive to short-term instructional changes, and be useful in informing treatment decisions (Martens & Ardoin, 2010). Consultants and consulting teams will need to be familiar with these two assessment traditions as well as various conventions (based on both statistical and visual analysis) for making inter- and intra-subject comparisons. Although CBM is widely used in RTI models for academic performance problems, more research is needed to develop measures that meet the criteria above in school-wide efforts to address children's behavior problems.

Third, the ability to sustain implementation of strong, individualized, and evidence-based treatments at Tier 3 of an RTI model outside *of special education will be an important challenge for consulting teams.* At present, special education is still positioned as the strongest, most intense treatment in a tiered service delivery model. This makes sense given that the structure of special education is designed to allow for individualized, direct instruction. That is, special education classrooms are characterized by low teacher–student ratios (sometimes involving 1:1 assistance), the freedom to select curriculum materials, and the ability to adjust the pace of instruction as specified in each child's IEP. We know that special education programs are costly to implement over time (Reschly, 1988), and Tier 3 interventions share many of these same features. If these interventions are to be sustained for any length of time beyond an initial assessment period, consulting teams will likely need to either obtain the resources necessary to support implementation in regular education or shift responsibility for implementation to special education.

In conclusion, the conceptual and empirical bases of school consultation have evolved considerably since the first edition of this book was published in late 1996. As we have noted here, the modern practice of school consultation occurs within the context of high-stakes, team-based service delivery that demands evidence-based practice. School consultation is further embedded in a context of tiered services that links prereferral intervention, positive behavioral supports, and RTI approaches to eligibility determination. We anticipate (and hope) that effective consultation practice will continue to evolve as advances in research inform the problem-solving, social influence, and support and development tasks comprising our integrated model. Regardless of the context in which it is provided, however, effective school consultation will continue to require the accomplishment of goals under each of these three tasks. As such, we would like to end this volume by reminding readers of the definition of school consultation offered in Chap. 1. That is, at its heart, school consultation remains a cooperative relationship between a specialist (consultant) and a staff member (consultee), the goals of which are to improve the learning and adjustment of a student (client) and to potentially increase the consultee's ability to prevent similar problems in the future.

References

Achenbach, T. M., & Rescorla, L. A. (2001). *Manual for the ASEBA school-age forms & profiles.* Department of Psychiatry: Burlington University of Vermont.

Addi-Raccah, A., & Arviv-Elyashiv, R. (2008). Parent empowerment and teacher professionalism. *Urban Education, 43*, 394–415.

Albee, G. W. (1959). *Mental health and manpower trends.* New York: Basic Books.

Albee, G. W. (1968). Conceptual models and manpower requirements in psychology. *American Psychologist, 23*, 317–320.

Aldrich, S. F., & Martens, B. K. (1993). The effects of behavioral problem analysis versus instructional environment information on teachers' perceptions. *School Psychology Quarterly, 8*, 110–124.

Algozzine, B., Ysseldyke, J. E., Christenson, S., & Thurlow, M. L. (1983). A factor analysis of teachers' intervention choices for dealing with students' behavior and learning problems. *The Elementary School Journal, 84*, 189–197.

Allegretto, S. A., Corcoran, S. P., & Mishel, L. (2004). *How does teacher pay compare? Methodological challenges and answers.* Washington, DC: Economic Policy Institute.

Allington, R. L. (1980). Teacher interruption behaviors during primary-grade oral reading. *Journal of Educational Psychology, 72*, 371–377.

Alpert, J., & Silverstein, J. (1985). Mental health consultation: Historical, present, and future perspectives. In J. R. Bergan (Ed.), *School psychology in contemporary society: An introduction* (pp. 281–315). Columbus, OH: Merrill.

Alpert, J. L., & Yammer, D. M. (1983). Research in school consultation: A content analysis of selected journals. *Professional Psychology, 14*, 604–612.

American Psychological Association. (2002). Ethical principles of psychologists and code of conduct. *American Psychologist, 57*, 1060–1073.

Anderson, C. M., & Long, E. S. (2002). Use of a structured descriptive assessment methodology to identify variables affecting problem behavior. *Journal of Applied Behavior Analysis, 35*, 137–154.

APA Presidential Task Force on Evidence-based Practice. (2006). Evidence-based practice in psychology. *American Psychologist, 61*, 271–285.

Apter, S. J. (1977). The public schools. In B. Blatt, D. Biklen, & R. Bogdon (Eds.), *An alternative textbook in special education.* Denver, CO: Love Publishing.

Archer, R. P., Maruish, M., Imhof, E. A., & Piotrowski, C. (1992). Psychological test usage with adolescent clients: 1990 survey findings. *Professional Psychology: Research & Practice, 22*, 247–252.

Ardoin, S. P., Witt, J. C., Suldo, S. M., Connell, J. E., Hoenig, J. L., Resetar, J. L., et al. (2004). Examining the incremental benefits of administering a maze and three versus one curriculum-based measurement reading probes when conducting universal screening. *School Psychology Review, 33*, 218–233.

Armbruster, B. B., Stevens, R. J., & Rosenshine, B. (1977). *Analyzing content coverage and emphasis: A study of three curricula and two tests. (Technical Report No 26)*. Urbana, IL: University of Illinois.

Astor, R. A., Pitner, R. O., & Duncan, B. B. (1998). Ecological approaches to mental health consultation with teachers on issues related to youth and school violence. *Journal of Negro Education, 65*, 336–355.

Axelrod, S. (1993). Integrating behavioral technology into public schools. *School Psychology Quarterly, 8*, 1–9.

Babinski, L. M., & Rogers, D. L. (1998). Supporting new teachers through consultee-centered group consultation. *Journal of Educational and Psychological Consultation, 9*, 285–308.

Bahr, M. W., Whitten, E., Dieker, L., Kocarek, C. E., & Manson, D. (1999). A comparison of school-based intervention teams: Implications for legal and ethical reforms. *Exceptional Children, 66*, 67–83.

Bandura, A. (1977). *Social learning theory*. Englewood Cliffs, NJ: Prentice-Hall.

Barlow, D. H., Hayes, S. C., & Nelson, R. O. (1984). The scientist practitioner (pp. 3–37). New York: Pergamon.

Barone, S. G. (1995). The egalitarian virus. *Education Weekly, March 1*, 35.

Barry, B., & Watson, M. R. (1996). Communication aspects of dyadic social influence in organizations: A review and integration of conceptual and empirical developments. In B. R. Burleson (Ed.), *Communication yearbook 19* (pp. 269–317). Thousand Oaks, CA: Sage.

Bass, B. M. (1981). *Stodgill's handbook of leadership* (rev.th ed.). New York: Free Press.

Becker, W. C. (1988). Direct instruction: Special issue. *Education and Treatment of Children, 11*, 297–402.

Begeny, J. C., & Martens, B. K. (2006). Assessing pre-service teachers' training in empirically-validated behavioral instruction practices. *School Psychology Quarterly, 21*, 262–285.

Bell, P. F., Lentz, F. E., & Graden, J. L. (1992). Effects of curriculum-test overlap on standardized achievement test scores: Identifying systematic confounds in educational decision making. *School Psychology Review, 21*, 644–655.

Bennett, R. E. (1984). Information management in educational service delivery. In C. A. Maher, R. J. Illback, & J. E. Zins (Eds.), *Organizational psychology in the schools: A handbook for professionals* (pp. 385–401). Springfield, IL: Thomas.

Bennis, W. G. (1969). *Organization development: Its nature, origins, and prospects*. Reading, MA: Addison-Wesley.

Bergan, J. R. (1977). *Behavioral consultation*. Columbus, OH: Merrill.

Bergan, J. R. (1995). Evolution of a problem-solving model of consultation. *Journal of Educational and Psychological Consultation, 6*, 111–123.

Bergan, J. R., & Kratochwill, T. R. (1990). *Behavioral consultation and therapy*. New York: Plenum.

Bergan, J. R., & Neumann, A. J. (1980). The identification of resources and constraints influencing plan design in consultation. *Journal of School Psychology, 18*, 317–323.

Bergan, J. R., & Tombari, M. L. (1975). The analysis of verbal interactions occurring during consultation. *Journal of School Psychology, 13*, 209–226.

Bergan, J. R., & Tombari, M. L. (1976). Consultant skill and efficiency and the implementation and outcomes of consultation. *Journal of School Psychology, 14*, 3–14.

Berkowitz, L., & Daniels, L. R. (1963). Responsibility and dependence. *Journal of Abnormal Psychology, 66*, 429–436.

Blachman, B. A., Ball, E. W., Black, R., & Tangel, D. M. (2000). *Road to the code: A phonological awareness program for young children*. Baltimore, MD: Brookes.

Blake, R. R., & Mouton, J. S. (1976). *Consultation*. Reading, MA: Addison-Wesley.

Borman, G. D., & Dowling, N. M. (2008). Teacher attrition and retention: A meta-analytic and narrative review of the research. *Review of Educational Research, 78*, 367–409.

Bossard, M. D., & Gutkin, T. B. (1983). The relationship of consultant skill and school organizational characteristics with teacher use of school based consultation services. *School Psychology Review, 12*, 50–56.

Brandenburg, N. A., Friedman, R. M., & Silver, S. E. (1990). The epidemiology of childhood psychiatric disorders: Recent prevalence findings and methodologic issues. *Journal of the American Academy of Child and Adolescent Psychiatry, 29*, 76–83.

Brehm, J. W. (1966). *A theory of psychological reactance*. New York: Academic Press.

Brophy, J. E. (1983). Classroom organization and management. *The Elementary School Journal, 83*, 265–285.

Browder, D. M., & Shear, S. M. (1996). Interspersal of known items in a treatment package to teach sight words to students with behavor disorders. *The Journal of Special Education, 29*, 400–413.

Brown, D., Pryzwansky, W. B., & Schulte, A. C. (2006). *Psychological consultation and collaboration: Introduction to theory and practice* (6th ed.). Boston: Pearson/Allyn & Bacon.

Buffum, A., Mattos, M., & Weber, C. (2009). *Pyramid response to intervention: RTI, professional learning communities, and how to respond when kids don't learn*. Bloomington, IN: Solution Tree.

Burns, M. K., Deno, S. L., & Jimerson, S. R. (2007). Toward a unified response-to-intervention model. In S. R. Jimerson, M. K. Burns, & A. M. VanDerHeyden (Eds.), *Handbook of response to intervention: The science and practice of assessment and intervention* (pp. 428–440). New York: Springer.

Burns, M. K., Ganuza, Z. M., & London, R. M. (2009). Brief experimental analysis of written letter formation: Single-case demonstration. *Journal of Behavioral Education, 18*, 20–34.

Burns, M. K., & Gibbons, K. A. (2008). *Implementing response-to-intervention in elementary and secondary schools: Procedures to assure scientific-based practices*. New York: Routledge/Taylor & Francis Group.

Burns, M. K., Peters, R., & Noell, G. H. (2008). Using performance feedback to enhance implementation fidelity of the problem-solving team process. *Journal of School Psychology, 46*, 537–550.

Burns, M. K., & Senesac, B. V. (2005). Comparison of dual discrepancy criteria to assess response to intervention. *Journal of School Psychology, 43*, 393–406.

Burns, M., & Symington, T. (2002). A meta-analysis of prereferral intervention teams: Student and systemic outcomes. *Journal of School Psychology, 40*, 437–447.

Burns, M. K., Wiley, H. I., & Viglietta, E. (2008). Best practices in effective problem-solving teams. In A. Thomas & J. Grimes (Eds.), *Best practices in school psychology-V* (pp. 1633–1644). Bethesda, MD: National Association of School Psychologists.

Busse, R. T., Kratochwill, T. R., & Elliott, S. N. (1995). Meta-analysis for single-case outcomes: Applications to research and practice. *Journal of School Psychology, 33*, 269–285.

Busse, R. T., Kratochwill, T. R., & Elliott, S. N. (1999). Influences of verbal interactions during behavioral consultations on treatment outcomes. *Journal of School Psychology, 37*, 117–143.

Caplan, G. (1961). *An approach to community mental health*. New York: Grune & Stratton.

Caplan, G. (1963). Types of mental health consultation. *American Journal of Orthopsychiatry, 3*, 470–481.

Caplan, G. (1964). *Principles of preventive psychiatry*. New York: Basic Books.

Caplan, G. (1970). *The theory and practice of mental health consultation*. New York: Basic Books.

Caplan, G. (1974). *Support systems and community mental health*. New York: Behavioral Publications.

Caplan, G. (1986). Recent developments in crisis intervention and in the promotion of support services. In M. Kessler & S. E. Goldston (Eds.), *A decade of progress in primary prevention* (pp. 235–260). Hanover, NH: University Press of New England.

Caplan, G. (1989). *Population-oriented psychiatry*. New York: Plenum.

Caplan, G. (1993a). Epilogue. In W. P. Erchul (Ed.), *Consultation in community, school and organizational practice: Gerald Caplan's contributions to professional psychology* (pp. 205–213). Washington, DC: Taylor & Francis.

Caplan, G. (1993b). Mental health consultation, community mental health, and population- oriented psychiatry. In W. P. Erchul (Ed.), *Consultation in community school, and organizational practice: Gerald Caplan's contributions to professional psychology* (pp. 41–55). Washington, DC: Taylor & Francis.

Caplan, G., & Bowlby, J. (1948). The aims and methods of child guidance. *Health Education Journal, 6,* 1–8.

Caplan, G., & Caplan, R. B. (1980). *Arab and Jew in Jerusalem: Explorations in community mental health.* Cambridge, MA: Harvard University Press.

Caplan, G., & Caplan, R. B. (1999). *Mental health consultation and collaboration.* Prospect Heights, IL: Waveland Press, Inc. (Original work published 1993).

Caplan, G., Caplan, R. B., & Erchul, W. P. (1994). Caplanian mental health consultation: Historical background and current status. *Consulting Psychology Journal: Practice and Research, 46*(4), 2–12.

Caplan, G., Caplan, R. B., & Erchul, W. P. (1995). A contemporary view of mental health consultation: Comments on "Types of mental health consultation" by Gerald Caplan (1963). *Journal of Educational and Psychological Consultation, 6,* 23–30.

Caplan, G., & Killilea, M. (1976). *Support systems and mutual help: Multidisciplinary explorations.* New York: Grune & Stratton.

Carkhuff, R. R. (1969). *Helping and human relations Vol. 1: Selection and training.* New York: Holt, Rinehart & Winston.

Carter, J., & Sugai, G. (1989). Survey of prereferral practices: Responses from state departments of education. *Exceptional Children, 55,* 298–302.

Cash, R. E. (2009). President's message: The future of school psychology: I dreamed a dream. *NASP Communiqué, 37*(8), 2.

Cataldo, M. F., Kahng, S., DeLeon, I. G., Martens, B. K., Friman, P. C., & Cataldo, M. (2007). Behavioral principles, assessment, and therapy. In M. L. Batshaw, N. J. Roizen, & L. Pelligrino (Eds.), *Children with Disabilities* (6th ed., pp. 539–555). Baltimore, MD: Paul H. Brookes Publishing Co.

Chard, D. J., Vaughn, S., & Tyler, B. J. (2002). A synthesis of research on effective interventions for building reading fluency with elementary students with learning disabilities. *Journal of Learning Disabilities, 35,* 386–406.

Chin, R., & Benne, K. D. (1969). General strategies for effecting change in human systems. In W. G. Bennis, K. D. Benne, & R. Chin (Eds.), *The planning of change* (2nd ed.). New York: Holt, Rinehart & Winston.

Christenson, S. L., & Sheridan, S. M. (Eds.). (2001). *Schools and families: Creating essential connections for learning.* New York: Guilford.

Christenson, S. L., & Ysseldyke, J. E. (1989). Assessing student performance: An important change is needed. *Journal of School Psychology, 27,* 409–425.

Cialdini, R. B., Vincent, J. B., Lewis, S. K., Catalan, J., Wheeler, D., & Darby, B. L. (1975). Reciprocal concessions procedure for inducing compliance: The door-in-the-face technique. *Journal of Personality and Social Psychology., 31,* 206–215.

Cihak, D. F., Kirk, E. R., & Boon, R. T. (2009). Effects of classwide positive peer "Tootling" to reduce the disruptive classroom behaviors of elementary students with and without disabilities. *Journal of Behavioral Education, 18,* 267–278.

Clark, E. G., & Leavell, H. R. (1958). Levels of application of preventive medicine. In H. R. Leavell & E. G. Clark (Eds.), *Preventive medicine for the doctor in his community: An epidemiologic approach* (2nd ed., pp. 13–39). New York: McGraw-Hill.

Cohen, M. D., March, J. G., & Olsen, J. P. (1972). A garbage can model of organizational choice. *Administrative Science Quarterly, 17,* 1.

Cohen, S., & Wills, T. A. (1985). Stress, social support, and the buffering hypothesis. *Psychological Bulletin, 98,* 310–357.

Cohn, M. M., & Kottkamp, R. B. (1993). *Teachers: The missing voice in education.* Albany, NY: State University of New York Press.

Conoley, J. C. (1981a). Advocacy consultation: Promises and problems. In J. C. Conoley (Ed.), *Consultation in schools: Theory, research, procedures* (pp. 157–178). New York: Academic Press.

Conoley, J. C. (1981b). The process of change: The agent of change. In J. C. Conoley (Ed.), *Consultation in schools: Theory, research, procedures* (pp. 1–10). New York: Academic Press.

Conoley, J. C., & Conoley, C. W. (1982). *School consultation: A guide to practice and training.* New York: Pergamon.

Conoley, J. C., & Conoley, C. W. (1992). *School consultation: Practice and training* (2nd ed.). Boston: Allyn & Bacon.

Conoley, J. C., & Gutkin, T. B. (1986). School psychology: A reconceptualization of service delivery realities. In S. N. Elliott & J. C. Witt (Eds.), *The delivery of psychological services in schools: Concepts, processes and issues* (pp. 393–424). Hillsdale, NJ: Erlbaum.

Conoley, J. C., & Wright, C. (1993). Caplan's ideas and the future of psychology in the schools. In W. P. Erchul (Ed.), *Consultation in community, school, and organizational practice: Gerald Caplan's contributions to professional psychology* (pp. 177–192). Washington, DC: Taylor & Francis.

Costenbader, V., Swartz, J., & Petrix, L. (1992). Consultation in the schools: The relationship between preservice training, perception of consultative skills, and actual time spent in consultation. *School Psychology Review, 21,* 95–108.

Cowen, E., & Hightower, A. D. (1990). The Primary Mental Health Project: Alternative approaches in school-based preventive services. In T. B. Gutkin & C. R. Reynolds (Eds.), *The handbook of school psychology* (2nd ed., pp. 775–795). New York: Wiley.

Cowen, E. L., Trost, M. A., Lorion, R. P., Dorr, D., Izzo, L. D., & Isaacson, R. V. (1975). *New ways in school mental health: Early detection and prevention of school maladaptation.* New York: Human Sciences Press.

Crothers, L., Hughes, T., & Morine, K. (2008). *Theory and cases in school-based consultation: A resource for school psychologists, school counselors, special educators, and other mental health professionals.* New York: Routledge.

Cubberley, E. P. (1916). *Public school administration: A statement of the fundamental principles underlying the organization and administration of public education.* Boston, MA: Houghton Mifflin.

Curtis, M. J., Castillo, J. M., & Cohen, R. (2008). Best practices in system-level change. In A. Thomas & J. Grimes (Eds.), *Best practices in school psychology-V* (pp. 887–901). Bethesda, MD: National Association of School Psychologists.

Curtis, M. J., & Zins, J. E. (1988). Effects of training in consultation and instructor feedback on acquisition of consultation skills. *Journal of School Psychology, 26,* 185–190.

Daly, E. J., Johnson, S., & LeClair, C. (2009). An experimental analysis of phoneme blending and segmenting skills. *Journal of Behavioral Education, 18,* 5–19.

Daly, E. J., Martens, B. K., Barnett, D., Witt, J. C., & Olson, S. C. (2007). Varying intervention delivery in response-to-intervention: Confronting and resolving challenges with measurement, instruction, and intensity. *School Psychology Review, 36,* 562–581.

Daly, E. J., Martens, B. K., Hamler, K., Dool, E. J., & Eckert, T. L. (1999). A brief experimental analysis for identifying instructional components needed to improve oral reading fluency. *Journal of Applied Behavior Analysis, 32,* 83–94.

Daly, E. J., III, Martens, B. K., Skinner, C. H., & Noell, G. H. (2009). Contributions of applied behavior analysis. In T. B. Gutkin & C. R. Reynolds (Eds.), *The handbook of school psychology* (4th ed., pp. 84–106). New York, NY: John Wiley & Sons.

Daly, E. J., Witt, J. C., Martens, B. K., & Dool, E. J. (1997). A model for conducting a functional analysis of academic performance problems. *School Psychology Review, 26,* 554–574.

Daly, J. A., & Wiemann, J. M. (Eds.). (1994). *Strategic interpersonal communication.* Hillsdale, NJ: Erlbaum.

Darling-Hammond, L., Berry, B. T., Haselkorn, D., & Fideler, E. (1999). Teacher recruitment, selection, and induction: Policy influences on the supply and quality of teachers. In L. Darling-Hammond & G. Sykes (Eds.), *Teaching as the learning profession: Handbook of policy and practice* (pp. 183–232). San Francisco: Jossey-Bass.

Davis, H., & Salasin, S. (1975). Utilization of evaluation. In M. Guttentag & E. Struening (Eds.), *Handbook of evaluation research* (Vol. 1, pp. 621–666). Beverly Hills: Sage.

Davis, J. M., & Sandoval, J. (1992). A pragmatic framework for systems-oriented consultation. *Journal of Educational and Psychological Consultation, 2,* 201–216.

Davison, M., & McCarthy, D. C. (1988). *The matching law: A research review*. Hillsdale, NJ: Erlbaum.

Delmolino, L. M., & Romanczyk, R. G. (1995). Facilitated communication: A critical review. *The Behavior Therapist, 18*, 27–30.

DeVoe, J., Peter, K., Noonan, M., Snyder, T., & Baum, K. (2005). *Indicators of school crime and safety 2005*. Washington, DC: U.S. Departments of Education and Justice.

deVoss, G. G. (1979). The structure of major lessons and collective student activity. *Elementary School Journal, 80*, 8–18.

Diagnostic and Statistical Manual of Mental Disorders Fourth Edition – Text Revision (DSM-IV-TR). (2000). Washington DC: American Psychiatric Association.

DiGennaro, F. D., Martens, B. K., & Kleinmann, A. E. (2007). A comparison of performance feedback procedures on teachers' implementation integrity and students' inappropriate behavior in special education classrooms. *Journal of Applied Behavior Analysis, 40*, 447–461.

DiGennaro, F. D., Martens, B. K., & McIntyre, L. L. (2005). Increasing treatment integrity through negative reinforcement: Effects on teacher and student behavior. *School Psychology Review, 34*, 220–231.

Dougherty, A. M. (2009). *Psychological consultation and collaboration in school and community settings* (5th ed.). Florence, KY: Cengage/Brooks/Cole.

Doyle, W. (1985). Recent research on classroom management: Implications for teacher preparation. *Journal of Teacher Education, 36*, 31–35.

Drasgow, E., & Yell, M. L. (2001). Functional behavioral assessments: Legal requirements and challenges. *School Psychology Review, 30*, 239–251.

Duhon, G. J., Mesmer, E. M., Gregerson, L., & Witt, J. C. (2009). Effects of public feedback during RTI team meetings on teacher implementation integrity and student academic performance. *Journal of School Psychology, 47*, 19–37.

Dunst, C. J., & Trivette, C. M. (1987). Enabling and empowering families: Conceptual and intervention issues. *School Psychology Review, 16*, 443–456.

DuPaul, G. D. (1992). How to assess attention-deficit hyperactivity disorder within school settings. *School Psychology Quarterly, 7*, 60–74.

DuPaul, G. J., Jitendra, A. K., Volpe, R. J., Tresco, K. E., Lutz, J. G., Vile Junod, R. E., et al. (2006). Consultation-based academic interventions for children with ADHD: Effects on reading and mathematics achievement. *Journal of Abnormal Child Psychology, 34*, 633–646.

Durand, V. M., & Crimmins, D. B. (1988). Identifying the variables maintaining self-injurious behavior. *Journal of Autism and Developmental Disorders, 18*, 99–117.

D'Zurilla, T. J., & Goldfried, M. R. (1971). Problem solving and behavior modification. *Journal of Abnormal Psychology, 78*, 107–126.

Eckert, T. L., Martens, B. K., & DiGennaro, F. D. (2005). Describing antecedent-behavior-consequence relations using conditional probabilities and the general operant contingency space: A preliminary investigation. *School Psychology Review, 34*, 520–528.

Ehrhardt, K. E., Barnett, D. W., Lentz, F. E., Stollar, S. A., & Reifin, L. H. (1996). Innovative methodology in ecological consultation: Use of scripts to promote treatment acceptability and integrity. *School Psychology Quarterly, 11*, 149–168.

Elliott, S. N., Turco, T., & Gresham, F. M. (1987). Consumers' and clients' pretreatment acceptability ratings of classroom group contingencies. *Journal of School Psychology, 25*, 145–154.

Elliott, S. N., & Von Brock Treuting, M. (1991). The Behavior Intervention Rating Scale: Development and validation of a pretreatment acceptability and effectiveness measure. *Journal of School Psychology, 29*, 43–51.

Elliott, S. N., Witt, J. C., Galvin, G., & Peterson, R. (1984). Acceptability of positive and reductive interventions: Factors that influence teachers' decisions. *Journal of School Psychology, 22*, 353–360.

Epstein, M., Cullinan, D., & Sabatino, D. (1977). State definitions of behavior disorders. *Journal of Special Education, 11*, 417–425.

Epstein, M. H., Matson, J. L., Repp, A., & Helsel, W. J. (1986). Acceptability of treatment alternatives as a function of teacher status and student level. *School Psychology Review, 15*, 84–90.

Erchul, W. P. (1987). A relational communication analysis of control in school consultation. *Professional School Psychology, 2*, 113–124.

Erchul, W. P. (1992a). On dominance, cooperation, teamwork, and collaboration in school-based consultation. *Journal of Educational and Psychological Consultation, 3*, 363–366.

Erchul, W. P. (1992b). Social psychological perspectives on the school psychologist's involvement with parents. In F. J. Medway & T. P. Cafferty (Eds.), *School psychology: A social psychological perspective* (pp. 425–448). Hillsdale, NJ: Erlbaum.

Erchul, W. P. (Ed.). (1993a). *Consultation in community, school, and organizational practice: Gerald Caplan's contributions to professional psychology*. Washington, DC: Taylor & Francis.

Erchul, W. P. (1993b). Reflections on mental health consultation: An interview with Gerald Caplan. In W. P. Erchul (Ed.), *Consultation in community, school and organizational practice: Gerald Caplan's contributions to professional psychology* (pp. 57–72). Washington, DC: Taylor & Francis.

Erchul, W. P. (1993c). Selected interpersonal perspectives in consultation research. *School Psychology Quarterly, 8*, 38–49.

Erchul, W. P. (1999). Two steps forward, one step back: Collaboration in school-based consultation. *Journal of School Psychology, 37*, 191–203.

Erchul, W. P. (2009). Gerald Caplan: A tribute to the originator of mental health consultation. *Journal of Educational and Psychological Consultation, 19*, 95–105.

Erchul, W. P., & Chewning, T. G. (1990). Behavioral consultation from a request-centered relational communication perspective. *School Psychology Quarterly, 5*, 1–20.

Erchul, W. P., & Conoley, C. W. (1991). Helpful theories to guide counselors' practice of school-based consultation. *Elementary School Guidance & Counseling, 25*, 204–211.

Erchul, W. P., Covington, C. G., Hughes, J. N., & Meyers, J. (1995). Further explorations of request-centered relational communication within school consultation. *School Psychology Review, 24*, 621–632.

Erchul, W. P., DuPaul, G. J., Grissom, P. F., Vile Junod, R., Jitendra, A. K., Mannella, M., et al. (2007). Relationships among relational communication processes and consultation outcomes for students with ADHD. *School Psychology Review, 36*, 111–129.

Erchul, W. P., DuPaul, G. J., Bennett, M. S., Grissom, P. F., Jitendra, A. K., Tresco, K. E., et al. (2009). A follow-up study of relational processes and consultation outcomes for students with ADHD. *School Psychology Review, 38*, 28–37.

Erchul, W. P., Grissom, P. F., & Getty, K. C. (2008). Studying interpersonal influence within school consultation: Social power base and relational communication perspectives. In W. P. Erchul & S. M. Sheridan (Eds.), *Handbook of research in school consultation* (pp. 293–322). New York: Taylor & Francis Group/Routledge.

Erchul, W. P., Hughes, J. N., Meyers, J., Hickman, J. A., & Braden, J. P. (1992). Dyadic agreement concerning the consultation process and its relationship to outcome. *Journal of Educational and Psychological Consultation, 3*, 119–132.

Erchul, W. P., & Martens, B. K. (1997). *School consultation: Conceptual and empirical bases of practice*. New York: Plenum.

Erchul, W. P., & Martens, B. K. (2002). *School consultation: Conceptual and empirical bases of practice* (2nd ed.). New York: Kluwer/Plenum.

Erchul, W. P., & Raven, B. H. (1997). Social power in school consultation: A contemporary view of French and Raven's bases of power model. *Journal of School Psychology, 35*, 137–171.

Erchul, W. P., Raven, B. H., & Ray, A. G. (2001). School psychologists' perceptions of social power bases in teacher consultation. *Journal of Educational and Psychological Consultation, 12*, 1–23.

Erchul, W. P., Raven, B. H., & Whichard, S. M. (2001). School psychologist and teacher perceptions of social power in consultation. *Journal of School Psychology, 39*, 483–497.

Erchul, W. P., Raven, B. H., & Wilson, K. E. (2004). The relationship between gender of consultant and social power perceptions within school consultation. *School Psychology Review, 33*, 582–590.

Erchul, W. P., & Schulte, A. C. (1993). Gerald Caplan's contributions to professional psychology: Conceptual underpinnings. In W. P. Erchul (Ed.), *Consultation in community, school, and organizational practice: Gerald Caplan's contributions to professional psychology* (pp. 3–40). Washington, DC: Taylor & Francis.

Erchul, W. P., & Schulte, A. C. (2009). Behavioral consultation. In A. Akin-Little, S. G. Little, M. A. Bray, & T. J. Kehle (Eds.), *Behavioral interventions in schools: Evidence-based positive strategies* (pp. 13–25). Washington, DC: American Psychological Association.

Erchul, W. P., & Sheridan, S. M. (Eds.). (2008a). *Handbook of research in school consultation: Empirical foundations for the field.* New York: Taylor & Francis Group/Routledge.

Erchul, W. P., & Sheridan, S. M. (2008b). Overview: The state of scientific research in school consultation. In W. P. Erchul & S. M. Sheridan (Eds.), *Handbook of research in school consultation: Empirical foundations for the field* (pp. 3–12). New York: Taylor & Francis Group/Routledge.

Erchul, W. P., Sheridan, S. M., Ryan, D. A., Grissom, P. F., Killough, C. E., & Mettler, D. W. (1999). Patterns of relational communication in conjoint behavioral consultation. *School Psychology Quarterly, 14,* 121–147.

Erikson, E. H. (1959). *Identity and the life cycle: Selected papers by Erik H. Erikson. Psychological Issues Monograph, 1(1), 18–166.* New York: International Universities Press.

Ervin, R. A., & Schaughency, E. (2008). Best practices in accessing the systems change literature. In A. Thomas & J. Grimes (Eds.), *Best practices in school psychology-V* (pp. 853–873). Bethesda, MD: National Association of School Psychologists.

Esler, A. N., Godber, Y., & Christenson, S. L. (2008). Best practices in school-family partnerships. In A. Thomas & J. Grimes (Eds.), *Best practices in school psychology-V* (pp. 917–936). Bethesda, MD: National Association of School Psychologists.

Esquivel, G. B., Lopez, E. C., & Nahari, S. (Eds.). (2007). *Handbook of multicultural school psychology.* Mahwah, NJ: Erlbaum.

Eysenck, H. J. (1952). The effects of psychotherapy: An evaluation. *Journal of Consulting Psychology, 16,* 319–324.

Fagan, T. K., & Wise, P. S. (2007). *School psychology: Past, present, and future* (3rd ed.). Bethesda, MD: National Association of School Psychologists.

Flugum, K. R., & Reschly, D. J. (1994). Prereferral interventions: Quality indices and outcomes. *Journal of School Psychology, 32,* 1–14.

Folger, J. P., & Puck, S. (1976, April). *Coding relational communication: A question approach.* Paper presented at the meeting of the International Communication Association, Portland, OR.

Ford, J. B., & Zelditch, M., Jr. (1988). A test of the law of anticipated reactions. *Social Psychology Quarterly, 51,* 164–171.

Forness, S. R., & Knitzer, J. (1992). A new proposed definition and terminology to replace "Serious Emotional Disturbance" in individuals with disabilities education act. *School Psychology Review, 21,* 12–20.

Freedman, J. L., & Fraser, S. C. (1966). Compliance without pressure: The foot-in-the-door technique. *Journal of Personality and Social Psychology, 4,* 195–202.

French, J. R. P., Jr., & Raven, B. H. (1959). The bases of social power. In D. Cartwright (Ed.), *Studies in social power* (pp. 150–167). Ann Arbor, MI: Institute for Social Research.

French, W., & Bell, C. H. (1978). *Organization development* (2nd ed.). Englewood Cliffs, NJ: Prentice-Hall.

Friedrich, J., & Douglass, D. (1998). Ethics and the persuasive enterprise of teaching psychology. *American Psychologist, 53,* 549–562.

Friend, M., & Cook, L. (2000). *Interactions* (3rd ed.). New York: Addison-Wesley/Longman.

Frisby, C. L. (2009). Cultural competence in school psychology: Established or elusive construct? In T. B. Gutkin & C. R. Reynolds (Eds.), *Handbook of school psychology* (4th ed., pp. 855–885). New York: Wiley.

Fuchs, L. S., & Fuchs, D. (1986a). Effects of systematic formative evaluation: A meta-analysis. *Exceptional Children, 53,* 199–208.

Fuchs, L. S., & Fuchs, D. (1986b). Linking assessment to instructional intervention: An overview. *School Psychology Review, 15,* 318–323.

Fuchs, D., & Fuchs, L. S. (1989). Exploring effective and efficient prereferral interventions: A component analysis of behavioral consultation. *School Psychology Review, 18,* 260–279.

Fuchs, L. S., & Fuchs, D. (1998). Treatment validity: A unifying concept for reconceptualizing the identification of learning disabilities. *Learning Disabilities Research & Practice, 13*, 204–219.

Fuchs, D., Fuchs, L. S., & Bahr, M. W. (1990). Mainstream assistance teams: A scientific basis for the art of consultation. *Exceptional Children, 57*, 128–139.

Fuchs, D., Fuchs, L. S., Bahr, M. W., Fernstrom, P., & Stecker, P. M. (1990b). Prereferral intervention: A prescriptive approach. *Exceptional Children, 56*, 493–513.

Fuchs, L. S., Fuchs, D., Hamlett, C. L., & Allinder, R. M. (1991). Effects of expert system advice within curriculum-based measurement on teacher planning and student achievement in spelling. *School Psychology Review, 20*, 49–66.

Fuchs, D., Mock, D., Morgan, P. L., & Young, C. L. (2003). Responsiveness to intervention: Definitions, evidence, and implications for the learning disabilities construct. *Learning Disabilities Research & Practice, 18*, 157–171.

Gallessich, J. (1982). *The profession and practice of consultation*. San Francisco: Jossey-Bass.

Gettinger, M. (1986). Issues and trends in academic engaged time of students. *Special Services in the Schools, 2*, 1–17.

Gettinger, M. (1988). Methods of proactive classroom management. *School Psychology Review, 17*, 227–242.

Getty, K. C., & Erchul, W. P. (2009). The influence of gender on the likelihood of using soft social power strategies in school consultation. *Psychology in the Schools, 46*, 447–458.

Giangreco, M. F. (1989). *Making related service decisions for students with severe handicaps in public schools: Roles, criteria, and authority*. Unpublished doctoral dissertation, Syracuse University.

Gibbon, J., Berryman, R., & Thompson, R. L. (1974). Contingency spaces and measures in classical and instrumental conditioning. *Journal of the Experimental Analysis of Behavior, 21*, 585–605.

Gillat, A., & Sulzer-Azaroff, B. (1994). Promoting principals' managerial involvement in instructional improvement. *Journal of Applied Behavior Analysis, 27*, 115–129.

Gilliam, J. E. (1979). Contributions and status rankings of educational planning committee participants. *Exceptional Children, 45*, 466–468.

Goldbaum, J., & Rucker, C. N. (1977). Assessment data and the child study team. In J. A. C. Vautour & C. N. Rucker (Eds.), *Child study team training program: Book of readings*. Austin, TX: Special Education Associates.

Goldstein, A. P., & Martens, B. K. (2000). *Lasting change: Methods for enhancing generalization of gain*. Champaign, IL: Research Press.

Goldstein, S., Strickland, B., Turnbull, A. P., & Curry, L. (1980). An observational analysis of the IEP conference. *Exceptional Children, 46*, 278–286.

Good, R. H., & Salvia, J. (1988). Curriculum bias in published, norm-referenced reading tests: Demonstrable effects. *School Psychology Review, 17*, 51–60.

Good, R. H., & Kaminski, R. (2002). *Dynamic Indicators of Basic Early Literacy Skills* (6th ed.). Eugene, OR: Institute for Development Development of Educational Achievement. Retrieved from http://dibels.uoregon.edu/

Good, T. L. (1983). Classroom research: A decade of progress. *Educational Psychologist, 18*, 137–144.

Good, T. L., & Brophy, J. E. (2000). *Looking in classrooms* (8th ed.). New York: Longman.

Gordon, R. (1983). An operational classification of disease prevention. *Public Health Reports, 98*, 107–109.

Gordon, R. (1987). An operational classification of disease prevention. In J. A. Steinberg & M. M. Silverman (Eds.), *Preventing mental disorders* (pp. 20–26). Rockville, MD: U.S. Department of Health and Human Services.

Gouldner, A. W. (1960). The norm of reciprocity: A preliminary statement. *American Sociological Review, 35*, 161–178.

Graden, J. L., Casey, A., & Christenson, S. L. (1985). Implementing a prereferral intervention system: I. The model. *Exceptional Children, 51*, 377–384.

Graden, J. L., Stollar, S. A., & Poth, R. L. (2007). The Ohio Integrated Systems Model: Overview and lessons learned. In S. R. Jimerson, M. K. Burns, & A. M. VanDerHeyden (Eds.), *Handbook of response to intervention: The science and practice of assessment and intervention* (pp. 288–299). New York: Springer.

Grant, W. V., & Snyder, T. D. (1986). *Digest of education statistics 1985–1986*. Washington, DC: Government Printing Office.

Gravois, T. A., Groff, S., & Rosenfield, S. (2009). Teams as value-added consultation services. In T. B. Gutkin & C. R. Reynolds (Eds.), *Handbook of school psychology* (4th ed., pp. 808–820). New York: Wiley.

Gresham, F. M. (1985). Behavior disorder assessment: Conceptual, definitional, and practical considerations. *School Psychology Review, 14*, 495–509.

Gresham, F. M. (1989). Assessment of treatment integrity in school consultation and prereferral intervention. *School Psychology Review, 18*, 37–50.

Gresham, F. M. (1991). Conceptualizing behavior disorders in terms of resistance to intervention. *School Psychology Review, 20*, 23–36.

Gresham, F. M. (2007). Evolution of the response-to-intervention concept: Empirical foundations and recent developments. In S. R. Jimerson, M. K. Burns, & A. M. VanDerHeyden (Eds.), *Handbook of response to intervention: The science and practice of assessment and intervention* (pp. 10–24). New York: Springer.

Gresham, F. M. (2009). Using response to intervention for identification of specific learning disabilities. In A. Akin-Little, S. G. Little, M. A. Bray, & T. J. Kehle (Eds.), *Behavioral interventions in schools: Evidence-based positive strategies* (pp. 205–220). Washington, DC: American Psychological Association.

Gresham, F. M., & Gansle, K. A. (1992). Misguided assumptions of DSM-III-R: Implications for school psychological practice. *School Psychology Quarterly, 7*, 79–95.

Gresham, F. M., Gansle, K. A., & Noell, G. H. (1993a). Treatment integrity in applied behavior analysis with children. *Journal of Applied Behavior Analysis, 26*, 257–263.

Gresham, F. M., Gansle, K., Noell, G. H., & Cohen, S. (1993b). Treatment integrity of school-based behavioral intervention studies: 1980–1990. *School Psychology Review, 22*, 254–272.

Gresham, F. M., & Kendell, G. K. (1987). School consultation research: Methodological critique and future research directions. *School Psychology Review, 16*, 306–316.

Gresham, F. M., & Noell, G. H. (1993). Documenting the effectiveness of consultation outcomes. In J. E. Zins, T. R. Kratochwill, & S. N. Elliott (Eds.), *Handbook of consultation services for children: Applications in educational and clinical settings* (pp. 249–273). San Francisco: Jossey-Bass.

Gresham, F. M., & Reschly, D. J. (1986). Social skills deficits and low peer acceptance of mainstreamed learning disabled children. *Learning Disability Quarterly, 9*, 23–32.

Grigorenko, E. L. (Ed.). (2008). *Educating individuals with disabilities*. New York: Springer.

Grossman, H. J. (1983). *Classification in mental retardation*. Washington, DC: American Association on Mental Deficiency.

Guarino, C. M., Santibañez, L., & Daley, G. A. (2006). Teacher recruitment and retention: A review of the recent empirical literature. *Review of Educational Research, 76*, 173–208.

Gursky, D. (2000/2001). Supply and demand: The teacher shortage: How bad is it? What's being done about it? *American Teacher, 85*, 12–13. 17.

Gutkin, T. B. (1980). Teacher perceptions of consultation services provided by school psychologists. *Professional Psychology, 11*, 637–642.

Gutkin, T. B. (1981). Relative frequency of consultee lack of knowledge, skill, confidence, and objectivity in school settings. *Journal of School Psychology, 19*, 57–61.

Gutkin, T. B. (1986). Consultees' perceptions of variables relating to the outcomes of school-based consultation interactions. *School Psychology Review, 15*, 375–382.

Gutkin, T. B. (1999a). Collaborative versus directive/prescriptive/expert school-based consultation: Reviewing and resolving a false dichotomy. *Journal of School Psychology, 37*, 161–190.

Gutkin, T. B. (1999b). The collaboration debate: Finding our way through the maze: Moving forward into the future: A response to Erchul (1999). *Journal of School Psychology, 37*, 229–241.

Gutkin, T. B., & Conoley, J. C. (1990). Reconceptualizing school psychology from a service delivery perspective: Implications for practice, training, and research. *Journal of School Psychology, 28*, 203–223.

Gutkin, T. B., & Curtis, M. J. (1982). School-based consultation: Theory and techniques. In C. R. Reynolds & T. B. Gutkin (Eds.), *The handbook of school psychology* (pp. 796–828). New York: Wiley.

Gutkin, T. B., & Curtis, M. J. (1990). School-based consultation: Theory, techniques, and research. In T. B. Gutkin & C. R. Reynolds (Eds.), *The handbook of school psychology* (2nd ed., pp. 577–611). New York: Wiley.

Gutkin, T. B., & Curtis, M. J. (2009). School-based consultation: The science and practice of indirect service delivery. In T. B. Gutkin & C. R. Reynolds (Eds.), *Handbook of school psychology* (4th ed., pp. 591–635). New York: Wiley.

Gutkin, T. B., Henning-Stout, M., & Piersel, W. C. (1988). Impact of a district-wide behavioral consultation prereferral intervention service on patterns of school psychological service delivery. *Professional School Psychology, 3*, 301–308.

Gutkin, T. B., & Hickman, J. A. (1988). Teachers' perceptions of control over presenting problems and resulting preferences for consultation versus referral services. *Journal of School Psychology, 26*, 395–398.

Haley, J. (1987). *Problem-solving therapy* (2nd ed.). San Francisco: Jossey-Bass.

Halpin, A. (1966). *Theory and research in administration*. New York: Macmillan.

Hanley, G. P., Iwata, B. A., & McCord, B. E. (2003). Functional analysis of problem behavior: A review. *Journal of Applied Behavior Analysis, 36*, 147–185.

Hanushek, E. A. (1992). The trade-off between child quantity and quality. *Journal of Political Economy, 100*, 84–117.

Happe, D. (1982). Behavioral intervention: It doesn't do any good in your briefcase. In J. Grimes (Ed.), *Psychological approaches to problems of children and adolescents* (pp. 15–41). Des Moines, IA: Iowa Department of Public Instruction.

Harding, J., Wacker, D. P., Cooper, L. J., Millard, T., & Jensen-Kovalan, P. (1994). Brief hierarchical assessment of potential treatment components with children in an outpatient clinic. *Journal of Applied Behavior Analysis, 27*, 291–300.

Haring, N. G., Lovitt, T. C., Eaton, M. D., & Hansen, C. L. (1978). *The fourth R: Research in the classroom*. Columbus, OH: Charles E. Merrill.

Harris, A. M., & Cancelli, A. A. (1991). Teachers as consultees: Enthusiastic, willing, or resistant participants? *Journal of Educational and Psychological Consultation, 2*, 217–238.

Hayes, S. C. (1981). Single case experimental design and empirical clinical practice. *Journal of Consulting and Clinical Psychology, 49*, 198–211.

Heller, K., & Monahan, J. (1977). *Psychology and community change*. Homewood, IL: Dorsey.

Henning-Stout, M. (1993). Theoretical and empirical bases of consultation. In J. E. Zins, T. R. Kratochwill, & S. N. Elliott (Eds.), *Handbook of consultation services for children: Applications in educational and clinical settings* (pp. 15–45). San Francisco: Jossey-Bass.

Herrnstein, R. J. (1961). Relative and absolute strength of response as a function of frequency of reinforcement. *Journal of the Experimental Analysis of Behavior, 4*, 267–272.

Herrnstein, R. J. (1970). On the law of effect. *Journal of the Experimental Analysis of Behavior, 13*, 243–266.

Hersch, C. (1968). The discontent explosion in mental health. *American Psychologist, 23*, 497–506.

Hintze, J. M. (1998). Review of school consultation: Conceptual and empirical bases of practice. *Journal of Educational and Psychological Consultation, 9*, 165–169.

Hintze, J. M., & Christ, T. J. (2004). An examination of variability as a function of passage variance in CBM progress monitoring. *School Psychology Review, 33*, 204–217.

Hiralall, A. S., & Martens, B. K. (1998). Teaching classroom management skills to preschool staff: The effects of scripted instructional sequences on teacher and student behavior. *School Psychology Quarterly, 13*, 94–115.

Hoff, K., & Zirkel, P. (1999). The IDEA's final regulations: Our Top Ten list for school psychologists. *NASP Communique, 28*(4), 6–7.

Hobbs, N. (1963). Strategies for the development of clinical psychology. *American Psychological Association Division of Clinical Psychology Newsletter, 16*, 3–5.

Hobbs, N. (1964). Mental health's third revolution. *American Journal of Orthopsychiatry, 34*, 822–833.

Hobbs, N. (1966). Helping disturbed children: Psychological and ecological strategies. *American Psychologist, 21*, 1105–1115.

Hollingshead, A. B., & Redlich, F. C. (1958). *Social class and mental illness: A community study.* New York: Wiley.

Holloway, E. (1995). *Clinical supervision: A systems approach.* Thousand Oaks, CA: Sage.

Holtgraves, T. (1992). The linguistic realization of face management: Implications for language production and comprehension, person perception, and cross-cultural communications. *Social Psychology Quarterly, 55*, 141–159.

Holtgraves, T., & Yang, J. (1990). Politeness as universal: Cross-cultural perceptions of request strategies and inferences based on their use. *Journal of Personality and Social Psychology, 59*, 719–729.

Howell, W. G., West, M. R., & Peterson, P. E. (2007). What Americans think about their schools. *Education Next, 7*(4), 13–26.

Hughes, J. N. (1986). Ethical issues in school consultation. *School Psychology Review, 15*, 489–499.

Hughes, J. N. (1992). Social psychology foundations of consultation. In F. J. Medway & T. P. Cafferty (Eds.), *School psychology: A social psychological perspective.* Hillsdale, NJ: Erlbaum.

Hughes, J. N., & Falk, R. (1981). Resistance, reactance, and consultation. *Journal of School Psychology, 19*, 134–142.

Hughes, J. N., Grossman, P., & Barker, D. (1990). Teacher expectancies, participation in consultation, and perceptions of consultant helpfulness. *School Psychology Quarterly, 5*, 167–179.

Hughes, J. N., Erchul, W. P., Yoon, J., Jackson, T., & Henington, C. (1997). Consultant use of questions and its relationship to consultee evaluation of effectiveness. *Journal of School Psychology, 35*, 281–297.

Hyman, I., Duffey, J., Caroll, R., Manni, J., & Winikur, D. (1973). Patterns of interprofessional conflict resolution on school child study teams. *Journal of School Psychology, 11*, 187–195.

Ikeda, M. J., Neessen, E., & Witt, J. C. (2008). Best practices in universal screening. In A. Thomas & J. Grimes (Eds.), *Best practices in school psychology-V* (pp. 103–114). Bethesda, MD: National Association of School Psychologists.

Illback, R. J., & Pennington, M. A. (2008). Organization development and change in school settings: Theoretical and empirical foundations. In W. P. Erchul & S. M. Sheridan (Eds.), *Handbook of research in school consultation: Empirical foundations for the field* (pp. 225–245). New York: Taylor & Francis Group/Routledge.

Ingersoll, R. S. (2001). Teacher turnover and teacher shortages: An organizational analysis. *American Educational Research Journal, 38*, 499–534.

Ingraham, C. L. (2000). Consultation through a multicultural lens: Multicultural and cross-cultural consultation in schools. *School Psychology Review, 29*, 320–343.

Ingraham, C. L. (2008). Studying multicultural aspects of consultation. In W. P. Erchul & S. M. Sheridan (Eds.), *Handbook of research in school consultation: Empirical foundations for the field* (pp. 269–291). New York: Taylor & Francis Group/Routledge.

Iscoe, I. (1993). Gerald Caplan's conceptual and qualitative contributions to community psychology: Views from an old timer. In W. P. Erchul (Ed.), *Consultation in community, school, and organizational practice: Gerald Caplan's contributions to professional psychology* (pp. 87–98). Washington, DC: Taylor & Francis.

Jackson, P. (1968). *Life in classrooms.* New York: Holt, Rinehart & Winston.

Jenkins, J. R., & Pany, D. (1978). Standardized achievement tests: How useful for special education? *Exceptional Children, 44*, 448–453.

Jimerson, S. R., Burns, M. K., & VanDerHeyden, A. M. (2007). Response to intervention at school: The science and practice of assessment and intervention. In S. R. Jimerson,

M. K. Burns, & A. M. VanDerHeyden (Eds.), *Handbook of response to intervention: The science and practice of assessment and intervention* (pp. 3–9). New York: Springer.

Jimerson, S. R., & Furlong, M. J. (Eds.). (2006). *The handbook of school violence and school safety: From research to practice.* New York: Routledge.

Jitendra, A. K., DuPaul, G. J., Volpe, R. J., Tresco, K. E., Vile Junod, R. E., Lutz, J. G., et al. (2007). Consultation-based academic intervention for children with attention deficit hyperactivity disorder: School functioning outcomes. *School Psychology Review, 36,* 217–236.

Johnson, P. (1976). Women and power: Toward a theory of effectiveness. *Journal of Social Issues, 32*(3), 99–110.

Johnson, K. R., & Layng, T. V. J. (1996). On terms and procedures: Fluency. *The Behavior Analyst, 19,* 281–288.

Johnston, J. M., & Pennypacker, H. S. (1980). *Strategies and tactics of human behavioral research.* Hillsdale, NJ: Lawrence Erlbaum Associates.

Jones, E. E., & Pittman, T. S. (1982). Toward a general theory of strategic interaction. In J. Suls (Ed.), *Psychological perspectives of self* (Vol. 1, pp. 231–263). Hillsdale, NJ: Erlbaum.

Jones, K. M., Wickstrom, K. F., Noltemeyer, A. L., Brown, S. J., Schuka, J. R., & Therrien, W. J. (2009). An experimental analysis of reading fluency. *Journal of Behavioral Education, 18,* 35–55.

Joyce, B., & Showers, B. (1981). Improving inservice training: The messages of research. *Educational Leadership, 39,* 379–385.

Joyce, B. R., & Showers, B. (2002). *Student achievement through staff development* (3rd ed.). Alexandria, VA: Association for Supervision and Curriculum Development.

Kavale, K. (1990). Effectiveness of special education. In T. B. Gutkin & C. R. Reynolds (Eds.), *Handbook of school psychology* (2nd ed., pp. 868–898). New York: John Wiley.

Kazdin, A. E. (1980). Acceptability of alternative treatments for deviant child behavior. *Journal of Applied Behavior Analysis, 13,* 259–273.

Kazdin, A. E. (1994). *Behavior modification in applied settings.* Pacific Grove, CA: Brooks/Cole.

Kelly, J. G. (1993). Gerald Caplan's paradigm: Bridging psychotherapy and public health practice. In W. P. Erchul (Ed.), *Consultation in community, school, and organizational practice: Gerald Caplan's contributions to professional psychology* (pp. 75–85). Washington, DC: Taylor & Francis.

Kern, L., Childs, K. E., Dunlap, G., Clarke, S., & Falk, G. D. (1994). Using assessment-based curricular intervention to improve the classroom behavior of a student with emotional and behavioral challenges. *Journal of Applied Behavior Analysis, 27,* 7–19.

Kipnis, D. (1994). Accounting for the use of behavior technologies in social psychology. *American Psychologist, 49,* 165–172.

Kirby, J. H. (1985). *Consultation: Practice and practitioner.* Muncie, IN: Accelerated Development.

Kiresuk, T. J., Smith, A., & Cardillo, J. E. (Eds.). (1994). *Goal attainment scaling: Applications, theory and measurement.* Hillsdale, NJ: Erlbaum.

Knoff, H. M. (2008). Best practices in implementing statewide positive behavioral support systems. In A. Thomas & J. Grimes (Eds.), *Best practices in school psychology-V* (pp. 749–763). Bethesda, MD: National Association of School Psychologists.

Kounin, J. (1970). *Discipline and group management in classrooms.* New York: Holt, Rinehart & Winston.

Kratochwill, T. R., Clements, M. A., & Kalymon, K. M. (2007). Response to intervention: Conceptual and methodological issues in implementation. In S. R. Jimerson, M. K. Burns, & A. M. VanDerHeyden (Eds.), *Handbook of response to intervention: The science and practice of assessment and intervention* (pp. 25–52). New York: Springer.

Kratochwill, T. R., Elliott, S. N. & Stoiber, K. C. (2002). Best practices in school-based problem-solving consultation. In A. Thomas & J. Grimes (Eds.), *Best practices in school psychology-IV* (pp. 583–608). Bethesda, MD: National Association of School Psychologists.

Kratochwill, T. R., Hoagwood, K. E., Levitt, J. M., Olin, S., Romanelli, L. H., Frank, J. L., et al. (2009). Evidence-based intervention and practices in school psychology: Challenges and opportunities for the profession. In T. B. Gutkin & C. R. Reynolds (Eds.), *Handbook of school psychology* (4th ed., pp. 497–521). New York: Wiley.

Kratochwill, T. R., VanSomeren, K. R., & Sheridan, S. M. (1989). Training behavioral consultants: A competency-based model to teacher interview skills. *Professional School Psychology, 4*, 41–58.

Lalli, J. S., Browder, D. M., Mace, F. C., & Brown, D. K. (1993). Teacher use of descriptive analysis data to implement interventions to decrease students' problem behaviors. *Journal of Applied Behavior Analysis, 26*, 227–238.

Lambert, N. M. (1976). Children's problems and classroom interventions from the perspective of classroom teachers. *Professional Psychology, 7*, 507–517.

Lannie, A. L., & Martens, B. K. (2008). Targeting performance dimensions in sequence according to the Instructional Hierarchy: Effects on children's math work within a self-monitoring program. *Journal of Behavioral Education, 17*, 356–375.

Larson, J. (2008). Best practices in school violence prevention. In A. Thomas & J. Grimes (Eds.), *Best practices in school psychology-V* (pp. 1291–1308). Bethesda, MD: National Association of School Psychologists.

Lentz, F. E., & Daly, E. J. (1996). Is the behavior of academic change agents controlled metaphysically? An analysis of the behavior of those who change behavior. *School Psychology Quarterly, 11*, 337–352.

Levinson, H. (1972). *Organizational diagnosis*. Cambridge, MA: Harvard University Press.

Lewin, K. (1952). Group decision and social change. In G. E. Swanson, T. M. Newcomb, & E. L. Hartley (Eds.), *Readings in social psychology* (2nd ed., pp. 459–473). New York: Holt, Rinehart & Winston.

Lewis, T. J., & Newcomer, L. L. (2002). Examining the efficacy of school-based consultation: Recommendations for improving outcomes. *Child and Family Behavior Therapy, 24*, 165–181.

Lieberman, M. A., Yalom, I. D., & Miles, M. B. (1973). *Encounter groups: First facts*. New York: Basic Books.

Lippitt, G., & Lippitt, R. (1986). *The consulting process in action* (2nd ed.). San Diego, CA: University Associates.

Lipsey, M. W., & Wilson, D. B. (1993). The efficacy of psychological, educational, and behavioral treatment: Confirmation from meta-analysis. *American Psychologist, 48*, 1181–1209.

Lloyd, J. W., Singh, N. N., & Repp, A. C. (Eds.). (1991). *The regular education initiative: Alternative perspectives on concepts issues and models*. Sycamore, IL: Sycamore.

Lortie, D. C. (1975). *Schoolteacher: A sociological study*. Chicago: University of Chicago Press.

Luiselli, J. K., Reed, D. D., & Martens, B. K. (2010). Academic problems. In J. C. Thomas & M. Hersen (Eds.), *Handbook of Clinical Psychology Competencies (Volume III, pp. 1685–1706)*. New York: Springer.

Lundervold, D., & Bourland, G. (1988). Quantitative analysis of treatment of aggression, self-injury, and property destruction. *Behavior Modification, 12*, 591–617.

Mace, F. C., & Lalli, J. S. (1991). Linking descriptive and experimental analyses in the treatment of bizarre speech. *Journal of Applied Behavior Analysis, 24*, 553–562.

Maher, C. A., & Bennett, R. E. (1984). *Planning and evaluating special education services*. Englewood Cliffs, NJ: Prentice-Hall.

Malecki, C. K., & Demaray, M. K. (2007). Social behavior assessment and response to intervention. In S. R. Jimerson, M. K. Burns, & A. M. VanDerHeyden (Eds.), *Handbook of response to intervention: The science and practice of assessment and intervention* (pp. 161–171). New York: Springer.

Mannino, F. V., & Shore, M. F. (1971). *Consultation research in mental health and related fields*. Public Health Monograph No. 79. Washington, DC: U.S. Government Printing Office.

Mannino, F. V., & Shore, M. F. (1975). The effects of consultation: A review of the literature. *American Journal of Community Psychology, 3*, 1–21.

Marks, E. S. (1995). *Entry strategies for school consultation*. New York: Guilford.

Marston, D., Muyskens, P., Lau, M., & Canter, A. (2003). Problem-solving model for decision making with high-incidence disabilities: The Minneapolis experience. *Learning Disabilities Research & Practice, 18*, 187–200.

Martens, B. K. (1992). Contingency and choice: The implications of matching theory for classroom instruction. *Journal of Behavioral Education, 2*, 121–137.

Martens, B. K. (1993a). A behavioral approach to consultation. In J. E. Zins, T. R. Kratochwill, & S. N. Elliott (Eds.), *Handbook of consultation services for children: Applications in educational and clinical settings* (pp. 65–86). San Francisco: Jossey-Bass.

Martens, B. K. (1993b). A case against magical thinking in school-based intervention. *Journal of Educational and Psychological Consultation, 4*, 185–189.

Martens, B. K. (1993c). Social labeling, precision of measurement, and problem solving: Key issues in the assessment of children's emotional problems. *School Psychology Review, 22*, 308–312.

Martens, B. K. (1996). *Helping teachers design effective shool-based interventions.* Invited workshop at the Syracuse City School District Summer Academy for School Psychologists, Syracuse, NY.

Martens, B. K., & Ardoin, S. P. (2002). Training school psychologists in behavior support consultation. *Child and Family Behavior Therapy, 24*, 147–163.

Martens, B. K., & Ardoin, S. P. (2010). Assessing disruptive behavior within a problem-solving model. In G. G. Peacock, R. A. Ervin, E. J. Daly, & K. W. Merrell (Eds.), *Practical handbook in school psychology: Effective practices for the 21st century* (pp. 157–174). New York: Guilford.

Martens, B. K., Deery, K. S., & Gherardi, J. P. (1991). An experimental analysis of reflected affect versus reflected content in consultative interactions. *Journal of Educational and Psychological Consultation, 2*, 117–132.

Martens, B. K., & DiGennaro, F. D. (2008). Behavioral consultation. In W. P. Erchul & S. M. Sheridan (Eds.), *Handbook of research in school consultation: Empirical foundations for the field* (pp. 147–170). New York: Taylor & Francis Group/Routledge.

Martens, B. K., DiGennaro, F. D., Reed, D. D., Szczech, F. M., & Rosenthal, B. D. (2008). Contingency space analysis: An alternative method for identifying contingent relations from observational data. *Journal of Applied Behavior Analysis, 41*, 69–81.

Martens, B. K., & Eckert, T. L. (2000). The essential role of data in psychological theory. *Journal of School Psychology, 38*, 369–376.

Martens, B. K., Eckert, T. L., Begeny, J. C., Lewandowski, L. J., DiGennaro, F., Montarello, S., et al. (2007). Effects of a fluency-building program on the reading performance of low-achieving second and third grade students. *Journal of Behavioral Education, 16*, 39–54.

Martens, B. K., Eckert, T. L., Bradley, T. A., & Ardoin, S. P. (1999). Identifying effective treatments from a brief experimental analysis: Using single-case design elements to aid decision making. *School Psychology Quarterly, 14*, 163–181.

Martens, B. K., Erchul, W. P., & Witt, J. C. (1992). Quantifying verbal interactions in school-based consultation: A comparison of four coding schemes. *School Psychology Review, 21*, 109–124.

Martens, B. K., & Gertz, L. E. (2009). Brief experimental analysis: A decision tool for bridging the gap between research and practice. *Journal of Behavioral Education, 18*, 92–99.

Martens, B. K., Hiralall, A. S., & Bradley, T. A. (1997). A note to teacher: Improving student behavior through goal setting and feedback. *School Psychology Quarterly, 12*, 33–41.

Martens, B. K., & Kelly, S. Q. (1993). A behavioral analysis of effective teaching. *School Psychology Quarterly, 8*, 10–26.

Martens, B. K., Kelly, S. Q., & Diskin, M. T. (1996). The effects of two sequential-request strategies on teachers' acceptability and use of a classroom intervention. *Journal of Educational and Psychological Consultation, 7*, 211–221.

Martens, B. K., & McIntyre, L. L. (2009). The importance of treatment integrity in school-based behavioral intervention. In A. Akin-Little, S. G. Little, M. A. Bray, & T. J. Kehle (Eds.), *Behavioral interventions in schools: Evidence-based positive strategies* (pp. 59–71). Washington, DC: American Psychological Association.

Martens, B. K., Peterson, R. L., Witt, J. C., & Cirone, S. (1986). Teacher perceptions of school based interventions. *Exceptional Children, 53*, 213–223.

Martens, B. K., Steele, E. S., Massie, D. R., & Diskin, M. T. (1995). Curriculum bias in standardized tests of reading decoding. *Journal of School Psychology, 33*, 287–296.

Martens, B. K., & Witt, J. C. (2004). Competence, persistence, and success: The positive psychology of behavioral skill instruction. *Psychology in the Schools, 41*, 19–30.

Martens, B. K., Witt, J. C., Daly, E. J., & Vollmer, T. (1999). Behavior analysis: Theory and practice in educational settings. In C. R. Reynolds & T. B. Gutkin (Eds.), *Handbook of school psychology* (3rd ed., pp. 638–663). New York: John Wiley & Sons.

Martin, R. (1978). Expert and referent power: A framework for understanding and maximizing consultation effectiveness. *Journal of School Psychology, 16*, 49–55.

McDougal, J. L., Chafouleas, S. M., & Waterman, B. (2006). *Functional behavioral assessment and intervention in schools: A practitioner's guide – grades 1–8*. Champaign, IL: Research Press.

McDougal, J. L., Clonan, S. M., & Martens, B. K. (2000). Using organizational change procedures to promote the acceptability of prereferral intervention services: The school-based intervention team project. *School Psychology Quarterly, 15*, 149–171.

McDougall, L. M., Reschly, D. J., & Corkery, J. M. (1988). Changes in referral interviews with teachers after behavioral consultation training. *Journal of School Psychology, 26*, 225–232.

McIntyre, L. L., Gresham, F. M., DiGennaro, F. D., & Reed, D. D. (2007). Treatment integrity of school-based interventions with children in the *Journal of Applied Behavior Analysis* from 1991–2005. *Journal of Applied Behavior Analysis, 40*, 659–672.

McKee, W. T., & Witt, J. C. (1990). Effective teaching: A review of instructional environmental variables. In T. B. Gutkin & C. R. Reynolds (Eds.), *The handbook of school psychology* (2nd ed., pp. 823–894). New York: John Wiley.

McKerchar, P. M., & Thompson, R. H. (2004). A descriptive analysis of potential reinforcement contingencies in the preschool classroom. *Journal of Applied Behavior Analysis, 37*, 431–444.

Medway, F. J. (1979). How effective is school consultation? A review of recent research. *Journal of School Psychology, 17*, 275–281.

Medway, F. J., & Updyke, J. F. (1985). Meta-analysis of consultation outcome studies. *American Journal of Community Psychology, 13*, 489–504.

Merrell, K. W., Ervin, R. A., & Gimpel, G. A. (2006). *School psychology for the 21st century: Foundations and practices*. New York: Guilford.

Merrell, K. W., & Shinn, M. R. (1990). Critical variables in the learning disabilities identification process. *School Psychology Review, 19*, 74–82.

Meyers, A. B., & Coleman, A. R. (2004). Review of *School Consultation: Conceptual and Empirical Bases of Practice* (2nd ed.). *Journal of Educational and Psychological Consultation, 15*, 111–116.

Meyers, J., Parsons, R. D., & Martin, R. (1979). *Mental health consultation in the schools*. San Francisco: Jossey-Bass.

Meyers, J., Proctor, S. L., Graybill, E. C., & Meyers, A. B. (2009). Organizational consultation and systems intervention. In T. B. Gutkin & C. R. Reynolds (Eds.), *Handbook of school psychology* (4th ed., pp. 921–940). New York: Wiley.

Miltenberger, R. G. (2008). *Behavior modification: Principles and procedures* (4th ed.). Belmont CA: Thomson Wadsworth.

Mintzberg, H. (1983). *Power in and around organizations*. Englewood Cliffs, NJ: Prentice-Hall.

Morison, P. (1992). Testing in American schools: Issues for research and policy. *Social Policy Report, 6*, 1–27.

Morris, R. J., & Mather, N. (Eds.). (2008). *Evidence-based interventions for students with learning and behavioral challenges*. New York: Routledge/Taylor & Francis Group.

Motta, R. W., Little, S. G., & Tobin, M. I. (1993). The use and abuse of human figure drawings. *School Psychology Quarterly, 8*, 162–169.

Mrazek, P. J., & Haggerty, R. J. (Eds.). (1994). *Reducing risks for mental disorders: Frontiers for preventive intervention research*. Washington, DC: National Academy Press.

National Center for Educational Statistics. (2009). *Digest of educational statistics, 2008.* Washington, DC: U. S. Department of Education. Retrieved July 30, 2009 from http://nces. ed.gov/fastfacts/

Neef, N. A., Iwata, B. A., Horner, R. H., Lerman, D., Martens, B. K., & Sainato, D. S. (Eds.). (2004). *Behavior analysis in education (2nd Ed.): From the Journal of Applied Behavior Analysis Reprint Series (Vol. 3).* Lawrence, KS: Society for the Experimental Analysis of Behavior.

Neef, N. A., Iwata, B. A., & Page, T. J. (1977). The effects of known-item interspersal on acquisition and retention of spelling and sight words. *Journal of Applied Behavior Analysis, 10,* 738.

Neef, N. A., & Noone Lutz, M. (2001). Assessment of variables affecting choice and application to classroom interventions. *School Psychology Quarterly, 16,* 239–252.

New York State Education Department. (2009). *Regulations of the Commissioner of Education.* Albany, NY: The University of the State of New York.

Ng, S. H., & Bradac, J. J. (1993). *Power in language: Verbal communication and social influence.* Newbury Park, CA: Sage.

No Child Left Behind Act of 2001, 20 U.S.C.6301 (2002).

Noell, G. H. (2008). Research examining the relationships among consultation process, treatment integrity, and outcomes. In W. P. Erchul & S. M. Sheridan (Eds.), *Handbook of research in school consultation: Empirical foundations for the field* (pp. 323–341). New York: Taylor & Francis Group/Routledge.

Noell, G. H., & Witt, J. C. (1996). A critical reevaluation of five fundamental assumptions of behavioral consultation. *School Psychology Quarterly, 11,* 189–203.

Noell, G. H., & Witt, J. C. (1999). When does consultation lead to intervention implementation? Critical issues for research and practice. *Journal of Special Education, 33,* 29–35.

Noell, G. H., Witt, J. C., Gilbertson, D. N., Ranier, D. D., & Freeland, J. T. (1997). Increasing teacher intervention implementation in general education settings through consultation and performance feedback. *School Psychology Quarterly, 12,* 77–88.

Noell, G. H., Witt, J. C., LaFleur, L. H., Mortenson, B. P., Ranier, D. D., & LeVelle, J. (2000). A comparison of two follow-up strategies to increase teacher implementation in general education following consultation. *Journal of Applied Behavior Analysis, 33,* 271–284.

Norcross, J. C., Beutler, L. E., & Levant, R. F. (Eds.). (2006). *Evidence-based practices in mental health: Debate and dialogue on the fundamental questions.* Washington, DC: American Psychological Association.

North Carolina Department of Public Instruction, Exceptional Children's Division. (2007). *Policies governing services for children with disabilities.* Raleigh, NC: North Carolina Department of Public Instruction, Exceptional Children's Division.

Office of Special Education Programs Technical Assistance Center on Positive Behavioral Interventions and Supports. (n.d.). *School-wide PBS.* Retrieved July 17, 2009, from http://www.pbis.org/school/default.aspx.

O'Keefe, D. J., & Medway, F. J. (1997). The application of persuasion research to consultation in school psychology. *Journal of School Psychology, 35,* 173–193.

Ost, D. H. (1991). The culture of teaching: Stability and change. In N. B. Wyner (Ed.), *Current perspectives on the culture of schools* (pp. 79–93). Brookline, MA: Brookline Books.

Owens, R. G. (1981). *Organizational behavior in education.* Englewood Cliffs, NJ: Prentice-Hall. pp. 3–40.

Paclawskyj, T. R., Matson, J. L., Rush, K. S., Smalls, Y., & Vollmer, T. R. (2000). Questions about behavioral function (QABF): A behavioral checklist for functional assessment of aberrant behavior. *Research in Developmental Disabilities, 21,* 223–229.

Parsons, R. D., & Meyers, J. (1984). *Developing consultation skills.* San Francisco: Jossey-Bass.

Peterson, L., Homer, A., & Wonderlich, S. (1982). The integrity of independent variables in behavior analysis. *Journal of Applied Behavior Analysis, 15,* 477–492.

Pfeiffer, S. I. (1980). The school-based interprofessional team: Recurring problems and some possible solutions. *Journal of School Psychology, 18,* 388–394.

Pfeiffer, S. I. (1981). The problems facing multidisciplinary teams: As perceived by team members. *Psychology in the Schools, 18,* 330–333.

Piersel, W. C., & Gutkin, T. B. (1983). Resistance to school-based consultation: A behavioral analysis of the problem. *Psychology in the Schools, 20*, 311–320.

Ponti, C. R., Zins, J. E., & Graden, J. L. (1988). Implementing a consultation-based service delivery system to decrease referrals for special education: A case study of organizational considerations. *School Psychology Review, 17*, 89–100.

Ramirez, S. Z., Lepage, K. M., Kratochwill, T. R., & Duffy, J. L. (1998). Multicultural issues in school-based consultation: Conceptual and research considerations. *Journal of School Psychology, 36*, 479–509.

Rathvon, N. (2008). *Effective school interventions: Evidence-based strategies for improving student outcomes* (2nd ed.). New York: Guilford.

Raven, B. H. (1965). Social influence and power. In I. D. Steiner & M. Fishbein (Eds.), *Current studies in social psychology* (pp. 371–381). New York, NY: Holt, Rinehart & Winston.

Raven, B. H. (1992). A power/interaction model of interpersonal influence: French and Raven thirty years later. *Journal of Social Behavior and Personality, 7*, 217–244.

Raven, B. H. (1993). The bases of power: Origins and recent developments. *Journal of Social Issues, 49*, 227–251.

Raven, B. H., & Kruglanski, A. W. (1970). Conflict and power. In P. G. Swingle (Ed.), *The structure of conflict* (pp. 69–109). New York, NY: Academic Press.

Raven, B. H., & Litman-Adizes, T. (1986). Interpersonal influence and social power in health promotion. In Z. Salisbury, S. Kar, & J. Zapka (Eds.), *Advances in health education and promotion* (pp. 181–210). Greenwich, CT: JAI Press.

Raven, B. H., Schwarzwald, J., & Koslowsky, M. (1998). Conceptualizing and measuring a power/interaction model of interpersonal influence. *Journal of Applied Social Psychology, 28*, 307–332.

Reddy, L. A., Barboza-Whitehead, S., Files, T., & Rubel, E. (2000). Clinical focus of consultation outcome research with children and adolescents. *Special Services in the Schools, 16*, 1–22.

Reed, D. D., Critchfield, T. S., & Martens, B. K. (2006). The generalized matching law in elite sport competition: Football play calling as operant choice. *Journal of Applied Behavior Analysis, 39*, 281–297.

Reed, D. R., & Martens, B. K. (2008a). Treatment of chronic breath-holding in an adult with severe mental retardation: A clinical case study. *International Journal of Behavioral Consultation and Therapy, 4*, 251–258.

Reed, D. D., & Martens, B. K. (2008b). Sensitivity and bias under conditions of equal and unequal academic task difficulty. *Journal of Applied Behavior Analysis, 41*, 39–52.

Reimers, T. M., Wacker, D. P., Cooper, L. J., & De Raad, A. O. (1992). Acceptability of behavioral treatments for children: Analog and naturalistic evaluations by parents. *School Psychology Review, 21*, 628–643.

Reimers, T. M., Wacker, D. P., & Koeppl, G. (1987). Acceptability of behavioral interventions: A review of the literature. *School Psychology Review, 16*, 212–227.

Reppucci, N. D., & Saunders, J. T. (1974). Social psychology of behavior modification: Problems of implementation in natural settings. *American Psychologist, 29*, 649–660.

Reschly, D. J. (1988). Special education reform: School psychology revolution. *School Psychology Review, 17*, 459–475.

Reschly, D. (2004). Paradigm shift, outcomes, criteria, and behavioral interventions: Foundations for the future of school psychology. *School Psychology Review, 33*, 408–416.

Reschly, D. J. (2008). School psychology paradigm shift and beyond. In A. Thomas & J. Grimes (Eds.), *Best practices in school psychology-V* (pp. 3–16). Bethesda, MD: National Association of School Psychologists.

Reschly, D. J., & Bergstrom, M. K. (2009). Response to intervention. In T. B. Gutkin & C. R. Reynolds (Eds.), *Handbook of school psychology* (4th ed., pp. 434–460). New York: Wiley.

Reschly, D. J., Tilly, W. D., & Grimes, J. P. (Eds.). (1999). *Special education in transition: Functional and noncategorical programming*. Longmont, CO: Sopris West.

Reynolds, C. R. (1981). The fallacy of "Two years below grade level for age" as a diagnostic criterion for reading disorders. *Journal of School Psychology, 19*, 350–358.

Reynolds, C. R., Gutkin, T. B., Elliott, S. N., & Witt, J. C. (1984). *School psychology: Essentials of theory and practice*. New York: Wiley.

Reynolds, C. R., & Shaywitz, S. E. (2009). Response to intervention: Ready or not? Or, from wait-to-fail to watch-them-fail. *School Psychology Quarterly, 34*, 130–145.

Roach, A. T., & Elliott, S. N. (2009). Consultation to support inclusive accountability and standards-based reform: Facilitating access, equity, and empowerment. *Journal of Educational and Psychological Consultation, 19*, 61–81.

Robinson, J. A., & Falconer, J. (1972). Mental health consultation to schoolteachers. In J. Zusman & D. L. Davidson (Eds.), *Practical aspects of mental health consultation* (pp. 88–95). Springfield, IL: Thomas.

Rogers, L. E., & Escudero, V. (Eds.). (2004). *Relational communication: An interactional perspective to the study of process and form*. Mahwah, NJ: Erlbaum.

Rogers, L. E., & Farace, R. V. (1975). Analysis of relational communication in dyads: New measurement procedures. *Human Communication Research, 1*, 222–239.

Rosenfield, S. (1992). Developing school-based consultation teams: A design for organizational change. *School Psychology Quarterly, 7*, 27–46.

Rosenfield, S., & Gravois, T. A. (1999). Working with teams in the school. In C. R. Reynolds & T. B. Gutkin (Eds.), *Handbook of school psychology* (3rd ed., pp. 1025–1040). New York: Wiley.

Sandoval, J., Lambert, N., & Davis, J. (1977). Consultation from the consultee's perspective. *Journal of School Psychology, 15*, 334–342.

Sarason, I. G., & Sarason, B. R. (1986). Experimentally provided social support. *Journal of Personality and Social Psychology, 50*, 1222–1225.

Sarason, S. B. (1971). *The culture of the school and the problem of change*. Boston, MA: Allyn & Bacon.

Sarason, S. B. (1982). *The culture of the school and the problem of change* (2nd ed.). Boston: Allyn & Bacon.

Sarason, S. B. (1996). *Revisiting "The culture of the school and the problem of change.*. New York: Teachers College Press, Columbia University.

Sarason, S. B., Levine, M., Goldenberg, I. I., Cherlin, D. L., & Bennett, E. M. (1966). *Psychology in community settings: Clinical, educational, vocational, social aspects*. New York: Wiley.

Scheeler, M. C., Bruno, K., Grubb, E., & Seavey, T. L. (2009). Generalizing teaching techniques from university to K-12 classrooms: Teaching preservice teachers to use what they learn. *Journal of Behavioral Education, 18*, 189–210.

Schein, E. H. (1969). *Process consultation: Its role in organization development*. Reading, MA: Addison-Wesley.

Schlenker, B. R. (1980). *Impression management: The self-concept, social identity, and interpersonal relations*. Monterey, CA: Brooks/Cole.

Schulberg, H. C., & Killilea, M. (1982). Community mental health in transition. In H. C. Schulberg & M. Killilea (Eds.), *The modern practice of community mental health: A volume in honor of Gerald Caplan* (pp. 40–94). San Francisco: Jossey-Bass.

Schulte, A. C., & Osborne, S. S. (2003). When assumptive worlds collide: A review of definitions of collaboration in consultation. *Journal of Educational and Psychological Consultation, 14*, 109–138.

Schulte, A. C., Osborne, S. S., & Erchul, W. P. (1998). Effective special education: A United States dilemma. *School Psychology Review, 27*, 66–76.

Scott, T. M. (2001). A schoolwide example of positive behavioral support. *Journal of Positive Behavior Interventions, 3*, 88–94.

Shapiro, E. S., & Derr, T. F. (1987). An examination of overlap between reading curricula and standardized achievement tests. *The Journal of Special Education, 21*, 59–67.

Sheridan, S. M., & Kratochwill, T. R. (1992). Behavioral parent-teacher consultation: conceptual and research considerations. *Journal of School Psychology, 30*, 117–139.

Sheridan, S. M., & Kratochwill, T. R. (2008). *Conjoint behavioral consultation: Promoting family-school connections and interventions* (2nd ed.). New York: Springer.

Sheridan, S. M., Kratochwill, T. R., & Elliott, S. N. (1990). Behavioral consultation with parents and teachers: Applications with socially withdrawn children. *School Psychology Review, 19*, 33–52.

Sheridan, S. M., Welch, M., & Orme, S. F. (1996). Is consultation effective? A review of outcome research. *Remedial and Special Education, 17*, 341–354.

Shinn, M. R. (1986). Does anyone care what happens after the refer-test-place sequence: The systematic evaluation of special education program effectiveness. *School Psychology Review, 15*, 49–58.

Shinn, M. R. (1989). *Curriculum-based measurement: Assessing special children.* New York: Guilford.

Shinn, M. R. (2002). Best practices in using curriculum-based measurement in a problem-solving model. In A. Thomas & J. Grimes (Eds.), *Best practices in school psychology* (4th ed., pp. 671–698). Bethesda, MD: National Association of School Psychologists.

Showers, B. (1990). Aiming for superior classroom instruction for all children: A comprehensive staff development model. *Remedial and Special Education, 11*, 35–39.

Simonsen, B., & Sugai, G. (2009). School-wide positive behavior support: A systems-level application of behavioral principles. In A. Akin-Little, S. G. Little, M. A. Bray, & T. J. Kehle (Eds.), *Behavioral interventions in schools: Evidence-based positive strategies* (pp. 125–140). Washington, DC: American Psychological Association.

Singer, J., Bossard, M., & Watkins, M. (1977). Effects of parental presence on attendance and input of interdisciplinary teams in an institutional setting. *Psychological Reports, 41*, 1031–1034.

Sirotnik, K. A. (1983). What you see is what you get – consistency, persistency, and mediocrity in classrooms. *Harvard Educational Review, 53*, 16–31.

Skinner, C. H., McLaughlin, T. F., & Logan, P. (1997). Cover, copy, and compare: A self-managed academic intervention effective across skills, students, and settings. *Journal of Behavioral Education, 7*, 295–306.

Slonski-Fowler, K. E., & Truscott, S. D. (2004). General education teachers' perceptions of the prereferral intervention team process. *Journal of Educational and Psychological Consultation, 15*, 1–39.

Smith, M. L., & Glass, G. V. (1977). Meta-analysis of psychotherapy outcome studies. *American Psychologist, 32*, 752–760.

Smith, D. K. (1984). Practicing school psychologists: Their characteristics, activities, and populations served. *Professional Psychology: Research and Practice, 15*, 798–810.

Steege, M. W., & Watson, T. S. (2008). Best practices in functional behavioral assessment. In A. Thomas & J. Grimes (Eds.), *Best practices in school psychology-V* (pp. 337–347). Bethesda, MD: National Association of School Psychologists.

Stein, L. I. (1971). Male and female: The doctor – nurse game. In J. P. Spradley & D. W. McCurdy (Eds.), *Conformity and conflict: Readings in cultural anthropology* (pp. 185–193). Boston: Little, Brown.

Stenger, M. K., Tollefson, N., & Fine, M. J. (1992). Variables that distinguish elementary teachers who participate in school-based consultation from those who do not. *School Psychology Quarterly, 7*, 271–284.

Sterling-Turner, H. E., Robinson, S. L., & Wilczynski, S. M. (2001). Functional assessment of distracting and disruptive behaviors in the school setting. *School Psychology Review, 30*, 211–226.

Sterling-Turner, H. E., & Watson, T. S. (2002). An analog investigation of the relationship between treatment acceptability and treatment integrity. *Journal of Behavioral Education, 11*, 39–50.

Stokes, T. F., & Baer, D. M. (1977). An implicit technology of generalization. *Journal of Applied Behavior Analysis, 19*, 349–367.

Sugai, G. M., & Tindal, G. A. (1993). *Effective school consultation.* Pacific Grove, CA: Brooks/Cole.

Supply and demand: The teacher shortage: Teacher recruitment: Pulling out all the stops (2001, March). *American Teacher, 10–11*, 17.

Szasz, T. S. (1960). The myth of mental illness. *American Psychologist, 15*, 113–118.

Tagiuri, R., & Litwin, G. H. (1968). *Organizational climate: Explorations of a concept*. Boston, MA: Harvard University Press.

Tannen, D. (1994). *Talking from 9 to 5: Women and men in the workplace: Language, sex, and power*. New York: Avon Books.

Tardy, C. H. (1994). Counteracting task-induced stress: Studies of instrumental and emotional support in problem-solving contexts. In B. R. Burleson, T. L. Albrecht, & I. G. Sarason (Eds.), *Communication of social support: Messages interactions relationships, and community* (pp. 71–87). Thousand Oaks, CA: Sage.

Task Force on Promotion and Dissemination of Psychological Procedures. (1995). Training in and dissemination of empirically-validated psychological treatments. *The Clinical Psychologist, 48*, 3–23.

Taylor, L. L. (2008). Comparing teacher salaries: Insights from the U.S. census. *Economics of Education Review, 27*(1), 48–57.

Telzrow, C. F. (1999). IDEA amendments of 1997: Promise or pitfall for special education reform? *Journal of School Psychology, 37*, 7–28.

Tharp, R. G., & Wetzel, R. J. (1969). *Behavior modification in the natural environment*. New York: Academic Press.

Thurlow, M. L., & Ysseldyke, J. (1982). Instructional planning: Information collected by school psychologists vs. information considered useful by teachers. *Journal of School Psychology, 20*, 3–10.

Tilly, W. D. (2008). The evolution of school psychology to science-based practice: Problem solving and the three-tiered model. In A. Thomas & J. Grimes (Eds.), *Best practices in school psychology-V* (pp. 17–35). Bethesda, MD: National Association of School Psychologists.

Tindall, R. H. (1979). School psychology: Development of a profession. In G. D. Phye & D. J. Reschly (Eds.), *School psychology: Perspectives and issues* (pp. 3–24). New York: Academic Press.

Tombari, M. L., & Bergan, J. R. (1978). Consultant cues and teacher verbalizations, judgments, and expectancies concerning children's adjustment problems. *Journal of School Psychology, 16*, 212–219.

Touchette, P. E., MacDonald, R. F., & Langer, S. N. (1985). A scatter plot for identifying stimulus control of problem behavior. *Journal of Applied Behavior Analysis, 18*, 343–351.

Trickett, E. J. (1993). Gerald Caplan and the unfinished business of community psychology: A comment. In W. P. Erchul (Ed.), *Consultation in community school, and organizational practice: Gerald Caplan's contributions to professional psychology* (pp. 163–175). Washington, DC: Taylor & Francis.

Truscott, S. D., Cohen, C. E., Sams, D. P., Sanborn, K. J., & Frank, A. J. (2005). The current state(s) of prereferral intervention teams. *Remedial & Special Education, 26*, 130–140.

Tysinger, P. D., Tysinger, J. A., & Diamanduros, T. (2009). Teacher expectations on the directiveness continuum in consultation. *Psychology in the Schools, 46*, 319–332.

Ullmann, L. P., & Krasner, L. (1969). *A psychological approach to abnormal behavior*. Englewood Cliffs, NJ: Prentice-Hall.

United States Department of Education. (1987). *Ninth annual report to Congress on the implemention of the Education of the Handicapped Act (Vol. 1)*. Washington, DC: U.S. Department of Educational Series, Special Education Programs.

Vaughn, S., & Fuchs, L. S. (2003). Redefining learning disabilities as inadequate response to instruction: The promise and potential problems. *Learning Disabilities Research & Practice, 18*, 137–146.

Vernberg, E. M., & Reppucci, N. D. (1986). Behavioral consultation. In F. V. Mannino, E. J. Trickett, M. F. Shore, M. G. Kidder, & G. Levin (Eds.), *Handbook of mental health consultation (DHHS Publication No. ADM 86-1446)* (pp. 49–80). Washington, DC: U.S. Government Printing Office.

Volpe, R. J., DiPerna, J. C., Hintze, J. M., & Shapiro, E. S. (2005). Observing students in classroom settings: A review of seven coding schemes. *School Psychology Review, 34*, 454–474.

Von Brock, M. B., & Elliott, S. N. (1987). The influence of treatment effectiveness information on the acceptability of classroom interventions. *Journal of School Psychology, 25*, 131–144.

Walster, E., & Festinger, L. (1962). The effectiveness of "overheard" persuasive communications. *Journal of Abnormal and Social Psychology, 65*, 395–402.

Walster, E., Walster, G. W., & Berscheid, E. (1978). *Equity theory and research*. Boston, MA: Allyn & Bacon.

Watson, T. S., & Sterling-Turner, H. (2008). Best practices in direct behavioral consultation. In A. Thomas & J. Grimes (Eds.), *Best practices in school psychology-V* (pp. 1661–1672). Bethesda, MD: National Association of School Psychologists.

Webster, R. E., McInnis, E. D., & Craver, L. (1986). Curriculum biasing effects in standardized and criterion-referenced reading achievement tests. *Psychology in the Schools, 23*, 205–213.

Weeks, M., & Gaylord-Ross, R. (1981). Task difficulty and aberrant behavior in severely handicapped students. *Journal of Applied Behavior Analysis, 14*, 19–36.

Weinstein, C. S. (1991). The classroom as a social context for learning. *Annual Review of Psychology, 42*, 493–525.

Wilkinson, L. A. (2006). Monitoring treatment integrity: An alternative to the "consult and hope" strategy in school-based behavioural consultation. *School Psychology International, 27*, 426–438.

Wilson, K. E., Erchul, W. P., & Raven, B. H. (2008). The likelihood of use of social power strategies by school psychologists when consulting with teachers. *Journal of Educational and Psychological Consultation, 18*, 101–123.

Witt, J. C. (1990). Collaboration in school-based consultation: Myth in need of data. *Journal of Educational and Psychological Consultation, 1*, 367–370.

Witt, J. C. (1997). Talk is not cheap. School is not cheap. *School Psychology, 12*, 281–292.

Witt, J. C., Daly, E. M., & Noell, G. (2000). *Functional assessments: A step-by-step guide to solving academic and behavior problems*. Longmont, CO: Sopris West.

Witt, J. C., & Elliott, S. N. (1985). Acceptability of classroom management strategies. In T. R. Kratochwill (Ed.), *Advances in school psychology* (Vol. 4, pp. 251–288). Hillsdale, NJ: Erlbaum.

Witt, J. C., Hannafin, M. J., & Martens, B. K. (1983). Home-based reinforcement: Behavioral covariation between academic performance and inappropriate behavior. *Journal of School Psychology, 21*, 337–348.

Witt, J. C., Noell, G. H., La Fleur, L. H., & Mortenson, B. P. (1997). Teacher usage of interventions in general education: Measurement and analysis of the independent variable. *Journal of Applied Behavior Analysis, 30*, 693–696.

Witt, J. C., & Martens, B. K. (1983). Assessing the acceptability of behavioral interventions used in classrooms. *Psychology in the Schools, 20*, 510–517.

Witt, J. C., & Martens, B. K. (1984). Adaptive behavior: Tests and assessment issues. *School Psychology Review, 13*, 478–484.

Witt, J. C., & Martens, B. K. (1988). Problems with problem-solving consultation: A re-analysis of assumptions, methods, and goals. *School Psychology Review, 17*, 211–226.

Witt, J. C., Martens, B. K., & Elliott, S. N. (1984). Factors affecting teachers' judgments of the acceptability of behavioral interventions: Time involvement, behavior problem severity, and type of intervention. *Behavior Therapy, 15*, 204–209.

Witt, J. C., Miller, C. D., McIntyre, R., & Smith, D. (1984). Effects of variables on parental perceptions of staffings. *Exceptional Children, 51*, 27–32.

Witt, J. C., Moe, G., Gutkin, T. B., & Andrews, L. (1984). The effect of saying the same thing in different ways: The problem of language and jargon in school-based consultation. *Journal of School Psychology, 22*, 361–367.

Witt, J. C., Noell, G. H., LaFleur, L. H., & Mortenson, B. P. (1997). Teacher usage of interventions in general education: Measurement and analysis of the independent variable. *Journal of Applied Behavior Analysis, 30*, 693–696.

Witt, J. C., & Robbins, J. R. (1985). Acceptability of reductive interventions for the control of inappropriate child behavior. *Journal of Abnormal Child Psychology, 13*, 59–67.

0

Wolery, M., Bailey, D. B., & Sugai, G. M. (1988). *Effective teaching: Principles and procedures of applied behavior analysis with exceptional students.* Boston: Allyn & Bacon.

Woodcock, R. W., McGrew, K. S., & Mather, N. (2001). *Woodcock-Johnson III tests of achievement.* Itasca, IL: Riverside Publishing.

Wosinska, W., Cialdini, R. B., Barrett, D. W., & Reykowski, J. (Eds.). (2001). *The practice of social influence in multiple cultures.* Mahwah, NJ: Erlbaum.

Wyner, N. B. (Ed.). (1991). *Current perspectives on the culture of schools.* Brookline, MA: Brookline Books.

Yeaton, W. H., & Sechrest, L. (1981). Critical dimensions in the choice and maintenance of successful treatments: Strength, integrity, and effectiveness. *Journal of Consulting and Clinical Psychology, 49,* 156–167.

Yoshida, R. K., Fenton, K. S., Maxwell, J. P., & Kaurman, M. J. (1978). Group decision-making in the planning team process: Myth or reality? *Journal of School Psychology, 16,* 237–244.

Ysseldyke, J. E., Christenson, S. L., Thurlow, M. L., & Bakewell, D. (1989). Are different kinds of instructional tasks used by different categories of students in different settings? *School Psychology Review, 18,* 98–111.

Ysseldyke, J. E., & Marston, D. (1990). The use of assessment information to plan instructional interventions: A review of the research. In T. B. Gutkin & C. R. Reynolds (Eds.), *The handbook of school psychology* (2nd ed., pp. 661–682). New York: John Wiley.

Ysseldyke, J. E., Pianta, B., Christenson, S., Wang, J. J., & Algozzine, B. (1983) An analysis of prereferral interventions. *Psychology in the Schools, 20,* 184–190.

Yukl, G., & Falbe, C. M. (1991). Importance of different power sources in downward and lateral relations. *Journal of Applied Psychology, 77,* 525–535.

Zigler, E., & Phillips, L. (1961). Psychiatric diagnosis and symptomatology. *Journal of Abnormal and Social Psychology, 63,* 69–75.

Zins, J. E. (1995). Has consultation achieved its primary prevention potential? *Journal of Primary Prevention, 15,* 285–301.

Zins, J. E., Curtis, M. J., Graden, J. L., & Ponti, C. R. (1988). *Helping students succeed in the regular classroom: A guide for developing intervention assistance programs.* San Francisco: Jossey-Bass.

Zins, J. E., & Erchul, W. P. (2002). Best practices in school consultation. In A. Thomas & J. Grimes (Eds.), *Best practices in school psychology-IV (pp. 625–643).* Bethesda, MD: National Association of School Psychologists.

Zins, J. E., Kratochwill, T. R., & Elliott, S. N. (Eds.). (1993). *The handbook of consultation services for children: Applications in educational and clinical settings.* San Francisco: Jossey-Bass.

Zubin, J. (1967). Classification of the behavior disorders. In P. R. Farnsworth, O. McNemar, & Q. McNemar (Eds.), *Annual review of psychology* (Vol. 18, pp. 373–406). Palo Alto, CA: Annual Reviews.

Author Index

A

Achenbach, T.M., 133
Addi-Raccah, A., 163
Albee, G.W., 8, 106
Aldrich, S.F., 114
Algozzine, B., 169, 170
Allegretto, S.A., 162
Allinder, R.M., 134
Allington, R.L., 69
Alpert, J.L., 13, 159
Anderson, C.M., 54, 132
Andrews, L., 154
Apter, S.J., 63, 74, 182
Archer, R.P., 188
Ardoin, S.P., 121, 128, 131, 135,
    136, 218
Armbruster, B.B., 186
Arviv-Elyashiv, R., 163
Astor, R.A., 87
Axelrod, S., 65

B

Babinski, L.M., 176
Baer, D.M., 122, 151, 174
Bahr, M.W., 23, 36–38, 108, 167, 173
Bailey, D.B., 145
Bakewell, D., 70, 181
Ball, E.W., 205
Bandura, A., 168
Barboza-Whitehead, S., 5
Barker, D., 168
Barnett, D.W., 74, 145, 190, 121
Barone, S.G., 41
Barrett, D.W., 44
Barry, B., 34
Bass, B.M., 53
Baum, K., 162
Becker, W.C., 70

Begeny, J.C., 109
Bell, C.H., 99
Bell, P.F., 186
Benne, K.D., 31, 41–43, 109
Bennett, E.M., 102
Bennett, M.S., 4, 38–40, 110, 111, 167, 171,
    174, 215, 216
Bennett, R.E., 99
Bennis, W.G., 99
Bergan, J.R., 13–15, 22, 34–38, 41, 47,
    80, 83, 91–97, 107, 115–117, 121,
    123, 127, 128, 132, 165, 172, 193,
    203, 204, 213
Bergstrom, M.K., 19–21, 24, 25, 28, 29, 99
Berkowitz, L., 49
Berry, B.T., 164
Berryman, R., 133
Berscheid, E., 48
Beutler, L.E., 5, 21
Blachman, B.A., 205, 206
Black, R., 205
Blake, R.R., 99
Boon, R.T., 114
Borman, G.D., 164
Bossard, M.D., 67, 68
Bourland, G., 151
Bowlby, J., 84
Bradac, J.J., 57
Braden, J.P., 168
Bradley, T.A., 123, 136
Brandenburg, N.A., 187
Brehm, J.W., 50
Brophy, J.E., 69, 160
Browder, D.M., 132, 209
Brown, D.K., 13, 14, 21, 87, 97, 102, 103,
    132, 171, 172
Brown, S.J., 125, 128, 138, 139
Bruno, K., 122
Buffum, A., 24–28

Burns, M.K., 11, 17, 19, 21–23, 25–27, 135,
        138, 172, 174, 191
Busse, R.T., 6, 176

C
Cancelli, A.A., 39, 165
Canter, A., 76
Caplan, G., 3, 4, 8, 13, 15, 18, 30, 32, 39,
        51, 52, 54, 80, 83–90, 92, 97, 98,
        100–103, 105–107, 114, 120, 165,
        166, 170, 194, 214
Caplan, R.B., 3, 13, 30, 39, 52, 80, 83, 88, 89,
        165, 171, 176
Cardillo, J.E., 38
Carkhuff, R.R., 8
Caroll, R., 69
Carter, J., 172
Casey, A., 22, 108, 173
Cash, R.E., 29
Castillo, J.M., 14, 99
Catalan, J., 118
Cataldo, M.F., 149, 151, 191
Chafouleas, S.M., 130
Chard, D.J., 113
Cherlin, D.L., 102
Chewning, T.G., 40, 110, 111, 168
Chin, R., 31, 41–43, 109
Christenson, S.L., 14, 22, 70, 108, 169, 173,
        181, 191
Christ, T.J., 135
Cialdini, R.B., 44, 118
Cihak, D.F., 114
Cirone, S., 108
Clark, E.G., 84, 85
Clements, M.A., 11, 22
Clonan, S.M., 76, 108, 173
Cohen, C.E., 22, 172–173
Cohen, M.D., 65
Cohen, R., 14, 99
Cohen, S., 86, 109
Cohn, M.M., 161–163
Coleman, A.R., viii, 236
Connell, J.E., 128, 135
Conoley, C.W., 52, 90, 100, 102, 103, 110, 113
Conoley, J.C., 30–32, 43, 52, 61, 100, 102,
        103, 110, 111, 113, 118, 119, 166
Cook, L., 39
Cooper, L.J., 138, 154
Corcoran, S.P., 162
Corkery, J.M., 108, 155
Costenbader, V., 77, 106, 107, 159
Covington, C.G., 111
Cowen, E.L., 8, 84
Craver, L., 186

Crimmins, D.B., 131
Critchfield, T.S., 148
Crothers, L., 14
Cubberley, E.P., 63
Cullinan, D., 182
Curry, L., 68
Curtis, M.J., 5, 7, 10, 14, 29, 34, 95, 99, 106,
        109, 110, 113, 117, 124, 125, 174

D
Daley, G.A., 164
Daly, E.J., 10, 28, 34, 74, 116, 129–131, 138,
        143–145, 147–149, 189, 190, 193, 202,
        218
Daly, E.M., 202
Daly, J.A., 34, 193
Daniels, L.R., 49
Darby, B.L., 118
Darling-Hammond, L., 164, 167
Davis, H., 99
Davis, J.M., 14, 61
Davison, M., 148
Deery, K.S., 117
DeLeon, I.G., 149, 191
Delmolino, L.M., 142
Demaray, M.K., 35
Deno, S.L., 21
De Raad, A.O., 154
Derr, T.F., 186
DeVoe, J., 162
deVoss, G.G., 70
Diamanduros, T., 168
Dieker, L., 23
DiGennaro, F.D., 15, 23, 30, 33, 80, 96,
        108–109, 116, 121, 124, 128, 129, 131,
        137, 152, 154, 165, 174, 218
DiPerna, J.C., 128
Diskin, M.T., 114, 186
Dool, E.J., 28, 138, 147, 189, 193
Dorr, D., 8
Dougherty, A.M., 14
Douglass, D., 40
Dowling, N.M., 164
Doyle, W., 70, 160
Drasgow, E., 128, 130, 179
Duffey, J., 69
Duffy, J.L., 14
Duhon, G.J., 23
Duncan, B.B., 87
Dunst, C.J., 40, 120
DuPaul, G.D., 187
DuPaul, G.J., 37, 193
Durand, V.M., 131
D'Zurilla, T.J., 91–93, 107

E

Eaton, M.D., 145
Eckert, T.L., 131, 132, 136–138, 142
Ehrhardt, K.E., 121
Elliott, S.N., 5, 6, 38, 40, 95, 109, 115,
    153–154, 176, 215
Epstein, M.H., 154, 182
Erchul, W.P., 4, 5, 9, 11, 13, 18, 20, 22,
    30, 33, 35–41, 45, 47–57, 59, 61,
    83, 84, 87, 89–91, 95, 97, 102, 105,
    106, 110, 111, 118, 119, 121, 122,
    166, 167, 168, 171, 174, 176, 194,
    202, 212–216
Erikson, E.H., 85
Ervin, R.A., 28, 99
Escudero, V., 36
Esler, A.N., 14
Esquivel, G.B., 11
Eysenck, H.J., 8, 106

F

Fagan, T.K., 5, 10, 11, 31, 63, 65
Falbe, C.M., 53
Falconer, J., 166
Falk, R., 40, 50
Farace, R.V., 36–38
Fenton, K.S., 68
Fernstrom, P., 36, 167
Festinger, L., 52
Fideler, E., 164
Files, T., 5
Fine, M.J., 170
Flugum, K.R., 76
Folger, J.P., 110
Ford, J.B., 55
Forness, S.R., 184, 188
Frank, A.J., 22, 173
Frank, J.L., 5, 21
Fraser, S.C., 118
Freedman, J.L., 118
Freeland, J.T., 106
French, J.R.P., Jr., 31, 43–45, 48,
    49, 119
French, W., 99
Friedman, R.M., 187
Friedrich, J., 40
Friend, M., 39
Friman, P.C., 149, 191
Frisby, C.L., 14
Fuchs, D., 11, 36–38, 108, 134, 135, 155, 167,
    173, 186
Fuchs, L.S., 36–38, 108, 134, 135, 155, 167,
    173, 186, 217
Furlong, M.J., 162

G

Gallessich, J., 9, 48, 97–98, 100
Galvin, G., 154
Gansle, K.A., 109, 183
Ganuza, Z.M., 138
Gaylord-Ross, R., 130
Gertz, L.E., 128, 136, 138
Gettinger, M., 65, 70, 190
Getty, K.C., 36, 54, 57
Gherardi, J.P., 117
Giangreco, M.F., 71
Gibbon, J., 133
Gibbons, K.A., 11, 17, 19,
    25–27, 135
Gilbertson, D.N., 106
Gillat, A., 124
Gilliam, J.E., 68
Gimpel, G.A., 28
Glass, G.V., 5, 8, 142
Godber, Y., 14
Goldbaum, J., 68
Goldenberg, I.I., 102
Goldfried, M.R., 91–93, 107
Goldstein, A.P., 174, 175
Goldstein, S., 68, 69
Good, R.H., 28, 129, 135,
    146, 186, 198, 203,
    204, 215
Good, T.L., 160, 181
Gordon, R., 85
Gouldner, A.W., 48
Graden, J.L., 10, 18, 22, 25, 27, 77, 108,
    173, 186
Grant, W.V., 63
Gravois, T.A., 22, 23, 173
Graybill, E.C., 14, 99
Gregerson, L., 23
Gresham, F.M., 5, 6, 17, 18, 25, 29,
    47, 106, 109, 116, 125, 153,
    154, 159, 183, 184,
    186, 187
Grigorenko, E.L. (Ed.)., viii, 230
Grimes, J.P., 10
Grissom, P.F., 36
Groff, S., 22, 173
Grossman, H.J., 183
Grossman, P., 168
Grubb, E., 122
Guarino, C.M., 164
Gursky, D., 162
Gutkin, T.B., 5, 7, 29, 31, 32, 34,
    39, 61, 65–67, 77–79, 95,
    106, 109–111, 113, 115,
    118, 119, 125, 154, 166,
    167, 169, 173, 174

H

Haggerty, R.J., 85
Haley, J., 40
Halpin, A., 66–68, 80
Hamler, K., 138
Hamlett, C.L., 134
Hanley, G.P., 109, 129
Hannafin, M.J., 66
Hansen, C.L., 145
Hanushek, E.A., 160
Happe, D., 108, 109
Harding, J., 138
Haring, N.G., 145
Harris, A.M., 39, 165
Haselkorn, D., 164
Hayes, S.C., 116, 138
Heller, K., 14
Helsel, W.J., 154
Henington, C., 40
Henning-Stout, M., 39, 173
Herrnstein, R.J., 148
Hersch, C., 6–8, 106
Hickman, J.A., 124, 168
Hightower, A.D., 84
Hintze, J.M., 128, 135
Hiralall, A.S., 121, 123
Hoagwood, K.E., 5, 21
Hobbs, N., 7, 8, 106
Hoenig, J.L., 128, 135
Hoff, K., 11
Hollingshead, A.B., 7, 8
Holloway, E., 40
Holtgraves, T., 57
Homer, A., 154
Horner, R.H., 20, 144
Howell, W.G., 163
Hughes, J.N., 32, 40, 50, 111,
        168, 171
Hughes, T., 14
Hyman, I., 69

I

Ikeda, M.J., 19, 85
Illback, R.J., 14
Imhof, E.A., 188
Ingersoll, R.S., 164
Ingraham, C.L., 14
Isaacson, R.V., 8
Iscoe, I., 98
Iwata, B.A., 109, 129,
        144, 209
Izzo, L.D., 8

J

Jackson, P., 160, 167
Jackson, T., 40
Jenkins, J.R., 186
Jensen-Kovalan, P., 138
Jimerson, S.R., 21, 25, 162
Jitendra, A.K., 37, 193
Johnson, K.R., 146
Johnson, P., 51, 52
Johnson, S., 138
Johnston, J.M., 138
Jones, E.E., 55
Jones, K.M., 119, 125, 128,
        138, 139
Joyce, B.R., 121, 175

K

Kahng, S., 149, 191
Kalymon, K.M., 11, 22
Kaminski, R., 28, 129, 135,
        146, 198, 203,
        204, 215
Kaurman, M.J., 68
Kavale, K., 134, 142, 143, 191,
        192, 217
Kazdin, A.E., 151, 153, 154
Kelly, J.G., 70, 102
Kelly, S.Q., 114
Kendell, G.K., 106, 159
Kern, L., 138
Killilea, M., 8, 9, 83
Killough, C.E., 33
Kipnis, D., 40
Kirby, J.H., 100
Kiresuk, T.J., 38
Kirk, E.R., 114
Kleinmann, A.E., 109
Knitzer, J., 184, 188
Knoff, H.M., 20
Kocarek, C.E., 23
Koeppl, G., 153
Koslowsky, M., 52
Kottkamp, R.B., 161–163
Kounin, J., 69
Krasner, L., 188
Kratochwill, T.R., 5, 6, 11, 13,
        14, 21, 22, 29, 35, 36,
        47, 80, 83, 91, 92, 94–96,
        108, 116, 121, 123, 127,
        128, 132, 165, 172,
        176, 193
Kruglanski, A.W., 47

L

La Fleur, L.H., 122
Lalli, J.S., 132
Lambert, N.M., 61, 115
Langer, S.N., 116, 132
Lannie, A.L., 145
Larson, J., 11
Lau, M., 76
Layng, T.V.J., 146
Leavell, H.R., 84, 85
LeClair, C., 138
Lentz, F.E., 121, 186
Lepage, K.M., 14
Lerman, D.C., 144
Levant, R.F., 5, 21
LeVelle, J., 121
Levine, M., 102
Levinson, H., 99
Levitt, J.M., 5
Lewandowski, L.J., 137
Lewin, K., 55
Lewis, S.K., 118
Lewis, T.J., 5
Lieberman, M.A., 8
Lippitt, G., 50
Lippitt, R., 50
Lipsey, M.W., 142
Litman-Adizes, T., 51
Little, S.G., 188
Litwin, G.H., 66
Lloyd, J.W., 10
Logan, P., 111, 138
London, R.M., 138
Long, E.S., 132
Lopez, E.C., 11
Lorion, R.P., 8
Lortie, D.C., 161, 163
Lovitt, T.C., 145
Luiselli, J.K., 128, 144, 145, 147, 181
Lundervold, D., 151
Lutz, J.G., 37, 193

M

MacDonald, R.F., 116, 132
Mace, F.C., 132
Maher, C.A., 99
Malecki, C.K., 25
Mannella, M., 37–40
Manni, J., 69
Manson, D., 23
March, J.G., 65
Marks, E.S., 14, 99

Marston, D., 76, 134, 143
Martens, B.K., 10, 15, 23, 28–30, 32,
    33, 36, 40, 66, 70, 74, 76, 80, 94–96,
    108, 109, 111, 113, 114, 116–118,
    120, 121, 123–125, 128–133,
    136–138, 141, 143–145,
    147–149, 152, 154, 155, 165,
    173–175, 177, 181, 183, 186,
    188–191, 193, 194, 218
Martin, R., 14, 40, 43, 45, 49, 50, 57, 61, 96,
    118, 119, 124
Maruish, M., 188
Massie, D.R., 186
Mather, N., 28, 204
Matson, J.L., 116, 132, 154
Mattos, M., 24
Maxwell, J.P., 68
McCarthy, D.C., 148
McCord, B.E., 109, 129
McDougal, J.L., 76–78, 80, 108, 130, 173
McDougall, L.M., 108, 115, 117, 155
McGrew, K.S., 204
McInnis, E.D., 186
McIntyre, L.L., 29, 109, 124, 125, 154, 155, 186
McIntyre, R., 68
McKee, W.T., 114
McKerchar, P.M., 132
McLaughlin, T.F., 111, 138
Medway, F.J., 6, 32, 106, 108
Merrell, K.W., 28, 185
Mesmer, E.M., 23
Mettler, D.W., 33
Meyers, A.B., 14, 99
Meyers, J., 14, 51, 57, 99, 111, 124, 168
Miles, M.B., 8
Millard, T., 138
Miller, C.D., 68
Miltenberger, R.G., 128, 130
Mintzberg, H., 43
Mishel, L., 162
Mock, D., 11
Moe, G., 154
Monahan, J., 14
Montarello, S., 137
Morgan, P.L., 11
Morine, K., 14
Morison, P., 65
Morris, R.J., 28
Mortenson, B.P., 122
Motta, R.W., 188
Mouton, J.S., 99
Mrazek, P.J., 85
Muyskens, P., 76

N

Nahari, S., 11
Neef, N.A., 144, 149, 209
Neessen, E., 19, 85
Neumann, A.J., 96, 213
Newcomer, L.L.., 5
Ng, S.H., 57
Noell, G., 28, 121, 123, 129, 202
Noell, G.H., 5, 6, 23, 95, 106, 109, 122–124, 130, 144, 147
Noltemeyer, A.L., 125, 128, 138, 139
Noonan, M., 162
Noone Lutz, M., 149
Norcross, J.C., 5, 21

O

O'Keefe, D.J., 32
Olin, S., 5, 21
Olsen, J.P., 65
Olson, S.C., 74, 145, 190
Orme, S.F., 6, 107
Osborne, S.S., 33, 34, 41
Ost, D.H., 165
Owens, R.G., 64, 66, 67, 70, 71, 80, 98, 109

P

Paclawskyj, T.R., 116, 132
Page, T.J., 209
Pany, D., 186
Parsons, R.D., 14, 51, 57, 124
Pennington, M.A., 14
Pennypacker, H.S., 138
Peter, K., 162
Peterson, L., 154
Peterson, P.E., 163
Peterson, R.L., 108, 154
Peters, R., 23
Petrix, L., 77, 159
Pfeiffer, S.I., 68
Phillips, L., 7
Piersel, W.C., 66, 76–78, 173
Piotrowski, C., 188
Pitner, R.O., 87
Pittman, T.S., 55
Ponti, C.R., 10, 18, 77
Poth, R.L., 25
Proctor, S.L., 14, 99
Pryzwansky, W.B., 13, 21, 87, 171
Puck, S., 110

R

Ramirez, S.Z., 14
Ranier, D.D., 106
Rathvon, N., 28
Raven, B.H., 31, 40, 43–61, 96, 97, 105, 118, 119, 122, 167, 202, 212–214
Ray, A.G., 52, 53, 59, 97, 122
Reddy, L.A., 5
Redlich, F.C., 7, 8
Reed, D.R., 116, 128, 131, 144, 148, 154, 181
Reifin, L.H., 121
Reimers, T.M., 153, 154
Repp, A.C., 10, 154
Reppucci, N.D., 91, 92, 107, 118
Reschly, D.J., 10, 19–21, 24, 25, 28, 29, 76, 99, 108, 134, 155, 177, 179, 181, 182, 184, 185, 187, 190, 217–219
Rescorla, L.A., 133
Resetar, J.L., 128, 135
Reykowski, J., 44
Reynolds, C.R., 29, 115, 186
Roach, A.T., 40
Robbins, J.R., 154
Robinson, J.A., 166
Robinson, S.L., 109, 130
Rogers, D.L., 176
Rogers, L.E., 36–38
Romanczyk, R.G., 142
Romanelli, L.H., 5, 21
Rosenfield, S., 22, 77, 173, 187
Rosenshine, B., 186
Rosenthal, B.D., 116, 131
Rubel, E., 5
Rucker, C.N, 68
Rush, K.S., 116, 132
Ryan, D.A., 33

S

Sabatino, D., 182
Sainato, D.S., 144
Salasin, S., 99
Salvia, J., 186
Sams, D.P., 22, 173
Sanborn, K.J., 22, 173
Sandoval, J., 14, 61
Santibañez, L., 164
Sarason, B.R., 86
Sarason, I.G., 86
Sarason, S.B., 67, 70, 78, 102, 122, 165, 167
Saunders, J.T., 92, 107, 118
Schaughency, E., 99

Scheeler, M.C., 122
Schein, E.H., 91
Schlenker, B.R., 55
Schuka J.R., 125, 128, 138, 139
Schulberg, H.C., 9, 83
Schulte, A.C., 9, 13, 21, 22, 33, 34, 41, 83,
    87, 171
Schwarzwald, J., 52
Scott, T.M., 165
Seavey, T.L., 122
Sechrest, L., 152, 153
Senesac, B.V., 135, 191
Shapiro, E.S., 128, 186
Shaywitz, S.E., 29
Shear, S.M., 209
Sheridan, S.M., 5, 6, 11, 13, 14, 18, 21,
    107, 108
Shinn, M.R., 75, 115, 135, 151, 182, 185, 191
Shore, M.F., 87, 106, 108
Showers, B., 121, 175
Silver, S.E.., 187
Silverstein, J., 13
Simonsen, B., 20
Singer, J., 68
Singh, N.N., 10
Sirotnik, K.A., 181
Skinner, C.H., 111, 130, 138, 144, 147
Slonski-Fowler, K.E., 23
Smalls, Y., 116, 132
Smith, A., 38
Smith, D.K., 68
Smith, M.L., 5, 8, 142
Smith, R.G., 38
Snyder, T.D., 63, 162
Stecker, P.M., 36, 167
Steege, M.W., 28
Steele, E.S., 186
Stein, L.I., 51, 52
Stenger, M.K., 170, 171
Sterling-Turner, H., 14
Sterling-Turner, H.E., 109, 130, 154
Stevens, R.J., 186
Stoiber, K.C., 95
Stokes, T.F., 122, 151, 174
Stollar, S.A., 25, 121
Strickland, B., 68
Sugai, G.M., 14, 20, 145, 172
Suldo, S.M., 128, 135
Sulzer-Azaroff, B., 124
Swartz, J., 77, 159
Symington, T., 22, 172, 174
Szasz, T.S., 6, 7, 106
Szczech, F.M., 116, 131

T
Tagiuri, R., 66
Tangel, D.M., 205
Tannen, D., 52
Tardy, C.H., 86, 120
Taylor, L.L., 162
Telzrow, C.F., 177, 178
Tharp, R.G., 7, 45, 91, 92, 107, 118
Therrien, W.J., 125, 128, 138, 139
Thompson, R.H., 132
Thompson, R.L., 133
Thurlow, M.L., 70, 169, 181
Tilly, W.D., 10, 19, 22, 25–27
Tindal, G.A., 14
Tindall, R.H, 10
Tobin, M.I., 188
Tollefson, N., 170
Tombari, M.L., 34, 35, 37, 38,
    41, 95, 96, 107, 115,
    117, 204
Touchette, P.E., 116, 132
Tresco, K.E., 37–39, 110, 111,
    167, 171, 174, 193,
    215, 216
Trickett, E.J., 124
Trivette, C.M., 40, 120
Trost, M.A., 8
Truscott, S.D., 22, 23, 172
Turco, T., 154
Turnbull, A.P., 68
Tyler, B.J., 113
Tysinger, J.A., 168
Tysinger, P.D., 168

U
Ullmann, L.P., 188
Updyke, J.F., 6

V
VanDerHeyden, A.M., 25
VanSomeren, K.R., 108
Vaughn, S., 113, 186, 217
Vernberg, E.M., 91
Viglietta, E., 22
Vile Junod, R.E., 37, 193
Vile Junod, R.J., 37–40
Vincent, J.B., 118
Vollmer, T.R., 10, 116, 130, 132, 143
Volpe, R.J., 128
Von Brock, M.B., 109
Von Brock Treuting, M., 38, 215

W

Wacker, D.P., 138, 153, 154
Walster, E., 52
Walster, G.W., 48
Waterman, B., 130
Watkins, M., 68
Watson, M.R., 34
Watson, T.S., 14, 28, 109, 154
Weber, C., 24, 63, 64
Webster, R.E., 186
Weeks, M., 129
Weinstein, C.S., 69
Welch, M., 6, 107
West, M.R., 163
Wetzel, R.J., 7, 45, 91, 92, 107, 118
Wheeler, D., 118
Whichard, S.M., 52, 53, 97, 167
Whitten, E., 23
Wickstrom, K.F., 125, 128, 138, 139
Wiemann, J.M., 34, 193
Wilczynski, S.M., 109, 130
Wiley, H.I., 22
Wilkinson, L.A., 95
Wills, T.A., 86
Wilson, D.B., 142
Wilson, K.E., 53, 57, 59, 97
Winikur, D., 69
Wise, P.S., 5, 10, 11, 31, 63, 65
Witt, J.C., 10, 19, 23, 28, 36, 40, 66, 68, 69,
     74, 85, 95, 106, 108–111, 114–116,
     120–123, 129, 130, 143, 145, 147,
     152–154, 174, 183, 189–191, 193, 202

Wolery, M., 145–147
Wonderlich, S., 154
Woodcock, R.W., 204,
     214, 215
Wosinska, W., 44
Wright, C., 166
Wyner, N.B., 165

Y

Yalom, I.D., 8
Yammer, D.M., 159
Yang, J., 57
Yeaton, W.H., 152, 153
Yell, M.L., 128, 130, 179
Yoon, J., 40
Yoshida, R.K., 68
Young, C.L., 11
Ysseldyke, J.E., 70, 108,
     114, 134, 143, 169, 181,
     190, 191
Yukl, G., 53

Z

Zelditch, M., Jr., 55
Zigler, E., 7
Zins, J.E., 5, 10, 18, 40,
     77, 91, 102,
     117, 124
Zirkel, P., 11
Zubin, J., 7

Subject Index

A

Ability training approach, 134, 143
Activity segment, 69. *See also* Instructional
 arrangement
Allocated time, 135, 190
Applied behavior analysis (ABA), 21, 28, 108,
 142–144, 147, 149, 151
Aptitude X treatment interaction, 134
Assessing the school as an organization,
 98–100
A VICTORY model, 99–101, 105

B

Basal curriculum, 181, 190
Behavioral
 assessment, 15, 28, 91, 92, 93, 109, 110,
 120, 125, 127, 128–134, 143
 contract, 149, 150
 regularities, 66–70
Behavioral consultation
 assumptions, 91, 92, 93, 109, 110, 120,
 129, 130, 143, 15
 interview objectives, 35, 93–95, 107, 108,
 115, 116, 127, 155
 stages, 35–37, 93–95, 107, 173
Behavioral psychology, 7, 83, 91–97
Behavior analysis
 limitations, 151
 principles, 14, 91, 92, 105, 107–109,
 142–145, 149, 152, 153
 procedures, 91, 93, 108, 125, 127–129,
 132, 137, 142–147, 149–151, 153,
 154, 191
Benchmark, assessment in RTI, 25–26
Brief experimental analysis, 28, 128, 129,
 136–139, 180
Building team, 14, 75, 76, 80. *See also*
 Multidisciplinary team

Bureaucracy

 assumptions, 64–65
 principles of administration, 64

C

Caregiver, 3, 31, 111, 121, 131
Child Behavior Checklist (CBCL), 133, 188
Classical organizational theory, 64–69, 79
Client, 3–8, 12, 13, 15, 25, 32, 36, 40, 47, 56,
 59, 64, 87–90, 92, 93, 96, 105–108,
 110, 111, 113, 119, 125, 127, 128,
 132, 137, 143, 144, 165, 168, 172,
 175–193, 202, 203, 215, 219
Client-centered focus, 108
Clinical psychology, 9
Coaching, 106, 123, 124, 175, 176
Collaboration
 vs. consultation, 33–34, 36, 41, 79, 84, 89,
 103, 168
 as myth, 110
Communication
 lateral, 65, 66
 vertical, 66
Community Mental Health Centers Act
 (P. L. 88–164), 9
Community mental health concepts, 83
Community mental health movement, 9, 83, 106
Compartmentalized instruction, 63, 65
Conceptual relevance, 107, 142, 152
Confidentiality, 30, 79, 80, 89, 101–103
Consideration, 67, 75, 80
Consultant
 as change agent, 30, 31
 internal/external distinction, 13, 48, 50,
 97–101, 105, 122, 173, 202
Consultant-consultee relationship
 Caplan's view, 87–90, 92, 101, 106,
 165–166

as cooperative, 12, 40, 41, 96, 102, 110,
    111, 174, 219
Consultation
    barriers to, 77, 114
    vs. collaboration, 33–34, 41, 84, 89, 103, 168
    contracting, 98, 100, 193
    effectiveness, 5–6, 35, 36, 38, 53, 61,
        76, 87, 93, 94, 96, 107, 108, 111,
        115, 144, 159, 167–169,
        171–176, 193
    history, 99, 170
    integrated model, 13–15, 22, 29, 80,
        83–103, 105, 109, 110–125, 127,
        192–194, 219
    journals, 4, 5
    outcomes, 5, 6, 13, 15, 34, 35, 37–41, 49,
        53, 89, 96, 105, 106, 112, 124–125,
        127, 143, 154, 167–169
    paradoxes of, 32, 61, 64, 78–80, 164
    tasks of, 29, 60, 86, 95, 97, 101, 103, 105,
        111–113, 115–120, 127, 175, 176,
        202, 203, 212, 213, 214, 219
Consultation Analysis Record (CAR), 34–36,
    95, 96
Consultative interview
    problem analysis (PAI), 22, 35, 38, 93, 94,
        110, 115–116, 123, 124, 127, 128,
        130, 131, 133, 134, 154, 155, 193,
        202–214
    problem evaluation (PEI), 22, 35, 93–95,
        110, 116–117, 127, 155, 211,
        214–21
    problem identification (PII), 22, 34, 35, 36,
        37, 38, 39, 93, 94, 110, 115, 117,
        122, 124, 127, 128, 131, 132, 155,
        172, 193, 194–204, 213
    tactics, 55, 92, 107, 108, 115, 117, 119
Consultee, 3–6, 12, 13, 18, 31–43, 45, 47–52,
    54–57, 59–61, 80, 86–97, 101–103,
    105–112, 115–125, 127, 128, 131,
    136, 144, 154, 155, 159–176, 193,
    194, 202, 204, 219
Contingency space analysis, 133
Continuum of services, 9, 178, 179, 180, 217,
    218. *See also* Range of services
Core characteristics, 29, 80, 113, 174
Coupling
    pooled, 70, 71
    reciprocal, 70, 71
    sequential, 70, 71, 78, 80, 113
Crisis/crisis model, 12, 39, 52, 83–86, 97, 106,
    107, 111, 114, 120, 124, 170
Crisis intervention, 9, 12, 84
Cross-cultural factors in consultation, 14

Curriculum-based measurement (CBM), 15,
    21, 28, 109, 121, 125, 127–129,
    134–139, 144, 218
Curriculum content validity, 186

D

Data-based decision making, 11, 124, 142, 193
*Diagnostic and Statistical Manual (4th
    Ed-Text Revision; DSM-IV-TR)*,
    177, 182, 183, 184, 185
Direct assessment phase, 131, 132–134
Directed rehearsal, 124
Direct observation, 77, 93, 127, 128, 132
*Disorders First Diagnosed in Infancy,
    Childhood, or Adolescence,* 184
Division of labor, 64, 65
Dominance, 36–38, 110
Domineeringness, 36–38, 110
Door-in-the-face, 118
Dual discrepancy approach/method in RTI,
    26–27, 135, 191
Due process requirements, 178, 179
Duration recording, 128
Dyadic social influence, 34, 96
Dynamic Indicators of Basic Early Literacy
    Skills (DIBELS), 28, 129, 135, 138,
    146, 198, 199, 201–205, 211–215

E

Ecological perspective, 191
Educationally Related Support Services
    (ERSS), 78
Education For All Handicapped Children Act
    (P. L. 94–142), 9, 20, 22,
    178, 217
Effect size (*ES*) statistics, 5, 28, 142, 143,
    144, 153. *See also* Meta-analysis
Egalitarian virus, 41
Empirical data, 141
Empirically supported interventions, 20
Empirical-rational approach
    to change, 42, 43, 109, 174
Empowerment philosophy, 40, 120
Enrichment program, 72, 73
Entry in school consultation, 97–103
Ethical Standards of the American
    Psychological Association, 142
Evaluation report, 75
Event recording, 128
Exception principle, 80
Exclusionary criteria, 184
Experimental control, 129, 138

F

Fifteen-minute consultation, 171–172
Focus groups, 77
Foot-in-the-door (FITD), 118
Free, appropriate public education (FAPE),
    177–179
Functional assessment, 15, 108, 115, 116,
    129–143, 152, 174, 179, 180,
    202–203
Functional behavior assessment, 28, 128–134,
    136, 143

G

Gatekeeper role within school psychology,
    10, 179
Generalization, 32, 33, 87, 109, 122, 145–147,
    151, 174, 175, 215
Goals, 7, 8, 10, 12, 19, 22, 24, 26, 27, 38, 40,
    50, 56, 60, 63, 65–57, 70, 72, 75,
    84, 88, 93–95, 99, 100, 106–108,
    111, 113, 115, 116, 120, 122–125,
    127, 129, 136, 141, 143, 145,
    151–153, 165, 167, 172–175, 178,
    182, 190–192, 196, 197, 199,
    203–205, 211–213, 215, 217–219
Group norms, 66, 67, 80

H

Handicapping conditions
    emotionally disturbed, 66, 73, 93, 123,
        173, 177, 178, 182–185, 187–188
    mentally retarded, 20, 73, 133, 179,
        183–185
    specific learning disability (SLD), 4, 10,
        11, 18, 20, 27, 32, 40, 68, 72–74,
        93, 128, 135, 173, 177, 179,
        182–187, 217, 218
Home-based reinforcement, 66, 80, 150
Human relations movement, 64, 66–70
Human services consultation, 3–6. *See also*
    Consultation

I

Implementation scripts, 121–122. *See also*
    Protocols, implementation
Inclusive Elementary and Special Education
    Training Program,
Index of interview control, 35, 38
Indirect assessment phase, 131–132
Individualized education program (IEP), 68,
    73–75, 134, 178, 179, 189, 217, 219

Individuals with Disabilities Education Act
    (IDEA), 9–12, 15, 20, 108, 130,
    150, 178–180, 182, 217, 218
Individuals with Disabilities Education Act of
    1997 (IDEA 1997), 11, 15, 20, 108,
    130, 178, 179
Individuals with Disabilities Education
    Improvement Act of 2004 (IDEIA
    2004), 11, 15, 18–20, 23, 28, 32,
    108, 172, 173, 179–181, 218
Influence
    ethical concerns, 33, 39, 40, 97
    mode of, 57, 60, 97
    power/interaction model, 43, 57–60, 96
Influencing agent, 42, 44, 50, 51, 54–58, 60
Initiating structure, 67, 68
Instructional arrangement, 69, 132
Instructional hierarchy
    acquisition, 145
    adaptation, 146
    fluency, 145
    generalization, 146
Instructional interventions, 77, 128, 144, 147,
    148, 187, 191
Instructional match, 148, 191
Integrated model of school consultation, 13,
    22, 29, 80, 83–103, 105, 110–125,
    127, 193. *See also* Consultation,
    integrated model
Interpersonal influence. *See* Influence
Invoking the power of a third party, 54–55, 97,
    118, 122

L

Leader Behavior Description Questionnaire
    (LBDQ), 67
Leadership style, 66, 67, 98
Least restrictive environment, 9, 150, 178,
    180, 187, 217

M

Mainstreaming, 10, 217
Maintenance, 7, 121, 123, 145, 146, 174–176, 192
Matching law, 148
Mental health collaboration, 89, 103. *See also*
    Collaboration
Mental health consultation
    assumptions, 87
    parables, 52
    sources of consultee difficulty, 89–90
    theme interference reduction, 90, 106
    types, 88

Meta-analysis, 5, 6, 21, 134, 142, 174
Motivation Assessment Scale (MAS), 131, 132
Multiaxial classification, 184
Multicultural factors in consultation, 14
Multidisciplinary team, 9, 22, 68, 179
Mutual help groups, 8, 86. *See also* Social support

N
Needs assessment, 77
No Child Left Behind Act of 2001 (NCLB), 11, 12, 15, 19, 23, 108, 141, 163, 218
Normative-re-educative approach to change, 42
Norm-referenced test, 75, 186

O
"One Right Model" of public education, 182, 189
Organizational behavior theory, 64, 70–71
Organizational climate, 66, 68, 80, 99
Organization development model of consultation, 14, 98
Outcome expectancy, 168

P
Paradox, 64, 78, 79, 164
Paradox of School Psychology, 32, 61
Paraprofessional, 4, 7, 8, 32
Parents, 7, 8, 11, 28, 66, 68, 69, 71, 74–76, 84, 89, 90, 92, 99, 130, 131, 141, 159, 162, 163, 164, 178, 187, 207
Performance feedback, 23, 106, 113, 121, 122, 123–124, 175
Planning team, 78, 173
P.L. 94-142; Individuals with Disabilities Education Act. *See* Individuals with Disabilities Education Act (IDEA)
Positive behavioral interventions, 15, 179, 188
Positive behavior support (PBS), 20, 28, 72, 128, 179, 180
Power. *See* Social power
Power-coercive approach to change, 42–43
Prereferral intervention
programs, 76, 107, 173
teams, 10, 12, 22, 23, 114, 172, 173, 174

Prevention
population-oriented, 9, 12, 84–85, 97
primary, 9, 18, 83, 84, 124
secondary, 9, 18, 84, 85, 124
tertiary, 9, 18, 84–86, 124
Problem attributions, 114
Problem solving, 13, 15, 17–30, 35, 41, 55, 66, 80, 83, 85–88, 90–93, 95, 97, 103, 105, 107, 108, 110–120, 124, 127, 136, 139, 159, 165, 168, 170–174, 176, 202, 212, 215, 217–219
Problem-solving system in RTI, 24–25
Problem-solving team (PST), 22–24, 30, 55, 66, 68, 73, 75, 79, 159, 172–174, 187, 188
Professional support, 10, 13, 15, 41, 43, 80, 105, 111
Programmatic isolation, 71, 218
Programming common stimuli, 122
Progress monitoring, 23, 24, 26–28, 134, 135, 138, 139, 151, 173, 201, 202, 211
Project PASS, 37, 38, 193, 202, 203, 215, 216
Prompting (in errorless learning), 146, 147
Prompting (procedures for)
graduated guidance, 144, 146, 147
least-to-most, 146
most-to-least, 146, 147
prompt and fade, 146–147
prompt and test, 146
time delay, 146, 147
Protocols, implementation, 121–122, 175
Psychoeducational evaluation, 75, 180, 184
Psychological services
direct/indirect distinction, 31–32
Psychotherapy, 3, 4, 8, 12, 31, 90, 106, 175
Pull-out program, 63, 66, 71, 73, 180
Punishment
Type I, 150
Type II, 150
Push-in program, 63, 73, 180

Q
Questions About Behavioral Function (QABF), 116, 132–133

R
Range of services, 63–64, 71, 80
Reactance, 50, 51
Recitation, 69

Recording
  event, 128
  interval, 128, 137
  percentage, 128
  sequential, 131–133
Reducing the power of a third party, 54–55, 97
Referral, 3, 10, 12, 18, 20, 22, 29, 32, 68,
        75–78, 80, 107, 114, 169, 172–174,
        187, 189, 192, 219
Refer-test-place sequence, 64, 74–76, 217
Regular education initiative (REI), 10
Reinforcement
  automatic, 130, 132
  differential, 137, 148–150
  positive, 45, 123, 129–130, 133, 143, 144,
        148–150, 152, 155
  social negative, 124, 129–130, 148
  social positive, 123, 129, 148, 150
Reinforcer dimensions, 149, 153
Relational communication, 35–37, 40, 111, 174
Relational control, 110, 119
Remedial assistance, 73, 180
Resistance to intervention, 77, 79, 100, 111,
        119, 154
Resource room, 66, 73, 180, 217
Response cost, 150
Response to intervention (RTI), 11, 13, 15,
        17–30, 32, 38, 55, 64, 76, 99, 100,
        108, 128, 129, 134, 135, 138, 139,
        159, 172–174, 179, 180, 188,
        218–219
Role structuring, 102, 202

S
SBIT project, 173, 174
Scatterplot analysis, 116, 132
School-based intervention, 13, 33, 109, 111,
        114, 116, 121, 125, 127, 134, 137,
        139, 141–155, 173, 190–192
School psychology, 5, 9, 21, 29, 31, 32, 46,
        53, 54, 61, 166, 167
Scientific method, 141
Scientist-practitioner perspective, 13, 14
Scientist-practitioner training, 13, 14, 21
Scope and sequence charts, 190
Seatwork, 69, 70, 77, 116, 130, 132,
        160, 188
Second Paradox of School Psychology, 61, 79
Section 504 of the Vocational Rehabilitation
        Act, 178, 179
Self-contained classroom, 72, 73
Self-efficacy, 124, 168, 169, 171
Single-case experimental research, 116, 136, 138

Skill area X proficiency level matrix, 146
Skill training approach, 74, 78, 137
Social influence, 13, 15, 31, 34, 39–41, 43–45,
        54, 55, 60–61, 80, 83, 89, 96–98,
        103, 105, 111–113, 117–120, 122,
        127, 175, 202–203, 212, 213, 214,
        219. See also Influence
Social labeling, 188
Social power
  bases of social power model, 31, 43, 45
  coercive power
    impersonal, 45–47, 53, 59
    personal, 47–48, 53, 55, 56, 61
  expert power
    negative, 47, 50, 119
    positive, 46, 49, 52–54, 97, 118, 119,
        122, 202, 213, 214
  harsh bases, 53, 54, 59
  informational power
    direct, 46, 51–54, 97, 119, 122
    indirect, 47, 51–52, 119
  legitimate power
    formal/position power, 46, 48–49,
        53–55, 98, 119
    legitimacy of equity, 46, 48–49, 53, 56,
        59, 119, 213
    legitimacy of reciprocity, 46, 48–49,
        53, 55, 56, 61, 119, 122, 213
    legitimacy of responsibility/
        dependence, 46, 48–49, 53, 54, 56,
        97, 119
  referent power
    negative, 47, 50, 119
    positive, 46, 49, 52–54, 97, 118, 119,
        122, 202, 212
  reward power
    impersonal, 45–47, 52, 53, 119
    personal, 47–48, 53, 55, 56, 119, 122,
        214
  soft bases, 53–54, 59, 97
Social support
  emotional support, 86, 90, 120
  instrumental support, 86, 90, 120
  supporting teachers, 12, 22, 66, 120, 121,
        153, 167
Special education, 4, 18, 32, 63, 98, 108, 143,
        172, 178, 217
Specific learning disability (SLD), 10, 11, 18,
        20, 27, 128, 135, 173, 179, 183,
        185-187, 217, 218
Staffing, 68, 75. See also Multidisciplinary
        team
Stage-setting devices, 55, 59
Standard protocol system in RTI, 24–25

Standards of practice, 121, 183
State regulations, 75, 173, 181–185, 187–188
Stimulus control, 144–145, 147, 152
Stimulus generalization, 145, 147
Strategic interpersonal communication, 34, 193
Student Learning in Context (SLIC)
    model, 191
Support. *See* Professional support; Social
    support
Support services, 74, 78
Systematic formative evaluation, 128,
    134–137, 139, 180, 203, 218

T
Target of influence 42, 44, 50, 60
Teacher consultant model 180
Teacher-directed small group, 69–70
Teachers
    challenges/constraints, 67, 113, 159,
        162–163, 165, 171, 172, 181, 188,
        189, 195, 208, 213
    expectations for consultation, 159, 167–169
    occupational role, 162, 167
    reasons for seeking consultation, 114, 146,
        152, 169–170
    recruitment issues, 159, 164, 167
    retention issues, 159, 164, 214
    rewards, 11, 19, 46, 52, 53, 55, 56, 100,
        141, 149, 159, 161–163, 214

    salary, 161–162, 164
    shortage, 164
Tier 1, tier 2, and tier 3 interventions, 24–28,
        73, 79, 85, 114, 187, 189, 218, 219
Time out, 116, 121, 137, 150, 151, 160
Time sampling, 109, 121, 128
Topic determination, 14–15
Treatment
    acceptability, 109, 142, 153–154
    integrity, 23, 29, 38, 116, 122, 125, 142,
        154–155, 211, 214, 215
    strength, 142, 152, 153

U
Universal screening, 19, 24, 26, 28, 135–136

V
Verbal praise, 118, 149, 150

W
Words read correctly per minute (WCPM),
    136–137

Y
Young, attractive, verbal, intelligent, and
    successful (YAVIS), 8

Breinigsville, PA USA
13 January 2011
253226BV00005B/15/P